Starting & Running an Online Business

FOR DUMMIES®

2ND EDITION

Starting & Running an Online Business

FOR

DUMMIES®

2ND EDITION

by Kim Gilmour, Dan Matthews and Greg Holden

WILEY

A John Wiley and Sons, Ltd, Publication

Starting & Running an Online Business For Dummies®, 2nd Edition

Published by
John Wiley & Sons, Ltd
The Atrium
Southern Gate
Chichester
West Sussex
PO19 8SQ
England

Email (for orders and customer service enquiries): cs-books@wiley.co.uk

Visit our Home Page on www.wiley.com

For general information on our other products and services, please contact our Customer Care Department within the U.S. at 877-762-2974, outside the U.S. at 317-572-3993, or fax 317-572-4002.

For technical support, please visit www.wiley.com/techsupport.

Wiley also publishes its books in a variety of electronic formats and by print-on-demand. Some content that appears in standard print versions of this book may not be available in other formats. For more information about Wiley products, visit us at www.wiley.com.

British Library Cataloguing in Publication Data: A catalogue record for this book is available from the British Library

ISBN: 978-1-119-99138-0 (paperback), 978-1-119-99279-0 (ebook), 978-1-119-99424-4 (ebook), 978-1-119-99423-7 (ebook)

Printed and bound in Great Britain by Bell & Bain Ltd., Glasgow, United Kingdom

10 9 8 7 6 5 4 3 2 1

WILEY

About the Authors

Kim Gilmour is a freelance journalist and author with more than 13 years of experience demystifying the world of technology for small businesses and consumers. As senior researcher/writer at *Which? Computing*, the UK's biggest computing magazine, she has conducted high-profile news investigations, product reviews and tutorials and is still a regular contributor. She was also features editor at *Internet Magazine*, one of the first publications to help businesses get online and guide them through the rise and subsequent fall of the dotcom boom. Prior to this she was assistant editor at an Australian business technology title. Kim's articles have appeared in *Web User, PC Pro* and *Computer Shopper,* amongst others. She is the author of *Digital Photography for the Older and Wiser, Spotify For Dummies* (October 2011) and is co-author of *eBay.co.uk for Business All-in-One For Dummies* and *Starting and Running a Business All-in-One 2e.* All books are published by Wiley.

Dan Matthews: Dan Matthews is Group Online Editor of Caspian Publishing, which produces magazines, websites, and events for an audience of UK entrepreneurs. Primarily working on realbusiness.co.uk, Dan writes about stellar business success stories as well as up-and-coming start-ups.

He was previously Group Online Editor of Crimson Business Publishing, with responsibility for sites such as startups.co.uk and growingbusiness.co.uk. He has contributed to a range of business magazines, including being contributing editor of *Real Business Magazine* and *Growing Business Magazine*, and is the co-author of *Starting a Business on eBay.co.uk For Dummies.*

Greg Holden: Greg Holden started a small business called Stylus Media, which is a group of editorial, design, and computer professionals who produce both print and electronic publications. The company gets its name from a recording stylus that reads the traces left on a disk by voices or instruments and translates those signals into electronic data that can be amplified and enjoyed by many. He has been self-employed for the past ten years. He is an avid user of eBay, both as a buyer and seller, and he recently started his own blog.

One of the ways Greg enjoys communicating is through explaining technical subjects in nontechnical language. The first edition of *Starting an Online Business For Dummies* was the ninth of his more than 30 computer books. He also authored *eBay PowerUser's Bible* for Wiley Publishing. Over the years, Greg has been a contributing editor of *Computer Currents* magazine, where he writes a monthly column. He also contributes to *PC World* and the University of Illinois at Chicago alumni magazine. Other projects have included preparing documentation for an electronics catalog company in Chicago and creating online courses on Windows 2000 and Microsoft Word 2000.

Greg balances his technical expertise and his entrepreneurial experience with his love of literature. He received an M.A. in English from the University of Illinois at Chicago and also writes general interest books, short stories, and poetry. Among his editing assignments is the monthly newsletter for his daughters' grade school.

After graduating from college, Greg became a reporter for his hometown newspaper. Working at the publications office at the University of Chicago was his next job, and it was there that he started to use computers. He discovered, as the technology became available, that he loved desktop publishing (with the Macintosh and LaserWriter) and, later on, the World Wide Web.

Greg loves to travel, but since his two daughters were born, he hasn't been able to get around much. He was able to translate his experiences into a book called *Karma Kids: Answering Everyday Parenting Questions with Buddhist Wisdom*. However, through the Web, he enjoys traveling vicariously and meeting people online. He lives with his family in an old house in Chicago that he has been rehabbing for – well, for many years now. He is a collector of objects such as pens, cameras, radios, and hats. He is always looking for things to take apart so that he can see how they work and fix them up. Many of the same skills prove useful in creating and maintaining Web pages. He is an active member of Jewel Heart, a Tibetan Buddhist meditation and study group based in Ann Arbor, Michigan.

Dedication

Kim: For Audrey.

Greg: To my best friend Ann Lindner, who makes everything possible.

Authors' Acknowledgements

Kim: I am so grateful to all the people whose businesses are featured in this book – their entrepreneurship is truly exciting and I wish them every continued success.

I'd also like to acknowledge everyone whose excellent knowledge and advice made updating this book possible. In particular, huge thanks to Scott at Scott Parker Consultancy for reviewing the design sections; Bernie from BN Nyman & Co for his expert legal guidance and Sean McManus for his online marketing expertise.

Thank you also to Jo Jones and Ben Kemble at John Wiley for their assistance and Isabel Atherton at Creative Authors for all her help.

I can't finish without thanking my parents, Brian and Liem, for being so patient and supportive throughout this entire process and my daughter Audrey for being such an inspiration.

Dan: Dan would like to thank Simon, Sam, Kelly and Wejdan at John Wiley for their guidance, support and ultimately patience in producing this book. He'd also like to thank Gemma for her patience and serenity, and Charles, Rebecca and Kate at Real Business for being all-round good eggs!

Greg: One of the things I like best about this book is that it's a teaching tool that gives me a chance to share my knowledge – small business owner to small business owner – about computers, the Internet, and communicating your message to others in an interactive way. As any businessperson knows, most large-scale projects are a team effort.

The most successful entrepreneurs also tend to be the ones who were the most generous with their time and experience. They taught me that the more helpful you are, the more successful you'll be in return.

I want to thank all those who were profiled as case studies, particularly John Moen of Graphic Maps, who pops up all through the book.

I would also like to acknowledge some of my own colleagues who helped prepare and review the text and graphics of this book and who have supported and encouraged me in other lessons of life. Thanks to Ann Lindner, whose teaching experience proved invaluable in suggesting ways to make the text more clear, and to my assistant Ben Huizenga.

For editing and technical assignments, I was lucky to be in the capable hands of the folks at Wiley Publishing.

Thanks also to Neil Salkind and David and Sherry Rogelberg of Studio B, and to Terri Varveris of Wiley Publishing for helping me to add this book to the list of those I've authored and, in the process, to broaden my expertise as a writer.

Last but certainly not least, the future is in the hands of the generation of my two daughters, Zosia and Lucy, who allow me to learn from the curiosity and joy with which they approach life.

Publisher's Acknowledgements

We're proud of this book; please send us your comments through our Dummies online registration form located at www.dummies.com/register/.

Some of the people who helped bring this book to market include the following:

Commissioning, Editorial, and Media Development

Project Editor: Jo Jones

(Previous Edition: Kelly Ewing and Simon Bell)

Commissioning Editor: Claire Ruston

(Previous Edition Samantha Spickernell)

Assistant Editor: Ben Kemble

Technical Editors: Sarah Laing and Mark Leach

Proofreader: Charlie Wilson

Publisher: David Palmer

Production Manager: Daniel Mersey

Cover Photos: © iStock / evirgen

Cartoons: Ed McLachlan

Screenshots: Microsoft product screenshots reprinted with permission from Microsoft Corporation

Composition Services

Project Coordinator: Kristie Rees

Layout and Graphics: Carl Byers, Joyce Haughey, Laura Westhuis

Proofreader: Lauren Mandelbaum

Indexer: Claudia Bourbeau

Publishing and Editorial for Consumer Dummies

    Kathleen Nebenhaus, Vice President and Executive Publisher

    Kristin Ferguson-Wagstaffe, Product Development Director

    Ensley Eikenburg, Associate Publisher, Travel

    Kelly Regan, Editorial Director, Travel

Publishing for Technology Dummies

    Andy Cummings, Vice President and Publisher

Composition Services

    Debbie Stailey, Director of Composition Services

Contents at a Glance

Table of Contents

Introduction

· ·

You've been thinking about starting your own business, but until now, it was just a dream. After all, you're a busy person. You have a full-time job, whether it's running your home or as part of the rat race. Perhaps you've been through a life-changing event and are ready to move in a new direction.

Well, we have news for you: *now* is the perfect time to turn your dream into reality by starting your own web-based business. People just like you are making money and enriching their lives by starting up online. Opening hours don't exist, but you can work when you need to, and the location of your business makes no difference. Anyone can run a small business from the comfort of a home office – even if it's just your spare bedroom. And you can make money online in an ever increasing number of ways, such as running your own blog, starting a business on eBay or dreaming up something entirely unique.

If you like the idea of being in business for yourself, but you don't have a particular product or service in mind at the moment, keep a lookout for openings and ideas: what could you put online that isn't there already? The Internet is home to many diverse businesses that have 'made it' in their own way. Among the entrepreneurs we interviewed for this book are a woman who sells waterproof cushion covers online, ,a writer who attracts new business through his blog, a painter and the founders of an online comic bookstore. With help from this book, you can transform a simple idea into your very own online empire.

About This Book

You say you wouldn't know a merchant account, domain name or click-through if you sat next to one on a train? Don't worry: the Internet (and this book) levels the playing field, so a novice has almost as good a chance at succeeding as the MBA-clutching whiz kids you hear about.

The Internet is a vital part of what makes a business these days. Whether you've been in business for 20 years or 20 minutes, the keys to success are the same:

- **Having a good idea:** If you have something to sell that people have an appetite for, and if your competition is thin on the ground, your chances of success are good.

- **Working hard:** When you're your own boss, you can make yourself work harder than any of your former bosses ever could. If you put in the effort and persevere through the inevitable ups and downs, you'll come up smiling.

- **Preparing for success:** One of the most surprising and useful things we can discover from online businesspeople is that if you believe that you will succeed, you stand a much better chance of doing so. Believe in yourself and go about your plans like they're dead certs. Together with your good ideas and hard work, your confidence will pay off.

If you're the cautious type who wants to test the waters before you launch your new business on the Internet, let this book lead you gently over the learning curve. After you're online, you can master techniques to improve your presence. Even if you aren't among the lucky small business owners who make a fortune by connecting to the Net, the odds are very good that you'll make new friends, build your confidence and have fun too.

Conventions Used in This Book

In this book, we format important bits of information in special ways to make sure that you notice them right away:

- **In This Chapter lists:** Chapters start with a list of the topics that we cover. This list represents a kind of table of contents in miniature.

- **Numbered lists:** When you see a numbered list, follow the steps in a specific order to accomplish the task.

- **Bulleted lists:** Bulleted lists (like this one) indicate things that you can do in any order or list related bits of information.

- **Web addresses:** When we describe activities or sites of interest on the World Wide Web, we include the address, or Uniform Resource Locator (URL), in a special typeface like this: `http://www.wiley.com/`. Because popular web browsers such as Microsoft Internet Explorer and Mozilla Firefox don't require you to enter the entire URL, this book uses the shortened addresses. For example, if you want to connect to the Wiley Publishing site, you can get there by simply entering the following in your browser's Go To or Address bar: `www.wiley.co.uk`. However, we sometimes list *secure* websites prefaced with `https://`, and you'll need to type this in to access them.

Don't be surprised if your browser can't find an Internet address you type or if a web page that's depicted in this book no longer looks the same. Although the sites were current when the book was written, web addresses (and sites themselves) can be pretty fickle. Try looking for a missing site by using an Internet search engine. Or try shortening the address by deleting everything after the `.co.uk` (or `.com` or `.org.uk`).

Foolish Assumptions

This book assumes that you've never been in business but that you're interested in setting up your own commercial site on the Internet. We assume that you're familiar with the Internet and have been surfing for a while.

We also assume that you have or are ready to get the following:

- ✔ **A computer and a broadband Internet connection:** Chapter 2 explains exactly what kind of stuff you need.

- ✔ **Instructions on how to think like a businessperson:** We spend big chunks of this book encouraging you to set goals and do the sort of planning that successful businesspeople need to do.

- ✔ **Just enough technical know-how:** You don't have to do it all yourself. Plenty of entrepreneurs decide to partner with someone or hire an expert to perform design and technical work. This book gives you your options, as well as a basic vocabulary, so that you can work productively with the consultants you hire.

How This Book Is Organised

This book is divided into five parts. Each part contains chapters that discuss stages in the process of starting an online business: designing the website, getting it hosted, choosing what shape your business will take and figuring out what you plan to sell.

Part 1: Strategies and Tools for Your Online Business

In Part I, we describe what you need to do and how you need to *think* in order to start your new business. Throughout the part, you find case studies profiling entrepreneurs and describing how they started their online businesses. Within these pages, we tell you what software you need to create web pages and perform essential business tasks, along with any computer upgrades that will help your business run more smoothly. You also discover how to choose a web host and find exciting new ways to make money online.

Part II: Establishing Your Online Presence

This part explains how to create a compelling and irresistible website, one that attracts paying customers around the world and keeps them coming back to make more purchases. This part also includes options for attracting and keeping customers, making your site secure and updating and improving your online business.

Part III: Running and Promoting Your Online Business

Your work doesn't end after you put your website online or start to make a few sales. In fact, what you do after you open your virtual doors for business can make the difference between a site that says, 'Buy from me!' and one that says, 'Get out quick!' In this part, we describe cost-effective marketing and advertising techniques that you can do yourself to increase visibility and improve customer satisfaction. You discover how to create a smooth shopping experience for your customers, how to accept payments and how to provide good customer service. You also find out about ways to increase visibility with search services.

Part IV: The Necessary Evils: Law and Accounting

This part delves into some less-than-sexy but essential tasks for any online business. You find out about general security software designed to make commerce more secure on the Internet. We also discuss copyrights, trademarks, data protection and other legal concerns for anyone wanting to start a company in an increasingly competitive atmosphere online. Finally, you get an overview of basic accounting practices for online businesses and suggestions of accounting tools that you can use to keep track of your e-commerce activities.

Part V: The Part of Tens

Filled with tips, cautions, suggestions and examples, the Part of Tens presents many titbits of information that you can use to plan and create your own business presence on the Internet, including ten hot new ways to make money on the web.

Icons Used in This Book

Starting & Running an Online Business For Dummies also uses special graphical elements called *icons* to get your attention. Here's what they look like and what they mean:

This icon flags practical advice about particular software programs or about issues of importance to businesses. Look to these tips for help with finding resources quickly, making sales or improving the quality of your online business site. This icon also alerts you to software programs and other resources that we consider to be especially good, particularly for those new to the industry.

This icon points out potential pitfalls that can develop into major problems if you're not careful.

This icon alerts you to important facts and figures to keep in mind as you grow your online business.

This icon calls your attention to interviews we conducted with online entrepreneurs who provide tips and instructions for running an online business.

This icon points out technical details that may be of interest to you. A thorough understanding, however, isn't a prerequisite to grasping the underlying concept. Non-techies are welcome to skip items marked by this icon altogether.

Where to Go from Here

We've made this book into an easy-to-use reference tool that you should be comfortable with, no matter what your level of experience. You can use this book in a couple of ways: as a cover-to-cover read or as a reference for when you run into problems or need inspiration. Feel free to skip straight to the chapters that interest you. You don't have to scour each chapter methodically from beginning to end to find what you want. The web doesn't work that way, and neither does this book!

Want a snapshot of what it takes to get online and be inspired by one woman's online business success story? Jump ahead to Chapter 1. Want to find out how to accept credit-card payments? Check out Chapter 11.

If you're just starting out and need to do some essential business planning, see Chapter 2. If you want to prepare a shopping list of business equipment, see Chapter 3. Part II is all about the essential aspects of creating and operating a successful online business, from organising and marketing your website to providing effective online customer service and security. Later chapters cover advertising, legal issues and accounting. So start where it suits you and come back later for more.

Part I
Strategies and Tools for Your Online Business

In this part . . .

What all does starting an online business involve? In this part, we answer that question with a brief overview of the whole process. The following chapters help you set your online business goals, draw up a blue-print for meeting those goals, and explore new ways to market your goods and services.

And just as dentists prepare their drills and carpenters assemble their tools, you need to gather the necessary hardware and software to keep your online business running smoothly. So, in this part, we discuss the business equipment that the online store owner needs and suggest ways that you can meet those needs even on a limited budget.

Let the step-by-step instructions and real-life case studies in this part guide you through the process of starting a successful business online.

Chapter 1

Opening Your Own Online Business in Ten Easy Steps

....

In This Chapter

▶ Finding a unique niche for your business

▶ Identifying a need and targeting your customers

▶ Turning your website into an indispensable resource

▶ Exploring innovative ways to market your business

▶ Evaluating your success and revising your site

....

*B*uying goods and services online is everyday practice in modern Britain – many people don't think twice these days about using the Internet to purchase groceries, clothes or music; and booking flights and hotels online is just what people *do*. Meanwhile, online marketplaces like eBay continue to thrive.

That's why starting up an online business is no longer a novelty. It's a fact of life for individuals and established companies alike.

E-commerce – the practice of selling goods and services through a website – is here to stay. Every year it becomes easier to conduct commerce online. Even if you have no business experience, ordinary people like you and us can take advantage of constantly updated software and services that make creating and maintaining web pages and transacting online business easier. Marketing your business is also within easy reach of individuals on a budget, with excellent tools available to help you compete with the big guys and attract the punters.

All you need is a good idea, a bit of startup cash, computer equipment, and a little help from your friends.

One of our goals in this book is to be friends who provide you with the right advice and support to get your business off the ground and turn it into a big success. In this chapter, we give you a step-by-step overview of the entire process of coming up with and launching your business.

Realising That Online Business Is the Norm

Now is the perfect time to start your online business. Did you know that the UK has the world's biggest online economy per capita, worth a breathtaking £100 billion a year? That's according to a 2010 survey by the Boston Consulting Group commissioned by Google (for more cool stats, see www.connectedkingdom.co.uk). Separate the online economy into an industry and it would be the UK's fifth biggest – outweighing the hefty transport, construction and utility sectors.

Nowadays having an online presence is essential, even if your business operates mainly in the 'real world'. In recent years, we've felt the pain of the credit crunch – but the online economy has stayed afloat. More people have turned to the web to streamline their businesses and cut down on costly shop front rentals and other overheads. Apart from operating your own website, eBay is *the* place to set up shop, and we dedicate a whole chapter to getting your business on there.

Other well-known web-based service providers like Google, Microsoft, PayPal and Amazon are helping small entrepreneurs to energise their businesses. Bloggers continue to rule Internet culture, and every business seems to have a Twitter account or Facebook page from which to promote their special deals. Ordinary people who create popular YouTube videos can make money from advertising revenue generated through the site or use it as a platform to publicise their businesses.

Broadband is commonplace and customers no longer have an age to wait for websites to load quickly; so these days you can be comfortable with delivering more snazzy content to your customers such as video and audio offerings (although our attention spans seem to be shorter than ever, so making it straightforward for people to find what they're after is still a good idea!).

Anything is possible, but you may have concerns about the future of e-commerce. We promise your fears will quickly evaporate when you read this book's case studies of our friends and colleagues who do business online. They're either thriving or at least treading water, and they enthusiastically encourage others to take the plunge.

It's still a great time to start an online business. Simply put, consumers and businesses are smarter than they were a decade ago. Sarah-Lou Reekie, an online entrepreneur, says:

> *There are more experts in the field so that it is easier to make things happen. The world is far more au fait and switched on to the web. The number of people able to access the web and order products and services is*

far higher. People aren't as nervous as they were to put through credit cards. After an amazingly short time, the web has changed from an unknown and somewhat scary medium to something as easy as ABC.

Step 1: Identify a Need

The fact is, no matter how good you are, you always have room for improvement. Even those at the top of their business game, like Tesco, Topshop and Innocent Smoothies, are always looking over their shoulder at the competition. But the chances are that someday someone else will come along and do what you do either cheaper or better or both. The same goes for the web, and it's this fact that you should keep in mind when you're coming up with your business ideas.

A hotbed of commerce

The Internet is a hotbed of commerce – and it just keeps getting hotter. Read what the experts are saying:

- After a short dip in 2008 and 2009 during the credit crunch, Internet shopping is back in vogue. The Interactive Media in Retail Group (IMRG) found that in July 2010, Brits spent an average of £81 per person, an 18 per cent increase on 2009.

- PayPal, the transaction service run by eBay, predicted that £9 billion would be spent online during Christmas 2010, with more than 30 million people taking the plunge – each with an average spend of £289 during this time! The most popular factor when buying online at Christmas is, overwhelmingly, finding a bargain, with 63 per cent of survey respondents citing this as an important factor. Free delivery and the sheer convenience of shopping online are the other main reasons.

- Research from credit card company Visa suggests that apart from doing more of our shopping online, we're looking to the web to find out how to do things more cheaply and doing our research before making a purchase.

You'd be mad not to take advantage of all this consumer activity, but a word of warning: the fragile economy of late means that every penny counts with your customers, and you must be upfront about your costs. Webcredible (www.webcredible.co.uk), a consultancy that helps improve customers' experiences on websites, says that 41 per cent of its survey respondents abandon their transactions if they're faced with hidden charges at the checkout. In addition, about a third of shoppers go elsewhere if they're forced to register on the website in order to make a purchase. Other reasons include no phone number and having to submit unnecessary personal details. Speed, convenience and honesty are what you need to remember!

From an everyday point of view, e-commerce and the web have been around for more than 15 years now. But people are identifying new products and ways to sell them all the time. Think of the things that didn't exist when the first websites were created: MP3s, wireless modems, DVDs, social networking, web-based email, smart phones. Success is never guaranteed. It depends on you – your energy, dedication and enthusiasm; as well as your initial business idea.

Your first job is to identify your market (the people who'll be buying your stuff or using your service) and determine how you can best meet its needs. After all, you can't expect web surfers to flock to your online business unless you identify services or items that they really need. Who are you targeting and why? Is your market likely to splash out on what you're promoting? Is there a genuine need for your product? Ask around and gauge the reaction of your friends and family. Ask them to be honest, or you could be losing real money (how many people pitch their ridiculous business idea on the TV programme *Dragon's Den* genuinely thinking they have a great idea because their mother or spouse has told them so?). Listen out for any constructive feedback that may help develop your site into a better offering.

Getting to know the marketplace

The *Internet* is a worldwide, interconnected network of computers to which people can connect either from work or home, and through which you can natter via email, learn new things from the web, and buy and sell items using credit and debit cards.

The Internet is a perfect venue for individuals who want to start their own business, who can cope with using computers and who believe that the web is the place to do it. You don't need much money to get started, after all. If you already have a computer and an Internet connection and can create your own web pages (which this book helps you with), making the move to your own business website may cost as little as a few hundred pounds. After you're online, the overheads are pretty reasonable too: you can get your website hosted online for as little as £5 a month.

With each month that goes by, the number of Internet users increases expo-nentially. In turn, this creates a vibrant money-making marketplace for the savviest Internet businesses. To illustrate, the Interactive Media in Retail Group (IMRG) shows that UK consumers spent £4.8 billion in September 2010; that's 24 per cent higher than 2009 figures. Online Christmas sales for 2010 were expected to be 16 per cent higher than in 2009.

Not convinced? Well, how about the fact that despite the difficult budget cuts and the rise in Value Added Tax (VAT), the IMRG predicts that online retail-ers are better placed to weather the storm – there's simply so much variety online, and consumers are becoming increasingly savvy when heading to the Internet to snap up a bargain. The Internet has become fertile ground for innovative businesses. Just look at Google; it's become one of the world's largest media companies with a value of tens of billions of pounds.

Many people decide to start an online business with little more than a casual knowledge of the Internet. But when you decide to get serious about going online, it pays to know how the land lies and who's walking on it with you.

One of your first steps should be to find out what it means to do business online and figure out whether your idea fits in the market. For example, you need to realise that customers are active, not passive, in the way that they absorb information; and that the Net was established within a culture of people sharing information freely and helping one another.

Some of the best places to find out about the culture of the Internet are blogs (or *web logs*: they're online journals usually written by people who aren't qualified writers; but that doesn't mean their insights are no less valid), forums where people exchange messages online, the trending topics on the microblog service Twitter and reviews on sites like Ciao.co.uk. Visiting websites devoted to topics that interest you personally can be especially helpful, and you may even end up participating! Also visit some leading commerce websites (in other words, where people buy and sell items online), such as eBay.co.uk, Amazon.co.uk, ASOS.com and Play.com, and take note of ideas you like. Pay special attention to the design and the way you *drill down* through the website to find what you're after – think of something you're interested in and see how few steps it takes for you to get to the item you're after. Remember that appearance and function are as important as the stuff you're selling.

'Cee-ing' what's out there

The more information you have about the 'three Cs' of the online world, the more likely you are to succeed in doing business online:

- **Competitors:** Familiarise yourself with who's already out there. Work out whether space for you exists and how you plan to fill that space. Don't be intimidated by competitors' existence – people will come to you if you do it a whole lot better!

- **Customers:** Who's gonna visit your website, and how will you get them there? Just like with any business, you must encourage demand for your products and make potential customers aware that you exist.

- **Culture:** Every demographic has its own culture. If you're selling clothes to teenagers then your online business will look and feel very different than the site of someone selling stair-lifts to the elderly. What's their style? How do they talk? What will they expect to see when they arrive at your site?

As you take a look around the Internet, notice the kinds of goods and services that tend to sell, as well as who's doing the selling. You have to be either different, better or, at least, more talked about than these guys. Keep the four Cs in mind if you want achieve this goal:

- ✔ **Cheapness:** Online businesses tend to sell items at a discount compared with high street shops in the real world – at least, that's what shoppers expect.

- ✔ **Customise:** Anything that's hard-to-find, personalised or, better yet, unique, sells well online.

- ✔ **Convenience:** Shoppers are looking for items that are easier to buy online than at a bricks-and-mortar shop – a rare book that you can order in minutes from Amazon.co.uk (www.amazon.co.uk) or a bespoke item made by a craftsperson selling via Not on the High Street (www.not onthehighstreet.com).

- ✔ **Content:** Consumers go online to breeze through news and features available free or through a subscription, such as newspapers and TV channels. Some of these news sites exist online only, and many authoritative are blogs dedicated to popular subjects.

Visit one of the tried-and-tested indexes to the Internet, such as Yahoo! (www. yahoo.co.uk), Microsoft's Bing (www.bing.com) or the top search service Google (www.google.co.uk). Enter a word or phrase in the site's home page search box that describes the kinds of goods or services you want to provide online. Find out how many existing businesses already do what you want to do. Better yet, determine what they *don't* do and set a goal of meeting that need yourself.

Working out how to do it better

The next step is to find ways to make your business stand out from the crowd. Direct your energies toward making your site unique in some way. Can you provide things that others don't offer? The things that set your online business apart from the rest can be as tangible as half-price sales, contests, seasonal sales or freebies. Or they can be features of your site that make it higher quality or make it a better user experience than your competitors. Maybe you want to concentrate on making your customer service better than anyone else (see the nearby sidebar 'Mama locates her online niche' on how one mum made that happen and is now enjoying a business with a £120,000 turnover).

What if you can't find other online businesses doing what you want to do? In this case, you've either struck gold (you've come up with an idea that no one else has thought of) or struck out (the business doesn't exist because it's a bad idea). In e-commerce, being first often means getting a head start and being more successful than latecomers, even if they have more resources than you do. The Internet is crowded, however, and genuinely new ideas are getting harder to come by. But don't let that put you off trying something new and outlandish. It just might work!

Mama locates her online niche

When Christianne James left her job as a city banker and became a mum, she had her hands full and needed a job she could fit around her busy life. In early 2008, when the time came to pay the kids' school fees, she decided to start 4little1s (www.4little1s.com) – an online store selling items she was familiar with: baby products.

With the baby market so competitive, Christianne decided to focus on top customer service and choosing beautiful baby bedding, furniture and other special lines that aren't typically available in high street stores.

'We pride ourselves on customer service and this can be seen in responding to customers' queries and questions even at 11 p.m.; seven days a week,' she points out to Kim (who knows this is true, because Christianne responded to an email she sent her in the middle of the night UK time – Kim was in Australia having lunch at the time!).

Christianne needed to find the right niche rather than pit her business against the big companies like Mothercare, John Lewis and Mamas and Papas, which target the entire baby market. She explains: 'A small company can be very agile and respond quickly to new products. We can sell before the larger companies have even considered taking on new products. We are right on the edge of innovation and there are lots of mums out there with some great products.'

(continued)

(continued)

Christianne is very proficient with computers but doesn't call herself a techie, so at the outset she and her business partner appointed an expert company to create a professional-looking website. She says, 'My business partner had worked in IT for a number of years so that helped particularly when dealing with the website company that created our site and ensured we were not being taken advantage of.' She runs the e-commerce side of things using Actinic software that integrates into her accounting system.

Christianne now maintains the site with her husband and as of 2010 the business turned over £120,000 a year – up from first year turnover of £20,000. Running the business herself means she can drop the kids off and pick them up from school and nursery while still managing to keep the business running, although she is thinking about setting up a real-life storefront too.

'The use of mobile technology, such as Blackberry and iPhone devices, has also helped us become more flexible and able to run the business around busy family life,' she says. 'Having a partner that understands the business and the importance of it is crucial to family life too.'

Her other advice is to find a good accountant who can help with company formation and structure right through to dealing with annual accounts and VAT. Another top tip is to keep overheads down. 'Do you really need offices to operate from?' she asks. 'Or can you initially run from a home office instead?'

These days, 4little1s has come a long way to simply being a way to pay off those school fees. It's 'growing and providing an income,' Christianne enthuses.

Step 2: Know What You're Offering

Business is all about identifying customers' needs and figuring out exactly what goods or services you're going to provide to meet those needs. The same applies both online and off.

To determine what you have to offer, make a list of the items you plan to sell or the services that you plan to provide to your customers. Next, you need to decide where you're going to obtain them. Are you going to create sale items yourself? Are you going to purchase them from a supplier? Jot down your ideas on paper and keep them close at hand as you develop your business plan.

The Internet is a personal, highly interactive medium. Be as specific as possible with what you plan to do online. Don't try to do everything; the medium favours businesses that do one thing well. The more specific your business, the more personal the level of service you can provide to your customers.

Step 3: Come Up with a Virtual Business Plan

The process of setting goals and objectives and then working out how you'll attain them is essential when starting a new business. What you end up with is a *business plan*. A good business plan should be your guide not only in the startup phase, but also as your business grows. It should provide a blueprint for how you run your business on a day-to-day basis and can also be instrumental in helping you obtain a bank loan or any other type of funding.

To set specific goals for your new business, ask yourself these questions:

- ✔ Why do you want to start a business?
- ✔ Why do you want to start a business online?
- ✔ What would attract you to a website (regardless of what it's selling)?
- ✔ Why do you enjoy using some websites and not others?
- ✔ Why are you loyal to some websites and not others?

These questions may seem simple, but many businesspeople never take the time to answer them. Make sure that you have a clear game plan for your business so that your venture has a good chance of success over the long haul. (See Chapter 2 for more on setting goals and envisioning your business.)

You can link your plan to your everyday tasks by taking the following steps:

1. **Write a brief description of your business and what you hope to accomplish with it.**

2. **Draw up a marketing strategy.**

3. **Anticipate financial incomings and outgoings. (See Chapter 15 for specifics.)**

Consider using specialised software to help you prepare your business plan. Programs such as Business Plan Pro by Palo Alto Software (www.paloalto.co.uk) lead you through the process by making you consider every aspect of how your business will work. If you don't want to splash out on software, take a look at one of the many free guides to business plans out there. Business Link (www.businesslink.gov.uk), the government network that supports small businesses, is one of the best places to start.

Working at home?

If you use part of your home as a base for your business (and plenty of fledgling entrepreneurs do), then you should get on top of how that will affect your taxes. For example, the rooms you use may qualify for business rates instead of council tax, and you may also have to pay capital gains tax when you come to sell the property. Get the lowdown in Chapter 15. Better news is that you should get some tax relief on household bills, and you can claim VAT (if you're registered) or capital allowances back on household purchases made in your business's name. For example, office furniture, a lick of paint and stationery may be a bit cheaper.

Step 4: Get Your Act Together and Set Up Shop

One of the great advantages of opening a shop on the Internet rather than on the high street is the savings you should be able to make.

Know your budget

Showcasing your products online instead of in a real life shop means that you won't have to pay rent, decorate or worry about lighting and heating the place. Instead of renting a space and putting up furniture and fixtures, you can buy a domain name, sign up with a hosting service, create some web pages and get started with an investment of only a few hundred pounds, or maybe even less.

You still need to anticipate how much it'll cost to set up shop, and factor in any freelance costs.

In addition to your virtual showroom, you also have to find a real place to conduct the operations and logistics of your business. You don't necessarily have to rent a warehouse or other large space. Many online entrepreneurs use a home office or even just a corner in a room where computers, books and other business-related equipment sit. Why pay for the extra overheads?

Christianne James set up 4little1s on a budget of £7,000, the bulk of which comprised initial stock (for more on Christianne, see the sidebar 'Mama locates her online niche').

Finding a host for your website

Although doing business online means that you don't have to rent space in a shopping centre or open a real, physical shop, you do have to set up a virtual space for your online business. You do so by creating a website and finding a company to host it. In cyberspace, your landlord is called a web hosting service. A web *host* is a company that, for a fee, makes your site available 24 hours a day by maintaining it on a special computer called a web *server*.

Professional web hosts are cheap. The landscape for web hosting has changed a lot in recent years. Previously, a lot of people set up their own web pages using free space provided by their Internet Service Provider (ISP), the company that services their Internet connection.

But the small amount of free space provided by ISPs and the increasing complexity of websites means it's probably a better option – at least in the long run – to find a professional host for your website. These days, many ISPs offer business services and will double up as web hosts too, such as Zen Internet (www.zen.co.uk) or BT (www.bt.co.uk).

Paying for your web space (it doesn't have to be much) will give you some-one to complain to should things go wrong too.

Many web hosts provide you with easy starter tools to create and publish your own web pages, but some nifty free tools also exist that you can install on your own web space to help you create great looking pages (for more on this, see Chapters 3 and 5). If you do want some hand-holding, companies like 1and1 (www.1and1.co.uk), Easyspace (www.easyspace.co.uk), and Fasthosts (www.fasthosts.co.uk) are just a few web hosts that provide you with tools that you can use to create an online shop front.

Many hosts also provide you with easy tools to install blog, e-commerce and forum software with a click of a mouse onto your site. It pays to look at reviews, shop around to see what suits your needs and technical ability, and find out how much customer support the hosts will give you – for more, see Chapter 3. Figure 1-1 shows web host 1&1's home page, where a range of hosting packages is available.

Assembling the equipment you need

Think of all the equipment you *don't* need when you set up shop online: you don't need shelving, a cash register, a car park, fancy displays or lighting . . . the list goes on and on. You may need some of those for your home, but you don't need to purchase them especially for your online business itself.

Figure 1-1:
Take the time to choose an affordable web host that makes it easy for you to create and maintain your site.

Keeping track of your inventory

You can easily overlook inventory and setting up systems for processing orders when you're just starting out. But as Lucky Boyd, an entrepreneur who started MyTexasMusic.com and other websites, pointed out to Greg, you need to make sure you have a 'big vision' early in the process of creating your site. In his case, a big vision meant having a site that could handle lots of visitors and make purchasing easy for them. In other cases, it may mean having sufficient inventory to meet demand.

A fine line exists between having enough inventory and having too much, however. When you first start off, you need to dip your toe in the water – you don't want to end up with excess stock hanging around. Many online businesses keep track of their inventory by using a database that's connected to their website. When someone orders a product from the website, that order is automatically recorded in the database, which then produces an order for replacement stock or, in some cases, you may be notified on email about dwindling stock levels.

In this kind of arrangement, the database serves as a so-called *back end* or *back office* to the web-based shop front. This sophisticated arrangement is not for beginners so you might want to hire a web developer to do the setup for you. There are also some great all-in-one solutions that allow you to combine inventory management with an online storefront, such as the free osCommerce and Zen Cart or the e-commerce software Actinic, and an increasing number of web-based services can help you get started too. For more see Chapter 5.

For doing business online, your most important piece of equipment is your computer. Other hardware, such as scanners, printers, cameras, modems, backup drives and monitors, are also essential. You need to make sure that your computer equipment is up to scratch because you're going to be spending a lot of time online: answering emails, checking orders, revising your website and marketing your product. Expect to spend anywhere between £500 and £5,000 for equipment, if you don't have any to begin with. (Oh, and you'll need a comfortable desk and chair too, to avoid the strain of sitting for lengthy periods.)

Some equipment such as computer monitors and scanners are worth buying second-hand, especially if they're still under warranty and have been treated well. Computers are cheap, though, and it pays to invest in one that will accommodate the extra use you'll get out of it as you move forward. (For more suggestions on buying business hardware and software, see Chapter 2.)

Choosing the right software for your needs

You can build a website by either doing it yourself or paying someone else to do it for you. The first option is cheaper, but nine times out of ten, the latter produces something a lot more sophisticated. It's also far more practical to work with someone at the outset rather than getting them in halfway through. Try searching for *web design*, and you'll be confronted with a long list of businesses that offer design skills. Pick one that's reputable, has good references and allows you to contact current customers for their views on the service.

However, we see no reason why you can't do a lot of the building work yourself if you're determined enough – but this means you need to put in a lot of extra research and invest in the right kind of software. This needn't cost a lot of money; some solutions are actually free!

For the most part, the programs you need in order to operate an online business are the same as the software you use to surf the Internet. But you may need a wider variety of tools than you'd use for simple information gathering.

Because you're going to be in the business of information *providing* now, as well as information gathering, you need programs such as the following:

- ✔ **A content publishing platform or content management system:** You'll need to design and publish your site, and publishing platforms like Wordpress (www.wordpress.com) make it easy for most people to post articles, photo galleries and news on their sites. It may be a little tricky to install one on your web space initially, but when you're set it's very easy to log in to the Wordpress control panel to design your site's look and feel. You don't need to be a master of HyperText Markup Language (HTML), either.

If your site gets more complicated than just a few pages on a blog – or you plan to expand it in the future – then you can install a content management system. Technically speaking, Wordpress is a kind of content management system, but fully-fledged ones like Joomla! (www.joomla.com) and Drupal (www.drupal.com) let you add different kinds of content to your site (like videos, polls, forums, a shop front) and keep track of everything that's on it; from photos and videos to articles and inventory listings. You can easily display news, change the layout of your page without losing any of the content and much more besides.

Those of you with basic sites that you don't see yourself updating often could use a WYSIWYG web page editor. Pronounced *wizzy-wig*, this stands for What You See Is What You Get. As you edit your page, the editing screen displays what the final website will look like rather than just its underlying code. In the past, much WYSIWYG software tended to be clunky to use and disregarded web standards. Microsoft discontinued its popular one called FrontPage, and released an improved version called Microsoft Expression Web. Other popular affordable editors include CoffeeCup and NetObjects Fusion.

✔ **Graphics software:** If you decide to create your business website yourself instead of finding someone to do it for you, you need a program that can help you create or edit images and logos that you want to include on your site. Image-editing software like Adobe Photoshop Elements or Corel Paint Shop Pro will do the job.

✔ **Shop-front software:** Some content management tools include shop-front software elements or you can purchase software that leads you through the process of creating a fully fledged online business and getting your pages on the web.

✔ **Accounting programs:** You can write your expenses and income on a sheet of paper. But it's far more efficient to use software that acts as a spreadsheet, helps you with billing and even calculates VAT.

Step 5: Get Help

Conducting online business does involve relatively new technologies, but they aren't impossible to figure out. In fact, the technology has become quite accessible. Many people who start online businesses find out how to create web pages and promote their companies by reading books, attending classes or networking with friends and colleagues. Of course, just because you *can* do it all doesn't mean that you have to. You may be better off hiring help, either to advise you in areas where you aren't as strong or simply to help you tackle the growing workload – and help your business grow at the same time.

Hiring technical bods

Spending money up front to hire professionals who can point you in the right direction can help you maintain an effective web presence for years to come. Many businesspeople who usually work alone (us included) hire knowledgeable individuals to do design or programming work that they'd find impossible to tackle otherwise.

Don't be reluctant to hire professional help in order to get your business off the ground. The web is full of developers that can provide customers with web access, help create websites and host sites on their servers. The expense for such services may be relatively high at first – probably several thousand pounds – but it'll pay off in the long term. Choose a designer carefully and check out the sites he's designed by getting in contact with customers and asking whether they're satisfied. Don't just tell a designer your business plan; send him the document (omitting your projected finances), explaining in fine detail exactly what your business aims are and how the website will fulfil those aims. Web design isn't all about snazzy graphics and bells and whistles: it's all about delivery, ease of use and accessibility.

When planning to employ a technical or design bod, draw up a simple contract that ensures you retain all copyrights to the work he undertakes, and make it clear from the outset that you'll have ultimate control of the site. You don't want a developer to 'lock you out' of your own site, making it difficult to change things around should you need to. For more legalities, see Chapter 14.

Who are the people in your neighbourhood?

Try to find an expert or helper right in your own town. Ask around your school, university or workplace, as well as any social venue you attend. Your neighbours may even be able to help you with various projects, including your online business . . . and your online business just may be able to help them too.

Just like finding a good tradesperson, positive word of mouth is the ideal way to find a reputable web designer.

If you're stumped and don't know anyone who's had their site built, try looking at some local websites that you like the look of – many designers will place a small link to their portfolio at the bottom of the site's main page and they may well live nearby. You might be able to find some further examples of the designer's work. Can you find what you're looking for? Does the site load quickly and without errors?

Don't work in a vacuum. Get involved with mailing lists and discussion groups online. Make contacts through these mediums and strike up relationships with people who can help you. Try UK Business Forums (`www.ukbusinessforums.co.uk`) to start with and go from there.

If you do find a business partner, make sure that the person's abilities balance your own. If you're great at sales and public relations, for example, find a writer, web page designer or someone who's good with the accounts to partner with.

Gathering your team

Many fast-growing businesses are family affairs. For example, Dave Cresswell and his brother Steve started an online comic store, Comic Domain (www.comicdomain.co.uk), and husband-and-wife team Jean and Geoff Sewell turned their successful real-life craft shop, The Cotton Patch, into a successful online store (www.cottonpatch.co.uk).

Early on, when you have plenty of time for planning, you probably won't feel a pressing need to hire others to help you. Many people wait to seek help when they have a deadline to meet or are in a financial crunch. Waiting to seek help is okay – as long as you realise that you probably *will* need help, sooner or later.

Of course, you don't have to hire family and friends, it's just that they'll probably be more sympathetic to your startup worries. They'll probably work harder for you and may even lend a hand for free.

If you feel you have to hire someone from the outside world, you must find people who are reliable and can make a long-term commitment to your project. Keep these things in mind:

- ✔ Because the person you hire will probably work online quite a bit, pick someone who already has experience with computers and the Internet.

- ✔ Online hiring works the same as hiring offline: you should always review a *curriculum vitae* (*CV*; or work history) get a couple of references, and ask for samples of the candidate's work.

- ✔ Choose someone who responds promptly and in a friendly manner and who demonstrates the talents you need.

- ✔ We can't stress how important it is to set timeframes and milestones on when you want things delivered – don't just agree on some wishy-washy dates. That way you'll know whether everything's going to plan.

- ✔ Ensure that you set boundaries before work begins and that you retain ultimate control of your website. The experts are there to help and guide you, but ultimately you're the one paying for the job.

Step 6: Designing and Planning Your Website

Even the most prolific eBay.co.uk sellers (see Chapter 10) usually complement their shop with their own website. Luckily, websites are becoming easier to create. You don't have to know a line of HTML in order to create an okay-looking web page yourself. (Chapter 5 walks you through the tasks involved in organising and designing web pages. Also, see Chapter 6 for tips on making your web pages content-rich and interactive.)

Make your business easy to find online. Pick an easy-to-remember web address (otherwise known as a *domain name* or a *URL*). If the ideal `.com` or `.co.uk` name isn't available, you can try one of the newer domain suffixes, such as `.biz`, but this suffix hasn't really hit mainstream consciousness yet. Plans are afoot for even more suffixes – a potentially limitless supply which means you could have `.yourbrandname` domain names. The impact of this remains to be seen – for now, `.com` and `.co.uk` names are still the most recognised. (See Chapter 3 and Chapter 8 for more information on domain name aliases.)

Making your site content-rich

The words and pictures of a website (as well as the products) are what attract visitors and keep them coming back on a regular basis. And the more compelling and useful the content, the higher your website ranks in search engines like Google – which results in more visits.

By compelling content, we're talking about words, headings or images that make visitors want to continue reading. You can make your content compelling in a number of ways:

- ✔ **Call to action:** Provide a call to action, such as 'Buy two get one free' or 'Receive special offers. Subscribe to our weekly newsletter!'.

- ✔ **Encourage browsing:** Readers have short attention spans. Provide a link that explains how visiting parts of the site will benefit them. ('Visit our News and Offers page to find out how to win double discounts this month.')

- ✔ **Briefly and concisely summarise your business and its mission:** Make it sound important. Online bookstore The Book Depository (`www.the bookdepository.co.uk`) clearly and proudly proclaims 'Free delivery worldwide on all our books'.

✔ **Pictures:** Use a digital camera to capture images of your sale items (or of the services you provide), as we describe in Chapter 5, and post them on a web page.

✔ **Timely language:** Let people know your great deal won't last forever – for example 'Offer expires 30 April' or 'Don't miss out! Act now'.

✔ **Keep it 'above the fold':** You hear this phrase a lot in design circles. It refers to the content you see on screen before scrolling down. All your compelling content should be located here to catch the reader's attention. The term originates from the old-style broadsheet newspapers like the New York Times or the Daily Telegraph whose urgent headlines are situated at the top half of the page, above the newspaper fold.

Don't forget the personal touch when it comes to connecting with your customers' needs. People who shop online don't get to meet the shop owner in person, so anything you can tell them about yourself helps make the process more personal and puts your visitors at ease. For example, Keith and Lauren Milsom's left-handed products shop, Anything Left Handed (shown in Figure 1-2), welcomes the visitor by explaining how their online store is the oldest and biggest specialist left-handed website in the world. There's also a link to a popular blog that talks about the various issues, light-hearted or otherwise, that left-handed people (Kim included!) have using various objects. According to a post on their blog, even pencils are designed for right-handed people, because the printing on them is upside down when held in the left hand! This post presents a good opportunity for Keith and Lauren to plug their 'left-handed' pencil, designed to confuse people who hold it in their right hand. The logo on it reads: 'It's a left-handed thing, you wouldn't understand!'

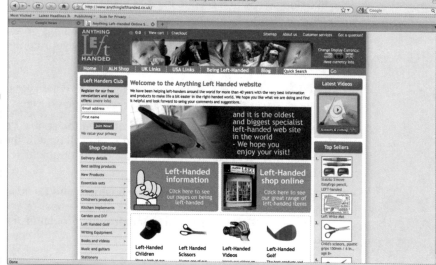

Figure 1-2: Personalise your business to connect with customers online, like Anything Left Handed.

Let your visitors know that they're dealing with real people, not remote machines and computer programs.

Sneaking a peek at other businesses' websites – to pick up ideas and see how they handle similar issues to your own – is a common and perfectly legitimate practice. Online, you can visit plenty of businesses that are comparable to yours from the comfort of your home office, and the trip takes mere minutes.

Copying other websites isn't clever and will land you in legal trouble, although no harm exists in gaining inspiration from what other people do well.

Establishing a brand and visual identity

When you start your first business on the web, you have to do a certain amount of convincing. You need to show customers that you're competent and professional. One factor that helps build trust is a visual identity. A site with an identity has a consistent look and feel no matter what part of the website you access. This is a lot easier to achieve in web design nowadays because of what's known as Cascading Style Sheets (CSS) – this is a file that defines the parameters of the pages on the website such as the column widths, fonts and their sizes, background images or colours, where the banner is placed and so on.

Should you ever decide to update your website's look and feel, you only need to edit the CSS file rather than every individual page. We talk more about this in Chapter 5. For example, take a look at Figure 1-3, as well as the example in the earlier sidebar 'Mama locates her online niche'. Both pages are from the 4Little1s website. Notice how in each the banner and sidebar are consistent in both images. Using these standard elements from page to page creates a brand identity that gives your business credibility and helps users find what they're looking for.

Establishing a brand is also important so your customers can feel immersed in your product. Take a look at a fashion or car magazine and look at the product advertisements. They convey a sense of luxury, aspiration and achievement. Ask yourself what you want *your* customers to feel when they use your product or service. Apart from the content, cool and warm colours, classic or contemporary fonts – these all make a difference. An architect might have a gallery of large photos that show off the buildings he's designed, each taken from a similar angle. And he might include a short bio of himself with a photo working or consulting with a client, as a way of showcasing his professionalism.

Figure 1-3:
Through careful planning and design, the 4little1s site maintains a consistent look and feel, or visual identity, on each page.

Testing your website

Unleashing your website to the world without giving it a test run can cause all sorts of issues. How easy is it for people to find what they're looking for? If you're too close to our own product, you can sometimes miss the obvious – for example, you might have categorised a product for sale in an area that makes sense to you, yet customers would never think to look there. Where do you think *your* visitors go?

Then you have the various browsers, such as Internet Explorer, Firefox, Safari and Chrome, that people use to access the web; not to mention the multiple mobile devices like Android phones and iPhones. Can your website display effectively on all these?

Typically, when Kim talks to both web design agencies who work for global clients as well as small businesses who've created a successful website on a shoestring, the only difference in their approaches is scale. Testing is important and doing it needn't be a mammoth effort. For example, a large company might get a number of focus groups to assess a preliminary website design or test-drive an early version of it, whereas you might ask some family and friends to look at a few sketches. Or you could give your site a technical check-up for free on sites like www.w3.org. We explain some low-fi techniques in Chapter 5.

Step 7: Process Your Sales

Many businesses go online and then are surprised by their own success. They don't have systems in place for completing sales, shipping goods in a timely manner, and tracking finances and stock.

An excellent way to plan for success is to set up ways to track your business finances and to create a secure online purchasing environment for your customers. That way, you can build on your success rather than be surprised by it.

Providing a means for secure transactions

Getting paid is the key to survival, let alone success. When your business exists online only, the payment process isn't always straightforward. Make your website a safe and easy place for customers to pay you. Provide different payment options and build customers' level of trust any way you can.

Although the level of trust among people who shop online is increasing steadily, a few web surfers are still squeamish about submitting credit-card numbers online. And fresh-faced businesspeople are understandably intimidated by the requirements of processing credit-card transactions. In the past, many online businesses used simple forms that customers had to print and mail along with a cheque. This arrangement is a pretty rare practice nowadays, because it slows down what should be a lightening quick transaction. Handling transactions in this manner today will raise some eyebrows among your customers and many will go elsewhere.

You can use numerous types of transaction software. PayPal and Google both operate their own, for example, and a host of independent businesses have also set up cheap alternatives. These services take a small percentage of the money you make every time you complete a sale; some are even free to set up – PayPal makes it easy for you to place 'Buy Now' buttons under your products. Customers expect to see this kind of transaction software when they shop online; gone are the days when the majority of e-shoppers paid over the phone or by post.

When you're able to accept credit cards, make your customers feel at ease by explaining what measures you're taking to ensure that their information is secure. Such measures include signing up for an account with a web host that provides a *secure server*, a computer that uses software to encrypt data and uses digital documents called *certificates* to ensure its identity. (See Chapters 7 and 11 for more on Internet security and secure shopping systems.)

The online payment service WorldPay lets small- and medium-sized businesses easily accept online payments, and it works with all major e-commerce software like Actinic or osCommerce. The process goes like this: when shoppers want to make a purchase, they use a *shopping trolley* or *cart* that acts as an electronic 'holding area' for items before they're purchased. Next, people can safely enter credit card and other personal information. The note stating that the payment area is protected by Secure Sockets Layer (SSL) encryption tells people that, even if a criminal intercepts their credit-card data, he won't be able to read it. Details are authenticated and checked for fraud by a system known as a *payment gateway*, and finally settled so funds are credited to the bank associated with the business's *internet merchant account*.

Safeguarding your customers' personal information is important, but you also need to safeguard your business. Many online businesses get burned by bad guys who submit fraudulent credit-card information. If you don't verify the information and submit it to your bank for processing, you're liable for the cost. Your payment gateway should check for fraud, but strongly consider signing up with a service that handles credit-card verification for you in order to cut down on lost revenue. The Anything Left Handed website (see the earlier section 'Making your site content-rich') uses a company called The 3rd Man to do an 'offline' fraud check for extra peace of mind.

How not to cook your books

What does *keeping your books* mean, anyway? In the simplest sense, it means recording all your business's financial activities – in other words, your incomings and outgoings, including any expenses you incur, all the income you receive, as well as your equipment and tax deductions. The financial side of running a business also means creating reports, such as profit-and-loss statements, that banks require if you apply for a loan. Such reports also give you good information about how well business is going, and where (if it all) things need to improve.

You can record all this information the old-fashioned way by writing it in ledgers and journals, or you can use a spreadsheet (like Microsoft Excel), or you can use accounting software. (See Chapter 15 for some suggestions of easy-to-use accounting packages that are great for financial novices.) Because you're making a commitment to using computers on a regular basis by starting an online business, using computers to keep your books too is only natural. Accounting software can help you keep track of expenses and provide information that may save you a headache when the tax authorities comes knocking.

After you've saved your financial data on your hard drive, make backups so that you don't lose information you need to do business. See Chapter 7 for ways to back up and protect your files.

Step 8: Provide Personal Service

The Internet, which runs on cables, networks and computer chips, may not seem like a place for the personal touch. But it's exactly that.

You might have heard the term *web 2.0*, a buzz word that describes the current socially-focused, collaborative websites that make it easy to communicate and share information and ideas with people around the world. With broadband and smart phones effectively meaning people are always contactable and 'on', don't be surprised if people get impatient if you don't respond within a day.

Technology didn't actually create the Internet and all its content; *people* did that. In fact, the Internet is the perfect place to provide your clients and customers with outstanding, personal customer service.

In many cases, customer service on the Internet is a matter of being available and responding quickly to all enquiries. You check your email regularly and respond promptly; you cheerfully solve problems and hand out refunds if needed.

By helping your customers, you help yourself too. You build loyalty as well as credibility among your clientele. For many small businesses, the key to competing effectively with larger competitors is to provide superior customer service. See Chapter 12 for more ideas on how you can offer great customer service.

Sharing your expertise

Your knowledge and experience are among your most valuable commodities. So you may be surprised when we suggest that you give them away for free. Why? It's a *try-before-you-buy* concept. Helping people for free builds your credibility and makes them more likely to pay for your services down the road.

We talk more about ways you can share your expertise and gain customers in Chapter 6. If you're an accountant, you could post advice pieces to fledgling entrepreneurs on blogs or news sites for free. Why free? Because visitors will remember sound advice down the line when they need to pay for financial expertise.

When your business is online, you can easily communicate what you know about your field and make your knowledge readily available. One way is to set up a web page that presents the basics about your company and your field of interest in the form of Frequently Asked Questions (FAQs). Another technique is to create your own email newsletter in which you write about what's new with your company and about topics related to your work. You could also set up a Facebook page dedicated to your business – if people become a 'fan' of your page, you can then broadcast updates that appear in their news feed. See Chapter 12 for more on communicating your expertise through FAQs, newsletters and advanced email techniques.

Greg's brother, who runs his own web business, was sceptical when Greg recommended to him that he include a page full of technical information explaining exactly what equipment he uses and describing the steps involved in audio restoration. He didn't think anyone would be interested; he also didn't want to give away his 'trade secrets'. *Au contraire, mon frère!* By and large, people who surf the Internet gobble up all the technical details they can find. The more you wow them with the names and model numbers of your expensive equipment, not to mention the work you go through to restore their old records, the more they'll trust you. And trust will get them to place an order with you. This approach doesn't necessarily work with any business; it often makes sense to keep things simple. But if you're selling a technical service – in other words anything that people are unlikely to understand easily – don't be afraid to let people know just how gifted you have to be to perform the task!

Making your site appealing

Entrepreneurs succeed by making their websites not only a place for sales and promotion but also an indispensable resource, full of useful links and other information, that customers want to visit again and again.

The Anything Left Handed website shown in Figure 1-4 (see the earlier section 'Making your site content-rich') has a comprehensive section on being left-handed – this explains everything from how products such as left-handed scissors and knives work, to how to make things easier for left-handed children. Some blog posts are hugely popular. 'Our left-handed articles are always very well received,' owner Keith Milsom says, 'and end up with hundreds of comments on them, which, apart from increasing the amount of content on our page, usually generates more ideas for new content than we ever have time to create.'

For any online business, knowing the names and addresses of people who visit and who don't necessarily make purchases is a gold mine of information. The business can use the contact information to send members special offers and news releases; the more regularly contact is maintained, the more likely casual shoppers or members will eventually turn into paying customers.

Figure 1-4:
The left-
handed
site has a
comprehen-
sive, free
resource to
being left-
handed.

You will, of course, need to ensure that visitors have *consented* to receive marketing material. Under data protection law, whenever you gather personal information such as a name and email address, you need to give people an opportunity there and then to opt-out from receiving further communications.

The concept of membership also builds a feeling of community among customers. By turning the e-commerce site into a meeting place for members who love Texas musicians, Lucky Boyd's MyTexasMusic.com helps those members make new friends and have a reason to visit the site on a regular basis. Community building is one way in which commerce on the web differs from traditional brick-and-mortar selling, and it's something you should consider too.

Another way to encourage customers to congregate at your site on a regular basis is to create a dedicated discussion area known as a *forum*. You can also display a Facebook 'Like' button on your site or a Google '+1' so visitors can become a fan of your page by just pasting a small bit of code on to your web page.

Emailing your way to the top

Email is, in our humble opinion, the single most important marketing tool that you can use to boost your online business. Becoming an expert email user increases your contacts and provides you with new sources of support too.

The two best and easiest email strategies are the following:

- ✔ Check your email as often as possible.
- ✔ Respond to email enquiries immediately.

Additionally, you can email enquiries about co-operative marketing opportunities to other websites similar to your own. Ask other online business owners whether they'll provide links to your site in exchange for you providing links to theirs. And always include a signature file with your message that includes the name of your business and a link to your business site. See Chapter 12 for more information on using email effectively to build and maintain relations with your online customers.

Note: We're encouraging you to use email primarily for one-to-one communication. The Internet excels at bringing individuals together. Mailing lists, desktop alerts and newsletters can use email effectively for marketing too. However, we're *not* encouraging you to send out mass quantities of unsolicited commercial email, a practice that turns off almost all consumers and that can get you in trouble with the law too.

Step 9: Promoting Your Business

The Internet is a noisy place, and the people who shout the loudest aren't usually the ones who get noticed – or rather, people will make a point of ignoring them because what they're saying is simply irrelevant. What's great about the Internet is that it's so easy to target niche demographics in a meaningful and relevant way.

To be successful, small businesses need to get the word out to the people who are likely to purchase what they have to offer. If this group turns out to be a narrow demographic, so much the better; the Internet is great for connecting to niche markets that share a common interest.

The Internet provides many unique and effective ways for small businesses to advertise, including search services, email, blogs, forums, electronic mailing lists and more.

Ensuring you're seen by search engines

How, exactly, do you get a highly ranked listing on the search engines such as Yahoo!, Bing and Google? Frankly, it's getting more difficult.

Getting your site ranked highly is big business, with specialist companies optimising the content on your pages to ensure that search engines place more relevance to *your* page as opposed to someone else's. Your website needs to be in ship-shape: no duplicate content, technically sound, free of bugs, regularly updated, relevant key words and so on. This practice (or art, depending on how you look at it) is called *search engine optimisation*, or SEO, and is a major part of your marketing toolkit. Some design agencies work together with SEO companies; or you could take a look at some great sites and blogs dedicated to search engines such as the long-running Search Engine Watch (`www.searchenginewatch.com`) and the popular blog of Kim's former colleague Malcolm Coles at `www.malcolmcoles.co.uk`.

We explain how search engines index your site in Chapter 13. Because the system is open to abuse, the way search engines rank your pages is extremely complex. Google has a free website optimiser (`www.google.com/websiteoptimizer`) that can help identify problems in the structure of your web page.

Advertising your website

Your website may be the cornerstone of your business, but if nobody knows it's out there, it can't help you generate sales.

The most familiar forms of online advertising are the *banner ads* (which run across the top of websites) and *skyscrapers* (which run vertically down the side of pages).

The sponsored, text-based advertisements that you find when conducting searches online or while browsing the web are affordable ways for you to advertise your website. The advertisements always relate to the type of thing the person is looking for or to the content of the page, so they're likely to be relevant.

This kind of advertising, currently led by Google, is called *pay per click* advertising. You only pay when someone clicks on your link, as opposed to paying just for the privilege of displaying your website. How much you pay depends on how much you're prepared to bid on certain search keywords, such as *holiday, Cotswolds* or *bed and breakfast* – it could be as little as £1 a click or as much as £5. The more money advertisers are prepared to pay, the more prominently their ads tend to appear.

Many small businesses put aside a budget to market their websites in this way, but targeting the right market can be hit and miss, so you need to be prepared to do your competitor research and take a look at some of the handy hints on websites such as Search Engine Watch (`www.searchenginewatch.com`).

You can advertise your website in loads of other places – Google Places lets you list it for free on its maps, and Yahoo! local will also place your business in its directory.

Chapter 12 contains everything you need to know about marketing with email newsletters.

Writing and sending a press release

Alerting the media to your new venture takes a lot of leg work, but if it means coverage in the long run – which in turn leads to sales – then it's all worth it.

Simply writing a release that says you've launched a business is no good. Is there some original research you've conducted with juicy stats that you can tie in to your website? Does your website sell something unusual and exclusive, such as a novelty gift that a journalist might want to feature in a Christmas buying guide?

A number of companies out there will distribute your press release, but it's a good idea to manually collate the contact details of a publication's features or news editor.

Using social media to create a buzz

You've heard all about Twitter and Facebook – and now Google Plus – these are powerful *social media* tools to help you promote your business.

Through these websites, you can communicate to your followers both on a one-to-one and a one-to-many basis. They can communicate back too. Perhaps they want to praise your product or offer up some constructive criticism.

Having your business out there, warts and all, can seem daunting if you know it's going to be a public target. But being on these websites puts you on the same footing as your customers. Look at the thousands of celebrities who have their own Twitter accounts. They often respond personally to fans, making people feel closer to them. Much of the time, negative comments can be turned into positives. If people know you've responded quickly (and as best you can) to any enquiries or complaints, they'll have trust in your brand.

Twitter lets you post updates of up to 140 characters called *tweets*. Thousands of tweets go on every second, so whatever you say should probably be witty, practical, exclusive or smart – that way people can *retweet* what you say to *their* follows, generating a snowball effect. That's what we mean about creating a buzz.

Step 10: Review, Revise and Improve

We go into more details about tweeting and a whole lot more in Chapter 9.

For any long-term endeavour, you need to establish standards by which you can judge its success or failure. You must decide for yourself what you consider success to be. After a period of time, take stock of where your business is and then take steps to do even better.

Taking stock

After 12 months online, web entrepreneur Lucky Boyd took stock. His site was online, but he wasn't getting many page views. He redid the site, increased the number of giveaways, and traffic rose. Now, he's preparing to redo all his web pages with the Hypertext Preprocessor programming language (PHP).

HTML is a mark-up language: it identifies parts of a web page that need to be formatted as headings, text, images and so on. You can use HMTL to include scripts, such as those written in the JavaScript language.

By creating pages from scratch using scripting languages like PHP you can make a site more dynamic and easier to update as opposed to the more 'static' HTML pages. You can rotate random images, process forms and compile statistics that track visitors by using PHP scripts, for example (although Google Analytics makes it a cinch to discover these facts and figures by pasting a small bit of code onto your web pages). The best thing about dynamic languages like PHP is that you can design web pages in a modular way so that you redesign and revise them more quickly than with HTML.

Another popular technique used on many web pages is called Ajax. This makes websites faster and more dynamic because they retrieve information in the background without you realising it. Services like Google Maps, where you can seamlessly zoom in to a location as if it's the most natural thing in the world, is one example of Ajax in action.

When all's said and done, your business may do so well that you can reinvest in it by buying new equipment or increasing your services. You may even be in a position to give something back to not-for-profits and those in need. Perhaps you'll have enough money left over to reward yourself too – as if being able to tell everyone 'I own my own online business' isn't reward enough. Who knows, you might even be featured in the next edition of this book!

The truth is, plenty of entrepreneurs are online for reasons other than making money. That said, it *is* important from time to time to evaluate how well you're doing financially. Accounting software, such as the programs that we describe in Chapter 15, makes it easy to check your revenues on a daily or weekly basis. The key is to establish the goals you want to reach and develop measurements so that you know when and if you reach those goals.

Updating your data

Getting your business online and then updating your site regularly is better than waiting to unveil the perfect website all at once. In fact, seeing your site improve and grow is one of the best things about going online. Over time, you can create contests, strike up relationships with other businesses and add more background information about your products and services.

Businesses on the web need to evaluate and revise their practices on a regular basis. Lucky Boyd of MyTexasMusic.com (see the earlier sidebar 'Keeping track of your inventory') studies reports of where visitors come from before they reach his site, and what pages they visit on the site, so that he can attract new customers. These types of statistics should also reveal what page people are on when they *leave* your site, whether a visit converts to a sale and whether they're repeat visitors and much more. Online business is a process of trial and error. The point is that experimenting with what promotions works and what don't needs to be an ongoing process and a long-term commitment. Taking a chance and profiting from your mistakes is better than not trying in the first place.

Chapter 2

Choosing and Equipping Your New Online Business

In This Chapter

▶ Picturing your successful online business

▶ Understanding your options: sales, services and auctions

▶ Making your online shop stand out from the crowd

▶ Buying or upgrading your computer hardware

▶ Assembling a business software suite

Starting your online business is like refurbishing an old house – something Greg is constantly doing. Both projects involve a series of recognisable phases:

✔ **The idea phase:** First, you tell people about your great idea. They hear the enthusiasm in your voice, nod their heads and say something like, 'Good luck.' They've seen you in this condition before and know how it usually turns out.

✔ **The decision phase:** Undaunted, you begin honing your plan. You read books (like this one), ask questions and shop around until you find just the right tools and materials to get you on your way. Of course, when you're up to your neck in work, you may start to panic, asking yourself whether you're really up for the task.

✔ **The assembly phase:** Undeterred, you forge ahead. You plug in your tools and go to work. Drills spin and sparks fly as your idea becomes reality.

✔ **The test-drive phase:** One fine day, out of the dust and fumes, your masterpiece emerges. You invite everyone over to enjoy the fruits of your labour. All those who were sceptical before are now awe-struck and full of admiration. Satisfied with the result, you enjoy your project for years to come.

If refurbishing a house doesn't work for you, think about restoring an antique car, planning an anniversary party or devising a mountain-climbing excursion in Tibet. The point is that starting an online business is a project like any other – one that you can construct and accomplish in stages. Right now, you're at the first stage of launching your new business. Your creativity is working overtime. You may even have some rough sketches that only a mother could love.

This chapter helps you get from concept to reality. Your first step is to imagine how you want your business to look and feel. Then you can begin to develop and implement strategies for achieving your dream. You've got a big advantage over those who started new businesses a few years ago: you've got thousands of predecessors to show you what works and what doesn't.

Starting Off on the Right Foot

As you travel along the path from idea to reality, you must also consider equipping your online business properly – just like you'd have to equip a traditional, bricks-and-mortar business. One of the many exciting aspects of launching a business online, however, is the absence of many *overheads* (that is, operating expenses). Many real world businesses resort to taking out loans to pay the rent and design their shop fronts, pay fees and purchase shop furniture. In contrast, the primary overhead for an online business is computer gadgetry. It's great if you can afford top-of-the-line equipment, but you'll be happy to know that the latest bells and whistles aren't absolutely necessary in order to build a business online and maintain it effectively. But in order to streamline the technical aspects of connecting to the Internet and creating a business website, some investment is always necessary.

Don't rush into a contract with a web designer or hosting company without researching the market and finding out exactly what you're getting for your money. Dan once made the mistake of paying upfront for a hosting and design package; he now believes that after they've got your money, they sit back and don't work hard for your business. You should demand an invoice for work done and make them tell you what they'll actually do for your business in the real world. A search engine optimisation package, for example, may be a waste of money as you could do it yourself (see Chapter 13 for more on search engines). Most importantly, make the company spell out a timeline of progress so that you have a rough idea of when you'll be ready to launch.

Mapping Out Your Online Business

How do you get off square one? Start by imagining the kind of business that's your ultimate goal. This step is the time to indulge in some brainstorming. Envisioning your business is a creative way of asking yourself the all-important questions: Why do I want to go into business online? What are my goals? Table 2-1 illustrates possible objectives and suggests how to achieve them.

By envisioning the final result you want to achieve, you can determine the steps you need to take to get there.

Table 2-1	Online Business Models	
Goal	*Type of website*	*What to Do*
Make big bucks	Sales	Sell items or get lots of paying advertisers
Gain credibility and attention	Marketing	Put your CV and samples of your work online
Turn an interest into a source of income	Hobby/special interest	Invite like-minded people to share your passion, participate in your site and generate traffic so that you can gain advertisers or customers

Getting inspired

You don't need to feel like you have to reinvent the wheel. A great idea doesn't necessarily mean something completely fresh that's never been done before (although if you have a great, new idea, then good for you!). Sometimes, spending just half an hour surfing the Net can stimulate your mental network. Find sites with qualities you want to emulate. Throughout this book, we suggest good business sites you can visit to find good models to follow.

Many people start up online selling to people just like themselves. For example, a motorbike enthusiast may start up a parts business or an informative site about the best bikes and where to buy them. If you're a hobby geek, then your own likes and dislikes have a lot of value. As you search the web for inspiration, make a list as you go of what you find appealing and jot down notes on logos, designs, text and *functionality* (how the site lets you access its features). That way, you'll have plenty of data to draw upon as you begin to refine what you yourself want to do.

Standing out from the crowd

The online world has undergone a population explosion. According to Internet Systems Consortium's Domain Survey (www.isc.org), in July 2010, 768.9 million computers that hosted websites were connected to the Internet, compared with 439.2 million in 2006 and 171.6 million in 2002. As an online entrepreneur, your goal is to make your mark – or to 'position yourself in the marketplace', as business consultants like to say. Consider the following tried-and-tested suggestions if you want your website to be a popular corner of the Internet:

- ✔ **Do something you know all about.** Experience adds value to the information you provide. Doing something that you have experience of also keeps you interested throughout the roller-coaster ride that is starting a business. Most importantly, in the online world, expertise sells.

- ✔ **Make a statement.** On your website, include a mission statement that clearly identifies what you do, the customers you hope to reach and how you're different from your competitors. Depending on what you plan to set up, this statement may be on the home page (in the form of a concise About Us statement) or in a frequently asked questions (FAQ) section of the site.

- ✔ **Include contact details.** We may be in a digital age, but people still crave the personal touch. You must prove that you're not a machine by keeping the language you use friendly, and including a phone number and email address is best practice. People are also very suspicious of websites that don't declare their address. (In addition, the legal requirements for a business website include putting your company name, registration number, registered office and VAT number on the site.)

- ✔ **Give something away for free.** We really can't stress this tip enough. Giveaways and promotions are proven ways to gain attention and develop a loyal customer base. You don't have to give away an actual product; you can offer words of wisdom based on your training and experience. Take a look at the hugely popular Money Saving Expert website at `www.moneysavingexpert.com`, which has allowed countless consumers to get great deals or learn about consumer rights without them forking out a penny.

- ✔ **Be obvious.** Money Saving Expert, which we list in the preceding bullet, does what it says on the tin. It helps if your website tells people what it does before they even get to the home page.

- ✔ **Find your niche.** Web space is a great place to pursue *niche marketing*. In fact, it often seems that the quirkier the item, the better it sells. Don't be afraid to target a narrow audience and direct all your sales efforts to a small group of devoted followers.

- ✔ **Do something you love.** The more you love your business, the more time and effort you're apt to put into it and, therefore, the more likely it is to be successful. Such businesses take advantage of the Internet's worldwide reach, which makes it easy for people with the same interests to gather at the same virtual location.

The top new economy millionaires have followed many, if not all the aforementioned strategies. Take Rightmove.co.uk. It was already making £8.9 million profit back in 2005, because its founders saw a trend towards people looking for property online. The founders built a simple and functional website and quickly cornered the burgeoning market. In March 2006, the company floated on the stock market and by 2007, 90 per cent of all UK real estate agents were Rightmove.co.uk members, advertising their properties via the website. In 2009, its profit had grown to a whopping £41.9 million!

Nick Robertson's ASOS.com (formally known as As Seen On Screen) jumped on people's insatiable appetite for the lifestyles of the rich and famous. The premise was simple: dress like the stars you worship. The website's meteoric success has allowed it to expand beyond its TV-based roots, and now it boasts a huge array of celebrity-inspired fashion. Oh, and the profitable company made £233 million in sales the year ending March 2010 – up 35 per cent on the previous year – and a profit of £14.6 million after tax. Not bad considering the economic climate!

Evaluating commercial websites

Is your website similar to others? How does it differ? (Or to put it another way: how is it better?) Your customers will be asking these questions, so you may as well start out by asking them as well.

Commercial websites – those whose Internet addresses usually end with .co. uk, .com or .biz – are the fastest-growing segment of the Net and this is the area you'll be entering. The trick is to be comfortable with the size and level of complexity of a business that's right for you. In general, your options are

- ✔ **A big commercial website:** The web means big business, and plenty of big companies create websites with the primary goal of supplementing a product or service that's already well known and well established. Just a few examples are the Ribena website (www.ribena.co.uk), the Pepsi World website (www.pepsiworld.com) and the Toyota website (www.toyota.com). True, these commercial websites were created by corporations with many millions of pounds to throw around, but you can still look at them to get ideas for your own site.

- ✔ **A mid-size site:** You can look at mid-sized companies too, which use the web as an extension of their brand. Brilliant examples of mid-sized companies are Ben & Jerry's ice cream (www.benjerry.co.uk) and Innocent Drinks (www.innocentdrinks.co.uk). Stephen Fry is famous for being a prolific Twitter user, but he writes far lengthier observations on his website, www.stephenfry.com. Sites such as CD Wow (www.cdwow.co.uk) and Play.com (www.play.com) are mid-sized companies, but their websites are as good as any blue chip you're likely to come across.

✔ **A site that's just right:** No prerequisites for prior business experience guarantee success on the web. Starting out as a single person, couple or family is also fine. In fact, we devote the rest of this book to helping you produce a top-notch, home-grown entrepreneurial business with the minimum of assistance. This chapter gets you off to a good start by examining the different kinds of business you can launch online and some business goals you should be setting yourself.

Checking Out Flavours of Online Businesses You Can Taste Test

If you're an excitable character, you may have to curb your enthusiasm as you comb the Internet for ideas. Use the following examples to create a picture of your business and then zero in on the kind of sites that can help you formulate its look and feel.

Selling consumer products

The web has always attracted those looking for unique items or something customised just for them. Consider taking your wares online if one or both of the following applies to you:

✔ You're a creative person who creates as a hobby the type of stuff people may want to buy (think artists, designers, model makers and so on). For example, Dan's mum is great at calligraphy, and he thinks she'd make a packet by selling her writing online.

✔ You have access to the sort of products or services that big companies simply can't replicate. Those items may mean regional foods, hand-made souvenirs or items for car enthusiasts; the list is truly endless – you just have to find your niche.

Innocent Drinks (www.innocentdrinks.co.uk) has never lost its 'community' feel, despite becoming bigger and bigger and moving on from simply selling smoothies to producing vegetable pots and fruit purees. Their website talks to you as if you're an old friend, and it even offers you fun things to do when you're bored such as browsing a gallery of past adverts or knitting tiny hats for their bottles in aid of charity. They even suggest calling their headquarters, Fruit Towers, on the Banana Phone. If that's not enough, you can contact any member of staff simply by clicking on their 'embarrassing' headshot. Their branding is brilliant and rare – try to match it (without copying), but remember that you must reflect your own business style and the people you want to sell to.

Punting what you're good at

Either through a website or through listings in indexes and directories, offering your professional services online can expand your client base dramatically. It also gives existing clients a new way to contact you or just see what's new with your business. Here are just a few examples of professionals who are offering their services online:

- ✔ **Solicitors:** John Pickering and Partners are personal injury solicitors (aren't they all nowadays) who specialise in severe diseases and critical injuries sustained at work. The firm is based in Manchester, but its website gives it a national and even global reach (www.johnpickering.co.uk). To give it a professional feel, something which is vital in this profession, the website features relevant news updates, information about claims and even information on how to choose a solicitor.

- ✔ **Nutritionists:** Registered nutritionist Jackie Farr has a simple, uncomplicated website (www.truenutrition.co.uk) that has easy-to-access sections defining nutritional therapy and describing a typical consultation (see Figure 2-1). Yet even before clicking through to these areas, the home page outlines who Jackie is, what nutritional therapy can do for you and how bad nutrition may be responsible for frequent infections, bad skin and lethargy.

- ✔ **Architects:** When the first edition of this book came out, we pointed out that the website of Robertson Francis Partnership, a chartered architect based in Cardiff, was under construction (www.rfparchitects.co.uk). Guess what? In 2011, the site *still* hadn't been built (ironic, eh?). Plenty of professional websites take an age to get up and running because people are too busy running their businesses. At least the architects put up their contact details on their holding page. If you're too busy running your business, at the very least do what these guys did and get something up there – even if it's just your name and address.

- ✔ **Music teachers:** Do a search on Gumtree (www.gumtree.com) or Google local (local.google.co.uk) and you'll see just how many music teachers are plying their wares online. Many don't have a website themselves, but are savvy enough to know that people will be searching for their services online.

We're busy people who don't always have the time to pore over the small print. Short and snappy nuggets of information draw customers to your site and make them feel as though they're getting something for free. One way you can put forth this professional expertise is by starting your own online newsletter. You get to be editor, writer and mailing-list manager. Plus, you get to talk as much as you want, network with tons of people who subscribe to your publication and put your name and your business before lots of people. Writer Sean McManus (profiled in Chapter 6) puts out a monthly newsletter that supplements his site (www.sean.co.uk), as do many of the other online businesspeople we mention in this chapter.

Figure 2-1:
A Kent nutritionist provides her contact information and fields of expertise on this simple, yet informative, web page.

Website designed by Scott Parker Consultancy (www.scottparker.co.uk)

Making money from your expertise

The original purpose of the Internet was to share knowledge via computers, and information is the commodity that has fuelled cyberspace's rapid growth. As the Internet and commercial online networks continue to expand, information remains key.

Collecting and disseminating data can be a profitable pastime. Think of all the websites where information is the chief commodity rather than clothes or music. The fact is, people love to get knowledge they trust from the comfort of their own homes.

Apart from the obvious online newspapers and blogs, here are just a few examples of the types of business that feed on our love of knowledge:

- ✔ **Search engines:** Some businesses succeed by connecting web surfers with companies, organisations and individuals that specialise in a given area. Yahoo! (www.yahoo.co.uk) is an obvious example. Originally started by two college students, Yahoo! has become an Internet behemoth by gathering information in one index so that people can easily find things online.

- ✔ **Links pages:** The Prize Finder (www.theprizefinder.com) lists thousands of current UK competitions and is updated daily. The site's been up and running for a decade and makes its money through *affiliate links* to other contest websites who advertise on the site. In the US, a similar site is Grandma Jam (`www.grandmajam.com`) run by Janet Marchbanks Aulenta. 'The key to succeeding at this type of site is to build up a regular base of users that return each day to find new contests – the daily upkeep is very important,' Janet says.

✔ **Personal recommendations:** The personal touch sells. Just look at Web 2.0 site Digg.com (more about Web 2.0 appears in Chapter 4). This guide to the online world provides web surfers with a central location where they can track down popular news stories. Despite various controversial redesigns, the site's premise remains the same: it works because real people submit the stories, and only the most popular stories make it to the top of page one. The users themselves are who 'digg' stories – the most popular ones rise up the rankings. Digg now has a My News page that delivers a personalised newspaper that's based on actions performed on Digg profiles you follow: if they 'digg' a story, it'll probably appear on your My News page.

Resource sites can transform information into money in several ways. In some cases, individuals pay to become members (such as Which?'s independent product tests at `www.which.co.uk`). Sometimes, businesses pay to be listed on a site. Other times, a site attracts so many visitors on a regular basis that other companies pay to post advertising on the site. Big successes – such as Facebook (`www.facebook.com`) and Digg (`www.digg.com`) – carry a healthy share of ads and strike lucrative partnerships with big companies as well.

Creating opportunities with technology

What could be more natural than using the web to sell what you need to get and stay online? The online world itself, by the very fact that it exists, has spawned all kinds of business opportunities for entrepreneurs:

✔ **Computers:** Some discount computer houses have made a killing by going online and offering equipment for less than conventional high street shops. Being on the Internet means that they save on overheads and then pass on those savings to their customers.

✔ **Web hosts:** These businesses house your website – your virtual home. Many, such as 1&1 (`www.1and1.co.uk`), are big concerns. Medium-sized companies, such as Positive Internet (`www.positiveinternet.com`), offer hosting services and similar levels of service too.

✔ **Software:** Matt Wright is well known on the web for providing free computer scripts that add important functionality to websites, such as processing information that visitors submit via online forms. Matt's Script Archive site (`www.scriptarchive.com`) receives 300,000 unique visitors a month and several prominent advertisements appear on his site, as well as an invitation for businesses to advertise on it.

Being a starving artist without starving

Being creative no longer means you have to live out of your flower-covered VW van, driving from art fairs to craft shows (unless you want to, of course). If you're simply looking for exposure and feedback on your creations, you can put samples of your work online. Consider the following suggestions for virtual creative venues (and revenues):

- ✔ **Display your artwork.** Thanks to tools that make it easy to display online galleries, you can showcase your work in a matter of minutes. Photographers, for example, can use sites like Shutterchance (www.shutterchance.com) and Flickr (www.flickr.com) to display their images. Through Flickr, Kim has sold several hundred pounds' worth of photographs after receiving enquiries from interested companies and publishers. One photograph, of a snow-covered taxi, has even been featured on two Christmas cards published by two separate card-making businesses. Meanwhile, Deviant Art (www.deviantart.com) displays all manner of creations and lets visitors purchase prints of the artwork and related merchandise such as hoodies and T-shirts, which generates income for the young artists who frequent the site. The personal website created by artist Alban Low (www.albanlow.com; see Figure 2-2) has received worldwide attention. (The upcoming sidebar, 'Painting a new business scenario', profiles Alban's site.)

- ✔ **Publish your writing.** These days every man and his dog seem to create *blogs* (web logs, or online diaries). The problem is that absolutely millions exist, and most aren't worth your time. However, the most successful are generating ad revenue. To find out how to create one yourself, check out Blogger (www.blogger.com). For inspiration, check out a successful independent blog, such as Seth Godin's (sethgodin.typepad.com) or a blog attached to an online newspaper.

- ✔ **Sell your music.** Singer-songwriter Sam Roberts sells his own CDs, videos and posters through his online shop (www.samrobertsband.com), and you can sell your tracks if you don't have your own website by listing them with Apple iTunes, Spotify (www.spotify.com) or independent digital music sites like Indmill (www.indmill.com).

- ✔ **Be a video star.** Once in a while, someone creates a funny or genuinely useful video on YouTube, and the entire world notices. Take South Shields mum Lauren Luke, who started uploading makeup tutorials from her bedroom on YouTube as a way to sell her eye-shadow products. Her videos have now notched up 100 million views and she's written for numerous publications such as the *Guardian* and *Glamour* magazine. Eventually, her success culminated in a book deal and she continues to upload videos. Check out her YouTube channel at www.youtube.com/panacea81.

Figure 2-2:
A British art-ist created a website to gain recognition and sell his creative work. It's quite basic – but it lets the artwork shine.

You can, of course, also sell all that junk that's been accumulating in your loft, as well as anything else you no longer want, on eBay.co.uk; see Chapter 10 for more information on this exciting business opportunity.

Marketing One-to-One with Your Customers

After you've reviewed websites that conduct the sorts of business ventures that interest you, you can put your goals into action. First you develop a mar-keting strategy that expresses your unique talents and services. People need encouragement if they're going to flock to your website, so try to come up with a cunning plan. One marketing ploy may be enough; we suggest coming up with five individual means to bring the customers in. For example, you can blog about your website, answer questions in forums, do a competition, go to networking events, start up a Facebook page and so on.

The fact is that online communities are often close-knit, long-standing groups of people who are good friends. The web, newsgroups and email allow you to communicate with these communities in ways that other media can't match.

Focusing on a customer segment

Old-fashioned business practices, such as getting to know your customers as individuals and providing personal service, are alive and well in cyberspace. Your No. 1 business strategy when it comes to starting your business online sounds simple: know your market.

But who is your market? On the Internet, it takes some work to get to know exactly who your customers are. Web surfers don't leave their names, addresses or even email addresses when they visit your site. Instead, when you check the raw, unformatted records (or *logs*) of the visitors who've connected to you, you see pages and pages of what appears to be computer gobbledygook. Special tools, such as Google Analytics, interpret the information and present it to you in easy-to-understand pie charts and bullet points.

How do you develop relationships with your customers?

- ✔ **Get your visitors to identify themselves.** Encourage them to send you emails, place orders, enter contests or provide you with feedback. (For more specific suggestions, see Chapter 6.)

- ✔ **Become an online researcher.** Find existing users who already purchase goods and services online that are similar to what you offer. Visit sites that are relevant to what you sell, and participate in discussions so that people can find out more about you.

- ✔ **Keep track of your visitors.** Count the visitors who come to your site and, more importantly, the ones who make purchases or seek out your services. Manage your customer profiles so that you can sell your existing clientele the items they're likely to buy.

- ✔ **Help your visitors get to know you.** Web space is virtually unlimited. Feel free to tell people about aspects of your life that don't relate directly to your business or to how you plan to make money. Consider Sean McManus, a technology author and journalist. His website (www.sean.co.uk), shown in Figure 2-3, includes the usual links to his serious books and articles, but also travel photos, a 3D version of his site you can view while wearing 3D glasses, games you can play on the site and even a 'Virtual Sean' you can 'chat' to, all of which show off Sean's fun and outgoing personality. He advises: 'The web is quite a sterile and unfriendly environment, compared to doing business in person. Use real photos of you and your team to make your business seem friendlier. It's okay to tell people about your hobbies and interests and to convey a bit of personality too, as long as you don't go too far and include a gallery of cat photos. Don't forget a headshot of yourself too, so people don't forget you're a real person!'

Figure 2-3:
What you put on your website about yourself and your interests encourages visitors to tell you about themselves.

After you get to know your audience, job No. 2 in your marketing strategy is to catch their attention. You have two ways to do this:

✔ **Make yourself visible.** In web-space, your primary task is simply making people aware that your site exists at all. You do so by getting yourself included in as many reputable and relevant indexes, search sites and business listings as possible. Never use automated services that try to get you listed on any old website because this could have a negative effect on your search result ranking – search engines may suspect you of manipulating the system and they may even ban your site from being indexed. Chapter 13 outlines some search engine optimisation (SEO) strategies for listing yourself with search engines.

As Google itself explains in its tips for webmasters, 'The best way to get other sites to create relevant links to yours is to create unique, relevant content that can quickly gain popularity in the Internet community. The more useful content you have, the greater the chances someone else will find that content valuable to their readers and link to it. Before making any single decision, you should ask yourself the question: Is this going to be beneficial for my page's visitors?'

✔ **Make your site an eye-catcher.** Getting people to come to you is only half the battle. The other half is getting them to shop when they get there. Combine striking images with promotions, offer useful information and provide ways for customers to interact with you. (See Chapters 5 and 6 for details.)

Painting a new business scenario

British artist Alban Low spent several years living in the peaceful French village of Cambieure, where he says his painting first 'came alive'. As he describes on his website, 'I used to love the daily comings and goings of the tractors and farmers . . . I often left the studio to paint the landscape around me. Sheltering in the shade was a necessity during July and August; the fig trees offered ample coverage with their huge leaves. The complex shapes, cool colours, abundant fruit and scenes beyond inspired me.' Alban returned to London in 2003 with the ability to see things in a completely new light. 'For so often I'd hurried past rivers, buildings, even railways, without a second thought. I began to notice their hidden beauty, arching bridges and competing colours.' He now uses his website as well as social media tools like Facebook, YouTube and blogs to showcase his work and drum up business.

Q. Why did you decide to set up a website to display your work?

A. Initially, as an online portfolio and because other people pressurised me to do so. My brother broke his leg and wanted a project to keep him sane. Also, he's very nice. He taught himself how to [design my site] then taught me how to keep it up-to-date and in order.

Q. Has your website raised your profile as an artist?

A. At first, it was useful as an online archive and I could mention it when I met people at exhibitions. Now it helps when other people talk about my work. To start with, I had a selling section, which just wasn't realistic. It has now helped gain commissions and exhibitions through its presence. I can refer to its content quickly and I can talk on the phone with a client while we both look through the pictures. I have approached many galleries over the past couple of years and having a website must have helped.

Q. How else do you use the web to gain interest in your work?

A. This is the most interesting question for me. I have started to use many different aspects of the web to fuel or help my professional practice. Last month, I got my first commission from New Zealand via Facebook. We used it for everything: checking details and showing the initial sketch and the final painting before it was packed off. And in this last year, I've used three different blogs to showcase and organise exhibitions. They're free to set up; nimble and easy to update. I've also had a Picasa account to hold images, which I've used to show galleries.

Lastly, I secured some television work on the strength of work I'm posting on YouTube (www. youtube.com/user/albanlow) to publicise my work. A director at TennisTV.com saw one of my animations and commissioned me to make an animation for their coverage. This was subsequently used by the BBC.

Q. What advice would you give an artist wanting to go online?

A. Start posting your work on Facebook as low-resolution images; involve friends as much as possible.

If you don't have much money to outlay, start with a blog. They're free and easier to update and adapt. If you involve other people in your work, they will also promote the sites and help you reach an audience outside your inner circle.

If your work is good and interesting, people will want to find out about you. The artwork is the initial point of contact for me and the web is a great support and a great tool.

Q. How much does your website cost to run?

A. My website was made for free and is hosted by my kind family. The cost of my domain name is nominal. I have no marketing budget and make headway through hard work and getting out into the real world too!

Getting involved in social media

Social media is just a fancy way of describing the current generation of socially focused websites that let people share content among themselves – be it a 140-character message on Twitter or a six-minute video on YouTube – with other like-minded individuals. Rather than conventional media like magazines, television and newspapers, the emphasis is on user-generated content.

Social media tools easily let you broadcast messages to all your friends or followers. From a commercial perspective, this means you can communicate bursts of information about your business, such as a clearance sale, to tens of thousands (or possibly even millions) of people in an instant. Because the content is only broadcast to people with an active interest in your business, they're more likely to engage with it rather than ignore it.

Many multinational companies such as Microsoft employ social media editors full time to help attract followers to their brand and keep fans informed about the latest products, competitions and other events. Social media's interactive nature means that people can comment on anything you post, such as pictures or important announcements, so you have to keep an eye on what's being said – good and bad – about your business.

Boosting your credibility

You need to transfer your confidence and sense of authority about what you do to anyone who visits you online. Convince people that you're an expert and a trustworthy person with whom they can do business.

Customers may have fewer reasons to be wary about using the Internet nowadays. But remember that the web as you know it has been around only a short time, and a large minority of people are still wary of surfing online, let alone shopping. Here, too, you can do a quick two-step in order to market your expertise.

Documenting your credentials

Feature any honours, awards or professional affiliations you have that relate to your online work. If you're providing professional or consulting services online, you may even make a link to your online CV. If you feel it's relevant, give details about how long you've been in your field and how you got to know what you know about your business.

If these forms of verification don't apply to you, all isn't lost. Just move to the all-important technique that we describe in the next section.

Convincing with must-have information

Providing useful, practical information about a topic is one of the best ways to market yourself online. One of the great things about starting an online business is that you don't have to incur the design and printing charges to get a brochure or flyer printed. You have plenty of space on your online business site to talk about your sales items or services in as much detail as you want. Try not to bore people though, will you!

What, exactly, can you talk about on your site? Here are some ideas:

- Provide detailed descriptions and photos of your sale items.
- Include a full list of clients you've worked for previously.
- Publish a page of testimonials from satisfied customers.
- Give your visitors a list of links to web pages and other sites where people can find out more about your area of business.
- Toot your own horn: explain why you love what you do and why you're so good at it.

Ask satisfied customers to give you a good testimonial. All you need is a sentence or two that you can use on your website. We mentioned The Prize Finder website earlier; it has success stories from previous prize winners as well as testimonials from advertisers listed on its site.

A site that contains compelling, entertaining content will become a resource that online visitors bookmark and return to on a regular basis. Be sure to update it regularly, and you'll have fulfilled the dream of any online business owner.

When using social media, it's crucial not to go overboard with the communication updates because you want to maintain that trust in your brand. You don't want people to think you're out to make a quick buck and are relentlessly pushing your products.

Creating customer-to-customer contact: Everybody wins

A 16-year-old cartoonist named Gabe Martin (www.gabemartin.com) put his cartoons on his website, called The Borderline. Virtually nothing happened. But when his dad put up some money for a contest, young Gabe started getting hundreds of visits and enquiries. He went on to create 11 mirror sites around the world, develop a base of devoted fans and sell his own cartoon book.

People regularly take advantage of freebies online by, for example, downloading *shareware* or *freeware* programs (programs that people develop and distribute for free). They get free advice from the web, and they find free companionship from chat rooms and discussion forums. Having already paid for network access and computer equipment, they actually *expect* to get something for free.

Your customers will keep coming back if you devise as many promotions, giveaways or sales as possible. You can also get people to interact through online forums or other tools, as we describe in Chapter 6.

In online business terms, anything that gets your visitors to click links and enter your site is good. Provide as many links to the rest of your site as you can on your home page. Many interactions that don't seem like sales do lead to sales, and your goal is always to keep people on your site for as long as possible.

See Chapters 5 and 6 for instructions on how to create hyperlinks and add interactivity to your website. For more about creating websites, check out *Creating Web Pages For Dummies,* 9th Edition, by Bud E. Smith and Arthur Bebak (Wiley).

Being a player in online communities

You may wait until the kids go off to school to tap away at your keyboard in your home office, but that doesn't mean that you're alone. Thousands of home-office workers and entrepreneurs just like you connect to the Net every day and share many of the same concerns, challenges and ups and downs as you.

Starting an online business isn't only a matter of creating web pages, scanning photos and taking orders. Marketing and networking are essential to making sure that you meet your goals. Participate in groups that are related either to your particular business or to online business in general. Here are some ways that you can make the right connections and get support and encouragement at the same time.

Becoming a forum fanatic

Businesspeople tend to overlook online discussion boards, forums and other groups because of admonitions about *spam* (pesky emails sent without permission by people trying to make money dishonestly) and other violations of *Netiquette* (the set of rules that govern online communications). However, when they join an online community and play an active role in helping others by answering questions and participating in discussions, online groups can be a wonderful resource for businesspeople. They attract knowledgeable consumers who are strongly interested in a topic – just the sort of people who make great customers.

A few forums especially intend to discuss small business issues and sales. Here are a few suggestions:

- ✔ www.uksmallbizworld.co.uk
- ✔ www.startups.co.uk/Forums
- ✔ www.ukbusinessforums.co.uk

You can also participate in discussion boards called *newsgroups*. The easiest way to access newsgroups is to use Google's web-based directory (groups. google.com).

Be sure to read a group or forum's FAQ page before you start posting. It's a good idea to *lurk before you post* – that is, simply read messages being posted to the group in order to find out about members' concerns. Stay away from groups that seem to consist only of get-rich-quick schemes or other scams. When you do post a message, be sure to keep your comments relevant to the conversation and give as much helpful advice as you can.

Some of the UK's most influential websites have a huge community of members participating in forums. Mumsnet (www.mumsnet.com) is a place for parents to discuss parenting-related issues; participate in live chats with prime ministers, opposition leaders and other top-ranking politicians; and make new friends. Parents are always online at all hours of the night chatting away in the wee hours as their little ones wake up for a feed. *The Times* calls it 'the most popular meeting point for parents'.

Being signature savvy

The most important business technique in communicating by either email or newsgroup postings is to include a signature file at the end of your message (see Figure 2-4). A *signature file* is a simple message that newsgroup and mail software programs automatically add to your messages (just like corporate emails). In the early days of the free web-based email service Hotmail, an automatic signature message was added to the bottom of every email that got sent out inviting recipients to try Hotmail for free. This led to an enormous spike in take-up, and the term *viral marketing* was born. By the time Microsoft purchased the then two-year-old company for £248 million at the end of 1997, the site had 9 million subscribers. Fourteen years on, it now boasts 364 million users, according to comScore.

Here's an example of author Sean McManus's signature file, which clearly lists the books he's written and a call to action for people to get 'FREE' chapters and bonus book content via his website.

Figure 2-4: A descriptive signature file on your messages serves as an instant business advertisement.

Exchanging emails

Email discussion groups or *discussion lists* work by exchanging email messages between members who share a common interest. They've become a little outdated now that online forums and tools such as Facebook make it so easy to exchange messages with more than one person at a time, but they're still around.

Each email message sent to the list is distributed to all the list's members. Any of those members can, in turn, respond by sending email replies. The series of back-and-forth messages develops into discussions.

The nice thing about a discussion list is that it consists only of people who've subscribed to the list or group, which means that they really want to be involved and participate.

Yahoo! Groups lets people start up their own online discussion groups, and members may receive new messages as emails as they happen or as a daily digest. They can post messages to a group via email too. The non-profit Freecycle network (www.freecycle.org), which lets people give away unwanted stuff for free, is a good example and is administered using Yahoo! Groups.

Adding ways to sell and multiply your profits

Many successful online businesses combine more than one concept of what constitutes electronic commerce. Chapter 8 discusses ways to sell your goods and services on your website, but the Internet offers other venues for promoting and selling your wares.

Selling through online classifieds

If you're looking for a quick and simple way to sell products or promote your services online without having to pay high overhead costs, consider taking out a classified ad in an online publication or a popular site like Craigslist (www.craigslist.org) or the online version of the Loot newspaper at www.loot.com.

The classifieds work the same way online as they do in print publications: you pay a fee and write a short description along with contact information, and the publisher makes the ad available to potential customers. However, online classifieds have a number of big advantages over their print equivalents:

- ✔ **Audience:** Rather than hundreds or thousands who may view your ad in print, tens of thousands, or perhaps even millions, can see it online.
- ✔ **Searchability:** Online classifieds are often indexed so that customers can search for particular items with their web browser. This index makes it easier for shoppers to find exactly what they want, whether it's a Hello Kitty figurine or a Martin guitar.
- ✔ **Time:** On the Net, ads are often online for a month or more.
- ✔ **Cost:** Some sites, such as Gumtree (www.gumtree.com) and Friday-Ad (www.friday-ad.co.uk), let you post classified ads for free.

On the downside, classifieds are often buried at the back of online magazines or websites, just as they are in print, so they're hardly well-travelled areas.

Also, most classifieds don't make use of the graphics that help sell and promote goods and services so effectively throughout the web.

Classifieds are an option if you're short on time or money. But don't forget that on your own online business site you can provide more details and not have to spend a penny.

Selling via online auctions

Many small businesses, such as antique dealerships or jewellery shops, sell individual merchandise through online auctions. eBay.co.uk and other popular auction sites provide effective ways to target sales items at collectors who are likely to pay top dollar for desirable goodies. If you come up with a system for finding things to sell and for turning around a large number of transactions on a regular basis, you can even turn selling on eBay into a full-time source of income. See Chapter 10 for more information about starting a business on eBay.co.uk.

Looking at Easyware (Not Hardware) for Your Business

Becoming an information provider on the Internet places an additional burden on your computer and peripheral equipment, such as your phone, printer/scanner and so on. When you're 'in it for the money', you may very well start to go online every day, perhaps for hours at a time, especially if you buy and sell on eBay.co.uk. The better your computer setup, the more photos, email messages and catalogue items you can store, and so on. In this section, we introduce you to many upgrades you may need to make to your existing technology.

Some general principles apply when assembling equipment (which we discuss in this section) and programs (which we discuss in a subsequent section, 'Considering Essential Software and Services for Your Online Business') for an online business:

- **Look on the Internet for what you need.** You can find just about everything you want to get you started.

- **Be sure to pry before you buy!** Don't pull out that credit card until you get the facts on what warranty and technical support your hardware or software vendor provides. Look for online reviews from ordinary customers: Amazon.co.uk has tons of customer reviews for hardware and software. Make sure that your vendor provides phone support 24 hours a day, 7 days a week. Also ask how long the typical turnaround time is in case your equipment needs to be serviced.

If you purchase lots of new hardware and software, remember to update your insurance by sending your insurer a list of your new equipment. Also consider purchasing insurance specifically for your computer-related items from a company such as Insure and Go (www.insureandgo.com) or Hiscox (business.hiscox.co.uk). For more on the importance of security, see Chapter 7.

Choosing the right computer for your online business

You very well may already have an existing computer setup that's adequate to get your business online and start the ball rolling. Or you may be starting from scratch and looking to purchase a computer for personal and/or business use. In either case, it pays to know what all the technical terms and specifications mean. Here are some general terms you need to understand:

- **Processor speed:** A processor's speed measure indicates how quickly it can perform functions. The central processing unit (CPU) of a computer is where the computing work gets done. Traditionally, processor speeds were measured in gigahertz (GHz) and megahertz (MHz), but today major manufacturers like Intel have ditched the technical jargon, choosing to use terms like Intel Pentium Dual Core. A faster processor is great, but you don't need the biggest and best processor out there for typical online business tasks. (For more on choosing the right processor, see the next section.)

- **Random access memory (RAM):** This is the memory that your computer uses to temporarily store information it needs to operate programs. RAM is usually expressed in millions of bytes, or megabytes (MB). The more RAM you have, the more programs you can run simultaneously. We recommend buying as much RAM as you can afford. Different types of RAM exist; DDR (double data rate) and the newer standard, DDR2, are the major types and they can dramatically improve the clock rate of a CPU.

- **Virtual memory:** This is a type of memory on your hard drive that your computer can 'borrow' to serve as extra RAM.

- **Network interface card (NIC):** You need this hardware add-on if you have a cable or DSL modem or if you expect to connect your computer to others on a network. Having an NIC usually provides you with Ethernet data transfer to the other computers. (*Ethernet* is a network technology that permits you to send and receive data at very fast speeds.) If you want to wirelessly network your desktop computer to a wireless router, you can buy a wireless networking dongle that plugs into your USB port without requiring an NIC. Modern laptops should already have built-in wireless access.

The Internet is teeming with places where you can find good deals on hardware. A great place to start is a review site, such as Ciao (www.ciao.co.uk) or Review Centre (www.reviewcentre.com), which allows customers to express their views about the equipment they've bought. Visit a few of these sites and select the most popular items.

Processor speed and memory

Computer processors are getting faster all the time; by the time you get it home another, faster, chip will already have hit the streets. In years past, a computer's processing speed was measured in megahertz or gigahertz but these numbers have become less and less relevant.

Now categories of chips such as Intel's dual-core and quad-core processors are better able to handle multiple tasks simultaneously. These are more efficient because they're essentially two processors in one, working in tandem so that the computer can process information faster. A handy decision-making tool on Intel's website at www.intel.com helps you decide on the type of processor you should be using for your computer, based on your business requirements.

Having as much memory as you can afford (RAM) is what we recommend. Memory acts like a 'buffer', allowing programs and large files to load and run quickly. Take a look at the memory required to run the types of applications listed in Table 2-2. Compared with earlier editions of this book, the amount of recommended RAM has increased several times over for applications such as Internet Explorer because they've become larger and more complex – but at the same time the price of memory has significantly decreased. (Note that these numbers are only estimates, based on the Windows versions of these products that were available at the time of writing.)

Table 2-2	Memory Requirements	
Type of Application	*Example*	*Amount of RAM Recommended*
Web browser	Internet Explorer	512MB
Word processor	Microsoft Word 2010	256MB (512MB recommended for advanced functionality)
Graphics program	Corel Paint Shop Pro Photo X2	512MB (768 recommended)
Accounting software	Microsoft Excel	256MB (512 recommended for advanced functionality)
Animation/presentation	Adobe Flash Player	128MB

We'd say that at least 4GB of RAM is necessary if you plan to work – in the last edition of this book we were only recommending at least 512MB of RAM, yet many computers now require this amount to run just one application! Memory is cheap so the more you can swing, the better it is in the long run.

Hard drive storage

Random access memory is only one type of memory your computer uses; the other kind, *hard drive*, stores information, such as text files, audio files, programs and the many essential files that your computer's operating system needs. Most of the new computers on the market come with hard drives that store hundreds of gigabytes of data. Even if you aren't doing a lot of graphics work, those of you using your computer for other tasks such as storing photographs will find your hard drive space being slowly eaten up. Applications, too, can take up a lot of storage space.

Most new computers come with hard drives that are around 500GB in size. Again, the more you can afford, the better.

DVD±RW or Blu-Ray drive

Having a recordable drive in your computer may not seem essential at first, but it can be unbelievably useful for storing backups of files. The DVD drive also performs essential installation, storage and data communications functions, such as installing software and saving and sharing data.

Recordable DVD drives should come as standard on modern computers. More and more computers now include higher capacity Blu-Ray drives that also let you watch or record high definition (HD) movies. You can fit 4.7GB (or more) of data on a conventional DVD±RW, and at least 25GB on Blu-Ray drives. DVD and Blu-Ray drives are backwards-compatible, meaning you can still read and write older CDs.

Be sure to protect your equipment against electrical problems that can result in loss of data or substantial repair bills. You can limit the damage caused by power outages or surges, or just by glitches in your computer programs, simply by saving your data. You can buy separate hard drives, as well as disks and data sticks on which you can store your most precious data. Keep backup data away from your workstation so that in the event of a fire or flood you still have a surviving copy.

Monitor

In terms of your online business, the quality or thinness of your monitor doesn't affect the quality of your website directly. Even if you have a poor-quality monitor, you can create a website that looks great to those who visit you. The problem is that you won't know how good your site really looks to customers who have high-quality monitors.

Flat-panel LCD (liquid crystal display) monitors are standard now, and the sizes available keep getting bigger and bigger. Back in 2003, Kim was reviewing 15-inch LCD monitors. Just a year later you could get 17-inch models for the same price, and by 2007, 19-inch and 21-inch monitors were hot items. Now you can get 25-inch (and bigger) LCDs and widescreen models too that are all perfectly affordable – and for the same price the 15-inch monitors were back in the day! (Current HD televisions are also computer friendly, allowing you to plug right into the display.) The main things you need to look out for when buying an LCD monitor have remained the same, however, and include:

- ✔ **Resolution:** The resolution of a computer monitor refers to the number of pixels (the tiny dots that you see on screen) it can display horizontally and vertically. A resolution of 640 x 480 means that the monitor can display 640 pixels across the screen and 480 pixels down the screen. Higher resolutions, such as 1,024 x 768, make images look sharper but require more RAM in your computer. Anything less than 640 x 480 is unusable these days.

- ✔ **Size:** Monitor size is measured diagonally, as with TVs. Big sizes are snazzy and may be in your budget, but may not be practical for a small home office.

  You could even consider working from *two* monitors to extend your workspace. The setup is simple: just plug both monitors into your computer and use the display settings under the Windows Control Panel to get monitor one and monitor two established. Your mouse pointer simply flows between two monitors. If you have an old monitor lying around the place, then this is a great option. Having two monitors gives you more 'real estate' to play with. You could use one screen for email and dealing with customer and administrative tasks, and the other for graphics work and website maintenance.

- ✔ **Response time:** Monitors need to react quickly in order to effectively display what's going on. Particularly for moving images, a slow response time (measured in milliseconds) means you get a shadowy effect known as 'ghosting' on screen. The lower the response time, the better. LCDs should suit your business just fine, but the emerging market is now in LED (light emitting diode) technology, which uses less energy than LCDs and can produce thinner and longer-lasting displays.

Keep in mind that lots of web pages seem to have been designed with 19-inch or 21-inch monitors in mind. The problem isn't just that some users (especially those with laptops) have 15-inch monitors, but you can never control how wide the viewer's browser window will be. And they may not even have their web browser window open to its maximum size when viewing your page. The problem is illustrated in the Yale Style Manual (www.webstyle guide.com), one of the classic references of website design.

Computer monitors display graphic information that consists of little units called *pixels*. Each pixel appears on-screen as a small dot – so small that it's hard to perceive with the naked eye, unless you magnify an image to look at details close up. Together, the patterns of pixels create different intensities of light in an image, as well as ranges of colour. A pixel can contain one or more bytes of binary information. The more pixels per inch (ppi), the higher a monitor's potential resolution. The higher the resolution, the closer the image appears to a continuous-tone image such as a photo. When you see a monitor's resolution described as 1,280 x 1,024, for example, that refers to the number of pixels that the monitor can display.

If you're one of the three people reading this who still regularly use a fax machine, you don't want it tying up your phone line and causing your customers to hear busy signals. Fax machines are virtually obsolete. Faxes themselves are still used in certain types of businesses, but you can sign up to electronic services that let you send faxes via your computer or receive your faxes and email them to you as attachments. Alternatively, if you must use a machine, then get a second dedicated phone line.

Image capture devices

When you're ready to move beyond the basic hardware and on to some jazzy value-adding add-ons, think about obtaining a tool for capturing photographic images. (By *capturing*, we mean *digitising* an image or, in other words, saving it in digital format.) Photos are often essential elements of business web pages: they attract a customer's attention, they illustrate items for sale in a catalogue and they can provide before-and-after samples of your work. If you're an artist or designer, having photographic representations of your work is vital.

Including a clear, sharp image on your website greatly increases your chances of selling your product or service. You have two choices for digitising: a scanner or digital camera.

Digital camera

Not so long ago, digital cameras cost thousands of pounds. These days, you can find a decent digital camera made by a reputable manufacturer, such as

Nikon, Fuji, Canon, Olympus, Panasonic or Kodak, for £100 to £200. You have to make an investment up front, but this particular tool can pay off for you in the long run. With the addition of a photo printer, you can even print your own photos. For mass production (such as flyers) you can use online printing services from companies like VistaPrint (www.vistaprint.co.uk) because these may be more cost effective than printing from a typical inkjet printer.

Don't hesitate to fork out the extra dough to get a camera that's easy to use and gives you good resolution (*resolution* is the measure of detail in a photograph).

You actually don't need a camera with top-notch resolution because online material is primarily intended to be displayed on computer monitors (which have limited resolution), and hundreds of low-cost devices out there have brilliant features. Anything 6 megapixels (Mp) and above will suffice, which is actually more than good enough to print a clear 10 x 8 sized photograph.

Megapixels are calculated by multiplying the number of pixels in an image – for example, when actually multiplied, 1,984 x 1,488 = 2,952,192 pixels or 2.9 megapixels. The higher the resolution, the fewer photos your camera can store at any one time because each image file requires more memory, but you can always reduce the resolution using your camera settings or buy a memory card with bigger capacity to solve the problem (Kim has a 4GB card that can store hundreds of photos).

Before being displayed by web browsers, you need to compress photographs (usually in a format called JPEG). Your camera can take images in JPEG format. (See Chapter 5 for more scintillating technical details on JPEG and GIF, another common format used for graphics like logos and scanned images.)

Also, smaller and simpler images (as opposed to large, high-resolution graphics) generally appear more quickly on the viewer's screen. You can often reduce the file size of images in your photo editing software quite dramatically without seeing any discernable loss in quality. If you make your customers wait too long to see an image, they're well within their rights to go to someone else's online shop.

When shopping for a digital camera, look for the following features:

✔ Easy to use, with accessible buttons

✔ Bundled image-processing software

✔ The ability to download image files directly to a memory card that you can easily transport to a computer's memory card reader

✔ A large, clear LCD screen that lets you see your images immediately

✔ Minimal *shutter lag* (the delay between pressing the shutter and the camera taking the image)

Digital photography is a fascinating and technical process, and you'll do well to read more about it in other books. Kim's actually written a book exclusively on the topic called *Digital Photography For the Older and Wiser* (Wiley; 2010). And you don't have to be old (or wise) to read it!

Scanners and multifunction devices

Scanning is the process of turning the colours and shapes contained in a photographic print or slide into digital information that a computer can understand. You place the image in a position where the scanner's camera can pass over it, and the scanner turns the image into a computer document that consists of tiny dots that make up an image called *pixels* (short for picture elements; 1 million pixels equals 1 megapixel). With flatbed scanners, you place the photo or other image on a flat glass bed, just like what you find on a photocopier. An optical device moves under the glass and scans the photo.

The best news about scanners is that they've been around for a while, which, in the world of computing, means that prices are going down all the time. Scanners are not a fast-moving market either, so you don't need to worry about getting one that's outdated. The bargain models are well under £50, and you can pick one up for around £30 if you use cost comparison websites, such as Pricerunner (www.pricerunner.co.uk) or Kelkoo (www.kelkoo.co.uk).

A type of scanner that has lots of benefits for small or home-based businesses is a multifunction device. You can find these units, along with conventional printers and scanners, at computer outlets or at the Pricerunner and Kelkoo. Multifunction devices save you a lot of desk space and are designed for home offices like yours. The average multifunction device can photocopy, scan and print photographs; you can also buy ones that combine a phone, fax and answering machine.

When choosing a printer or multifunction device, always remember that the cost of the device isn't its true cost. Printing costs can notch up – paper and ink can be expensive, particularly because manufacturers recommend you use their own brand of ink for best results. Ink cartridges often have a computer chip on them to deter third-party manufacturers from selling compatible inks; and photo paper is supposedly optimised for use with certain ink. Also, when buying a printer, try to choose one that uses separate ink cartridges for the printer colours (blue, magenta, cyan and black) rather than one containing all colours in the one unit. This is so you only need to replace the cartridge for the ink colour you're running low on.

Scan and deliver

Getting your photos online is so easy nowadays – by 2013, it's estimated that 124 billion photos will be hosted on Facebook (in 2009, the number stood at 15 billion). So the process is far from a technical minefield – it's very likely that you've shared photos on Facebook, and the latest smartphones also let you post your photos online to Facebook and Flickr from virtually wherever you are.

But your website isn't all about photographs from your digital camera. Scanners still play their part if, say, you're an artist and just want to scan in a few drawings for your website without having to go through the hassle of learning how to optimise them for the web. Or perhaps you have some old print photographs or negatives that you want to use for your site? Your local photo shop or copy centre can help. Many high street photographic shops, like Jessops and Snappy Snaps, for example, provide computer services that include scanning photos. You can also have the images placed online or on a CD when you develop your snaps.

Tell the technician that you want the image to appear on the web, so it should be optimised

in JPEG format. Also, if you have an idea of how big you want the final image to be when it appears online, tell that to the technician too. Jargon corner: the screen resolution your images need to be for online use should be around 72 pixels per inch; note that this is smaller than the print resolution they need to be for printing (300 dots per inch). The shop can save the image in the size that you want so you don't have to resize it later in a graphics program. However, getting images scanned at the biggest size you're willing to display or print it at is best, then you can scale down later – any image program will let you do this.

If you don't even want to buy a camera, you can always try Flickr (`www.flickr.com`), the online photo album that anyone can add to. People who post their pics can choose to allow others to use them for free through an open licensing scheme called Creative Commons. Usually, all you need to do is credit the author. Flickr allows you to contact photographers when you need to obtain their permission or download a higher-quality image.

Getting Online: Connection Options

Now you can get a broadband connection from a reputable company for £15 a month. You can also bundle Internet access up with your phone connection and even digital TV to save a bit more cash.

Dial-up is simply pointless. Broadband speeds in the UK are now exceptionally fast – BT has even been testing 1 gigabit broadband connections (which translates to practically lightning speed). The communications regulator, Ofcom, estimates that 70 per cent of UK households have a fixed broadband connection with more than a quarter able to achieve up to 10 megabit speeds.

Although on a typical home broadband connection it's slower to upload information to the web (such as your web pages) than it is to download, it's still much faster than dial-up. A broadband connection can save you an hour a day, which you can spend on planning, on stock checks or taking well-earned rests.

Broadband is a generic term describing the bandwidth of your Internet connection. It's broad, so more information can pass through it in a shorter space of time. *Asymmetrical Digital Subscriber Line* (ADSL) is the predominant form of broadband in the UK and transmits information via your phone line at different speeds depending on whether you're sending (uploading) or receiving (downloading) data. *Symmetrical Digital Subscriber Line* (SDSL) transmits information at the same speed in both directions.

Considering Essential Software and Services for Your Online Business

One of the great things about starting an Internet business is that you get to use software. As you probably know, the programs you use online are inexpensive (sometimes free), easy to use and install, and continually updated.

Like your website itself, you don't even need to install a lot of programs on your computer any more, and you needn't cram all your data onto your hard drive, either. All you need is a web browser and a broadband connection to conduct a raft of activities. This shift to moving services to the Internet is known as *cloud computing* (*cloud* describes the Internet). It's revolutionising the way people buy and sell, consume entertainment, communicate and create.

You're probably already using the cloud on a consumer level. If you use a web-based email service with one of the major providers like Google, Yahoo! or Microsoft, then you'll know how all your messages reside on their servers, ready for you to access at any time. You don't have to worry about your computer running out of storage space. Many of the leading providers also let you use your accounts with them to do things such as edit Word documents and spreadsheets, view PDF files, share photos and videos with friends and manage your website files and statistics.

And if you have a blog, then you'll know that all you need to do is log in to your website (or the blog host's) and start creating posts or redesigning the look and feel of your site – all from within the comfort of your web browser.

We talk more about cloud computing from a business perspective in Chapter 12. There's still a place for good old software that you download and install on your computer; particularly because it works in tandem with your online activities. For the rest of this section, we describe some programs you may not have as yet and that will come in handy when you create your online business.

Don't forget to update your insurance by sending your insurer a list of new software (and hardware) or even by purchasing insurance specifically for your computer-related items.

Anyone who uses firewall or antivirus software will tell you how essential these pieces of software are, for home or business use. Find out more about such software in Chapter 7. See Chapter 15 for suggestions of accounting software – other important software you'll need.

Web browser

A *web browser* is software that serves as a window to the images, colours, links and other content contained on the web. The most popular such program is still Microsoft Internet Explorer. But its market share has been eroded in recent years, making way for increasingly popular browsers such as Mozilla Firefox, Safari, Chrome and Opera, all of which are gaining new fans every day. See which one you like the best.

Your web browser is your primary tool for conducting business online, just as it is for everyday personal use. When it comes to running a virtual shop or consulting business, though, you have to run your software through a few more paces than usual. You need your browser to

- ✔ Preview the web pages you create
- ✔ Display animations, movie clips and other goodies you plan to add online
- ✔ Support some level of Internet security, such as Secure Sockets Layer (SSL), if you plan to conduct secure transactions on your site

In addition to having an up-to-date browser with the latest features, installing a few major browsers on your computer is a good idea. For example, if you use Microsoft Internet Explorer, be sure to download the latest copy of Firefox as well. That way, you can test your site to make sure that it looks good to all your visitors. Remember, too, that people use Apple Macs as well as PCs, laptops, palmtops and smartphones – and they also view web pages at different resolutions, depending on their monitor size and viewing preferences. Your website has to look good on all of them. Tools such as Browser Cam (www.browsercam.com) can help you see what your site looks like in several browsers.

Web page editor or content management platform

HyperText Markup Language (HTML) is a set of instructions used to format text, images and other web page elements so that web browsers can correctly display them. Meanwhile, keeping a site's font, body font, font sizes, page width, background images and other formatting consistent throughout an entire website relies on code called Cascading Style Sheets (CSS). The CSS attributes are usually contained in files ending in .css; in order to reflect changes across your entire website, you just edit the CSS files rather than painstakingly change every single HTML page.

Sounds complicated? Well, you don't have to master HTML or CSS in order to create your own web pages. Tools including *web page editors* and *content management systems* are available to help you format text, add images, make hyperlinks and do all the fun assembly steps necessary to make your website a winner.

Content management systems like Joomla! (www.joomla.com) and Drupal (www.drupal.com) make it easy to slot in all the elements you'll need for a seemingly complex page. Web page editors are a little outdated. But if you have a simple-to-manage site that doesn't sell products and will generally remain static (apart from say a blog or a news page), then a web page editor should still fit the bill.

For more detail on these tools and their benefits, see Chapters 1 and 3.

Taking email a step higher

You're probably very familiar with sending and receiving email messages or attaching files to them. But when you start an online business, you should make sure that email software has some advanced features:

- **Autoresponders:** Some programs automatically respond to email requests with a form letter or document of your choice.

- **Mailing lists:** With a well-organised address book, you can collect the email addresses of visitors or subscribers and send them a regular update of your business activities or, better yet, an email newsletter (so long as they're happy to receive it). As your customer base grows, you could consider a plug-in that helps you manage the list more effectively.

- **Signature files:** Your email software should automatically include a simple electronic signature at the end. Use this space to list your company name, your title and your website URL.

✔ **Anti-spam and security software:** Your security software may come with tools to filter out junk email (known as spam). It should also scan incoming emails for viruses.

✔ **Email marketing tools:** Services for small businesses like VerticalResponse (www.verticalresponse.com), which Sean McManus (see Chapter 6 and the earlier section 'Focusing on a customer segment') uses to send his monthly newsletter out to subscribers, let you create an email message to send to your customers in mere minutes.

In some cases, you can install software that works in conjunction with your existing email program (known as a plug-in). Because these functions are all essential aspects of providing good customer service, we discuss them in more detail in Chapter 12.

Discussion forum software

When your business site is up and running, consider taking it a step farther by creating your own discussion area, or forum, right on your website. This is a web-based discussion area where your visitors can compare notes and share their passion for the products you sell or the area of service you provide.

It does take a lot of effort and time to maintain a forum though, and not all websites are suited to one. As web consultant Scott Parker says, 'They are really hard to manage and get off the ground. Start off with a blog that allows feedback.' If you do go for the forum route, then popular forum software includes vBulletin (www.vbulletin.com) and the free phpBB (www.phpBB.com).

FTP software

FTP (File Transfer Protocol) is one of those acronyms you see time and time again as you move around the Internet.

In case you haven't used FTP yet, start dusting it off. When you create your own web pages, a simple, no-nonsense FTP program is the easiest way to transfer them from your computer at home to your web host. If you need to correct and update your web pages quickly (and you will), you'll benefit by having your FTP software ready and set up with your website address, username and password so that you can transfer files right away. See Chapter 3 for more about using File Transfer Protocol.

Image editors

You need a graphics-editing program either to create original artwork for your web pages or to crop and adjust your scanned images and digital photographs. In the case of adjusting or cropping photographic image files, the software you need almost always comes bundled with the scanner or digital camera, but you may need to upgrade to a more advanced program if you want to adjust the colours, clone out unwanted elements, remove red eyes and so on.

Plenty of free image-editing tools do great jobs. Google's Picasa (`http://picasa.google.com`) is highly functional, as is Microsoft's Windows Live Photo Gallery (`www.live.com`).

Pay a little and you can get even more creative with your graphics, if that's what you want. Two programs we like are Adobe Photoshop Elements (`www.adobe.co.uk`) and Corel Paint Shop Pro. These are available off-the-shelf in boxed form from computer outlets, but you can download both these programs from the web to use on a trial basis. After the trial period is over, you need to pay to upgrade and keep the program.

Many programs are available as *shareware*. The ability to download and use free (and almost free) software from shareware archives and many other sites is one of the nicest things about the Internet. Keep the system working by remembering to pay the shareware fees to the nice folks who make their software available to individuals like you and me.

Instant messaging

You may think that MSN Messenger, AOL Instant Messenger, Google Talk and Yahoo Messenger are just for chatting online, but instant messaging has its business applications too. Here are a few suggestions:

- If individuals you work with all the time are hard to reach, you can use a messaging program to tell you whether those people are logged on to their computers. The program allows you to contact them the moment they sit down to work (provided they don't mind your greeting them so quickly, of course).
- With a microphone, sound card and speakers, you can carry on voice conversations through your messaging software.

MSN Messenger enables users to do file transfers without having to use FTP software or attaching files to email messages.

The internet phone service Skype (www.skype.com) means you can make video and phone calls for free to other people with Skype accounts, as well as low cost calls to landlines. Skype also has an instant messaging system.

Backup software

Losing copies of your personal documents is one thing, but losing files related to your business can hit you hard in the pocket. That makes it even more important to make backups of your online business computer files. External hard drives are manufactured by companies including Iomega, Seagate, Freecom, Western Digital and more. These typically come with software that lets you automatically make backups of your files, but backup tools are also built into the latest Windows and Mac systems. Make sure that *all* your files are backed up, not just certain elements of your drive and, if you can afford it, back up onto *two* drives! Kim would have lost *all* the photographs of her daughter, Audrey, had she not backed up because her entire photo library was wiped out during an upgrade.

Chapter 3

Selecting the Right Web Host and Design Tools

*Y*ou *can* sell items online without having a website. But do you really want to? Doing real online business without some sort of online 'home base' is simply inefficient. The vast majority of online commercial concerns use their websites as the primary way to attract customers, convey their message and make sales. A huge number of micro-entrepreneurs use online marketplaces such as eBay (www.ebay.co.uk) to make money, but the sellers who depend on eBay for a regular income often have their own web pages too.

The success of a commercial website depends in large measure on two important factors: where it's hosted and how it's designed. These factors affect how easily you can create and update your web pages, what special features such as multimedia or interactive forms you can have on your site and how your site appears to your users. Some hosting services provide web page creation tools that are easy to use but that limit the level of sophistication you can apply to the page's design. Other services leave the creation and design up to you. Others still let you install popular, free web page creation and management tools with a click of a button, although it's up to you to design and maintain them. In this chapter, we provide an overview of your web hosting options as well as different design approaches that you can implement.

Plenty of websites and software packages claim that they can have your web site up and running online 'in a matter of minutes' using a 'seamless' process. The actual construction may indeed be quick and smooth – as long as you've done all your preparation work. This preparation work includes identifying your goals for going online, deciding what market you want to reach, deciding what products you want to sell, writing descriptions and capturing images of those products and so on. Don't forget, too, that maintaining your website is an ongoing process and you don't want to find that the package you're using makes it difficult for you to implement simple tweaks and changes.

Getting the Most from Your Web Host

An Internet connection and a web browser are all you need if you're just interested in surfing the web, consuming information and shopping for online goodies. But when you're starting an online business, you're no longer just a consumer; you're becoming a provider of information and consumable goods. In addition to a means to connect to the Internet, you need to find a hosting service that makes your online business available to your prospective customers.

A *web hosting service* is the online world's equivalent of a landlord. Just as the owner of a building gives you office space or room for a shop front, a hosting service provides you with space online where you can set up shop.

You can operate an online business without a website if you sell regularly on eBay. But even on eBay, you can create an About Me page or an eBay shop; eBay itself is your host in both cases. (You pay a monthly fee to eBay in order to host your shop. See Chapter 10 for more information.)

A web host provides space on special computers called *web servers* that are connected to the Internet all the time. Web servers are equipped with software that makes your web pages visible to people who connect to them by using a web browser. The process of using a web hosting service for your online business works roughly like this:

1. **You buy a domain name for your site (`yourbusinessname.co.uk`).**

   This is the address – or URL – people type into their web browsers when they want to access your website. (Most hosts include a domain name for your website as part of their business packages. Read the small print to make sure you'll be listed as the registrant contact, which allows you to retain control of your domain should you choose another host later down the line.) All devices, including servers, connected to the Internet are identified by an ugly and difficult-to-remember number called an

IP (Internet Protocol) address, but you can configure a domain name to point to the host IP address, so you won't need to type in the long number.

2. **You sign up with a web host.**

   Usually, you pay a fee, although some free hosts are around. In all cases, you're assigned space on a server, usually along with many other websites (for more, see the later section 'Exploring Web Hosting Options').

3. **You create your web pages.**

   You can do this in a number of ways. You can install a content management system (CMS) like Wordpress or Joomla! and begin creating and managing your site entirely online through your web browser (see 'Looking at Web Creation and Publishing Tools', later in the chapter). A CMS lets you upload images and templates directly through your browser (as if adding a photo to publish on Facebook, or uploading an attachment to Hotmail). The initial installation of your CMS involves a little technical configuration, but some hosts let you install them with just a few clicks. You may come across hosts who have their own bespoke web page creators that you can access from your website control panel. Alternatively, you can work in the traditional way by creating pages 'offline' using a web page editor (see the next step).

4. **If creating pages offline, you transfer your web page files (HyperText Markup Language, or HTML, documents, images and so on) from your computer to the host's web server.**

   You generally need special File Transfer Protocol (FTP) software to do the transferring. But many web hosts help you through the process by providing their own user-friendly web-based software. Most web editors have built-in FTP that let you transfer too. You'll need to provide your site's username and password, which you either create or are allocated when first acquiring your web space.

5. **You access your own site with your web browser and check the contents to make sure that all the images appear and that any hypertext links you created go to the intended destinations.**

   At this point, you're open for business – visitors can view your web pages by entering your web address in their browser's address bar. Check your site across as many browsers (Firefox, Chrome, Safari, Internet Explorer) as you can, and also try to view it across a range of platforms (Mac OS X Snow Leopard, Windows Vista, Windows 7 or a Linux-run PC). This is to ensure people can see your site correctly on different screens and devices.

6. **You market and promote your site to attract potential clients or customers.**

What's in a name?

Most hosts assign you a URL that leads to your directory (or folder) on the web server. For example, one of Kim's websites, hosted by Positive Internet, includes space on a server where she can store her web pages, and the address looks like this:

```
http://kgilmour.php5.truth.
posiweb.net/
```

This is a common form of URL that many web hosts use. The first part of the address is Kim's directory. The next parts are subdirectories assigned by her host (PHP happens to be a scripting language). The computer, in turn, resides in her provider's domain on the Internet: posiweb.net. Behind this URL is actually a host IP address, in this case 80.87.143.6.

However, for an extra fee, web hosts let you either buy a catchier domain name or let you tie an existing domain name to the longer URL. Kim's paid for the domain champagne comedy.com, a fan website dedicated to an Australian comedy series from the early 1990s, and by pointing this URL to her web space, you go to the exact place that the long-winded URL does.

You've no excuse for not having your own domain name because it's so cheap and easy to do. Some domain name registrars let you redirect traffic to your URL to a nominated website. This is different to actually *pointing* your domain to your website – you might have the registrar's advertising framed around your website, and search engines may not pick up on your domain name and its associations with your content.

Exploring Web Hosting Options

Hi! We're your friendly World Wide Web real estate agents. You say you're not sure exactly what kind of website is right for you, and you want to see all the options, from a tiny shop front in a shopping centre to your own landscaped corporate complex? Your wish is our command. In this part we show you around the many different business properties available in cyberspace.

Many hosts combine web hosting with access to some kind of web page or online store creation kit. Most of these tools are proprietary and unique to that particular host. In all cases, you simply follow the manufacturer's instructions. Most of these hosting services enable you to create your web pages by filling in forms; you never have to see a line of HTML code if you don't want to. Depending on which service you choose, you have varying degrees of control over how your site ultimately looks.

Others tend to be do-it-yourself projects. You sign up with the host, you choose the software and you create your own site. Competition between web hosts is fierce, so the distinction between these two types of categories is blurring. More and more companies are providing you, the end user, access to trusted and powerful 'open source' web page creation solutions that are free to use and ready to install in just a couple of minutes. This is great for you, because it streamlines the process of website creation. You have plenty of control over how your site comes into being and how it grows over time.

If you simply need a basic website and don't want a lot of choices, you could try experimenting with one of the kits. Your site may seem a little generic and basic, but setup is easy, and you can concentrate on marketing and running your business. However, if you're the independent type who wants to control your site and have lots of room to grow, consider taking on a do-it-yourself project. The sky's the limit as far as the degree of creativity you can exercise and the amount of blood, sweat and tears you can put in (as long as you don't make your site so large and complex that customers have a hard time finding anything, of course). These days getting started actually isn't too hard, particularly because plenty of online guidance is available in the form of web documentation and forums. And the more work you do, the greater your chances of seeing your business prosper.

Essentially, you're looking at four main types of hosting: free, dedicated, shared and managed hosting services. Also under the umbrella of hosting are cloud services (see Chapter 4).

Free web hosting

Plenty of free places exist on the web where you can start up blogs (www.blogger.com), photo albums (www.flickr.com), discussion groups (http://groups.yahoo.com) and the like – most of these are targeted at individuals, rather than businesses. Free web hosting is still possible for small businesses but it's not really a permanent or long-term solution for a dedicated online business. We recommend upgrading to a host that can offer you support when things go wrong. Many Web consultants recommend steering away from free hosts if you have a business, because you have little comeback if it goes down. Depending on the service, the ads that often accompany your site in exchange for the free hosting can be intrusive. You're also very limited with what you can do in terms of technical and visual design – space is often quite limited as well.

If you do want to use a free service, consider using it as an add-on to your regular business site. For example, you might leave your regular website pretty static apart from frequent updates to your blog. You could choose to link to an external Blogger-hosted blog from your regular website, so long as the blog is designed with your website's look and feel and provides visitors with a link back to where they came from.

Several 'free' hosts have since folded or shut down their operations due to lack of activity. The most famous of these is Yahoo! GeoCities, one of the original free website hosts, which flourished in the mid- to late-1990s. That said, several providers are still around that can help you get your business off the ground. These include:

- ✔ **Moonfruit:** One of the more impressive of the free sites. Moonfruit does not display ads, but you need to pay to get more features out of your site. It has a drag-and-drop website creator and pages look slick and professional. The free version only gives you 20 megabytes of space and up to 15 separate pages, but this is a good start if you're just taking your first few steps into web page creation land. Go to www.moonfruit.com to get started.

- ✔ **Bravenet:** Around since 1997, Bravenet provides free and paid hosting options. With the free option, you're limited in the types of files you can upload to your web space. It doesn't support the scripting language PHP, for example, so you can't add dynamic, interactive pages to your free site. You also only get a mere 5 megabytes worth of space – that's a lot if you're only including text, but it can add up when you start adding photographs. Still, you can use its free website builder and it supports FTP (File Transfer Protocol, a way to transfer files from your computer to your website). See www.bravenet.com for more.

- ✔ **Freeola:** Customers of this broadband ISP get unlimited web space, so if you're looking to change providers it might be worth taking a look at this company's options, particularly if you want more control over your site. If you register your domain with its sister company GetDotted you can have it point to the free web space. Otherwise, Freeola has 500 web addresses that you can use in conjunction with a chosen username (such as execs.co.uk or technicians.co.uk). All the terms and conditions are available at www.freeola.com. You can't use Freeola's servers to store and process credit card details, but you're free to link to third-party payment service providers like WorldPay or PayPal (see Chapter 11 for more on accepting payments).

- ✔ **Weebly:** This US-based free web page creation provider claims to have six million users worldwide. Website building is a breeze with a drag-and-drop interface that requires no technical knowledge. Weebly supports blogging, photo galleries, web form creation, visitor stats, the ability for multiple users to edit your site and much more. Did we mention all this is free? Currently the site doesn't even include advertising, apart from a small link back to the Weebly site. Your domain takes the form of yourname.weebly.com. For inspiration on how a Weebly site can work, take a look at cake-maker Danielle Versluis's creations at http://sweettreatsbydanielle.weebly.com.

Double-check that the site you choose lets you set up for-profit business sites for free.

Adding music, photos and artwork

Suppose that you've built a basic website, and you want to have music CDs, photos or artwork that can be printed and sold on clothing. You've created the art or saved the photos as GIF or JPEG image files, and you want to place them on products you can sell to friends, family or anyone who's interested. A popular service called PrintShop (www.printshop.co.uk) makes it easy for you to create and sell such products online for free. The hard part is deciding what you want to sell, how best to describe your sales items and how to promote your site. Getting your words and images online is remarkably straightforward:

1. **Go to the PrintShop signup page (www. printshop.co.uk/signup.asp), shown in the figure.**

2. **Enter your details, including your business name and web address.**

3. **Add details of the type of products you want to sell, such as T-shirts, hoodies, mugs, mouse mats and so on.**

4. **After submitting approval your application, PrintShop asks for any logos, pictures and text you'd like to be included in your shop.**

After all the information is in, PrintShop designs a shop for you within two working days (see figure). You can start selling straight away – PrintShop does the logistical, stock and admin bit, for a slice of your profits, of course.

PrintShop's services are essentially free, and you only 'pay' them when you make a sale. This system gives you modest profits (you get £2 for the sale of a T-shirt, £1 for a mug), but PrintShop holds all the stock and takes on the job of delivering your items. That vastly reduces the pressure on you and may be a great way to start your journey as an online entrepreneur. Maintaining stock levels and judging your cash flow are tricky things to master.

(continued)

(continued)

For no charge, PrintShop gives you:

✔ A branded shop front that looks like your website

✔ Free customer service for your buyers

✔ A range of products to feature your designs

✔ Plenty of colours to choose from

✔ No minimum stock levels

✔ The ability to sell in pounds, dollars and euros

Other similar providers that you can get up and running with straight away include CafePress (www.cafepress.com) and Zazzle (www.zazzle.com), but Printshop is UK-based so you have the added advantage of local support should you need it. Meanwhile Lulu.com, which we discuss in Chapter 17, lets you sell your own books online and has a UK support centre.

Shared hosting

Arguably, the most popular web hosting option around is shared hosting. Your website resides on the same server as hundreds or even thousands of other sites (one of Kim's sites is on the same server as around 500 sites; another is shared with around 1,800). Each website resides in its own partition on the server and visitors to your site shouldn't notice any difference because traffic restrictions are in place for all sites, easing the server load. (Sites that regularly exceed these restrictions risk having their sites taken offline unless they pay extra for a higher-bandwidth deal.)

You'll be able to upload your own files to the server and have access to databases, email and technical support. A dedicated, web-based control panel helps you manage everything easily with minimal technical knowledge required. Additionally, access to web-based publishing tools is well-supported.

Sharing resources with other sites cuts down significantly on cost and administration. You aren't responsible for maintaining the server: updates to the server software are administered by the hosting company rather than yourself.

However, secure websites (beginning with https://) may not be supported with a shared hosting option, and because you don't have total control over the overall server's security settings, for peace of mind you may wish to opt for a dedicated option (see the following section) if you're storing sensitive customer data.

Prices for shared hosting vary greatly depending on the type of host and the package you've chosen. You may be looking at anything from £30 to £120 a year for a typical deal that gives you ample web space and bandwidth, access to databases and publishing tools, and phone and web-based support. The number of shared hosts out there is endless. Browse the ads at the back of computer magazines for an idea of what's available. Companies include 1&1, Fasthosts, Heart Internet, Easyspace, 123-reg, Positive Internet and many more.

Dedicated hosting

Dedicated hosting costs a lot more than shared hosting (you're looking at around £100 a month) and involves a fair deal of technical know-how to maintain.

The advantage, however, is that you have your very own server on which to host your website (or websites) with a dedicated IP address (a numerical identifier allocated to all machines connected to the Internet, such as 58.178.44.163). The ability to have free rein on your server setup is an attractive option because you won't need to worry about traffic restrictions or running out of storage space. You can also securely host sensitive customer data. But the amount of configuration required means you'll most likely need a technical contact to set up the server and be available to perform periodic maintenance and updates. Companies in this area include 1&1 and sister company Fasthosts.

Managed hosting

This is like dedicated hosting (see the previous section), but with someone at the other end there to help you with installing and setting up the dedicated server, handling security issues, monitoring its traffic, ensuring uptime and so on. The weight off your shoulders in terms of not worrying about setting up your server is a bonus but it's an expensive solution and really only worthwhile for high-traffic enterprise sites. Companies in this space include NetBenefit and Rackspace.

For less cost than dedicated hosting you could consider a *virtual* private hosting service. Essentially, you get all the same administrative functions as you would on a dedicated server, but in reality the server is partitioned. The disadvantage is that you get less disk space than a dedicated host; you often share the same IP address when you access the server's functions and functions may run slower because you're also sharing resources with many other sites (although, as with shared hosting, your host limits the number of sites allocated to the server).

Looking at Web Creation and Publishing Tools

A carpenter has his favourite hammer and saw. A chef has an array of utensils and pots and pans. Likewise, a website creator has software programs that facilitate the presentation of words, colours, images and multimedia in web browsers.

It pays to spend time choosing a web page editor that has the right qualities. What qualities should you look for in a web page tool, and how do you know which tool is right for you? To help narrow the field, we've divided this class of software into different levels of sophistication. Pick the type of program that best fits your technical skills.

Investigating content management systems

A web-based content management system (CMS) or content publishing platform lets you produce a website without requiring a huge knowledge of HTML code (see the later sidebar 'Flipping your whizzy-wig') or other scripting languages. You log in to your website and publish content in much the same way as you would with a word processor. No need to waste your time buried in technical jargon – instead, you can concentrate on producing a functional website for your business. All your information is pulled out from a database, so you can swiftly access and edit posts from within the CMS at any time.

The most popular content management systems are free (plenty of commercial alternatives exist, but these tend to be tailored towards medium-sized to large businesses that have many thousands of pages to their websites). The free ones are *open source*, meaning you're free to edit the underlying code after it's installed on your website (although we wouldn't do that as we aren't technical boffins).

Joomla!, a free CMS which claims to run on 2.7 per cent of websites online, describes a CMS as: 'software that keeps track of every piece of content on your website, much like your local public library keeps track of books and stores them'.

Any kind of content is supported by a CMS, whether it be images, video, audio or text. You never need to worry about understanding how it works – it just *does*.

Dynamic websites

Gone are the days when a website just sat there, doing nothing. Now we see all kinds of intelligent interactivity popping up on them: live news updates on the BBC; product recommendations for you based on a purchase you've just made on Amazon; new webmail popping up in Hotmail without having to reload the page; built-in chat functions on Facebook; real-time recognition about the strength of the password you're changing on eBay; instant search suggestions and search results on Google that appear as you type a word.

These are all examples of dynamic websites that are constantly pulling up new content. You don't necessarily have to 'refresh' the page to see the changes. They all work by using state-of-the-art computer scripting languages and technologies.

Dymanic websites work in several ways. They can be database-driven, meaning they pull up information (text, photos, customer information such as the status of your online order) from a database on the server side (the website host). Alternatively, site content can change from the client side; the browser is able to pull up information from the web and have the changes appear on screen without the end-user having to manually refresh the page. One example we like is the puzzle and trivia site Sporcle.com. You can play thousands of fun word games (such as naming all the states in the US or identifying a list of wrinkly rock legends from the '60s and '70s as they look today). When you type an answer, Sporcle recognises whether you've typed a correct response and instantly fills in the blank accordingly without you having to hit Submit. You don't always need to provide answers in the order of the questions, so the timed games are rapid-fire and exciting.

Database-driven websites are easy to manage because information is stored in a way that won't involve redoing the entire site manually. Kim once had to update an online bookstore for a publishing company. All their books were assigned a caption and a category. When the company wanted to change the category of one of their books, the book's original image and caption remained on the site, but its listing changed to a different category and so was displayed on an alternative page. Had the site not been database-driven, this would have involved a lot of manual effort.

Most web hosts support dynamic websites. You need to figure out what components you want in your web server and whether your host will support these. What technology will sit on the server side? What database solution should you use? If you're choosing a dedicated hosting option, what software will run your server?

Stick to an *open source* (free to access) non-commercial solution comprising free operating system Linux, web server software Apache, scripting language PHP and the free, open source database MySQL (pronounced 'my sequel'). All are collectively known by the acronym LAMP. It's cheaper, and the open source nature means that there are more compatible apps and scripts out there to use.

Apache HTTP is the most popular web server software (`www.apache.org`), and it harks back to the birth of the World Wide Web. It's open source and installed on more than 100 million web servers.

For more tips for choosing a host and the features you might need, see the section 'Features to look for in your host', later in this chapter, and check out the case study 'Flexible hosting'.

Initial installation doesn't need to be tricky, either. Wordpress likes to peddle its 'famous five-minute install' and has loads of easy-to-follow documentation online. Your host needs to support the scripting language PHP and MySQL database. Most do, but double-check before you sign up. You usually get at least one database on which to store your content depending on your hosting package and you can create the database from your control panel. Here, we explain the most popular *free* CMS options available and how they can benefit your business (you can find a more comprehensive list of all content management systems on Wikipedia at `http://en.wikipedia.org/wiki/List_of_content_management_systems`):

- **Wordpress.org:** One the longest-running content management systems around, Wordpress.org is by far the most popular and people primarily use it to create blogs and news-based sites. However, you can create individual pages from them that don't look a thing like blogs (for instance, you can disable comments and timestamps). You can choose from a range of pre-loaded themes to help you design your website, which you can then customise in any way you want without losing your content. Or you can use your own custom theme. The beauty of Wordpress.org is that countless mini-applications called *plugins* are available that people have developed to work with the system; such as spam filtering tools, contact forms, polls and many more – and they're all free. Get started at `www.wordpress.org`. (Note: A version of Wordpress is at `www.wordpress.com` rather than `.org`, but it's hosted by Wordpress and is only designed to host blogs. You can't upload a custom theme or edit the underlying code. You also don't control the database or the software, so you can't customise it by adding plugins. This article clearly explains the differences between the two: `http://en.support.wordpress.com/com-vs-org`.) In Figure 3-1 you can see Wordpress.org in action on Kim's dashboard.

- **Joomla!:** This is a little more sophisticated to run than Wordpress but is very powerful stuff for businesses. You can slot in different content elements into your website, although if your site is only ever going to run to a few pages, it might be a bit too big for your needs. Take a look at Outdoor Photographer magazine's website at `www.outdoorphotographer.com`. It runs primarily on Joomla! and includes a poll, blog, contents, subscription forum, forum, plenty of tips and articles. See `www.joomla.com` for more.

- **Drupal:** Another content management system run by sites like The Economist (`www.economist.com`) and The White House (`www.whitehouse.gov`). Drupal is probably more technical to get started with than the others and more suitable for larger sites, but when everything is in place it should be straightforward for you to update. A large emphasis is on extending your website using one of the thousands of modules that people have developed for the system. Discover how it can help you at `www.drupal.com`.

Figure 3-1:
You can
use the
Wordpress.
org CMS to
create blogs
and newsy
websites,
but enough
customi-
sation exists
for you to
build stand-
alone pages
for your site.

Your CMS needn't be the be-all and end-all of your website. One of Kim's sites includes a discussion forum, which she's linked off her main Wordpress-powered page. The forum, running on the commercial software vBulletin, operates separately to the Wordpress system and requires a separate data-base. But she's designed it to include the same logo to keep a sense of familiar-ity. You could do the same with other elements of your site such as the online store front (see the later section 'Shop front solutions made easy'). The pos-sibilities are endless.

Considering programs that do it all

If you plan to do a great deal of business online, or even want to add the title of web designer to your list of talents (as some of the entrepreneurs profiled in this book have done), it makes sense to spend some money up front and use a web page tool that can do everything you want – today and for years to come.

The advanced programs that we describe here go beyond the simple designa-tion of content management. They not only let you edit web pages but also help you add interactivity to your site, link dynamically updated databases to your site and keep track of how your site is organised and updated. Some programs even transfer your web documents to your web host with a single menu option. This way, you get to concentrate on the fun part of running an online business – meeting people, taking orders, processing payments and the like.

Adobe Dreamweaver CS5

What's that you say? You can never have enough bells and whistles? The cutting edge is where you love to walk? Then Dreamweaver, a web authoring tool by Adobe, is for you. Dreamweaver is a feature-rich, professional piece of software.

Dreamweaver's strengths aren't so much in the basic features such as making selected text bold, italic or a different size; rather, Dreamweaver excels in producing *dynamic HTML* (which makes web pages more interactive through scripts) and HTML style sheets. Dreamweaver has ample FTP settings, and it gives you the option of seeing the HTML codes you're working within one window and the formatting of your web page within a second, WYSIWYG (What You See Is What You Get; see 'Flipping your whizzy-wig', below) window. The latest version, Dreamweaver CS5, is a complex and powerful piece of software. It lets you create Active Server pages and connect to the ColdFusion database, and it contains lots of templates and wizards. Dreamweaver is available for both Windows and Macintosh computers; find out more at the Adobe website (www.adobe.com/uk/products/dreamweaver).

Microsoft Expression Studio 4 Web Professional

Microsoft Expression products comprise a powerful combination of web and application design tools. The Web Professional product includes web design software called Microsoft Expression Web, which is a step up from FrontPage, which was discontinued several years ago. It does pretty much everything you'd want when creating a website. Although you don't need to know much code, it's a hefty product that requires a steep learning curve and is likely to be far too complex for a startup website. Features include the ability to design a template; create a web-based form; create web-standards-compliant pages; add images, videos, links and other elements; create a search page; bring old websites up to scratch; and more.

You need to understand how cascading style sheets (CSS) work to make the most out of Expression Web because the product relies so much on ensuring that websites are standards-compliant. Previously, FrontPage didn't adhere to those standards because they weren't yet in place. If you used to design websites with FrontPage and want to make the transition then you might like to access the handy list of resources at http://blogs.msdn.com/b/xwebsupport/archive/2010/05/14/resources-for-expression-web-users.aspx. The official Expression website is at www.microsoft.com/expression/products/Purchase.aspx.

TECHNICAL STUFF

Flipping your whizzy-wig

Web browsers are multilingual; they understand exotic-sounding languages such as FTP, HTTP and GIF, among others. But one language browsers don't speak is English. Browsers don't understand instructions such as 'Put that image there' or 'Make that text italic'. HyperText Markup Language, or HTML, is a translator, if you will, between human languages and web languages.

Thanks to modern web page creation tools like the systems we mentioned in the section 'Investigating content management systems', you don't have to master HTML in order to create web pages. Plenty of web page editors do almost all your English-to-HTML translations for you.

The secret of all these web page creation tools is their WYSIWYG (pronounced whizzy-wig) display. WYSIWYG stands for What You See Is What You Get. A WYSIWYG editor lets you see on-screen how your page will look when it's on the web (or at least preview it) rather than forcing you to type (or even see) HTML commands like this:

```
<H1> This is a Level 1
    Heading </H1>
<IMG SRC = "lucy.gif"> <BR>
<P>This is an image of
    Lucy.</P>
```

A WYSIWYG editor, such as CoffeeCup HTML Editor for Windows (www.coffeecup.com), shows you how the page appears even as you assemble it. Besides that, it lets you format text and add images by means of familiar software shortcuts such as menus and buttons. For Mac fans, iweb (part of iMovie; equipped with Mac OS X) works in a similar way. It's a very pretty way to create a website. You can even drag photos straight into the program and resize them on-screen!

Shop front solutions made easy

As with content management systems, you can create an online shop front for your website without needing to master HTML. Several options are available:

✔ Install the appropriate software on your server and create your store listings by logging into your website, in much the same way as you create a website using a CMS. Popular options include osCommerce (www.oscommerce.com) and ZenCart (www.zen-cart.com).

✔ Buy software that resides on your computer and create the pages on your website before sending them to your server. Actinic Catalog (www.actinic.co.uk) does this.

✔ Use a hosted solution, where a separate company manages the shop front process and lets you design and create your shop through your web browser. Actinic Express (www.actinic.co.uk/ecommerce-for-startups/express-online-shopping-cart.html) does this; as does ekmPowershop (see the nearby sidebar).

In all cases, you can integrate your shop front with a trusted payment provider like Paypoint.net, Worldpay or PayPal (see Chapter 11 for the lowdown) that's responsible for processing credit card payments and getting them to your account.

Most shop-front software provides you with predesigned web pages, called *templates*, which you can customise for your particular business (the extent to which you can customise the template may vary). A good shopping trolley system enables customers to select items and tally the cost at the checkout. It should also easily integrate with common electronic payment options, such as credit card purchases.

Plenty of options are out there, so do some research and weigh up the pros and cons of each. Consider the following features when selecting your checkout software:

- ✔ **The shop front:** The shop front contains the web pages that you create. Some packages include predesigned web pages that you can copy and customise with your own content. How flexible are these?

- ✔ **The inventory:** You can stock your virtual shop-front shelves by presenting your wares in the form of an online catalogue or product list. Can you easily export this inventory or import it from a spreadsheet?

- ✔ **The virtual delivery van:** Some shop-front packages streamline the process of transferring your files from your computer to the server. Instead of using FTP software, you publish information simply by clicking a button in your browser.

- ✔ **The checkout counter:** Most electronic shop-front packages give you the option to accept orders online with a credit card, but you may want to consider taking them by phone or fax too.

- ✔ **Idiotproof-ness:** Do you want handholding through the entire setup process, or do you want to take complete control of the shop-front design and layout (your designer may be able to help you with this)?

- ✔ **Managing customers and sales:** Besides providing you with all the software that you need to create web pages and get them online, electronic shop fronts instruct you on how to market your site and present your goods and services in a positive way. In addition, some programs provide you with a back room for your business, where you can record customer information, orders and fulfilment. Are there tools to help collect customer information (such as email addresses) that you can use for marketing and managing customer relations? Can you advertise sale items, or let customers enter a discount coupon code upon checkout?

ekmPowershop

ekmPowershop (www.ekmpowershop.com) bills itself as 'easy to use' and promises 'instant results'. It's meant for people with little or no experience of payment software, and for a monthly fee of £20, you can set up a fully operational e-commerce shop. Put simply, when you sign up to ekmPowershop, you get a blank space on its servers where you can add your logos, text, product categories and pictures of the products themselves. You have the choice of integrating the software onto an existing website (which we recommend; it gives your website design and content far more flexibility) or using it on its own as a place to sell your goods (but you'll be limited with how your site looks).

The service is good because the site is updated regularly, and the technologies that your site relies on aren't allowed to go out of date. ekmPowershop offers real customer support (not just a robot), and because you don't have to install any software, you're less likely to need help anyway. You also get a complimentary search engine submission and a secure server as standard.

To accept credit cards online you can link up to a payment service provider like WorldPay or PayPal (see Chapter 11 for more).

The difference between ekmPowershop and other e-commerce solutions like Actinic, Zencart and osCommerce is that ekmPowershop hosts all your e-commerce content (such as the product descriptions, images and category listings). This makes things easy from a setup perspective. But if you wanted to cancel your contract with them and move to another solution, it would be tricky to move because you'd need to export all your content and redesign your site again.

The standard service costs £19.99 a month plus an initial setup charge of £49.95. Again, the results aren't as good as if you'd employed a professional web design company and hosting service, but then the cost is tiny by comparison. Take a look at some of the customers who are using ekmPowershop. They range from the 02 arena's merchandise store (http://merchandise.theo2.co.uk) to The Bicycle Doctor (www.thebicycledoctor.net).

Online shop-front software is very affordable for businesses like yours. For instance, osCommerce and ZenCart are free (although you may have to hire a technical expert and designer to set it up), while Actinic Catalog costs £499 plus VAT. Actinic Express, the web-based solution, is £1 for the first month and £18 thereafter. For a startup like yours, we wouldn't expect you to be choosing a Rolls-Royce solution when the Toyota version does the job just fine.

REMEMBER

All software requires updating from time-to-time and the complexity of this may vary. Wordpress.org alerts you to the update and all you have to do is click a button!

Features to look for in your host

A shared hosting solution should cost from £5 to £10 a month for a small amount of web space, say 500 to 750 megabytes. Look for a host that doesn't limit the number of web pages that you can create. Also find one that gives you at least a couple of email addresses with your account and that lets you add extra addresses for a nominal fee. Finally, look for a host that gives you access to databases that support the online store front and content publishing solutions you plan to use.

The previous sections look at how to set up your own store front and web page creation tools. But some hosts like to promote their own solutions. Online store Cheesybug Toys (www.cheesybug.co.uk), which was established in 2000, uses shop creation software provided by its web host, 1&1 (www.1and1.co.uk). Figure 3-2 shows how its checkout screen looks.

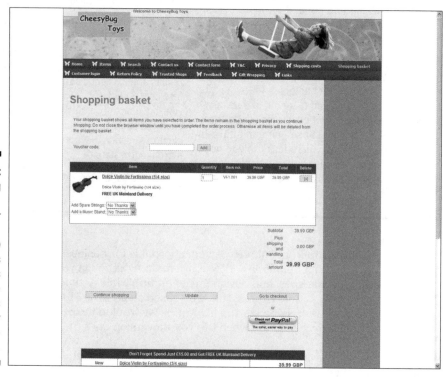

Figure 3-2: Cheesybug Toys (www. cheesy bug. co.uk) has designed its online store using tools provided by its web host, 1&1.

CASE STUDY

Flexible hosting

Doug Laughter knows how important it is to choose the right host. He and his wife Kristy own The Silver Connection, a business based in the United States, which sells sterling silver jewellery imported from India, Asia and Mexico. They began their business when Kristy brought back some silver jewellery from Mexico. The Silver Connection went online in April 1998 at www.silverconnection.com and is hosted by CrystalTech Web Hosting (www.crystaltech.com).

CrystalTech don't have a UK base and you might prefer choosing a local host for support purposes, but the following case study is a good reflection of what you should consider when you choose a host.

Q. Why did you choose CrystalTech as your web host?

A. CrystalTech is my second web host. I didn't have any problems with my previous host, but the issue of changing web hosts came down to the web development technology I wanted to choose for my site. I settled on CrystalTech because it supported the Web Application Server that I chose, which was a Windows platform running Internet Information Server. I also wanted to use Microsoft Access or Microsoft SQL Server for my database solution to support the development of Active Server Pages (ASP).

Q. What makes CrystalTech such a good web host?

A. It gives its clients access to a Control Centre that allows complete administrative control for the domain. Included in this are mail, FTP and Domain Name Systems with automatic ODBC (Open Database Connectivity) for databases. A client also gets access to several utilities that analyse traffic to your website. I also use the comprehensive knowledge base and online forums that carry on discussions about programming, website design, databases, networking and other topics.

Q. What kinds of customer service features do you use that other business owners should look for?

A. One feature that CrystalTech is very good with is notification. If web hosting or mail services will be offline for a certain amount of time, I receive an email in advance specifying exactly what is going to happen and when. I have always been treated very well by tech support when I have needed to call.

Q. What kinds of questions should small business owners and managers ask when they're shopping around for a hosting service? What kinds of features should they be looking for initially?

A. I would first suggest considering how you want to develop your website. Today's e-commerce site needs to be dynamic in nature, so the business needs to research and determine what web server application it will use. A web server application consists of the following:

- ✔ **Server Side Technology** (such as Active Server Pages, Adobe ColdFusion, Java Server Pages, PHP)

- ✔ **Database Solution** (such asMicrosoft SQL Server, MS Office Access, MySQL, Oracle

- ✔ **Server Application** (such as IIS, Apache, Oracle iPlanet)

- ✔ **Operating Platform** (either Windows or UNIX/Linux)

(continued)

(continued)

So the decision on how the e-commerce website will be developed and in what technology is a very key decision to make from the onset. Once this is decided, choose a web host that supports your web server application of choice.

Q. After the development platform is determined, what features should you look for?

A. Look for dedicated disk space for database applications. From 250MB to 500MB of disk space may be fine for your website files, but throw in a highly developed Microsoft SQL Server relational database management system, and you'll be paying for some additional space.

Also ask about how much data transfer you can do in a given period, how many email addresses are given with the domain and whether there's an application that lets you control and administer your entire website. If you don't have your own shopping trolley application, ask your host what it offers in this area. Specifically, find out what application it offers, how transactions are completed and how credit card purchases are processed. Finally, make sure there's an application that can analyse traffic, such as Webtrends, or SmarterStats.

You either choose or are allocated a password and username to log into your website. You log into your website with an FTP program or through your host's online dashboard, accessible through your web browser. Although you don't need to enter a password to view a website through a browser (well, at least for most sites), you do need a password to protect your site from being accessed with an FTP program. Otherwise, anyone can enter your web space and tamper with your files.

Many FTP programs are available for free on the Internet or you can purchase them cheaply. Check out some other programs on the market:

- ✔ FileZilla (www.filezilla-project.com; free)
- ✔ Coffee Cup Direct FTP (www.coffeecup.com; £24)
- ✔ Smart FTP (www.smartftp.com; £30 for a professional licence)

After you have your software tools together and have a user directory on your ISP's web server, it's time to put your website together. Basically, when Greg wants to create or revise content for his website, he opens the page in his web page editor, makes the changes, saves the changes and then transfers the files to his ISP's directory with his FTP program. Finally, he reviews the changes in his browser.

The web is global, and you don't necessarily have to choose a British host. We prefer it for obvious reasons like being able to contact them at local hours and being billed locally, but it's up to you.

What to look for in a web host

Along with providing lots of space for your HTML, image and other files (typically, you get anywhere from 100 megabytes to a few gigabytes of space), web hosting services offer a variety of related services, including some or all the following:

✔ **Email addresses:** You're likely to be able to get several email addresses for your own or your family members' personal use. Besides that, many web hosts give you special email addresses called *auto-responders*. These are email addresses, such as `info@yourcompany.com`, that you can set up to automatically return a text message or a file to anyone looking for information.

✔ **Domain names:** Virtually all the hosting options that we mention in this chapter give customers the option of obtaining a short domain name. But some web hosts simplify the process by providing domain-name registration in their flat monthly rates.

✔ **Web page software:** Some hosting services include web page authoring/editing software. Some web hosting services even offer web page forms that you can fill out online in order to create your own online shopping catalogue. All you have to provide is a digital image of the item you want to sell, along with a price and a description. You submit the information to the web host, which then adds the item to an online catalogue that's part of your site.

✔ **Multimedia/CGI scripts:** One big thing that sets web hosting services apart from part-time hosts is the ability to serve complex and memory-intensive content, such as Flash video files. They also let you process web page forms that you include on your site by executing computer programs called *CGI scripts*. These programs receive the data that someone sends you (such as a customer service request or an order form) and present the data in readable form, such as a text file, email message or an entry in a database. See Chapter 6 for more about how to set up and use forms and other interactive website features.

✔ **Shopping trolley software:** If part of your reason for going online is to sell items, look for a web host that can streamline the process for you. Most organisations provide you with web page forms that you can fill out to create sale items and offer them in an online shopping trolley, for example.

✔ **Automatic data backups:** Some hosting services automatically back up your website data to protect you against data loss – an especially useful feature because, in extreme cases, major data losses have been known to sink businesses. The automatic nature of the backups frees you from the worry and trouble of doing it manually.

✔ **Site statistics:** Virtually all web hosting services also provide you with site statistics that give you an idea (perhaps not a precisely accurate count, but a good estimate) of how many visitors you've received. Even better is access to software reports that analyse and graphically report where your visitors are from, how they found you, which pages on your site are the most frequently viewed and so on. You can do this yourself using something like Google Analytics (see Chapter 8).

✔ **Shopping and electronic commerce features:** If you plan to give your customers the ability to order and purchase your goods or services online by using their credit cards, be sure to look for a web host that provides you with secure commerce options. A *secure server* is a computer that can encrypt sensitive data (such as credit card numbers) that the customer sends to your site. For a more detailed discussion of secure electronic commerce, see Chapter 7.

✔ **Password protected website folders:** These are available to restrict access to specific areas of your site.

✔ **ASP.NET versus PHP; Microsoft SQL versus MySQL:** *Huh! Technical jargon! Someone hand me a strong drink.* What we mean here is what kind of databases and programming features does your host have that'll make your site dynamic and be able to run content management systems, contact forms, discussion forums, online store fronts and so on? Microsoft has one end of the market, and free, open-source solutions have the other.

Having so many hosting options available is the proverbial blessing and curse. It's good that you have so many possibilities and that the competition is so fierce because that can keep prices down. On the other hand, deciding which host is best for you can be difficult. In addition to asking about the preceding list of features, here are a few more questions to ask prospective web hosts to help narrow the field:

✔ **Do you limit file transfers?** Many services charge a monthly rate for a specific amount of electronic data that's transferred to and from your site. Each time a visitor views a page, that user is actually downloading a few kilobytes of data in order to view it. If your web pages contain, say, 1 megabyte of text and images and you get 1,000 visitors per month browsing the vast majority of your site, then your site accounts for 1 gigabyte of data transfer per month. If your host allocates you less than 1 gigabyte per month, it'll probably charge you extra for the amount you go over the limit.

✔ **What kind of connection do you have?** Your site's web page content appears more quickly in web browser windows if your server has a super-fast T1 or T3 connection.

Besides these questions, the other obvious ones to ask any contractor apply to web hosting services as well. These include questions like 'How long have you been in business?', 'Can I cancel my contract at any time?' and, 'Can you suggest customers who will give me a reference?'

The fact that we include a screen shot or mention of a particular web hosting service's site in this chapter or elsewhere in this book doesn't mean that we're endorsing or recommending that particular organisation alone. A number of companies can offer your business a good deal, so shop around carefully and find the one that's best for you. Check out the hosts with the best rates and most reliable service. Visit some other sites that they host and email the owners of those sites for their opinion of their hosting service. Ask around at forums (although take criticism with a grain of salt, as *every* big host is bound to get some negative feedback).

Competition is tough among hosting services, which means that prices are going down. But it also means that hosting services may seem to promise the moon in order to get your business. Be sure to read the small print and talk to the host before you sign a contract, and always get statements about technical support and backups in writing.

What's it gonna cost?

Because of the ongoing competition in the industry, prices for web hosting services vary widely. If you look in the classified sections in the back of magazines that cover the web or search on the Internet itself, you'll see ads for hosting services costing next to nothing. Chances are, these prices are for a basic level of service – web space, email addresses, domain name and software – which may be all you need.

The second level of service provides script processing, the ability to serve audio and video files on your site, database support, regular backups and extensive site statistics, as well as consultants who can help you design and configure your site. This more sophisticated range of features costs more and may set you back £20 to £50 a month, depending on the service level you require. At Easyspace.com, for example, you can conduct secure electronic commerce on your site as part of hosting packages that cost between £70 and £160 a year. MySQL database support starts at £70 a year.

Chapter 4

Profiting from Web 2.0 and Social Media Tools

. . . .

In This Chapter

▶ Taking advantage of round-the-clock availability and new communications

▶ Identifying new products and services

▶ Marketing your views, opinions, and commentary through your website and social media

▶ Creating your own business blog and Facebook page

▶ Making sure that your online business promotes community spirit

. . . .

*W*hen you open shop on the Internet, you don't just begin to operate in isolation. The whole point of the web is the fact that it's a community. It's the same for businesses as it is for individuals. Whether you like it or not, you're not alone. You have access to thousands, even millions, of other businesses that are in the same situation you are – or that went through the same kinds of uncertainties you're encountering before they achieved success.

This chapter is all about building your brand and attracting customers through fun, engaging and modern *social networking* tools. The Internet lets you actively participate with your customers even if you operate mainly (or entirely) online.

Here, you'll find a user friendly overview of the many new opportunities available to you when you start an online business, including tools, services and opportunities for partnering so that you can advertise your new business in ways that help you succeed without breaking your budget.

We also discuss new products and services you can sell which were never possible even just a few years ago.

Web 2.0 – What on Earth Does That Mean?

The phrase *Web 2.0* became popular about six or seven years ago. It doesn't just mean the second generation of the Internet, although faster connections and greater bandwidth underpin it. In essence, Web 2.0 refers to the ability to collaborate and share information online, in a way that people weren't capable of doing before.

Web 1.0 was all one-way traffic. A webmaster would stick something on a site, and you'd either read it or buy it. Now, users are demanding greater involvement in their web experiences. They don't just want to look at websites, they want to help build them; to create and be part of social networks.

New technologies have helped make this happen. Arguably, the essence of the web as a social tool was around all along, but it just didn't have the capability.

Massive names like social networking site Facebook (www.facebook.com), microblogging site Twitter (www.twitter.com) and all-encompassing search engine Google (www.google.co.uk) are underpinning the dominance of Web 2.0 services, linking people together in ways unthinkable just a few years ago.

Take Twitter for example. Hardly anyone understood the point of a tool that let you communicate in 140 characters or less what you were doing. But when celebrities suddenly caught on and used it to start 'Tweeting' about where they were and how they were really, truly feeling behind the glitz and the glamour, the traditional media began to feel threatened – and took notice.

Now you see the @ symbol before a Twitter username (like @stephenfry or @bbcnews) everywhere you go. People have it on business cards and email signatures. TV shows broadcast their Twitter usernames all the time and they don't even need to preface it with the twitter.com. During the 83rd Oscars broadcast, watched by millions around the world, the *hashtag #oscars* appeared on screen – a hashtag is a keyword prefaced by the hash (#) symbol. People put put hashtags after a Tweet so that other people can find all the Tweets related to that topic. When controversial actor Charlie Sheen suddenly joined in March 2011, he gained 1 million followers in 24 hours and started various hashtag trends including the phrases #winning and #tigerblood.

Facebook, Twitter, Google's video sharing site YouTube (www.youtube.com), bookmarking site Digg (www.digg.com), content management/blogging tool Wordpress (www.wordpress.com and www.wordpress.org), photo-sharing site Flickr (www.flickr.com), blogging host Tumblr (www.tumblr.com) and hundreds of other websites all rely on contributions from people like you and us to survive. Others still rely on you to make their sites a richer experience. The music-sharing service Spotify (www.spotify.com)

lets you listen to streaming music and create your own playlists online (see Kim's book, *Spotify For Dummies*, for more). But it also integrates with Facebook so you can share your playlists with others and see what all your other friends are listening to on the service.

Part of Web 2.0's popularity derives from people's desire to share information with like-minded friends – and talk a bit about themselves and their interests, too. If you can offer the ability for people to do this in an innovative way, then you're bound to build traffic quickly. The great thing about Web 2.0 is that other people populate the site, so you need fewer resources to get the thing going.

Wikis (websites that allow anyone to add their content), *social bookmarking* (the act of bookmarking your favourite websites for other like-minded people to share), *podcasting* (downloading audio files) and *vodcasting* (downloading visual files) have developed from the trend for sharing knowledge and new information. Now sites from the BBC to Google and Amazon use these cool tools.

Anyone can set up a podcast from their own home with a decent microphone and a computer hooked up to the Net. YouTube is full of people videoing themselves in front of a webcam.

The most famous example of a Wiki is Wikipedia.org, which has 3.5 million pages of content contributed by the public. The website is an encyclopaedia of people's knowledge, and despite the fact that anyone can edit it, it's almost totally accurate (save for a few high-profile entries that have had to be restricted to avoid hoax edits).

Web 2.0 isn't about self-indulgent kids – far from it. It brings people together. If it weren't for Twitter as a vehicle for mass organisation of protest movements, we wouldn't have seen the revolutions in the Middle East. And in the political world closer to home, constituents can contact their Members of Parliament and get updates on what's going on in their electorate. From an entertainment perspective, Twitter has also made live TV fun again – you can see what everyone else is thinking at the same time whenever something is broadcasting.

When it comes to your business, you can take advantage of these and many other emerging tools to get closer to your customers than ever before. We hope you can get inspired by some ideas in this chapter.

Getting to Grips with a New Generation of Business Tools

Being online means you enjoy advantages over businesses operating solely in the bricks-and-mortar marketplace. Email, blogging, social networking and the Internet in general give you much better access to your customers – and no equivalent exists in the offline world. You also have access to services such as search engines that can help you find suppliers and do business research and marketing. Conversely, people can find you too.

Sometimes, a big step towards success is simply being aware of all the opportunities available to you. The worst reason you can have for going online is simply that 'everybody's doing it'. Instead of focusing on one way of advertising or selling, take stock of all the aspects of online business that you can exploit. Then when you create your website, select a payment option or set up security measures, you do things right the first time around. The next few sections describe some advantages you need to make part of your business plan.

The shop is always open

One of the first reasons why entrepreneurs flock to the web is the ability to do business around the clock with customers all over the world. It may be 2 a.m. in the UK, but someone can still be making a purchase in Rome, Los Angeles or Sydney from your website or eBay shop.

If you're just starting out and you're trying to reach the widest possible audience of consumers, be sure your goods or services are:

- ✔ **Small:** That means they're easy to pack and easy to ship.
- ✔ **Something that people need and can use worldwide:** DVDs, CDs, mobile phone and digital camera batteries, computer products, action figures and sports memorabilia appeal to many.
- ✔ **Something that people can't find in their local area:** Many sites resell gourmet foodstuffs like spices and dried mushrooms that you can't easily find overseas, for example.

Make sure that you appeal to a small, niche segment of individuals around the world. Doing one thing extremely well is better than doing lots of things badly. That applies to all businesses, from the smallest start-ups to the biggest multinationals. Keeping your business lean and mean improves your chances of success.

New ways of communicating and listening

Nothing beats email, in our opinion, for reaching customers in a timely and friendly way. We know all about the immediacy of talking to people over the phone, the sophistication of desktop alerts and the benefits of print advertising. But phone calls can be intrusive, alerts are expensive and mag ads only work for certain types of business. As you can probably testify as a consumer, most people are wary of anyone who wants to market to them with an out-of-the-blue phone call that interrupts their day. Email messages can come in at any time of the day or night, but they don't interrupt what customers are doing. And if customers have already made a purchase from your company, they may welcome a follow-up contact by email, especially because they can respond to you at their own convenience. Not only that, but you can include links to products and services in emails that could tempt customers into further purchases. You can announce new product ranges, special offers, even an entirely new business.

One of the most popular online communications systems, instant messaging (IM), is useful for keeping in touch with business partners and colleagues. But be very wary of using it to approach current or potential customers. Consumers are used to dropping everything to answer instant messages from friends. When they discover that it's a marketing message, they're not going to be happy – it's the online equivalent of taking a telesales call when you're enjoying a nice bath.

Besides email newsletters, what kinds of communications strategies work with online shoppers? The following sections give a few suggestions.

Giving away a free sample

Greg was in the grocery shop the other day, looking at a hunk of luxury cheese that costs a pretty penny, wishing he could open up the package and taste-test it before handing over big bucks. The concept of the free sample is one that everyone loves – especially web surfers. Newspapers like the *Financial Times* do it by making the first few paragraphs of archived articles and selected columns (like Lex) available online; if you want to read the rest, you have to become a Standard or Premium member. Amazon.co.uk makes brief excerpts of selected CD tracks available on its website so that shoppers can listen to the music before deciding whether or not to buy the CD.

On the Internet, software producers have been giving away free samples for many years in the form of computer *shareware*: software programs that users can download and use for a specified period of time. After the time period expires, the consumers are asked (or required, if the program ceases to function) to pay a shareware fee if they want to keep the program. A tiny Texas company called id Software started giving away a stripped-down computer game on the Internet back in 1993, in the hope of getting users hooked on it so that they would pay for the full-featured version. The plan worked, and since then, more than 100,000 customers have paid as much as $40 (£22) for a full copy of the game, which is called Doom. id Software has gone on to create and sell many other popular games (and versions of Doom) since.

Giving out discounts

One reason shoppers turn to the Internet is to save money. Thanks to sites such as PriceRunner (`www.pricerunner.co.uk`), Kelkoo (`www.kelkoo.co.uk`) and Moneysupermarket.com (`www.moneysupermarket.com`), which allow you to compare prices on various websites for books, holidays, electrical equipment, car insurance or whatever you like, shoppers expect some sort of discount from the Internet. They love it if you offer special Internet-only prices on your website, give them money off or provide promotional offers like the one offered by Sky in Figure 4-1.

Figure 4-1: Use vouchers, discounts and Internet-only specials to entice more customers or drive them to a bricks-and-mortar shop.

© 2011 BskyB

Giving customers the chance to talk back

Another great thing about the Internet is that it gives customers the chance to get involved in the design and manufacture of products. They can create their own clothing ranges, sportswear or even artwork and have it sent to them by post. Moonpig, in Figure 4-2, is a good example of a brand that lets people customise a greeting card to their own tastes. You can even upload your own photos to appear on greeting cards.

Setting up chat rooms on your site doesn't make sense unless you have a solid user base of at least several hundred regular users who feel passionately about your goods and services and are dedicated enough to want to type real-time messages to one another and to you. However, discussion groups are practical, even for small businesses; you can set them up by installing software like phpBB or vBulletin on your site, or link to your Yahoo! Group. Find out more about making your website interactive in Chapter 6.

Figure 4-2:
The web enables manufacturers to put customers in charge of the design process.

Web APIs: The building blocks of Web 2.0

One of the biggest ways in which Web 2.0 has expanded is through a concept called a web API, or web Application Programming Interface. We aren't that clued up about how it all works from a technical perspective (we already feel a slight headache coming on just thinking about it), but in a nutshell it makes it easy for one website or application's content to be transported to another application and then displayed or used in different ways. This happens when the website opens up some of its functionality to developers.

You can see thousands of examples of these combinations (called *mashups*) on www. programmableweb.com/mashups. Some are practical, others are just plain fun. Some real-world examples of APIs in use include:

✔ You can share images uploaded onto Flickr or Apple's iPhoto on your Facebook profile.

✔ Gigero (www.gigero.com) shows you where your favourite artist is playing using Google Maps. It then links to the artist's tracks on the music streaming service Spotify and to the event page on last.fm.

✔ Rather than use the Twitter.com website to try to keep track of all the people you're following, Tweetdeck can help you manage the flow, as well as what friends using other social networking sites are up to. (Twitter recently bought Tweetdeck for £25m as it was so good.)

✔ #haiku (http://haiku.thehemp cloud.com) mashes up Twitter and Flickr by using posts tagged with #haiku and matching them up with similarly tagged photos from Flickr.

✔ Many websites, like that of the *New York Times*, now integrate with Facebook, so you can log in with your Facebook credentials to perform actions such as liking an article or leaving a comment that are then highlighted in your Facebook profile.

✔ You can search real-time status updates from Facebook (no login required) at www.funnystatus.com/Search Facebook.

Advertising on Facebook

Facebook is a free service for its users, so how do you think it makes money? It's not just through advertising *en masse* – that's a part of it, but just think of the wealth of information Facebook has on its users that other brands can use and make the most of.

When businesses advertise on Facebook, they can target their ads to certain demographics based on information that users have entered on their profiles.

This advertising goes beyond names, ages and locations. Interests, political preferences, sexual orientation, pages and posts that a user likes are often publicly revealed – all this is prime fodder to help businesses target the right customers for their products. When you advertise on Facebook you can narrow the fields down so that your wedding products business targets all engaged women between the ages of 25 and 40 who like reading, walking and music, if that's what you want.

You can create your short ad online and set a daily budget (which you can cancel at any time).

For more on Facebook ads and to see whether it's right for you, see www.facebook.com/facebookads.

Harnessing opinions

You can add a short survey to your website to help improve the experience for your visitors and identify areas for change. Setup only takes a few minutes using a third-party survey provider. Common examples include Kampyle (www.kampyle.com) and SurveyMonkey (www.surveymonkey.com), but many others exist.

Have a survey run for a few weeks to harness feedback on whether or not visitors liked your site, and then analyse the results.

Auctioning off your professional services

Making a living selling your design, consultation or other professional services isn't new. But the Internet provides you with new and innovative ways to get the word out about what you do. Along with having your own website in which you describe your experience, provide samples of your work and make references to clients you've helped, you can find new clients by auctioning off your services in what's known as a *reverse auction*. In a reverse auction, the provider of goods or services doesn't initiate a transaction – rather, the customer does.

The UK government is a big fan of reverse auctions as a way of getting the best price for contracts. For example, say the Department for Culture, Media and Sport needs a new stationery supplier. It advertises the contract in the form of a tender and invites bids; the lowest bid (from a reputable supplier) wins the deal. Even the Ministry of Defence is involved. Check out www. contracts.mod.uk if you don't believe us!

Elance Online, a reverse auction site based in the United States, enables professional contractors to offer their services and bid on jobs. (Go to www. elance.com and click Elance Online.) The site is ideal if you don't offer bits of content, such as stories or articles, but usually charge by the hour or by the job for your services. In this case, the customer is typically a company that needs design, writing, construction or technical work. The company posts a description of the job on the Elance site. Essentially, it's a request for bids or request for proposals: freelancers who've already registered with the site then make bids on the job. The company can then choose the lowest bid or choose another company based on its qualifications.

Exploring New Products and Services That You Can Sell

The choices you make when you first get started in e-commerce have an impact on how successfully you target your customers. One of the main choices is determining what you plan to sell online. Because you've made the decision to sell on the Internet, chances are good that you're a technology-savvy businessperson. You're open to new technologies and new ways of selling. The 21st century has seen an explosion in products and services that were unheard of just a decade or so ago. If you can take advantages of one of these opportunities, you increase your potential customer base.

Make your music available online

The iTunes Music Store (www.apple.com/uk/itunes), Spotify (www. spotify.com), Amazon (www.amazon.co.uk) and social music sites like last.fm (www.last.fm) have opened up immense opportunities for unsigned bands to get their music heard.

Then you have the promotional side of things – using social media like Facebook and MySpace to set up a band page and post samples of your music online. These days you don't need to have special media players to play your music. All computers nowadays come with that capability thrown in. The most popular format is still MP3/MP4, along with AAC (Advanced Audio Codec) and WAV (Waveform Audio Format). To a lesser extent, Windows Media Audio is also available (this isn't natively supported by Macs, but you can download workarounds).

Streaming music (which can include samples) is also possible via your web browser, so you don't need to download the individual music files. This is a useful way for you to deter people from downloading your entire album for free, without anyone paying for it.

As an artist, you can't just partner directly with the likes iTunes and Amazon MP3 (it would be the equivalent of your band going to an HMV store and trying to get it to stock your home-pressed CD). However, middlemen exist who do have relationships with these sites including TuneCore (www.tunecore.com), CDBaby (www.cdbaby.com) and DashGo (www.dashgo.com).

Making creative works work

Plenty of online marketplaces are around that act like real-life markets, with a range of stallholders peddling handmade wares from dresses made of vintage materials to innovative sculptures, jewellery and vases. eBay is the most obvious example because it sells just about anything, but unless people already know you and your designs, gaining exposure from them will be hard work. Kim knows of one jewellery seller who finds it hard to sell her relatively expensive but high-quality pieces on eBay when so many competitors are around with cheap designer rip-offs that overwhelm her listings.

That's why websites dedicated to showing off your special designs exist. The reality is that the majority of people won't gain a full-time income selling via these sites, but we certainly see no harm in giving your work more exposure. In a world of mass consumption, plenty of people still have an eye for individual artistic merit.

Etsy (www.etsy.com) is one of the most well-known places for people to sell their original works in a marketplace of like-minded creative types, and Deviant Art (www.deviantart.com) is populated by young people who've uploaded their graphic art to the website. Interested parties can purchase designs on T-shirts and the like through Deviant Art, with the creator earning the profits.

Another website, Not on The High Street (www.notonthehighstreet.com), is for people who want to find that extra special gift. When Kim's daughter was a baby she found a cute fabric guitar rattle for her on the site. Its maker sent Kim a personal email pointing out that because the guitars all use fabric remnants the end product would look slightly different to the photos displayed on the website – the maker was checking whether that was OK. Kim still has the rattle!

Providing groceries and household services

Small, easily shipped merchandise like golf balls or tools are undeniably well suited to online sales. But you don't need to restrict your online business to such items. Even perishable items like foodstuffs can be, and frequently are, purchased online. Initially, the field attracted *pure plays* – companies that devoted their sales activities solely to the Internet. They failed to compete with bricks-and-mortar shops.

The good news is that traditional bricks-and-mortar grocery shops are finding success by selling their products on the web as a way of supplementing their traditional in-store offering. The website for Riverford Organic Vegetables (`http://www.riverford.co.uk`), shown in Figure 4-3, gives its customers the convenience of veg and fruit boxes delivered to their door – but with an emphasis on quality. You can also top up your box with other grocery staples like milk, egg, bread and meat.

Figure 4-3: Regional grocers and food producers are widening their customer bases thanks to the web.

Big supermarkets such as Sainsbury's (`www.sainsburys.co.uk`) and Ocado (`www.ocado.co.uk`), which spend millions of pounds promoting, maintaining and selling through their websites, have conducted numerous studies into what makes people buy food online. Generally, people buy groceries this way for three main reasons:

✔ Cost savings

✔ Convenience

✔ Greater product variety

If you're able to offer food items that consumers can't find elsewhere, and at a competitive price, you should consider selling food online. People hate navigating multi-storey car parks and waiting in long queues at the checkout. People who live alone and who have difficulty getting out (such as the elderly or sick) naturally turn to buying their groceries online.

Are you interested in reaching online grocery shoppers online? The Food Standards Agency has a useful website (www.eatwell.gov.uk/keeping foodsafe/shoppingforfood/onlinemailorder) detailing the standards of quality, packaging and delivery you have to achieve.

Customers have plenty of rights in this area; for example you have to make descriptions of your products full and accurate, and you must send a confirmation email after your customer has ordered food. Non-food sellers also have to provide a cooling-off period of seven days, during which customers are allowed to change their minds and cancel orders. Also check out Food First (www.foodfirst.co.uk) for details and inspiration about the food industry.

Dealing in virtual currencies

Back in the dotcom boom era of the late 1990s, some questionable startup ideas existed that weren't quite ready for mainstream acceptance. But sometimes the strangest ideas resurface in different ways.

Take Beenz, the doomed *virtual currency* created by entrepreneur Charles Cohen that attracted a lot of publicity back in 1998. Beenz were similar to loyalty points but acted just like real money – the Beenz were sold to companies in local currencies, and these companies distributed the Beenz to consumers after they performed certain actions on their websites (such as making a purchase). People could then spend Beenz on goods or cash them in at a lesser rate, with Beenz.com (the company) earning money from the difference. But the big problem was that the system was marketed as a global currency rather than a loyalty-type scheme, which meant people could potentially use it to avoid tax if they traded in large amounts. The scheme hit regulatory problems as a result. Another problem was that many of the companies Beenz.com partnered with went bust when the bubble burst, and Beenz.com lost a huge chunk of its revenue. It closed in 2001 after being privately sold to a company (that itself later folded).

Fast-forward to today, and virtual currencies are still around (in a slightly different form). Virtual money that you can use to perform certain online tasks is big business. Social games like Farmville (a game you download to the Facebook platform) encourage people to spend money to buy credits, which they can then use to buy things like a virtual cow, pink barnyard or some crops for their farm.

Meanwhile, established virtual worlds like Second Life let residents spend real money in order to buy virtual money called Lindens. Then they can buy virtual land, clothes for their avatar or anything else that other residents have created or are willing to sell for Lindens. They also earn Lindens for working, for example as an assistant in a virtual store.

If Beenz.com had launched in a different time with a different business strategy, who knows where it might have ended up?

Facebook is in on the act now, trying to jump on Farmville's success bandwagon. With Facebook Credits, you spend money to buy credits that you can then spend on earning 'premium items' for third-party games you've downloaded to the Facebook platform. Facebook gets a cut of the money for providing the payment service (which some developers aren't too happy about, but if it wasn't for Facebook providing the platform for people to download and use the games and apps, no market for them would exist).

So, what does all this mean for your business? Facebook has made no mention of expanding Facebook Credits beyond the walls of Facebook, but seeing as it already lets you create a 'Like' button on your website, the Credits could possibly be used on other sites – like yours. And of course, another system may well take over in the future – we discuss new ways to charge for content in the section 'Adding Online Content and Commentary', later in this chapter.

Making the move to mobile

In 2009, Apple announced that people had downloaded 1 *billion* apps from its App Store. By 2010, that figure shot up to *10 billion*. These apps, which cover anything from the Angry Birds gaming phenomenon to a GPS-controlled pedometer, are available from the App Store and typically cost £0.60 to £1.20 each.

People can use their iTunes Music Store login to charge the apps to their account. They only need to type in their username and password; there's no hunting around for a credit card because these details are stored in your iTunes account. The other convenience is having all the apps sitting there in your iTunes account so you can download updates in one swift move. You even have what's known as *in-app* purchases, which are extra bells and whistles you can buy to enhance your apps. For instance, the Hipstamatic app for the iPhone emulates an old-style camera along with various 'films'. You can make an in-app purchase to buy virtual lenses and different filters that give your photos a unique effect.

The massive success of the Apple iPhone, Android-powered phones (which use Google Accounts) and the iPad – along with the countless apps available to download – illustrates how well digital products can sell with the right administration in place.

Making money from affiliate links

Affiliate marketing is a massive business. Say a clothes shop recruits a partner (or affiliate) who promotes a link from her website back to the clothing website. The affiliate gets paid if she generates a *lead* – someone follows the link and then performs an action, such as signing up to the clothes shop's newsletter or making a purchase. The affiliate gets either a flat referral fee or a percentage of the sale. The clothes shop knows that the referral has come from the affiliate's website because the link contains a unique identifying code that the shop can trace back to the affiliate.

Many intermediary companies facilitate the partnership between advertiser and publisher, from both technical and payment perspectives.

Affiliate marketing can be full of scam artists trying to promise riches for affiliates so long as they cough up a 'fee'. Never pay money upfront to become an affiliate. If you're interested in either marketing or becoming an affiliate, go with a large intermediary company like Affili.net (www.affili.net), which boasts partners like Red Driving School, World Wildlife Fund and Virgin Holidays. Also check out the long-established LinkShare (www.linkshare.co.uk) and Commission Junction (https://uk.cj.com).

Potential affiliates could try joining eBay's Partner Program or Amazon's affiliate program, Amazon Associates. You can display ads for certain products on Amazon and earn commission if someone clicks through to the Amazon website as a result.

Go to www.affiliates4u.com for more on affiliate marketing. A big conference called a4uexpo takes place every year in London and other European cities, and there you visit companies who are showcasing. You can find information at www.a4uexpo.com.

Adding Online Content and Commentary

Plenty of traditional publications have discovered that they can supplement home delivery and newsstand sales by providing some parts of their content online on a subscription-only basis. Typically, some content is available for free, but other stories are designated as *premium content*, made available only to subscribers who have paid to subscribe to the site and who can enter a valid username and password.

The online versions of the *Economist* (www.economist.com) and *The Spectator* (www.spectator.co.uk) both have premium content that's available only to paying subscribers. In the last decade, more newspapers started to offer extra content for free, reasoning that they'd make more money through advertising on a free website than through subscriptions on a paid-for model. This has had mixed results. In late 2010, *The Times* announced that it would break with current trends and start offering *walled* content: articles only available on a subscription-led basis. Long-term success of this remains to be seen, but early indicators suggest that this is the way forward.

In February 2011, both Google and Apple announced payment systems that publishers can use to charge for content. Google's solution, called One Pass (www.google.com/landing/onepass), lets readers access premium content by providing the system to manage and authenticate payments. People can access all their purchased content across mobile and desktop devices, and Google Checkout (see Chapter 11) is used as the payment system. Google takes 10 per cent of the cut. Apple's offering works in a similar way to its iTunes Music Store and App Store. However, at the time of writing, it takes 30 per cent of the cut.

The beauty of using Google and Apple to handle the administration means that it saves on the programming work involved to separate free and paid-for content on your website, while simultaneously handling the payment processing. It's also convenient for readers, because they can pay using their existing accounts and access paid content without having to log in separately to your website.

Publishers among you who would prefer to go it alone and avoid large computer companies taking a large slice of your revenue can still do that. Technically, restricting certain content only to those who have a username and password isn't that difficult. Most web server software enables webmasters to designate certain directories as password protected and others as freely available. If you're technically savvy and decide to operate your own web server, you can use the open-source application Apache to password-protect some parts of your website. The tricky part isn't in restricting the content but in creating the system that enables buyers to assign themselves usernames and passwords and pay for their subscriptions in the first place. It's best to hire a web designer or sign up with an e-commerce hosting service with support staff that can lead you through the process of setting up such systems.

Using social networks to build your fan base

In the next sections we focus on adding free content to the web that could help publicise your website and, as they say in the marketing world, add value.

Facebook

Many companies use social networking sites like Facebook to create pages, or public profiles, dedicated to their brand.

A public Facebook Page looks just like an individual's profile page, only it's about a product, service or public figure (like an actor, politician or singer). You can post status updates, photos, videos, notes and so on just as you would with a normal page, except your business name or product appears instead. The other difference is that the page is public and anyone can become a fan and view it, whereas many Facebook profile pages are restricted to friends only.

You do need to tread a fine line between blatantly promoting your services and providing a real benefit on a Facebook page. Post informative videos relating to your products, articles that people can respond to and discuss, and photos of new products or of events your customers may have attended.

Say you're a musician who creates a Facebook page. You can use it to inform fans about new album and single releases, and provide new video clips and photos, merchandise, tour dates and competitions. You can also use it to broadcast viewpoints and facilitate discussion with fans.

Make sure you aren't infringing trade marks, and realise that Facebook has ultimate control over whether your page stays or goes. Kim dabbled a little in Facebook pages by creating a fun one dedicated to the foodstuff tofu. It soon built up 20,000-plus followers. But after Facebook deemed tofu a generic term rather than one related to a real business, it considered Kim's page a contravention of its terms of service. Facebook then restricted Kim's publishing rights so that she was unable to post status updates and new photos. (She thought this was a little unfair, because fully operational pages exist that are dedicated to other generic things like bacon and rice...)

After you have your page up and running, Facebook provides an insights tool you can use to see how many people are viewing the videos and commenting on the posts. Such promotional activity often translates into product sales! You'll be surprised at how many people interact with your posts by 'liking' them, commenting on them or even posting photographs on the page themselves.

Creating a Facebook page is easy if you're familiar with how Facebook works, because it follows the same guidelines. Log in to Facebook and then go to `www.facebook.com/pages` and click Create a Page to get started. After your page gets at least 25 fans, you can create a custom URL for it – Kim's Facebook page devoted to her Digital Photography for the Older and Wiser book is, at the time of writing, accessible at `www.facebook.com/digital photos`. Figure 4-4 shows how her page looks.

For much more on using Facebook with your business, read *Facebook Marketing All-in-One For Dummies* (Wiley).

Twitter

Twitter is also a good place to promote your products, but Tweets can sometimes get lost in the crowd. Try displaying a sidebar of your Tweets on your homepage so that visitors can see a rolling commentary of what's new without necessarily having to be on Twitter. You can also publish your Tweets on your Facebook page. To find out how (it only takes a minute!) go to `http://twitter.com/about/resources/widgets`.

Figure 4-4:
Facebook makes it easy to give your brand or business a public profile and interactive presence on the web.

Blogging to build your brand

People have been speaking their minds for fun and profit for as long as media has existed to broadcast their words. Think about famous orators like Socrates, Lenin and Martin Luther King. What would they have done in the age of the Internet? They'd have started their own blogs, that's what!

A *weblog* (*blog* for short) is a type of online journal or diary that you can frequently update. Blogs can be about anything in particular or nothing at all: you can blog about your daily activities or travels and let your family and friends know what you've been up to lately, or you can get your views and opinions out in the world and develop a community of like-minded readers. Many blogs consist of commentary by individuals who gather news items or cool web pages and make them available to their friends (or strangers who happen upon their blogs). This vision, in fact, was the original idea behind blogs, and the concept followed by many of the most popular ones: highlighting little-known websites or articles or shops in the media that readers are too busy to visit, and providing alternative views and commentary about those websites, news stories or other current events.

Is it really possible to make a living by blogging? Yes. Many have become respected news sources in their own right, and bought up by larger media companies as a result. The technology news site Mashable, which tracks trends in Web 2.0 and social media, was started up in 2005 by then-19-year-old Pete Cashmore from his bedroom in Aberdeenshire, Scotland. It now receives 40 million page views a month and is one of the world's most profitable blogs, employing journalists around the globe.

Another technology blog, TechCrunch, was bought by AOL in a reported multi-million dollar deal. Months later, AOL also bought political website The Huffington Post for a mind-boggling $315 million, ($300 million of that was cash).

So, how about finding that niche and perhaps becoming the next big thing in blogging?

Of course, the best bloggers are good writers and have special knowledge that's in demand. If you plan to make money through blogging, it's absolutely essential that you have something to say. People aren't going to flock to a site that talks about daily life in a boring way.

Finding your niche

Blogging, like anything on the web, works when you identify a niche group and target that group by providing those people with content that they're likely to want. The challenge is finding something to say and putting time and energy into saying it on a regular basis. Although Greg has set up his own blog at `www.gregholden.com`, he finds it difficult to devote the time and commitment for daily contributions.

Academic faculty members who are published and well regarded in their fields also run popular blogs. Even CEOs are getting into it, although their position of responsibility makes their writing uncontroversial and therefore usually pretty boring.

What do you feel strongly about? What do you know well? Is there something you'd love to communicate and discuss every day? If so, that's what you should use to organise your blog. A blog can be about anything you like – and we mean anything. A prime example: the Appliance Blog (`www.appliance blog.com`), in which an appliance repairman in Springfield, Oregon, provides a daily diary of his service calls and repairs. Along the way, he provides links to the websites of major appliance manufacturers as well as a forum where you can ask questions about your own appliance problems. The repairman's blog isn't a place where you can find out what he had for breakfast or what he thinks about world peace; it focuses solely on what he knows, and it's a useful resource for anyone who's having a problem with an appliance.

One of the best-known blogs was the one created by an Iraqi citizen who went by the pseudonym Salam Pax. His blog – Where is Rael? – provided a compelling account of daily life in Iraq in 2002 and 2003, during the US military's campaign to topple the regime of Saddam Hussein.

Starting a blog

How, exactly, do you start a blog? The easiest way for beginners is to sign up for an account with an online blogging platform that streamlines the process. Some of the best known are

- Blogger (www.blogger.com)
- WordPress (www.wordpress.com and www.wordpress.org), which you can install onto your own website for more customisation
- Typepad (www.typepad.com)
- Tumblr (www.tumblr.com)
- Posterous (www.posterous.com)

Before the year 2000, you had to be a programmer to figure out how to create a blog on your web page. But a number of online services are available online to streamline the process for nonprogrammers. Blogger (www.blogger.com) lets you create your own blog for free, so it's a good place to start. Google owns Blogger, so the site enables you to participate in Google's AdWords program (see Chapter 13) as well, so you may gain some revenue from your blog. Those of you who already have a Google Account (used for accessing Google services, like Gmail) can use those credentials to log in to Blogger. As with any web-based content, you should do some planning and write down notes, such as

- A name for your blog
- What you want to talk about
- Some ideas for your first few blog entries

Then follow these steps:

1. **Start up your web browser, go to the Blogger home page (www.blogger.com) and log in using your Google Account details (if you don't have a Google Account, click Get Started and follow the simple sign-up instructions).**

   The Blogger account creation page appears.

2. **Fill out the form with a display name, password, gender (optional) and email address; read the terms of service; tick the Acceptance of Terms box; and click Continue.**

   The Name Your Blog page appears.

3. **Click Create Your Blog Now.**

   Come up with a title name for your blog; then add a blog address (URL) ending in blogspot.com. Click Check Availability to see whether that name is taken.

For example, if your blog is called ToolTime, your URL could be `tool time.blogspot.com`.

The Choose a Template page appears.

4. **Click the button beneath the graphic design (or template) you want to use and then click Continue.**

   After a few seconds, a page appears with the notice Your Blog Has Been Created!

5. **Click Start Blogging.**

   A page appears in which you type a title for your first posting and then type the posting itself (see Figure 4-5).

6. **Click the Publish Post button at the bottom of the page.**

   Your blog post is published online. That's how easy it is to set up a simple blog!

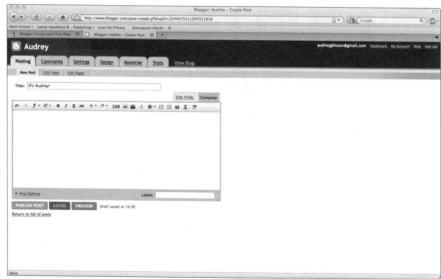

Figure 4-5:
Blogger makes it easy to create a blog for free and give it a graphic design.

©2011 Google

You can always change your template later or customise how it looks. Click the Design Tab to arrange page elements in your blog or the more user-friendly. Template Designer lets you choose from a range of layouts and colour schemes for your blog. Feeling extra ambitious? Customise everything in the template (such as the colours or banner) by clicking the Edit HTML link.

Building an audience

Blogs that are odd, quirky (one good site is Sleep Talkin' Man, `http://sleeptalkinman.blogspot.com`, where a wife records her husband's surreal night-time musings for posterity), based on dramatic human-interest situations such as wartime journals or that are politically oriented tend to be the most successful. That said, here are some ways to build up an audience for your blog:

✔ **Writing for other bloggers:** Your first audience will probably consist of family or friends, or other bloggers who live in the same geographic area or write about the same subjects you do. Contact those bloggers and ask them to exchange links with your blog; ask your other readers to spread the word about your blog too.

✔ **Sprinkling keywords, tags and categories:** Blogs are like other web pages: although their content changes frequently, search engines index them. The more keywords you include in your postings (including tags, which identify a post's subject and are used for people to search for all related posts) and the greater the range of subjects you cover, the more likely you are to have your blog turn up in a set of search results.

✔ **Posting consistently:** When readers latch on to a blog they like, they visit it frequently. You need to post something – anything – on a daily basis, or at least several times a week.

✔ **Syndicating your blog:** One way of spreading the word about your blog is providing a 'feed' of its latest contents, such as the headings of posts and the dates of the latest posts. This summary is automatically prepared in XML (eXtensible Markup Language) by most blogging tools. You make the feed of your blog available on its home page; web browsers and sites that aggregate (in other words, collect) the feeds from many of their favorite blogs can collect them and quickly know when the blogs have been updated.

If you can make a living at blogging or at least end up with some fun money at the end of each month, more power to you. But don't go into blogging with that attitude, or you'll lose interest right away. Look at a blog as another tool in your online business arsenal – another way of getting your message before the public, another vehicle for steering visitors to your online business. Unless your business is actually in creating original content, treat your blog as a venue where you talk about situations related to your products without directly selling them to the public. Try to build up a number of loyal readers and attract advertising revenue – or simply attract more customers to your website.

Building a Community

Studies consistently show that people who spend large amounts of time in community venues such as discussion forums end up spending money on the same website (eBay is the perfect example). It's a value proposition, but you can't attach a specific dollar value to it.

Community building on commercial websites doesn't necessarily involve discussion boards or chat rooms. Anything you can do to get your customers communicating with one another works. On Amazon.co.uk, a kind of community feel is created by the book reviews written by individual readers and the feedback system whereby people can rate whether or not a review has been helpful. Meanwhile Top 10 book lists and wishlists let visitors share their views.

Partnerships

The notion of online community cuts both ways: it's not only for consumers who visit websites and join communities, but for businesspeople like you too. Some of the liveliest and most popular online communities are eBay groups – discussion forums started by eBay members themselves. And among those, some of the most popular are the ones in which sellers share tips and advice about boosting their online incomes, finding merchandise to sell, identifying mystery items and so on.

Don't forget that even though you may run a business by yourself from your home, you're not really alone. If you need some encouragement, join a discussion group.

Market research

Given the sheer number of consumers who are on the web, it stands to reason that you can find out a lot about those individuals by going online. If you don't have any awareness of who your potential customers are and what they want, you may never get them to pull out their credit cards. You can do your own market research by going online to find your customers, listening to their views in chat rooms and on discussion forums, and doing some market research. Approach consumers who already buy the types of products or services that you want to sell.

Consult the Guerrilla Marketing books (gmarketing.com) for insights into different ways to reach your target consumers.

CASE STUDY

The pros and cons of publicity

When entrepreneur Andy Geldman decided to publish his own book, he never realised that the publicity drive would quickly lead to national press, a TV interview on Sky News and even a lengthy chat on Australian breakfast television! A link to the site accompanying his book was also a phenomenal success on the social bookmarking site Digg (see Chapter 13 for more on how this worked for Andy). However, publicity – no matter how positive – doesn't always mean financial success, as Andy discovered. People will still need to find your product and be persuaded to buy it!

His book, *Slurls* (www.slurls.com), is a humorous account of websites with unintentional double meanings (like cabin rentals at www.oldmanshaven.com). Kim enjoyed reading it so much she even wrote an endorsement for the book's back cover. Andy coined the word *Slurl* to describe these sites, got the book on Amazon.co.uk and hired a publicist to help get the story out there.

Q: Did you do any media training before embarking on the broadcast interviews?

A: Not intentionally! Just before doing the TV interviews I made a YouTube video that turned out to be excellent practice in getting the tone right, having answers prepared, eye contact, speed of speech etc. I was really glad I did it and would recommend others do the same for practice. Video yourself in a situation as close as possible to the real thing; and watch it back. Keep repeating it until you are happy with it. It's really tempting to think that if you know your subject well you can just do an interview straight off, but the reality is that you have to learn. TV and radio is nothing like a real-life conversation!

Q: You have a Facebook page dedicated to Slurls. How is that going?

A: I post small but frequent updates to keep it interesting and engage people. The key is little and often – for example 'Slurl of the Day' – to try to make people laugh and catch their attention enough for them to comment on and 'like'. Try to make the updates speak for themselves. It's been moderately successful, with 300 fans. Posts get a fair few 'likes' and comments.

Q: How much did you spend on promotion and has it been value for money considering all the publicity?

A: Roughly £3,000. Financially, it was not worth it. I did not break even. But the experience and learning from the interviews and publicity was worthwhile. I would be wary of doing it again. I wouldn't self-publish another book expecting to make any money, but I might consider it again for personal reasons.

Q: So is there anything about the approach you took that you would change?

A: I would have practised for the interviews earlier on (not just by accident!). I would probably not have turned down the tabloid coverage in favour of coverage from a quality newspaper. The latter did have knock-on effects and generated lots more publicity, but the story might have been a better fit with the tabloid and generated more sales.

Q: How did you come up with the press release?

A: It had to have a good personal story that said something about me, and it needed to be snappy, interesting and say what the book is, including good examples. It needed to use plain English. No business speak or buzz words.

The other aspect of market research that's perfectly executed with a web browser is research into your own online competitors – businesses that already do what you hope to do. It can be discouraging, at first, to discover companies that have already cleared the trail that you hoped to blaze. The chances of doing something absolutely unique on the web are small, but use the discovery as an educational opportunity to find out whether a market exists for your product and a way to sell it that differs from existing competitors. Take note of features displayed by your competitors' websites, such as the following:

- ✔ **Selling:** How does the website do its selling? Does it sell only in one location, or does its website supplement eBay.co.uk or Amazon.co.uk sales or a brick-and-mortar business? Does the site make suggestions about related items that a consumer may want (a practice known as up-selling)?

- ✔ **Design:** How does the site look? Is it well put together? What makes it attractive and does it draw you in? It's not the same to ask, Is it pretty? Many ugly websites, like the simple gossip site Popbitch (`www.pop bitch.com`), are also virtual gold mines.

- ✔ **Organisation:** How is the website organised? Is it easy to find specific products or information about them? How many navigational aids (navigation bars, drop-down menu lists, site maps and the like) does the site provide?

- ✔ **Depth:** How many levels of information does the website include ? The more information you offer on the site, the *stickier* (more able to hold a visitor's attention) the site becomes. Try to imagine how your customers will react to the content on your website; are they encouraged to plough on, uncovering new content, or better yet click through to buy some of your stuff?

In your review of the competition's web presentation, make a list of features that you can emulate as well as features you can improve on. Your goal shouldn't be to copy the site, but to discover your own unique niche and identify customers whose needs the other venue may not address.

Google Alerts are a fantastic way to 'eavesdrop' on what people are saying about your company in one easy-to-read email digest. Go to `www.google.com/alerts` and type in your company or website name, along with the type of alert you'd like (news, discussions, real time, video or all these). Select an email frequency (as it happens, once a day or once a week). Enter your email address and click Create Alert. It takes mere seconds to do. You don't even have to have a Google Account to create an alert, and you can unsubscribe by clicking on the link in any email digest you receive. (But if you set up more than one alert, then it's worth logging in to Google and keeping track of all your alerts from within its site.)

Part II
Establishing Your Online Presence

'My friends on the dock helped me
with the slogan.'

In this part . . .

*J*ust as business owners in the real world have to rent or buy a facility and fix it up to conduct their businesses, you have to develop an online storefront to conduct your online business. In this part, we explain how to put a virtual roof over your store and make the most of new technologies and techniques that'll help you and your customers get to know each other . You also find out about security strategies to protect your customers' privacy. In other words, this part focuses on the nuts and bolts of your website itself.

The web is the most exciting and popular place to open an online store. But merely creating a set of web pages isn't enough to succeed online. Your site needs to be compelling – even irresistible. This part shows you how to organise your site and fill it with useful content that attracts customers in the first place and encourages them to stay to browse. We also show you how to get your pages up and running quickly, to equip your site (and yourself) to handle many different kinds of electronic purchases, and to keep improving your site so that it runs more efficiently.

Chapter 5

Giving Your E-business Site Structure and Style

In This Chapter

▶ Creating a simple and well-organised business site

▶ Establishing a graphic identity through colour and type

▶ Using images to add interest to your site

▶ Working with a web designer

Standing out from the crowd and attracting attention on the web has become increasingly difficult now that practically everyone, from your local newsagent to international conglomerates, seems to be online trying to find their niches. Happily, technology has become far more sophisticated and user-friendly, so getting a professional-looking website online isn't the minefield it used to be. Rather than coding a website from scratch, you can choose easier ways to retain consistency in your website's structure and layout.

And despite the advances in making websites more flashy and interactive, web surfers will still leave your site in seconds if they can't find what they're looking for. They may be accustomed to seeing animations, add-ons and flashy gimmicks, but often the trick is to have no trick: keep your site simple, well-organised and content rich.

In this chapter, we present one of the best ways for a new business to attract attention online: through a clearly organised and eye-catching website. (Another strategy for attracting visitors – developing promotions and content that encourages interaction – is the subject of Chapter 6.)

Building the Right Structure

You may be tempted to rush into the process of designing and building your website, but although enthusiasm is always a good thing, you should try to think with a clear head and take time to plan what you're going to do. In design circles, the structure of your website is often called the *wireframe* and is developed before you even decide on the colour scheme of your website.

Whether you're setting off on a road trip across the country or building a new extension on your house, you progress more smoothly by drawing a blueprint of how you want to progress. Do you remember when you were a tiny little nipper and did your homework with a pencil and paper? Dig 'em out again and make a list of the elements you want to have on your site.

Structure is very important. A website with a well-thought-out structure is vital for usability and helps your customers find what they're looking for. It also helps you when you're optimising your site so it can be better indexed by search engines, because a website with a decent structure is looked upon far more favourably (for more on search engine optimisation, see Chapter 13).

Look over the items on your list and break them into two or three main categories. These main categories will branch off your *home page*, which functions as the grand entrance for your online business site. You can then draw a map of your site that assumes the shape of a triangle, as shown in Figure 5-1.

Figure 5-1: A home page is the point from which your site branches into more specific levels of information.

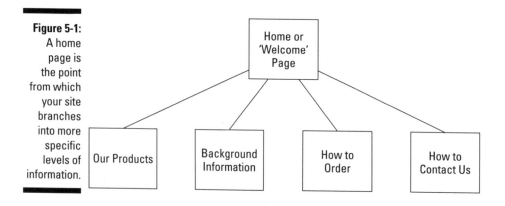

Note: The page heading 'Background Information' is a placeholder for detailed information about some aspect of your online business. Some websites have an 'About Us' page that explains the history of the company and why it's reputable. Kim was looking at the website of a manufacturer of blinds. The 'About Us' page revealed that it had more than 30 years of experience in manufacturing blinds in the local area, and had become so successful it had recently moved into a larger showroom. On the basis of that description, Kim decided to pay the manufacturer a visit the next day (and found out that it was, in fact, so popular that she had wait ten days before she could get a quote!). You can write about your experience with and love for what you buy and sell, or anything else that personalises your site and builds trust.

The example in Figure 5-1 results in a very simple website. But there's nothing wrong with starting out simple. Many web designers agree that the best plan is to group the site into broad areas and then subsections under them if necessary, but don't add too many levels.

Write all the elements of your website onto sticky notes and put them on the wall. Then move them around and group them until you have a sensible looking structure. You can even take this further by giving the sticky notes to potential users of your website and ask them to group them into what they think are logical layers. You may be surprised to see what they come up with. Asking people about the structure of your website is important, even if you just show them sketches on paper.

More 'complicated' websites with a lot of products might prefer the sticky note route. Many businesses have a three-layered arrangement for their website and divide the site into two sections, one about the company and one about the products or services for sale (see Figure 5-2).

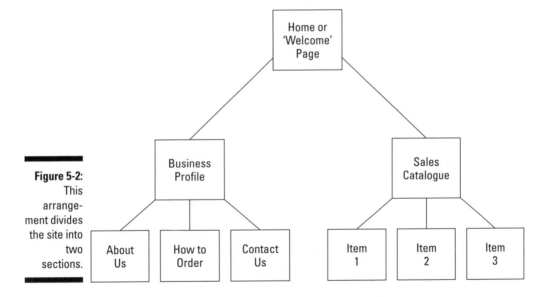

Figure 5-2: This arrangement divides the site into two sections.

Think of your home page as the lobby of a museum where you get the help of the friendly person at the information desk who hands you a list of the special exhibits you can visit that day and shows you a map so that you can begin to figure out how you're going to get from here to there. Remember to include the following items on your home page:

- ✔ The name of the shop or business.

- ✔ Your logo, if you have one.

- ✔ Links to the main areas of your site or, if your site isn't overly extensive, to every page.

- ✔ Contact information, such as your email address, phone/fax numbers and your business address so that people know where to find you in the Land Beyond Cyberspace. If you run a registered business, it's a legal requirement to put your company details including your registration number online – for the lowdown on the detail you need to provide, see Chapter 14.

Pepper your home page with keywords describing your business – that way, search engines that index your site know what your website is all about and people looking for a business like yours see your site before your competitors' sites. Headings, for instance, should all include the most important words that you think people will be searching for. We explain all about the art of search engine optimisation in Chapter 13.

Making them fall in love at first site

First impressions are critical on the web, where shoppers have the ability to jump from site to site with a click of the mouse button (or the tap of a finger if they're using a touch screen). A few extra seconds of downtime waiting for complex images or mini-computer programs such as *Java applets* to download can cause your prospective buyer to lose patience and you to lose a sale.

How do you make visitors to your welcome page feel like they're being greeted with open arms? Here are some suggestions:

- ✔ **Keep it simple.** Don't overload any one page with more than three or four images. Keep images 20K or less in size, if you can.

- ✔ **Find a fast host.** Some web servers have super-fast connections to the Internet and others use slower lines. Test your site; if your pages take more than a couple of seconds to appear, ask your host company why and find out whether they can move you to a faster machine.

- ✔ **Offer a bargain.** Nothing attracts attention as much as a contest, a giveaway or a special sales promotion. Make these offers visually prominent from other elements of your page. See Chapter 6 for more ideas.

- ✔ **Provide instant gratification.** Make sure that your most important information appears at or near the top of your page. Readers on the web don't like having to scroll through several screens' worth of material in order to get to the information they want.

Styling Up with Cascading Style Sheets

Just as the structure of your website is important, so is its style and layout. This is where *Cascading Style Sheets* (CSS) come in. CSS is a language that defines the way a page looks in areas such as fonts, font sizes, colour schemes, column widths and so on. You can also specify different fonts and colours for different parts of your website (such as how the sidebar looks). CSS is, from a technical perspective, a little tricky to get your head around – but it's no harder than getting to grips with HyperText Markup Language (HTML; see the nearby sidebar 'A quick HTML primer'). And there's no doubt that, in the long run, CSS saves you a lot of legwork when you want to retain consistency in the style and layout of your website.

We hear you say: doesn't HTML already let me style and lay out my site? Well, it does, but in an extremely clunky way. HTML wasn't designed with this kind of styling in mind. Put simply, CSS saves you a ton of running (or typing) around.

You won't necessarily need to know how to code a CSS file from scratch because web page editors have templates you can use to get started and then edit, but the web standards body W3C has a great beginners' tutorial at www. w3.org/Style/Examples/011/firstcss. You can also find loads of other free tutorials that understanding souls have put online for you to use.

You can embed CSS into your HTML files and paste the attributes into every HTML page, but this isn't very efficient. A better way is to create a separate, *external* CSS file that all your HTML pages can link to. These files end in the extension .css. Should you ever decide to update your website's look and feel, you only need to edit the external CSS file.

We should point out that working out how to use HTML and CSS is almost like learning a foreign language, but it's good to familiarise yourself with the basics even if you're hiring someone else to do the hard work – particularly if you just want to go under the bonnet and make a small tweak here and there. If you're going it alone rather than using a professional, then spend at least a few weeks getting to know HTML well before you have a crack at creating your website. Remember, people are put off easily by poor design and functionality, so yours has to work perfectly when you launch it.

You can typically edit CSS files within your content publishing program (such as Wordpress) or just go in to explore how they work (be careful not to overwrite anything unless you have a backup copy and know what you're doing, though!).

A quick HTML primer

Thanks to web page creation tools, you don't have to master HyperText Markup Language in order to create your own web pages, although some knowledge of HTML is helpful when it comes to editing pages and understanding how they're put together.

HTML is a markup language, not a computer programming language. You use it in much the same way that old-fashioned editors marked up copy before they gave it to typesetters. A markup language allows you to identify major sections of a document, such as body text, headings, title, and so on. A software program (in the case of HTML, a web browser) is programmed to recognise the markup language and to display the formatting elements that you've marked.

Markup tags are the basic building blocks of HTML as well as its more complex and powerful cousin, eXtensible Markup Language (XML). Tags enable you to structure the appearance of your document so that when it's transferred from one computer to another it looks the way you described it. HTML tags appear within carrot-shaped brackets. Most HTML commands require a *start tag* at the beginning of the section and an *end tag* (which usually begins with a backslash) at the end.

For example, if you place the HTML tags <B> and </B> around the phrase 'This text will be bold', the words appear in bold type on any browser that displays them, no matter if it's running on a Windows-based PC, a UNIX workstation, a Macintosh, a mobile smart phone, an iPad or any other computer.

Many HTML commands are accompanied by *attributes,* which provide a browser with more specific instructions on what action the tag is to perform. In the following lines of HTML, SRC is an attribute that works with the <IMG> tag to identify a file to display:

```
<IMG SRC="house.jpg">
```

Each attribute is separated from an HTML command by a single blank space. The equal sign (=) is an operator that introduces the value on which the attribute and command will function. Usually, the value is a filename or a directory path leading to a specific file that is to be displayed on a web page. The straight (as opposed to curly) quotation marks around the value are essential for the HTML command to work.

The web is simply growing too fast for HTML to keep up. The next standard, HTML5, has been many years in the making. It promises to make it far easier for search engines to understand exactly what's on a page because you can now use the language to specify each element of the page including headers, footers, stand-alone articles (such as blog posts), navigational aspects (such as the menu or sidebar) and more. What's even more exciting about HTML5 (from a techie standpoint, at least) is that it allows you to easily embed multimedia aspects within your site without having to resort to lengthy codes or plug-ins. And because designers now commonly use CSS to specify the style of a website such as its typeface and colour scheme, these parameters are now being phased out of HTML altogether.

Nip and Tuck: Establishing a Visual Identity

The prospect of designing a website may be intimidating if you haven't tried it before. But just remember that it really boils down to a simple principle: *effective visual communication that conveys a particular message.* The first step in creating graphics is not to open a painting program and start drawing, but rather to plan your page's message. Next, determine the audience you want to reach with that message and think about how your graphics can best communicate what you want to say. Some ways to do this follow:

- Gather ideas from websites that use graphics well – and learn from ones that do badly. UK magazines dedicated to the Internet and web design can help guide you in the right direction. Web User (www.webuser.co.uk) reviews websites for design and usability, as do .net (www.netmag.co.uk) and Web Designer (www.webdesignermag.co.uk).

- Use graphics consistently from page to page to create an identity and convey a consistent message. Using CSS in your web design helps with this (see the previous section in this chapter).

- Create graphics that meet visitors' needs and expectations. If you're selling fashions to teenagers, go for out-there graphics. If you're selling financial advice to OAPs, choose a distinguished and sophisticated typeface.

How do you become acquainted with your customers when you'll probably never meet them face to face? Check out what they're tweeting about on Twitter (www.twitter.com) and on Facebook groups and forums. Blogs are also a valuable source. You'd be amazed at what people blog about. Don't believe us? Go to www.blogger.com and type *sandwich* or some other obscure subject matter into the search bar. We guarantee you'll be met with a string of blog posts. Now try again with a term relevant to your business. Read the posted messages to get a sense of the concerns and vocabulary of your intended audience.

Using colour effectively

Without a suitable background for your web page, most web browsers simply default to white. And older browsers default to grey, which in most cases is rather drab and ugly. (In fact, the first browsers were unable to display a background colour at all, as Kim remembers rather fondly from when she used her first browser, back in 1995.)

White is perfectly acceptable as a background (it's the background colour of this book, after all!) but it might not match the style of your page. You might want something that stands out from the crowd. A subtle, titled background with a low-key pattern might be effective, so long as a visitor to the site can easily read your text over the top of it. A lightly tinted cream shade could also work.

Loads of professional-looking sites employ the best of both worlds: a patterned or darker-coloured background sits behind a main text box with a lighter background. As you can see in Figure 5-3, the Comic Domain website has a dark background with a slight texture to it, while still employing a clean, white box that includes all the necessary columns, navigation and promotional material. That way you don't need to feel constrained when it comes to choosing a background that might make your text unreadable.

Figure 5-3: Overlaying a dark or patterned background with a text box is an ideal way of making your website stand out, as Comic Domain has done.

You can use an image rather than a solid colour to serve as the background of a page. You specify an image in the HTML code of your web page (or in your web page editor), and browsers automatically *tile* the image, reproducing it over and over to fill up the current width and height of the browser window.

The same colour principles apply when it comes to the typeface you're using. In most cases, black for the main body text is absolutely fine, but sometimes a very dark grey is easier on the eye than solid black. You may want to make headings a different colour to your main body text, or use colours like red or blue to highlight special offers or competitions.

What you absolutely don't want to have happen is that the background makes the page unreadable. Keep in mind that the colours you use must have contrast so that they don't blend into one another. For example, you don't want to put purple type on a brown or blue background, or yellow type on a white background. Remember to use light type against a dark background, and dark type against a light background. That way, all your page's contents show up.

In HTML, colours are represented by what's known as *hexadecimal notation* (HEX). According to the web tutorial group W3Schools.com, HTML colours involve combining red, green and blue colour values with light values from darkest to lightest ranging from 0 (represented by 00) to 255 (represented by FF). Sixteen million possible combinations exist. Each colour value is specified as three pairs of two-digit numbers (red, green and blue), starting with the # sign. So, the value #000000 is pure black, and #FFFFFF is pure white. Red is represented by #FF0000: red is the strongest light value and no green or blue light exists. (The web tutorial group web tutorial group offers some useful info on this subject at www.w3schools.com/html/html_colors.asp.)

In the old days, web designers were very much preoccupied with only using a palette of 216 'web safe' colours for monitors that could only display a limited amount of colours. You'll find web safe charts and their associated HTML values all over the web, but they aren't as necessary nowadays because monitors can display a virtually unlimited palette of shades. However, it's still good practice to use standard colours for the main elements of your website.

Redesigning the colour scheme of your site is easy with CSS (see the earlier section 'Styling Up with Cascading Style Sheets'). All you need to do is edit external CSS files and the look of all your pages changes accordingly.

You can use colours to elicit a particular mood or emotion and also to convey your organisation's identity on the web. The right choice of colour can create impressions ranging from elegant to funky. The basic colour scheme chosen by the phone group T-Mobile (www.t-mobile.co.uk) conveys to customers its professionalism, yet also gives an impression of being with it – cool if you will. The comedian, writer and TV personality Danny Wallace (www.dannywallace.com) is popular with 20- to 30-somethings, and his website colour scheme complements his media profile: straight-talking yellow, black and white colours similar to what you'd find in a printed newspaper or blokey publication.

When selecting colours for your own web pages, also consider the demographics of your target audience. Do some research on what emotions or impressions are conveyed by different colours and which colours best match the remit or identity of your business. Refer to resources such as 1st Web Designer's article at www.1stwebdesigner.com/design/color-psychology-website-design, which emphasises the impact certain colours have on your emotions and state of mind and gives some great examples of global brands and how they use colours on their websites.

Sometimes your own instincts are the best way to decide what colours to use. Do you need to attract kids with wild designs? Or would that put off your older, more discerning customers (or the kids' parents, if they're the ones who'll be buying what you have to sell)? Pay attention to your gut reactions, then get feedback from your colleagues, and test your choice on a few sample members of your audience before you make your final decision.

The header of your website (where your business name and logo is displayed) is prime real estate and often the first place your visitors glance at. You can choose to lay a background banner image underneath this header – it can be 'stretchy' and go across the entire width of the viewer's browser, or be a fixed width. Your designer can help you to experiment. You can even choose to use a photograph rather than a colour, or a gently patterned background.

Using web typefaces like a pro

Your website's font should, like colour, convey a personality and align to your target audience. Professional lawyers won't be using the cartoon-like Comic Sans Serif font on their website, and dentists won't employ a novelty ghoulish font adorned with ghosts and pumpkins when listing their services – unless they only want to attract patients who have no fear of them!

But just because you fall in love with a particular typeface doesn't mean your audience will be able to admire it in all its beauty. The problem is that you don't necessarily have ultimate control over whether a given browser displays the specified typeface because you don't know for sure whether the individual user's system (Windows, Mac or Linux) has access to your preferred typefaces. If the particular font you specified isn't available, the browser falls back on its default font unless you specify an alternative (probably Helvetica or Times).

That's why, generally speaking, when you design web pages, you're better off picking a generic typeface that's built into virtually every computer's operating system. This convention ensures that your web pages look more or less the same no matter what web browser or what type of computer displays them.

Thankfully, common doesn't have to be ugly. You can use plenty of beautiful, timeless, web-safe fonts that most people have on their systems. These include (and are not limited to) Arial, Helvetica, Trebuchet MS, Gill Sans, Verdana, Palatino Linotype and Georgia. By designing your website using CSS (see the earlier section 'Styling Up with Cascading Style Sheets' and Figure 5-4) you specify the 'family' of fonts yours belongs to, so the browser can default back to a similar font if people's systems don't have the one you've indicated.

Still keen on a particular unconventional font? Well, you don't have to limit yourself to the same-old, same-old. There's a trick you can use with CSS called *@font-face* that lets you dictate your own font. If you're particularly enamoured by a nonstandard font, people with the latest versions of their browsers should be able to view the font you've referenced. For the specifics, see the primer at Mozilla Firefox's website: `http://hacks.mozilla.org/2009/06/beautiful-fonts-with-font-face`.

Sans-serif fonts are easier to read onscreen than serif fonts. A serif font has the little 'hooks' (called serifs) around the letters while sans-serif doesn't have them at all. You should also avoid using more than two or three fonts throughout your website – any more and things can look untidy.

Where, exactly, do you specify type fonts, colours and sizes for the text on a web page? Special HTML tags can do it, but the best way is to specify your font is by using CSS. The code should look something like this if you're using CSS within your HTML page:

```
<html>
<head>
<style type="text/css">
p.serif{font-family:"Trebuchet MS", Helvetica, sans-
          serif;}
p.sansserif{font-family:"Palatino Linotype", "Book
          Antiqua", Palatino, serif;}
</style>
</head>

<body>
<p class="serif">This sentence is in Trebuchet font.</p>
<p class="sansserif"> This sentence is in Palatino font.</
          p>

</body>
</html>
```

In the above example, the fonts displayed will look like this:

This sentence is in Trebuchet font.

You can find a great tutorial on designing fonts with CSS at the W3Schools.com website (www.w3schools.com/css/css_font.asp). There's even a 'try it yourself' page, shown below:

If your logo doesn't consist of a standard typeface and you want to make sure everyone sees it because it's integral to your brand, than scan the logo in or create the heading in an image-editing program and insert it into the page as a graphic image. Beware! *Never* do this for blocks of text. Search engines will think the text is a graphic image and won't be able to pick up the text on your site. This means they won't able to pick up on the keywords relevant to your site, and your website search engine ranking will suffer, along with your business. What's more, using images instead of text isn't an accessible form of web design because screen-reading software or people whose images are turned off can't pick up the words.

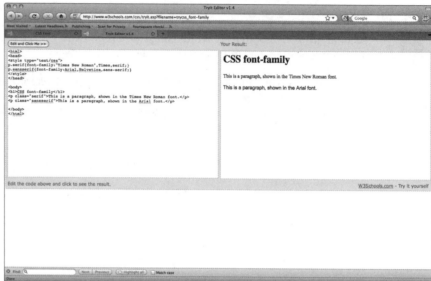

Figure 5-4:
By using
CSS to style
up your
fonts, you
can make
it easier for
people to
view your
fonts
regardless
of what sys-
tem they're
running.

Source: W3Schools.com.

Using a marketplace of artwork

Not everyone has the time or resources to scan or download photos, or
create their own original graphics. But that doesn't mean you can't add
graphic interest to your web page. So many free and cheap libraries on the
web are full of clip art, stock photography, icons and other small images that
people have created for anyone to use – some ask for an extremely reasonable usage fee and others don't ask for anything at all apart from a small
credit somewhere on your page or next to the image.

Here are some image sites you can try:

- ✔ **Iconfinder.com** (www.iconfinder.com): Search for nice icons you
  might want to use on your website. You can filter your search to show
  icons that the designers have allowed for commercial use.

- ✔ **iStockphoto** (www.istockphoto.com): Affordable, decent images. Most
  are sold royalty-free, which means you pay a one-time fee that lets you
  use an image multiple times.

You can also search for free images licensed under a global scheme called
Creative Commons. This is an open licensing scheme that, depending on the
type of licence, allows people to share their content on both commercial and
non-commercial sites. Usually, all the artists want in exchange is a credit. You
can go to www.flickr.com/creativecommons to see the millions of people
using the photo-sharing website Flickr who've licensed their content. Firefox also
has a built-in Creative Commons search within its browser search box; simply

click the drop-down arrow on the right and choose 'Creative Commons' from the list. Go to www.creativecommons.org to see an explanation of all the licences available; some of them are only intended for use on non-commercial sites.

Clip art can also provide a background pattern for a web page or highlight sales headings such as Free!, New! or Special! When Greg first started out in the print publications business, he bought catalogues of illustrations, literally clipped out the art and pasted it down. It's still called clip art, but now the process is different. In keeping with the spirit of exchange that's been a part of the Internet since its inception, some talented and generous artists have created icons, buttons and other illustrations in electronic form and offered them free for downloading, although clip art even in its digital form is a little dated. Try Clip Art Warehouse (www.clipart.co.uk) or Cool Clips (www.coolclips.com).

Be sure to read the copyright fine print *before* you copy graphics, particularly if you've been searching them using Google's image search or similar. All artists own the copyright to their work. It's up to them to determine how they want to give someone else the right to copy their work. Sometimes, the authors require you to pay a small fee if you want to copy their work, or they may restrict use of their work to non-commercial organisations or personal websites.

A picture is worth a thousand words

Some customers know exactly what they want from the get-go and don't need any help from you. But most customers love to shop around or could use some encouragement to move from one item or catalogue page to another. This is where images can play an important role.

Even if you use only basic clip art, such as placing spheres or arrows next to sale items, your customer is likely to thank you by buying more. A much better approach, though, is to take digital images of your sale items and provide compact, clear images of them on your site.

You don't need a fancy digital SLR – any compact digital camera will do the trick, so long as it has a few manual settings such as the ability to change the light sensitivity or shutter speed if necessary. If you're selling many items and want to include them in an online catalogue, the key is to keep the lighting, perspective and background as consistent as possible. For around £150, you can buy a portable home studio kit from somewhere like Jessops and use it to take photos of your products against a white background.

Depending on the item you're selling, it's also a good idea to take photos at their maximum resolution (detail) so visitors have the option to click an enlarged version of the item. You show a small, lower-quality photo on your site, and link it through to a larger image, perhaps in a separate window.

After you've got your photo, you can use image-editing software to tweak it so it looks nice and presentable. Free options for editing include Google's

Picasa (http://picasa.google.com) and Microsoft's Windows Live Photo Gallery (http://explore.live.com/windows-live-photo-gallery). Later down the line, it's well worth shelling out £60 or so for a popular product that gives you that little bit more creative control, such as the ability to overlay text and use more advanced editing techniques. Corel Paint Shop Pro and Adobe Photoshop Elements are the most well-known examples. (Powerful free programs like Paint.net and Gimp are worth a try, but these are a little more technical to use.)

When you've taken your image, here are the basic steps you need to take to get it online (some or all of them may be familiar if you're already using a digital camera):

1. **Transfer the image(s) to your computer.**

   You need to import images onto your computer using either the cable connected to your camera or a memory card reader. In most cases, you can use your image-editing software to organise the images you've imported – the latest versions of the major packages all let you do this. Don't keep transferring your images directly into one big folder, because as your collection grows it'll be a nightmare to sort down the line. Change the default file names that your digital camera assigned to your images to something meaningful, be it a product code or a short description of the photo.

   If you'd like to know more about digital photography, Wiley publishes many Dummies books on the subject. Kim's written a book called *Digital Photography for the Older and Wiser* (2010) – you don't actually need to be old or wise to get the most out of it!

2. **Crop the image.**

   Cropping an image is a good idea because it highlights the most important content and reduces the file size. Reducing the file size of an image should always be a primary goal – the smaller the image, the quicker it appears in someone's browser window. Cropping means that you resize the box around the image in order to select the portion of the image that you want to keep and leave out the parts of the image that aren't essential. (It's even better if you achieve a tight crop when you take the photograph in the first place.)

   Almost all scanning and graphics programs offer separate options for cropping an image and reducing the image size. By cropping the image, you eliminate parts of the image you don't want. This *does* reduce the image size, but it *doesn't* reduce the size of the objects within the image. Resizing the overall image size is a separate step, which enables you to change the dimensions of the entire image without eliminating any contents.

3. **Adjust contrast and brightness.**

   Your image-editing program includes brightness and contrast sliders that you can adjust with your mouse to improve the image (some also offer automatic, 'quick-fix' functions that are surprisingly accurate). If you're happy with the image as it is, leave the brightness and contrast set where they are.

4. Adjust the colour balance.

In some cases, you may want to adjust the way colours look in your photographs. Often, digital cameras interpret light a different way and colours can take on a tinge. Often, the automatic adjustment tool in your image-editing program can fix any colour problems – otherwise, tweak the colour control sliders.

5. Resize the image.

The old phrase 'good things come in small packages' is never more true than when you're improving your digital image. For instance, say your original digital image is 1,280 by 1,024 pixels wide. Well, that's way too massive to be displaying on your website – viewed at full size, that's about the same size as a 19-inch monitor! You need to resize the image in your editing program before uploading it to your web space. In Chapter 2, we note that digital images are made up of little bits (dots) of computerised information called *pixels*. The more pixels an image has, the higher its resolution, or detail. However, on the web you don't need to see images in massive detail. A typical photograph on the BBC News website ranges from just 300 pixels wide for an incidental photo accompanying a news piece to around 600 pixels for one that goes across a column and is one of the main focuses of an article.

6. Reduce the image size.

Although resizing the image makes it physically smaller because it has less pixels, it won't necessarily reduce the file size enough for it to load quickly in people's browsers. For that, you need to optimise your image for web viewing by *compressing* it. This involves a loss of quality but you'll be surprised how much you can reduce the image's file size without discerning a massive loss of quality. Many image-editing programs let you choose to save an image that's optimised for 'web quality'.

7. Export and save the file.

How and where you save your new image is up to you but one way is to export the image to folders dedicated to smaller-resolution versions of your images. Don't overwrite your original image as it's of best quality (modern-day image-editing programs keep the original so you can undo any changes, but it's best to be safe).

When you give your image a name, be sure to add the correct filename extension. For photographs, use .jpg. See the sidebar 'GIF versus JPG', later in this chapter, for more on image types.

We haven't mentioned scanning images here, but the principles of editing your scanned images are the same. When scanning items, scan at 72 pixels per inch (this is the suitable resolution for web-viewing) and resize your image accordingly. Any higher and your scan will be far too immense and you'll need to resize and compress it later.

Creating a logo

An effective logo establishes your online business's graphic identity in no uncertain terms. A logo can be as simple as a rendering of the company name that imparts an official typeface or colour. Whatever text it includes, a logo is a small, self-contained graphic object that conveys the group's identity and purpose.

A good logo effectively combines colour, type and graphics to convey an organisation's identity or mission. It should be instantly recognisable – think of companies like Apple, FedEx, Waitrose, Virgin and Shell.

Accommodating your viewers

Even though broadband connections are standard nowadays, that's still no excuse to cram your website with unnecessary multimedia content that overwhelms the entire experience. Sure, you can let people *click through* to these elements if you think they're relevant to your business, but having every single bell and whistle on your home page can get too much. Kim hates going to a website only to see (or even worse, hear) a video playing automatically – before she's even clicked a button! It's usually an advertisement, too, which makes it even worse.

Embedding a video is fine as long as it doesn't start playing automatically. Viewers should always have the choice of clicking 'play' first. And if you're a wedding photographer, of course you want to display quality images of your work, but don't squeeze dozens of your best photos on the front page – visitors will quickly get bored of waiting for them to load. Provide a link to let people visit your gallery pages if they want to browse further.

People's time is precious, and they might be busy doing other things online such as downloading music or a Windows security update, which can make other pages slow to load. Keeping your website streamlined and quick to load is essential. Some tips to reduce the file size of your pages include:

- Creating low-resolution alternatives to high-resolution graphics, such as thumbnails (postage-stamp-sized versions of larger images)

- Cropping images to keep them small

- Using line art whenever possible, rather than high-resolution photos

By using the same image more than once on a web page, you can give the impression of greater activity but yet not slow down the appearance of the entire page. Why? If you repeat the same image three times, your customer's browser has to download the image file only once. It stores the image in a storage area, called a *disk cache*, on the user's hard drive. To display the other instances of the image, the browser retrieves the file from the disk cache, so the second and third images appear much more quickly than the first one did.

Users can also disable image display altogether so that they don't see graphics on any of the sites they visit. The solution: always provide a simple textual alternative to your images (called ALT tags) so that if the user has disabled the display of a particular image then a word or two describing that image appears in its place. This is particularly important if a visually-impaired visitor has used a screen reader to translate text to audio. They'll then be able to know what sorts of images are being displayed on your page.

GIF versus JPEG

Website technology and HTML may have changed dramatically over the past few years, but for the most part, two main types of images exist as far as web pages are concerned: GIF and JPEG (also known as JPG). There's a third format, PNG, designed as a successor to GIF – but it's still not as widely used as GIF. GIF, JPEG and PNG use methods that compress computer image files so that the visual information contained within them can be transmitted easily over computer networks. Here's the lowdown on each:

✔ GIF stands for Graphics Interchange Format. GIF is best suited to text, line art or images with well-defined edges. Special types of GIF allow images with transparent backgrounds to be interlaced (broken into layers that appear gradually over slow connections) and animated.

✔ JPEG (pronounced 'jay-peg') stands for Joint Photographic Experts Group, the name of the group that originated the format. JPEG (JPG for short) is best for photos and continuous tones of greyscale or colour that need greater compression while minimising loss of quality.

✔ PNG stands for Portable Network Graphics and acts a lot like GIF while supporting a greater range of colours and transparency levels. However, it doesn't support animation. Most browsers will display PNG files but some older Internet Explorer browsers (prior to version 9) still can't display certain PNG files correctly and you have to apply a fix to your website to get around the problem.

If you don't think you can create a logo yourself and you aren't employing someone to do so, there's actually a website that gives budding designers the chance to win prize money in exchange for a logo design. For as little as $275, Logo Tournament (www.logotournament.com) lets you host a competition between designers to create your logo. You describe your company, its aims and what attributes you want your logo to convey, then watch the entries roll in from around the world. You might get a few dud submissions at the beginning (particularly if they start rolling in mere hours after you start a tournament), but from what we've seen on the site, there have been some fantastic submissions. In fact, the website is worth browsing just for the sheer amount of inspiration you can get from the public logos that are available to view.

A logo doesn't have to be a fabulously complex drawing with drop-shadows and gradations of colour. A simple, type-only logo can work as well. Pick a typeface you want, choose your graphic's outline version and fill the letters with colour.

Hiring a Professional Web Designer

Part of the fun of running your own business is doing things yourself. So it comes as no surprise that many of the entrepreneurs we interviewed in the course of writing this book do their own web page design, despite the extra time requirement and the fact that they aren't full-time design specialists. They discovered how to create websites by reading books and online tutorials or taking classes on the subject. But in many cases, the initial cost of hiring someone to help you design your online business can be a good investment in the long run.

Keep in mind that after you pay someone to help you develop a look, you may be able to implement it in the future more easily yourself. For example:

- A designer can help you install a content management system like Wordpress or Drupal onto your site and can customise the templates to suit your layout requirements. You can then maintain and update the site yourself – adding articles, photos, blog posts – without having to worry about any HTML. The same goes with any online shopping cart software (see Chapter 11) – you can add new lines, product descriptions and images without interfering with the structure of your site.

- If you need business cards, stationery, brochures or other printed material in addition to a website, hiring someone to develop a consistent look for everything at the beginning is worth the money.

- You can pay a designer to get you started with a logo, colour selections and page layouts. Then you can save money by adding text yourself.

- Consider the benefits of having your logo or other artwork drawn by a real artist or giving the work to someone who's just starting out.

Professional designers charge up to £100 per hour for their work (which is less than the average plumber). You can expect a designer to spend five or six hours creating a logo or template. But if your company uses that initial design for the foreseeable future, you're not really paying that much per year.

In this case, as in all others, ask friends and family to help first. Dan's got a couple of pals who are really artistic and have some technical knowledge too. If you're in the same boat, then you can save some serious cash.

Chapter 6

Attracting and Keeping Customers

- -

- -

As writers, we know only too well the challenge of staring at a totally white piece of paper or a blank computer screen. It's at times like these that Greg remembers his teacher telling him to 'let it flow' and worry about editing after he'd let his creative juices flow. That's good advice up to a point, especially for something like a blog. But when it comes to a business website, you have to get it just right before you invite people to have a look. You need to present the *right* content in the *right* way to make prospective clients and customers want to explore your site the first time and then return down the road.

One of our primary points in this chapter is that you need to express your main message on your business site up front. We do the same by explaining what we consider to be general content rules for an online business. You should:

- Remember that people who are online have short attention spans.

- Make it easy for visitors to find out who you are and what you have to offer.

- Be friendly and informal in tone, concise in length and clear in your material's structure.

- Develop the all-important one-to-one-relationship with customers and clients by inviting dialogue and interaction, both with you and with others who share the same interests.

In other words, you need to be straightforward about who you are and where you're coming from on your business site. This chapter is obviously about writing for the web. But the idea is not to be satisfied with generating just any old text. The goal is to craft exciting, well-organised and easily digestible information. What follows is how to put these objectives into action.

Including Features that Attract Customers

Half the battle with developing content for a business website is knowing what shoppers want and determining strategies for giving it to them. Identifying your target audience helps you devise a message that will make each potential customer think you're speaking directly to her. But you also should keep in mind some general concepts that can help you market successfully to all ages, both genders and every socioeconomic group.

Studies of how people absorb the information on a web page indicate that people don't really read the contents from top to bottom (or left to right, for that matter) in a linear way. In fact, most web surfers don't *read* in the traditional sense at all. Instead, they browse so quickly that you'd think they're on a timer. They skip through pages by clicking link after link, as broadband lets them absorb complex graphics and multimedia faster than ever before. On average, people stay on each web page for just a few seconds, unless they find something that really grabs them. Next time you're online for half an hour or so, press the Back button and check out the web pages you've visited; you'll be amazed at how many you've browsed.

In addition, lots of people are beginning to use smart phones, interactive mobile devices like the iPad and gaming consoles like Microsoft Xbox and Nintendo Wii to get online. These new devices only add to the 'can't hang about' web surfing trend. Because your prospective customers don't necessarily have tons of computing power or hours' worth of time to explore your site (plus they're using a multitude of different devices to access online content), the best rule is to keep it simple.

People who are looking for things on the web are often in a state of hurried distraction. Think about a television watcher browsing during a commercial or a harried parent stealing a few moments on the computer while the baby naps, or even, dare we say, while at work when she's supposed to be concentrating on other things. Imagine this person surfing with one hand on a mouse, the other dipping her hand into a packet of crisps. This person – your average customer – isn't in the mood to listen as you tell your fondest hopes and dreams for success, which started with selling sweets in the playground. Here's what this shopper is probably thinking:

'Look, I don't have time to read all this. My show is about to come back on, and I still need the loo.'

'What's this? Why does this page take so long to load? And I paid good money for ultra-fast broadband! I swear, sometimes I wish the web didn't have any graphics. Here, I'll click this. No, wait! I'll click that. Oh, no, now the baby is crying again.'

The following sections describe some ways to attract the attention of the distracted and get them to click exactly where you want them to go.

Don't be shy about what you have to say

Don't keep people in suspense about what your business does. People in general, and web users in particular, want to know what a business does and why. Make it hard for them to find out, and they'll be off without giving your business a second thought. Answer the golden questions, on the other hand, and you're well on your way to retaining them:

- Who are you, anyway?
- All right, so what are you selling?
- Well, then, why do I want to buy what you're selling?
- Why should I choose your site to investigate rather than all the others out there?

A 2010 survey by Forrester (www.forrester.com) revealed that 88 per cent of people have abandoned an online shopping trolley and failed to make a purchase – that's the same percentage as 2005, which suggests that retailers *still* need to step up their game if they want to get customers checking out of their stores.

Web surfers are opportunists and, in many cases, aren't particularly loyal. Many discover new sites as they trawl randomly through the web. If they find something easier and quicker, they'll move on. When it comes to web pages, it pays to put the most important components first: who you are, what you do and how you stand out from any competing sites. If you can, illustrate these points without using words – make the product completely self-explanatory (think Google) or brilliantly designed so that people naturally want to find out more.

If you have a long list of items to sell, you probably can't fit everything you have to offer right on the first page of your site. Even if you could, you wouldn't want to: as in a television newscast, it's better to prioritise the contents of your site so that the *breaking stories*, or the best contents, appear at the top, and then you arrange the rest of what's in your catalogue in order of importance.

Think long and hard before you use features that may scare people away instead of wowing them. We're talking about those *splash pages* that contain only a logo or short greeting and then reload automatically and take the visitor to the main body of a site (ironically, we've seen our fair share of web designers using them). We also don't recommend loading up your home page with Flash animations or Java applets that either take your prospective customers' browsers precious seconds to load or fail to load altogether for security reasons.

Encourage visitors to click, click, click!

Imagine multitasking web surfers arriving at your website with only a fraction of their attention engaged. Make the links easy to read and in obvious locations. Having a row of links at the top of your home page, each of which points the visitor to an important area of your site, is always a good idea (see Figure 6-1). Such links give visitors an idea of what your site contains in a single glance and immediately encourage viewers to click a primary subsection of your site and explore further (some websites are also designed so that subsections appear in a drop-down menu when their mouse hovers over the link). By placing an interactive table of contents right up front, you direct surfers right to the material they're looking for. The BBC News website continues to evolve its design to keep up with browsing trends, but it's always retained links to major news categories at the top of all its pages.

Figure 6-1:
Notice how http://news.bbc.co.uk uses lots of clearly labelled buttons to draw users' attention.

BBC News © 2011 BBC

The links can go at or near the top of the page on either the left or right side. The Dummies.com home page, shown in Figure 6-2, has links clearly categorised at the top of the page, but there's also an all-important search box to help people look for that perfect Dummies book (after all, there are thousands!).

Figure 6-2: Putting at least five or six links near the top of your home page is clearly a good idea!

If you want to be ranked highly by search engines (and who doesn't?), you have another good reason to place your site's main topics near the top of the page in a series of links. Search engines tend to favour the first 50 or so words that appear on a web page. If you can get your important keywords included in that index, the chances are better that your site will rank highly in a list of links returned by the service in response to a search. (See Chapter 13 for more on embedding keywords.)

You can easily link to local files on your website using your web publishing tool. To have the same links appear at the same location on every page, you only need to edit its *template* as appropriate. For example, in Wordpress, you can insert links to various sub-sections of your site into the 'Sidebar' and 'Header' templates, which you can access and edit from within the Wordpress dashboard.

Say a fictional furniture seller wants to link to his beds section, located at www.lotsofgreatfurniture.co.uk/beds.html. In HTML, the seller may use this format:

```
<a href="/beds.html">Beds and bedding</a>.
```

Note the forward slash symbol. And because the link is to an internal page, there's no need to type out the entire web address.

If your site uses directories, you can also link to the directory. If the furniture seller also had a blog at www.lotsofgreatfurniture.co.uk/blog, he could type

```
<a href="/blog/">Blog</a>
```

instead. Note that the main web page at the 'top' of a directory is called index.html by default, so typing

```
/blog/index.html
```

would also work. To link to a specific page, also use the same format. If in doubt, you can still type the entire URL, but it just adds more unnecessary code.

Presenting the reader with links up front doesn't just help your search engine rankings, it also indicates that your site is content rich and worthy of a thorough look.

Tell us a little about yourself

One thing you need to state clearly as soon as possible on your website is who you are and what you do, or what people can get out of using your website. Mashable, the blog that dishes out what's going on in the social media world, encapsulates what it does in a very slick way:

> *Social media news and web tips.*

Can you identify your primary goal in a single sentence? If not, try to boil down your goals to two or three sentences at the most. Whatever you do, make your mission statement more specific and customer-oriented than simply saying, 'Out to make lots of money!' Tell prospects what you can do for them; the fact that you have three kids at uni and need to make money to pay their tuition isn't really a customer's concern. Online grocer Ocado's upfront statement is, 'Quality groceries that won't cost the earth.' This not only reflects its desire to offer reasonably priced groceries, but also ties into its environmentallyfriendly ethos.

Add a search box

One of the most effective kinds of content you can add to your site is a search box, like we do on Dummies.com. A *search box* is a simple text-entry field that lets a visitor enter a word or phrase. By clicking a button labelled Go, Search or something of the sort, the search term or terms are sent to the site, where a script checks an index of the site's contents for any files that contain the terms. The script then causes a list of documents that contain the search terms to appear in the visitor's browser window. You usually see them at the top of the home page, right near the links to the major sections of the site. The Wiley.com page, shown in Figure 6-3, includes a search box in the upper right corner of the page.

For more on search options, see the section, 'Make Your Site Searchable', later in this chapter.

Figure 6-3: Many surfers prefer using a search box to clicking links.

Keep it snappy

Although Kim's always looking for freelance writing jobs, even she has to admit that you don't really need to hire a professional to make a website compelling. You're not writing an essay, a term paper or a book here. Rather, you need to observe only a few simple rules:

- Provide lots of links and hooks that readers can scan.

- Keep everything concise!

The key word to remember is *short*. Keep sentences brief and snappy. Limit paragraphs to one or two sentences in length. You may also want to limit each web page to no more than one or two screens in length (anything below one screen is known as *below the fold*) so that viewers don't have to scroll down too far to find what they want – even if they're on a laptop or smaller Internet appliance.

Making your content scannable

When you're writing something on paper, whether it's a letter to your mum or your shopping list, contents have to be readable. Contents on your website, on the other hand, have to be scannable. This principle, popularised by usability expert Jakob Nielsen back in the mid-90s, still holds true today. It all has to do with the way people absorb information online. Eyes that are staring at a computer screen for many minutes or many hours tend to jump around a web page, looking for an interesting bit of information on which to rest. In this section, we suggest ways to attract those tired eyes and guide them toward the products or services you want to provide.

Point the way with headings

One hard-to-miss web page element that's designed to grab the attention of your readers' eyes is a heading. Every web page needs to contain headings that direct the reader's attention to its most important contents. This book provides a good example. The chapter title (we hope) piques your interest first. Then the section headings and subheadings direct you to more details on the topics you want to read about.

Most graphics designers we've worked with label their heads with letters of the alphabet: A, B, C and so on. In a similar fashion, most web page editing tools designate top-level headings with the style Heading 1. Beneath this heading, you place one or more Heading 2 headings. Beneath each of those, you may have Heading 3 and, beneath those, Heading 4. (Headings 5 and 6 are too small to be useful, in our opinion.) The arrangement may look like the following.

```
Miss Cookie's Delectable Cooking School (Heading 1)
  Kitchen Equipment You Can't Live Without (Heading 2)
  The Story of a Calorie Counter Gone Wrong (Heading 2)
  Programmes of Culinary Study (Heading 2)
    Registration (Heading 3)
    Course Schedule (Heading 3)
```

Think about how your headings might look on other devices. Remember, more and more people use mobile devices to read content. Kim got an iPhone recently, and while she was out looking for a TV, she was busy searching reviews of the models in the store using the built-in Safari browser. (Many sites redirect phone users to stripped-down, mobile versions of their websites, which is another design area altogether.)

You can energise virtually any heading by telling your audience something specific about your business. Instead of 'Ida's Antique Shop', for example, say something like 'Ida's Antique Shop: The Perfect Destination for the Collector and the Crafter'. Instead of simply writing a heading like 'Stan Thompson, Pet Grooming', say something specific, such as 'Stan Thompson: We Groom Your Pet at Our Place or Yours'.

Become an expert list maker

Lists are simple and effective ways to break up text and make your web content easier to digest. They're easy to create and easy for your customer to view and absorb. For example, suppose that you import your own decorations, and you want to offer certain varieties at a discount during various seasons. Rather than bury the items you're offering within an easily overlooked paragraph, why not divide your list into subgroups of sale items so that visitors find what they want without being distracted?

You can use bulleted lists if, say, you're mentioning the types of items you stock and their order isn't that important. Numbered lists are good for sequential things, such as the easy three-step process involved in booking a holiday through your website or top five ways to cook with the item you're selling.

Creating lists is easy – if you're using a content publishing tool like Wordpress, all you need to do is type your items one after the other, highlight them all and click the appropriate icon that lets you place bullet points in front of each.

It's a good idea visually to make sure that all your lists are roughly the same length, and make sure that the style is consistent (for example, is the first letter of each point capitalised? Try to follow that through).

Figure 6-4 shows how Kim creates a bulleted list in Wordpress when posting to her blog.

Figure 6-4: A bulleted list, as seen on the editing page of Kim's blog, is an easy way to direct customers' attention to special promotions, sale items and other important product features.

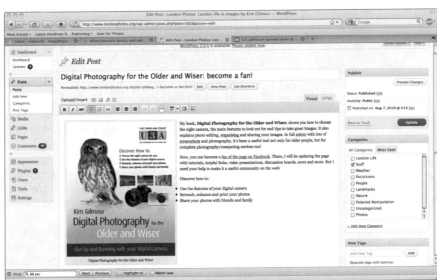

Your web page title: The ultimate heading

When you're dreaming up clever headings for your web pages, don't overlook the 'heading' that appears in the narrow title bar at the very top of your visitor's web browser window: the *title* of your web page.

The two HTML tags `<TITLE>` and `</TITLE>` contain the text that appears within the browser title bar. But you don't have to mess with these nasty HTML codes: all web page creation programs and publishing tools give you an easy way to enter or edit a title for a web page. With something like Wordpress, simply access your Settings page from within the dashboard, and type the site title into the box.

An effective title refers to your goods or services while grabbing the viewer's attention. If your business is called Myrna's Cheesecakes, for example, you may make your title 'Smile and Say Cheese! with Myrna's Cheesecakes'.

Remember, too, that the site title is what shows up when people find you on a search engine. So it's one of *the* most important things you need to get right for your site. Be sure to include your business name and a brief description too.

Many web editors let you vary the appearance of the bullet that appears next to a bulleted list item. For example, you can make it a hollow circle rather than a solid black dot, or you can choose a rectangle rather than a circle.

Lead your readers on with links

We mean for you to interpret your headings literally, not figuratively. In other words, we're not suggesting that you make promises on which you can't deliver. Rather, you should do anything you can to lead your visitors to your site and then get them to stay long enough to explore individual pages. You can accomplish this goal with a single hyperlinked word that leads to another page on your site:

> More . . .

We see this word all the time on web pages that present a lot of content. At the bottom of a list of their products and services, businesses place that word in bold type – **More . . .** – and we're always interested in finding out what more they could possibly have to offer.

Most blog publishing tools can be set to automatically link to more content if your blog post runs to more than a couple of paragraphs. In Wordpress settings, you can choose to display whole posts in your feed or just a summary.

Magazines use the same approach. On their covers you'll find taglines that refer you to the kinds of stories that you'll find inside. You can do the same kind of thing on your web pages. For example, which of the following links is more likely to get a response?

Next

Next: Paragon's Success Stories

Whenever possible, tell your visitors what they can expect to encounter as a benefit when they click a link. Give them a tease – and then a big pay-off for responding. Never use the words *Click here* for a link. It provides nothing tantalising for the reader and it also means nothing to search engines, which use link descriptions to help determine their content and importance.

Enhance your text with well-placed images

Images on your website can appear in the body of your page along with your text – this is called an *inline image*. You could also link to an *external image* that visitors access by clicking a link. The link may take the form of highlighted text or a small version of the image called a *thumbnail*.

The basic HTML tag that inserts an image in your document takes the following form:

```
<IMG SRC="URL">
```

This tag tells your browser to display an image (<IMG>) here. "URL" gives the location of the image file that serves as the source (SRC) for this image. Whenever possible, you should also include WIDTH and HEIGHT attributes (as shown a couple of paragraphs down) because they help speed up graphics display for many browsers.

Whenever possible, include what's known as *alt* or *alternative* text – a brief description of your image. Because search engines aren't great at recognising pictures (yet; Google is working on it), it's good practice to describe your image to help them index your site. Another important reason to include alt text is so that visually impaired people who use a screen reader to transcribe written words into audio can also know what images are on your page.

Here are all the tags in action:

```
<IMG HEIGHT=51 WIDTH=48 SRC="target.gif" ALT="Describe
        your photo here">
```

Most web page editors add the WIDTH and HEIGHT attributes automatically when you insert an image, and they also prompt you for some alt text. Typically, here's what happens:

1. **You click the location in the web page where you want the image to appear.**

2. **Then you click an Image toolbar button or choose Insert⇨Image to display an image selection dialog box.**

3. **Next you enter the name of the image you want to add (the alt text) and click OK.**

   The image is added to your web page. (For more information, see Chapter 5.)

A well-placed image points the way to text that you want people to read immediately. Think about where your own eyes go when you first connect to a web page. Most likely, you first look at any images on the page; then you look at the headings; and finally, you settle on text to read. If you can place an image next to a heading, you virtually ensure that viewers will read the heading.

Freebies: Everyone's favourite

No matter how much money you have in the bank, you're bound to respond to a really good deal. If you want sure-fire attention, use one of the following words in the headings on your online business site's home page:

- Free
- New
- Act (as in Act Now!)
- Sale
- Discount
- Win (although this word can sound like a scam if used in the wrong context)

Running competitions and prize draws

The word *free* and the phrase *Enter Our Competition* can give you a big bang for your buck when it comes to a business website. In fact, few things are as likely to get viewers to click into a site as the promise of getting something for nothing.

Giveaways have a number of hidden benefits too: everyone who enters sends you personal information that you can use to compile a mailing list or prepare marketing statistics, but bear in mind that for data protection reasons they must have the opportunity upon entering to opt out. Giveaways get people involved with your site, and they invite return visits – especially if you hold contests for several weeks at a time.

Of course, in order to hold a giveaway, you need to have something to *give away*. If you make baskets or sell backpacks, you can designate one of your sale items as the prize. If you can't afford to give something away, offer a big (perhaps 50 per cent) discount.

Be aware of the laws and regulations that cover competitions. You need to abide by the UK's Gambling Act (2005) and don't want to find yourself in legal hot water. Nor do you want to be promoting alcoholic drinks, cigarettes, drugs, weapons or anything else that might have legal restrictions in place.

In the UK, you need to make sure any *competition* involves an element of skill and give people an option to enter for free, otherwise you could be seen as holding a lottery (which is unlawful without a licence).

Completely free *prize draws* are allowed, too. Remember, that the cost of sending an entry into the draw above and beyond a first class stamp could be considered as a form of paying to enter. So give entrants free routes to entry: let them email you their details, fill in a form on your website or automatically put them into the draw when they buy a product from you.

Check out the law firm Pinsent Mason's guide to running a competition at `www.out-law.com/page-9216` and always seek independent legal advice before holding a competition or free draw. Another essential place to look at is the Gambling Commission's website at `www.gamblingcommission.gov.uk`, where you'll find an up-to-date summary of the gambling legislation in PDF form and, in their FAQ section, a rundown of what you can and can't do. The leaflet 'Running free competitions and prize draws' will help.

Following are some other points to consider:

- ✔ Unless you're sure that it's legal to allow web surfers from other countries to participate, you're safest limiting your contest to UK residents only.

- ✔ If you hold a competition on your webpage, include all the terms and conditions that explain who's eligible, who selects the winner, whether it's only open to UK residents and any rules of participation.

- ✔ Be sure to clearly state the starting and ending dates for receiving entries *as well as the time zone* you're referring to. This protects you if someone claims they entered the competition on time, but didn't.

- ✔ Define the rules of the contest clearly. Include exactly what the prize is, how many you'll give away and when you'll announce the winner.

If you do hold a contest, announce it at the top of your web page and hint at the prizes people can win. Use bold and big type to attract the attention of your visitors.

Expert tips and insider information

Giveaways aren't just for businesspeople in retail or wholesale salespeople who have merchandise they can offer as prizes in a contest. If your work involves professional services, you can give away something just as valuable: your knowledge. Publish a simple newsletter that you email to subscribers on a periodic basis. (See Chapter 12 for instructions on how to do so.) Or answer questions by email. Some website designers (particularly college students who are just starting out) work for next to nothing initially, until they build a client base and can charge a higher rate for their services.

Make your site searchable

Search boxes let visitors instantly scan the site's entire contents for a word or phrase. They put visitors in control right away and get them to interact with your site. They're popular for some very good reasons.

We recommend some sort of search utility for e-commerce sites. However, adding a search box to your site doesn't make much sense if you have only five to ten pages of content. Add search capability only if you have enough content to warrant searching. If your site has a sales catalogue driven by a database, it makes more sense to let your customers use a database search tool instead of adding one of the site search tools that we describe in this section and in Chapter 8.

Although search boxes require some technical programming, you can get around the problem by using tools and services that are already out there. Choose one of these options:

- ✔ **Let your web host do the work:** Some hosting services will do the indexing and creation of the search utility as part of their services.

- ✔ **Use a free site search service:** The server that does the indexing of your web pages and holds the index doesn't need to be the server that hosts your site. Google, Yahoo! and Bing, among others, will make your site searchable for free. In exchange, you display advertisements or logos in the search results you return to your visitors. For more on adding a search box, see Chapter 8.

- ✔ **Pay for a search service:** If you don't want to display ads on your search results pages, pay a monthly fee to get rid of them and integrate your site's look and feel into the search results. Google offers this service; prices are quite reasonable and depend on how many search queries your site attracts. (A typical small business attracting 50,000 queries a year pays £150 annually. And although we aren't expecting you'll be getting half a million search queries off the bat, if you're lucky enough to do so further down the line, that'll set you back £1210 annually at the time of writing – which still seems pretty fair). FreeFind (`www.freefind.com`) has some economy packages, a free version that forces you to view ads and a professional version priced at £19 per month for a site of 3,000 pages or less. It also comes with a 30-day money-back guarantee.

Writer Sean McManus, profiled later in this chapter, has gone beyond having a simple Search This Site text box on his site. He has one (as seen below in Figure 6-5), but also includes a sitemap at the bottom of his pages that provides a list of links to his site's most important contents.

Figure 6-5:
A Search
This Site
text box or
sitemap
page lets
visitors
instantly
match their
interests
with what
you have to
offer.

Writing Unforgettable Text

Quite often, business writing on the web differs from the dry, linear report writing you're called upon to compose (or worse yet, read) in the corporate world.

Never directly transpose something from your corporate brochure onto your website. Your visitors will fall asleep or, worse, head somewhere else! Online, you have the chance to express the real you. Sites that are funny, authors with a personality and content that's quirky are most read.

Striking the right tone

When your friends describe you to someone who's never met you, what do they describe first? Maybe it's your fashion sense or your collection of salt and pepper shakers. Your business also has a personality, and the more striking you make its description on your web page, the better. Use the tone of your text to define what makes your business unique and what distinguishes it from your competition.

Getting a little help from your friends

Blowing your own trumpet is a fine technique to use in some situations, but you shouldn't go overboard with promotional prose that beats readers over the head. Web readers are looking for objective information they can evaluate for themselves. An independent review of your site or your products carries far more weight than your own ravings about how great your site is. Sure, you know your products and services are great, but you're more convincing if your offerings can sell themselves, or you can identify third parties to endorse them.

CASE STUDY

Building an online presence takes time

Sean McManus is a UK-based writer specialising in business and technology. He launched his first website, www.sean.co.uk, way back in 1998. He now promotes his books and attracts new copywriting clients through his site, which runs to well over 300 pages. He also created Wild Mood Swings (www.wild moodswings.co.uk), which takes you to a different website depending on your mood, and JournalismCareers.com, which offers students advice on writing careers.

Q. What would you describe as the primary goal of your online business?

A. My work priorities have changed over time. Today, the main aim of the website is to help me secure new writing projects by bringing in enquiries from editors or companies that require writing services. Secondly, it helps me demonstrate my credibility by sharing my portfolio of work.

Equally important is the opportunity to connect with readers. Most of my visitors are people who are interested in reading the articles on my website, rather than people who want to commission more of the same. I don't see that as a problem at all. I learn a lot from the feedback from these visitors, which helps me to generate new project ideas.

Q. How many hours a week do you work on your business site?

A. It tends to go in bursts. Every year or so I'll invest a lot of time over a period of weeks or months to update the design. Most of the time I just spend a few hours a month on posting new content. I'd like to have more time to update the site but it's important not to confuse the website with the actual business. Any time I spend writing for my website – even the blog – is time I can't spend writing a book.

Q. How do you promote your site?

A. I make sure I include a plug for my website in all my communications materials including business cards, books, email signatures and even invoices. I use a strong call to action like 'Get a free chapter for my new book' to encourage people to visit.

Search engines are an important source of traffic so I try to ensure my site indexes well. I'm a writer, so I have a lot of text content, which search engines love.

Q. Has your online business been profitable financially?

A. Yes. I place adverts on most pages, and the adverts comfortably pay for the hosting costs. I've managed to attract some fantastic projects and opportunities through the website too.

Q. Apart from your website, how else do you promote your products and services?

A. I use Twitter (@musicandwords) to keep in touch with website visitors, and create an email newsletter using Vertical Response (www. verticalresponse.com) for those who register to receive it. A visit on the web can be so fleeting and then the site is forgotten, so these tools help me to build a relationship with people who come to the site and who might be interested in learning more about my work and visiting again another day. LinkedIn (www.linkedin.com) is a good business networking tool and has brought in some interesting enquiries. You'll still need to actively do business in other ways: meet clients, attend and run events, pick up the phone. It's important to have a website, but also to make it just one part of your strategy and not the be-all and end-all of your business. Even web-only businesses need offline promotion and public relations activities.

Q. What advice would you give to someone starting an online business?

A. I have several suggestions:

- ✓ **Learn the basics of what makes websites effective.** Even if you're going to outsource the design to somebody else, you need to take control of your own web strategy and make sure your site works for you. Your designers won't understand your business as well as you do, so you can't delegate responsibility for this. It pays to learn about usability too, the science of making websites easy to use.

- ✓ **Unless you're passionate about learning to design a website, outsource it.** It takes a lot of time and energy to learn to design a

website. A well-designed website inspires confidence in customers, while a poorly-designed one can drive them away.

- ✓ **Write descriptive content and update regularly.** Also, search engines love text so if you can write articles or blog posts that include the kind of words your potential customers use, you'll get more business leads.

- ✓ **Look for good-quality links to your website.** For example, are you a member of an association or trade body that might link to your website?

- ✓ **Be personal.** The web is quite a sterile and unfriendly environment compared to doing business in person. Use real photos of you and your team to make your business seem more friendly. It's okay to tell people about your hobbies and interests and to convey a bit of personality too, as long as you don't go too far and include a gallery of cat photos!

- ✓ **Test your site extensively.** Make sure it works on different browsers and devices and solicit feedback from your visitors. You'd be amazed how much you can learn from a quick one-line survey.

What's that you say? *Wired* magazine hasn't called to do an in-depth interview profiling your entrepreneurial skills? You haven't been listed as a trending topic on Twitter, or been given a thumbs-up vote by hundreds of fans on Digg or Facebook? Take a hint from what we and our colleagues do when we're writing computer books such as the one you're reading now: we fire up our email and dash off messages to anyone who may want to endorse our books – our mentors, our friends and people we admire in the industry.

People should endorse your business because they like it, not simply because you asked for an endorsement. If they have problems with your business setup, they can be a great source of objective advice on how to improve it. Then, after you make the improvements, they're more likely than ever to endorse it.

Satisfied customers are another source of endorsements. Approach your customers and ask whether they're willing to provide a quote about how you helped them. If you don't yet have satisfied customers, ask one or two people to try your products or services for free and then, if they're happy with your wares, ask permission to use their comments on your site. Your goal is to get a pithy, positive quote that you can put on your home page or on a page specifically devoted to quotes from your clients.

Don't be afraid to knock on the doors of celebrities too. Email an online reporter or someone prominent in your field and ask for an endorsement. People love to give their opinions and see their names in print. You just may be pleasantly surprised at how ready they are to help you.

Sharing your expertise

Few things build credibility and ensure return visits like a website that presents inside tips and goodies you can't get anywhere else. The more you can make your visitors feel that they're going to find something on your site that's rare or unique, the more success you'll have.

Tell what you know. Give people information about your field that they may not have. Point them to all sorts of different places with links.

Inviting Comments from Customers

Quick, inexpensive and *personal*: these are three of the most important advantages that the web has over traditional printed catalogues. The first two are obvious pluses. You don't have to wait for your online catalogue to get printed and distributed. On the web, your contents are published and available to your customers right away. Putting a catalogue on the web eliminates (or, if publishing a catalogue on the web allows you to reduce your print run, dramatically reduces) the cost of printing, which can result in big savings for you.

But the fact that online catalogues can be more personal than the printed variety is perhaps the biggest advantage of all. The personal touch comes from the web's potential for *interactivity*. Getting your customers to click links makes them actively involved with your catalogue.

Show off great reviews

Review sites are all over the web, with consumers happy to give their honest opinion on a product or service. Popular review websites include:

- ✔ UK-based Review Centre at www.reviewcentre.com
- ✔ Microsoft-owned Ciao at www.ciao.co.uk

✔ Travel and tourism reviews on www.tripadvisor.com and www.
booking.com

✔ The consumer group Which? at www.which.co.uk (only viewable to
subscribers)

After you've built up a loyal following, consider incorporating the ability for
customers to review your products on your own website, just like Amazon,
Argos and many others do. Specialist companies like BazaarVoice (www.
bazaarvoice.com) can help you do this, or you could add an extension or
plug-in into your existing content management system that lets people rate
an article or product on your website. Your web developer should be able to
do this for you. However, we don't advise doing this if you're just starting out,
because a lack of reviews makes it look like your items are unpopular!

Getting positive email feedback

Playing hide and seek is fun when you're amusing your baby niece, but it's
not a good way to build a solid base of customers. In fact, providing a way for
your customers to interact with you so that they can reach you quickly may
be the most important part of your website.

One way to do it is to add a simple _mailto_ link like this:

Questions? Comments? Send email to info@mycompany.com

A mailto link gets its name from the HTML command that programmers
use to create it. When visitors click the email address, their email program
opens a new email message window with your email address already entered.
That way, they have only to enter a subject line (and actually, you can even
specify a subject line using simple HTML), type the message and click Send
to send you their thoughts.

Most web page creation programs make it easy to create a mailto link. To rec-
reate the example we use in HTML, simply type:

```
Questions? Comments? Send email to
<a href="mailto:info@mycompany.com">info@mycompany.com</a>
```

Some drawbacks to this method exist, though. Publishing your email address
directly on your web page means that you're virtually certain to get unsolicited email messages (commonly called _spam_) sent to that address. Hiding
your email address behind generic link text (such as 'webmaster') rather
than typing out the address as we've done in the example may help reduce
your chances of attracting spam, but spammers are still likely to detect your
address in the underlying code.

The other disadvantage is that not everybody wants their email program to load when a mailto: link is clicked; it can get *very* annoying if you get no warning that this is about to happen. Kim has a web-based Gmail address and prefers to send messages through the Gmail website on her web browser rather than use her Mac's Mail program, which tends to be slow. Sometimes she clicks on 'Contact Us' links that use mailto: and immediately launch Mail, when she had been expecting a link to a contact form.

Including a *contact form* on your website can reduce spam and streamline the contact process for your visitors, as we describe in the following section.

Creating web page forms that aren't off-putting

You don't have to do much web surfing before you become intimately acquainted with how web page forms work, at least from the standpoint of someone who has to fill them out in order to sign up for web hosting or to download software.

When it comes to creating your own website, however, you become conscious of how useful forms are as a means of gathering essential marketing information about your customers. They give your visitors a place to sound off, ask questions and generally get involved with your online business.

Be clear and use common sense when creating your order form. Here are some general guidelines on how to organise your form and what you need to include:

- **Make it easy on the customer.** Whenever possible, add pull-down menus with pre-entered options to your *form fields* (text boxes that visitors use to enter information). That way, users don't have to wonder about things such as the level of detail you expect them to include in their address.

- **Validate the information.** You can use a programming language called JavaScript to ensure that users enter information correctly, that all fields are completely filled out (hey, you forgot the post code!) and so on. You may have to hire someone to add the appropriate code to the order form, but it's worth it to save you from having to call customers to verify or correct information that they missed or submitted incorrectly.

- **Provide a help number.** Give people a number to call if they have questions or want to check on an order.

- **Return an acknowledgment.** Let customers know that you've received their order and will be shipping the merchandise immediately or contacting them if you need more information.

As usual, good web page authoring and editing programs make it a cinch to create the text boxes, check boxes, buttons and other parts of a form that the user fills out. The other part of a form, the computer script that receives the data and processes it so that you can read and use the information, isn't as simple. See Chapter 12 for details.

Putting a form in needn't be a technical headache. You can use free ones like those from companies Response-O-Matic (www.response-o-matic.com) that are ad-supported (you can pay to remove these) and FormMail.to (www.formmail.to) that provide you with the script that receives that data and forwards it to you. Consider also free plug-ins available for content publishing tools like Wordpress (www.wordpress.org) and Joomla! (www.joomla.com).

Add a Like button

About 12 years ago, people liked to know who visited their website by linking to an online guestbook – you've probably gone to plenty of special events where they ask you to sign in and write a little something about the guests of honour, the place where the party is being held or the occasion marked by the event you're attending. Online guestbooks worked the same way, but today they're a little quaint, and they're also susceptible to spam and comment abuse. These days, enabling comments on your website's blog is one popular way to make your customers feel that they're part of a thriving community.

You can also tap into existing communities and bring your website to them by adding a Facebook Like (or Recommend) button or other interactive Facebook box to your website. You've probably seen them around.

For instance, let's say you add the Like button to your business's page where you're selling a great new handmade children's bib made of recycled vintage fabric. When visitors click the Like button, their activity – along with your website URL – appears on their friends' news feeds. If other people click on your website this way, a wave of activity may quickly spread.

Facebook also lets you add other plug-ins or mini-applications (called 'widgets') to your website, such as an activity box that displays the recent pages that visitors have Liked. If you've set up a Facebook page for your business (we explain how to do this in Chapter 12), then you can show off your thousands of fans by display a box that shows their profile pictures.

To see the whole range of what's available, see www.facebook.com/share. Here's how easy it is to add a Like button to one of your pages:

1. **Find out ways to share.**

   Go to www.facebook.com/share and click on the 'Like Button' link.

2. **Specify a web page you want people to Like.**

Under 'URL to like', type in the web address of your desired page.

3. **Choose the button's layout style from the drop-down menus.**

Standard format displays the Like button as well as the sentence, 'X amount of people like this. Be the first of your friends.' Other, more compact looks are available – how they appear shows up in real time on the page.

4. **Display faces or no faces by unticking or leaving the box ticked, as appropriate.**

Untick the box if you'd prefer not to show the profile photos of people who like your content.

5. **Type in a width for your button.**

By default, your widget is 450 pixels wide, about as long as this sentence on screen. This is usually fine, but you might want to experiment and reduce the pixel count to have the text wrap on to a second line (ideal if you're placing the button in a narrow column).

6. **Select either a Like or a Recommend button from the drop-down menu.**

You can have either word appear on your button, so select which one you prefer. The Recommend button is best for one-off articles, and the Like button is ideal for your main website page.

7. **Select a preferred look and feel from the drop-down menu.**

Choose the font and button styles (dark or light) that most closely align with your website's existing design.

8. **Generate the required code by clicking 'Get Code'.**

Here's what you need to paste into your website. You find two types of code here: iframe and XFBML. The latter is a unique Facebook code that web developers use which lets you find out more about who's interacted with your site. It's something you could adopt down the track, and Facebook explains how do go about using it on its developer pages. Here, we use the simpler iframe setup.

9. **Copy the code to your computer's clipboard.**

Facebook has made it easy to select the required code. Click within the iframe box and all the code should become automatically highlighted. Then copy it by pressing Ctrl+C.

10. **Launch your web editor or content publishing tool, and find the page on which you'd like to place the Like button.**

If you're working in a program that shows the HTML for a web page while you edit it, you can move on to Step 11. If, on the other hand, your editor hides the HTML from you, you have to use your editor's menu options to view the HTML source for your page. The exact menu command varies from program to program. For instance, Wordpress has an HTML tab at the top of the editing box. The HTML for the webpage you want to edit then appears.

11. **Place the Like button on a prominent part of your page.**

   How do you know where this spot is? Well, it depends on the publishing tool you're using. If you're looking at raw HTML files, you have to add the code in the BODY section of a web page. This is the part of the page contained between two HTML tags, <BODY> and </BODY>. Place your mouse cursor between these tags and within the area you want to add the button, and type in the tag <CODE> (this specifies that you're adding code). Then press Ctrl+V to paste in the Facebook code. When you've finished, type </CODE> to close the tag. If you're using Wordpress, you can click the Code button, paste the code in (Ctrl+V) and click the Code button again to close the code.

In Figure 6-6 Kim's website shows a simple form of the Like button.

If you're using a Mac, press Command+C instead of Ctrl+C when copying text and Command+V to paste text.

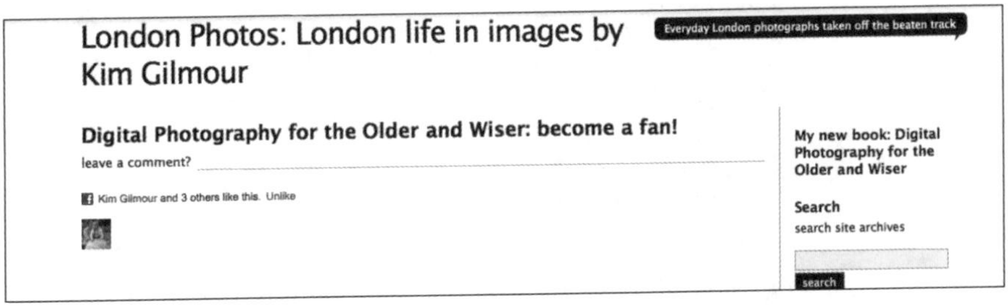

Figure 6-6:
Add a
Facebook
Like button
to your web
page.

London Photos: London life in images by
Kim Gilmour

Everyday London photographs taken off the beaten track

Digital Photography for the Older and Wiser: become a fan!
leave a comment? _____

Kim Gilmour and 3 others like this. Unlike

My new book: Digital
Photography for the
Older and Wiser

Search
search site archives

search

Now, when visitors to your web page click the Like button, this activity will appear on their Facebook profile page and on their other friends' news feeds. They can even add a comment to the activity (such as, 'I bought this great new book!').

Chit-chatting that counts

You've accomplished a lot by the time you've put your business online. Hopefully, you're already seeing the fruits of your labour in the form of email enquiries and orders for your products or services.

That's all good, but this is no time to rest on your laurels. After visitors start coming to your site, the next step is to retain those visitors. A good way to do so is by building a sense of community by posting a bulletin-board-type discussion area or forum.

A *forum* takes the form of back-and-forth messages on topics of mutual interest. Each person can read previously posted messages and either respond or start a new topic of discussion. For an example of a discussion area that's tied to an online business, visit the Australian Fishing (www.ausfish.com.au) discussion areas, one of which is shown in Figure 6-7.

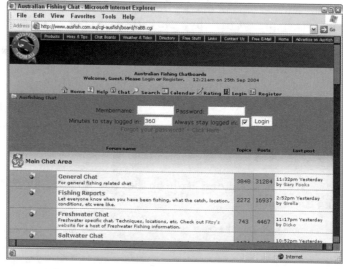

Figure 6-7:
A discussion area stimulates interest and interaction among like-minded customers.

The talk doesn't have to be about your own particular niche in your business field. In fact, the discussion will be more lively if your visitors can discuss concerns about your area of business in general, whether it's flower arranging, boat sales, tax preparation, clock repair, computers or whatever.

How, exactly, do you start a discussion area? The first step is to install a special computer script on the computer that hosts your website. (Again, discussing this prospect with your web hosting service beforehand is essential.) When visitors come to your site, their web browsers access the script, enabling them to enter comments and read other messages. Some web hosts provide a 'one-click' install of popular, free forum software like phpBB (www.phpBB.com) – all you need to do is specify the directory, or folder, you'd like the forum to appear in. You still need to keep the software up to date, though.

Here are some specific ways to prepare a discussion area for your site:

✔ Download a free forum or discussion-group script from either of these sites:

  • phpBB (www.phpBB.com)

  • Matt's Script Archive (www.worldwidemart.com/scripts)

✔ Buy a vBulletin licence (www.vbulletin.com), a hugely popular forum software that runs many popular websites like the celebrity gossip news site Digital Spy (www.digitalspy.co.uk). You'll probably need your web developer to help you install this.

To be able to run these forums, the information needs to be held in a database. It's likely that your computer will need to have the database management system *mySQL* (pronouned 'my sequel') enabled, as well as the scripting language PHP. Ask your web developer or web host for details. Tell them you're installing a forum and they'll probably understand what you're trying to do straight away.

Many, if not most, forums fail to take off, but don't take the lack of activity personally. We don't recommend persevering with a forum if you aren't attracting regular visitors and posters, because an inactive forum can make your website seem like a ghost town – not ideal for visitors who are expecting a hive of activity on your site! Not all businesses are suited to a forum either, so it's best to assess whether one will fill a niche or not. An alternative is to set up a Facebook page and facilitate discussions from there. See Chapter 12 for more.

Chapter 7

Building in Security Up Front

K eeping your business secure used to mean putting a strong lock on the door and installing an alarm system. But these days, online business is a huge target for organised criminal gangs. Whether it's through data theft or other intrusions by hackers, the threats to the security of your business are very real.

The whole idea of keeping one step ahead of these canny cyber gangs can seem intimidating, especially whenever you hear about big companies falling victim to cyber crime – if the big guys can't even keep their own data secure, how can you? These are real concerns, and the always-on nature of broadband and mobile phones means your office is constantly connected to the Internet. You'll also be entrusting your website with a third-party host, and most likely your email too – so you have to ensure the companies you're dealing with are putting in the right measures to keep your data secure. And let's not forget too that any intrusion into your website that takes it offline for any period of time is detrimental to your business.

Fortunately, you can take some down-to-earth measures, most of which involve nothing more than good old common sense. You don't need to spend lots of money to make your information and that of your all-important customers secure.

Some measures are easy to put into practice and are especially important for home-based businesspeople. Others are technically challenging to implement on your own. But even if you have your web host or a consultant do the work, you need to familiarise yourself with Internet security schemes. Doing so gives you the ability to make informed decisions about how to protect your online data. You can then take steps to lock your virtual doors so that you don't have to worry that your sensitive business information is easy pickings for hackers and other bogeymen.

Practising Safe Business

If you work from home, you'd be forgiven for thinking that your safety concerns are the same as when you're watching TV on a Saturday afternoon. Unfortunately, this isn't the case. By law you have responsibility for yourself and the people you employ. You've got equipment to take care of and possibly stock, as well as lots of precious data to keep safe – particularly customer data such as email and credit card details, which you must keep secure. Luckily, it doesn't take a brain surgeon to stay on the right side of employment law and keep your business interests safe.

Working from home can seem ideal but in reality you're often pestered by all manner of interruptions and distractions such as phone calls from relatives and friends who assume you aren't busy. So, knowing all too well that it's easier said than done, here are some simple steps that can help you set more clearly defined boundaries between work and domestic life, even when it all happens under the same roof.

When the computer is a group sport

It wasn't so long ago that a household had only one telephone, but even if you're a certain age, thinking back to those days is hard. Now it seems like everyone's entitled to their own computers, and with the proliferation of smart phones that are always connected to email along with the web and budget laptops that can get you online in a jiffy, that's virtually a reality for many these days.

There's a lot to be said for having at least two separate machines in your home – one for personal use and one for business use.

Logging on to your business computer with a username and password is good practice. Windows is designed to support multiple user profiles, or accounts. Even if you have only one computer, passwords can still provide a measure of protection. (For suggestions on choosing good passwords that are hard to crack, see the section 'Picking passwords that are hard to guess', later in this chapter.)

With user accounts, every person who uses the computer logs in with his username and password. Each person can pick his own background colour and desktop arrangement for his Windows user account. Each account has different permissions, or privileges, associated with it. As the manager, you'll probably have administrator privileges. The administrator is the user who has full control over the computer. He can install programs and hardware, and edit the privileges of other users. He can also get under the bonnet of the computer and tinker with the files that run the system. If a user without these privileges tries to do something for which he doesn't have permissions, such as download a game, Windows prompts the user to enter the administrator username and password (that's when your kid calls you for help). If the user doesn't know the username and password, he can't proceed with the task.

User accounts and passwords don't necessarily protect your business files, but they convey to your family members that they should use their own software, stick to their own directories and not try to explore your company data.

Folder Guard, a program by WinAbility Corporation (`www.winability.com/folderguard`), enables you to hide or password-protect files or folders on your computer. It also restricts access to other functions in Windows such as the Start Menu or the Control Panel. The software works with Windows 2000/XP/Vista/7. You can choose from the personal version ($39.95 or £25), which is intended for home users, or the business version ($79.95 or £50). A free 30-day trial version is available for download from the WinAbility website.

Your call centre

Even thrifty guys like us consider it a necessity, not a luxury, to get a separate phone line for business use (even if it's your mobile phone rather than a land line). Having a devoted phone line not only makes your business seem more serious, but also separates your business calls from your personal ones.

The next step is to set up your business phone with its own answering machine or voice mail. On your business voice mail, identify yourself with your business's name. This arrangement builds credibility and makes you feel like a real business owner. You can then install privacy features, such as caller ID, on your business line as needed.

If you're on a budget, you can use the Internet phone service Skype (recently acquired by Microsoft) to make phone calls over your Internet connection. Skype also lets you create an extra virtual phone line for your business. You get a proper number that people can call you on using any phone. Choose not only the country of origin, but the locality of your number (such as 020 for London or 01223 for Cambridge). To receive calls you need a broadband connection, Skype software on your computer or mobile phone and a headset or compatible handset. An optional webcam lets you do video calls. For more, see `www.skype.com`. Note that Skype isn't a substitute for emergency calls and the risk exists of your connection failing or experiencing occasional 'drop outs'. But it's well worth investigating, particularly as Skype could save you a bit of money when making phone calls.

Preparing for the worst

When you're lying awake at night, you can be anxious about all sorts of grim disasters: flood, fire, theft, computer virus, you name it. Prevention is always better than cure, so the following sections outline steps you can take to prevent problems. But, should a problem arise, you also find ways to recover more easily.

Insurance . . . the least you can do

We can think of ways to spend money that are a whole lot more fun than paying insurance premiums. But there we are every month, setting up direct debits to protect ourselves in case something goes wrong with our houses, cars, even ourselves and our pets. And yes, we have another item to add to the list: protecting our business investment by obtaining insurance that specifically covers us against hardware damage, theft and loss of data. Consultancy firm PricewaterhouseCoopers discovered that around four out of ten UK businesses were insuring against damage caused by data loss.

You can also obtain a policy that covers the cost of data entry or equipment rental that would be necessary to recover your business information.

 It's important that you take stock of everything that you consider an asset for your business and make sure that your policy covers it all. This will probably add to your standard home insurance, but it's worth the extra expense if the worst happens. Here are some specific strategies:

- Make a list of all your hardware and software and how much each item cost and store a copy of it in a place such as a fireproof safe or safety-deposit box, preferably in a different building to where your business is located.

- Take photos of your computer setup in case you need to make an insurance claim and put them in the same safe place.

- Save your electronic files on DVD or external hard drive and place them in a safe storage location, such as a safety-deposit box.

Investigate the many options available to you for insuring your computer hardware and software. Your current homeowner's or renter's insurance may offer coverage, but make sure that the money amount is sufficient for replacement. Also, what proof does the insurance company require from you to prove that you've sufficiently attempted to protect your computers from data loss?

You may also want to take a look at business insurance search engines and brokers that can give you some ideas of which provider best suits your needs. Some comparison websites include www.moneysupermarket.com, www.gocompare.com and www.confused.com.

Considering the unthinkable

The Gartner Group estimates that two out of five businesses that experience a major disaster will go out of business within five years. We'd guess that the three that get back up on their feet and running quickly are those that already had recovery plans in place. Even if your company is small, you need to be prepared for big trouble – not only for terrorist attacks and hackers trying to take down a network but natural disasters such as floods or tornadoes. A recovery effort may include the following strategies:

- ✔ **Backup power systems:** What will you do if the power goes out and you can't access the web? Consider an uninterruptible power supply (UPS). Many battery backup systems are around, such as APC Back-UPS CS (www.apcpower.co.uk), which instantly switches your computers to battery power when the electricity goes out so that you can save your data and switch to laptops. Even more important, make sure that your Internet service provider (ISP) or web host has a backup power supply so that your store can remain online in case of a power outage. Having a laptop, as well as a PC, can help too. Simply switch to your laptop in the event of a power cut, and you'll get an extra couple of hours (depending on the machine's battery life) to bridge the power gap.

- ✔ **Data storage:** This is probably the most practical and essential disaster recovery step for small or home-based businesses. Back up your files on a computer or external hard drive that's not located in the place where you physically work. You could consider storing your files with an online storage service. (See the section on online storage space in the box 'Low- and high-tech locks' later in this chapter.)

- ✔ **Telecommunications:** Having some alternate method of communication available in case your phone system goes down ensures that you're always in touch. The obvious choice is a mobile phone. Also set up a voice mailbox so that customers and vendors can leave messages for you, even if you can't answer the phone.

Creating a plan is a waste of time if you don't regularly set aside time to keep it up to date. Back up your data on a regular basis, purchase additional equipment if you need it and make arrangements to use other computers and offices if you need to – in other words, _implement_ your plan. You owe it not only to yourself but also to your customers to be prepared in case of disaster.

Antivirus Protection without a Needle

As an online businessperson you'll be downloading files and receiving them as email attachments, opening files on discs or Flash drives received from customers and vendors, and accessing all manner of websites. You'll also be exchanging emails with people you've never met.

Downloading files from known sources only is one handy tip to reduce the risk of viruses, worms and other so-called *malware*, but other ways for nasties to get onto your computer exist. Inadvertently accessing malicious websites that harbour dangerous computer code could adversely affect your computer – and your business. *Spyware* (see the later section 'Cleaning out adware and spyware') could find its way onto your computer – this is rogue software that allows hackers to remotely monitor your online activities, such as keystrokes, in order to steal precious data.

You probably know by now not to open any suspicious attachments on email that you aren't expecting – and many email programs and services scan your inbox before allowing you to download potentially dodgy files. But even the act of opening an email could lead to problems, particularly if you download images from unknown sources. And keeping your broadband-connected computer open to the elements could lead to intrusions.

Despite the risks, you don't need to worry if you take the right precautions and regularly monitor network activity. As we mention earlier in this chapter, prevention is better than cure, and plenty of ways exist to minimise any security risk. Antivirus group Sophos has some great best practice tips for your small business on minimising security risks, including a plain-English A–Z guide to threats to your computer and your data – visit www.sophos.com/security/best-practice. You'll also find many other practical resources on their site.

When it comes to protecting your computer, you're probably better off getting a fully-fledged security suite that protects you from viruses, spam, spyware, unwanted intrusions and other unauthorised activity. Some solutions include:

- ✓ **Norton Internet Security (www.symantec.co.uk):** Symantec manufactures the popular 'all-in-one' Norton Internet Security suite; a new edition comes out every year and costs around £50 for an annual subscription. It's readily available to purchase from computer stores or online and automates many security functions. For a larger setup, Norton Protection Suite is specifically designed for small to medium businesses and is available from Symantec resellers; see the Symantec website for pricing and availability.

- ✓ **AVG AntiVirus by AVG Technologies (www.avg.com):** Many prefer to use AVG's solution as it doesn't take up too much of a footprint on your computer (although Norton eats up far less resources than it did in the old days). There's a free version for home users and a more full-featured security suite edition that costs £38 for a year's subscription. For home networks with multiple computers, the bells-and-whistles business solution costs £189 for a year's subscription. This protects your file and mail servers as well as your workstations. The price may seem a lot to stump up, but AVG has a 30-day money-back guarantee. For more, see the AVG website.

✔ **Sophos Computer Security Small Business Edition** (`www.sophos.com`): Sophos is a British-based company with a global reach. You can download a trial version of its small business software on its website.

✔ **Internet Security Suite by McAfee** (`www.mcafeestore.com`): This is the leading competitor to Norton Internet Security. It's a most comprehensive program and costs £49.99. Check out the website and assess what they've got on offer.

You can often find special offers for the security suites on sites like `www.amazon.co.uk`.

Low- and high-tech locks

If you play the word game with a web surfer or website and say 'security', you're likely to get a response such as 'encryption'. But security doesn't need to start with software. The fact is, all the firewalls and passwords in the world won't help you if someone breaks into your home office and trashes it or makes off with the computer that contains all your files.

Besides insuring your computer equipment and taking photos in case you need to get it replaced, you can also invest in locks for your home office and your machines. They may not keep someone from breaking into your house, but they'll act as a deterrent and make it more difficult for intruders to carry off your hardware.

Here are some suggestions for how to protect your hardware and the business data that your computers contain:

✔ **Lock your office.** Everyone has locks on the outer doors of their house, but go a step further and install a deadbolt lock on your office door.

✔ **Lock your computers.** Kensington (`www.kensington.com`) offers a variety of computer locking systems for both desktop and laptop computers. Most laptops come with a Kensington lock slot, apart from some slimmer Mac offerings.

✔ **Locate your laptop:** Unbeknownst to someone who's up to no good, you can install an innovative theft recovery system called GadgetTrak on your hard drive. Then, if your laptop is stolen, the software tries to locate its coordinates using Wi-Fi technology. GadgetTrak even snaps a photo of the thief using your laptop's built-in webcam! Other similar innovative services are available. Although recovery isn't guaranteed the software may bring extra peace of mind.

✔ **Make backups:** Be sure to regularly back up your information on an external hard drive. Windows 7 and Mac OS X include built-in backup tools, but make sure that the software is backing up *all* essential files, and remember to back up every week or so. You may also consider signing up to an online backup service. That way, if you lose your computers and your extra storage drives for whatever reason, you have an online backup in a secure location. Major services include iDrive (`www.idrive.com`; $10 or £6.20 per month for a business account) and Carbonite (`www.carbonite.co.uk`; £42 per year).

Another area demands your attention on a regular basis. Viruses change all the time, and new ones appear regularly. The antivirus program you install one day may not be able to handle the viruses that appear just a month later. You may want to pick an antivirus program that gives free regular updates. Also check out CNet's www.download.com and take a look at the antivirus software reviews. People seem to feel quite passionate about viruses and they don't hold back on their opinions!

It seems like everyone has a mobile gadget these days, whether it's the latest do-it-all smartphone, a laptop, iPad or other portable computing device. But how many people secure these devices in case they were to get stolen? These mini-computers might hold sensitive company information on emails and texts. At the very least, you should make the device's storage area accessible with a password. You can also install protection software designed especially for mobile devices, such as Norton Smartphone Security, which offers a free trial (uk.norton.com/smartphone-security).

Installing Firewalls and Other Safeguards

You probably know how important a firewall is in a personal sense. It filters out unwanted intrusions such as executable programs that hackers seek to plant on your file system so they can use your computer for their own purposes. When you're starting an online business, the objectives of a firewall become different: you're protecting not just your own information but also that of your customers. In other words, you're quite possibly relying on the firewall to protect your source of income as well as the data on your computers.

Just what is a firewall, exactly? A *firewall* can be an application or hardware device that monitors the data flowing into or out of a computer network and that filters the data based on criteria that the owner sets up. Like a porter in the reception of a block of flats, a firewall scans the packets (small, uniform data segments) of digital information that traverse the Internet, making sure that the data is headed for the right destination and that it doesn't match known characteristics of viruses or attacks. Authorised traffic is allowed into your network. Attack attempts or viruses are either automatically deleted or cause an alert message to appear to which you must respond with a decision to block or allow the incoming or outgoing packets. A good firewall protects traffic going in and prevents suspicious traffic going out (a rogue program on your computer reporting to 'home base', for instance).

Keeping out Trojan horses and other unwanted visitors

A *Trojan horse* is a program that enters your computer surreptitiously and then attempts to do something without your knowledge. Some people say that such programs enter your system through a 'back door' because you don't immediately know that they've entered your system. Trojan horses may come in the form of an email attachment with the filename extension .exe (which stands for executable).

Cleaning out adware and spyware

You've also got to watch out for software that monitors your web surfing and other activities and reports them back to advertisers, potentially invading your privacy. This software is called *adware*, which is an unethical form of doing business because it sometimes hijacks your web browser (Internet Explorer, say) with commercial branding and forces you to use a particular search engine. Adware can also bombard you with pop-up advertising.

Ad-Aware isn't a firewall exactly, but it's a useful program that detects and erases any advertising programs you may have inadvertently downloaded from the Internet. Such advertising programs may be running on your computer, consuming your processing resources and slowing down operations.

Spyware programs, which install themselves and spy on your browsing habits so criminals can use your information for their own gain, are far worse than adware.

Ad-Aware, produced by Swedish company Lavasoft, deletes advertising software that, many users believe, can violate your privacy. Like any good security software, it offers 'real time' protection from malicious files, which means it's always on alert for threats. Figure 7-1 provides a typical screen shot that shows Ad-Aware Free running:

We recommend Ad-Aware; the home version is free and a more fully-featured Pro version is available for $29.95 (£18.50). You can also download a business version with a ten-user licence for $275 (£170) at:

```
http://www.lavasoft.com/products/ad_aware_business_
edition.php
```

Microsoft also has some great, free programs that protect against malware – take a look at www.microsoft.com/security_essentials. Always keep your browser software up to date too, because it blocks pop-ups and alerts you if a website is attempting to run any code on your system.

Figure 7-1:
Ad-Aware
screenshot.

Another popular, free program is called HijackThis. It was originally developed by a Dutch student Merijn Bellekom, and after gaining popularity security company Trend Micro bought the program. Find it at `free.antivirus.com/hijackthis`. However, unlike Ad-Aware, HijackThis doesn't distinguish between what's good and what's bad on your computer. For that, you should consult an expert. Post your HijackThis log on a technical support forum such as *Web User* magazine's HijackThis thread. Go to `www.webuser.co.uk/forums` and follow the link to 'HijackThis logs help and analysis'.

Positioning the firewall

These days, most home networks are configured so that the computers on the network can share information, as well as the same Internet connection. Whether you run a home-based business or a business in a discrete location, you almost certainly have a network of multiple computers. A network is far more vulnerable than a single computer connected to the Internet: a network has more entry points than a single computer, and more reliance is placed on each of the operators of those computers to observe good safety practices. And if one computer on the network is attacked, real potential exists for the others to be attacked as well.

You're probably acquainted with software firewalls. All the latest versions of Windows (after Windows XP Service Pack 2, which came out way back in 2004!) include a firewall that's on by default; check whether one is running by going to Start, then Control Panel and then System and Security.

If you're using a firewall supplied by another company, such as the one equipped with your security software, then you may use that in place of your Windows firewall. Don't run both at once because this may cause conflicts.

Software firewalls protect one computer at a time. In a typical business scenario, however, multiple computers share a single Internet connection through a router that functions as a gateway. Many network administrators prefer a *hardware firewall* – a device that functions as a filter for traffic both entering and leaving it. In most cases, a hardware firewall also functions as a router, but it can also be separate from the router. You position the device at the perimeter of the network where it can protect all the company's computers at once.

Companies that want to provide a website that the public can visit as well as secure email and other communications services create a secure sub-network of one or more specially hardened (in other words, secured because all unnecessary services have been removed from them) computers. This kind of network is sometimes called a *Demilitarised Zone* or DMZ.

Keeping your firewall up to date

Firewalls work by means of attack *signatures* (also called *definitions*), which are sets of data that identify a connection attempt as a potential attack. Some attacks are easy to stop: they've been attempted for years, and the amateur hackers who attempt intrusions don't give much thought to them. The more dangerous attacks are new ones. They have signatures that have emerged since you installed your firewall.

You quickly get a dose of reality and find just how serious the problem is by visiting one of the websites that keeps track of the latest attacks – we mention the online security company Sophos earlier in this chapter; it's worth signing up to one of their newsletters at `https://secure.sophos.com/security/notifications` (note the secure 's' in https://).

US-based SANS Internet Storm Center has reported that the 'survival time' for an unpatched computer (a computer that has security software that hasn't been equipped with the latest updates called *patches*) after connecting it to the Internet was only five minutes – a figure that seems to decrease every year. That means such a computer only has five minutes before someone tries to attack it. For a BBC Worldwide report, their unprotected test computer lasted only eight seconds! If that doesn't scare you into updating your security software, we don't know what will.

Keeping Your Wireless Network Secure

Being able to access the Internet from anywhere in the house using your laptop or other wireless Internet device gives you great freedom, but it's essential that your wireless network is secure – if anyone can hop on to your Internet connection with their laptop and not have to type in a password, then nearby spies could intercept fragments of sensitive data as it's transferred across the airwaves.

Neighbours could also use *your* Internet connection to download and share copyrighted music or movies, or conduct illegal activity online. This eats into your monthly download allowance and slows your Internet connection down. What's more, whatever dodgy activity they get up to could then be tied to you, not them – so it's crucial to keep that virtual lock on.

Thankfully, securing your wireless network these days and only letting authorised devices, such as your laptop, access it is relatively straightforward – it's just that so many people fail to do sort out this security.

Setting a password for your network

All your wireless devices should be talking to a device called a *router* (the gadget with the antennae sticking out of it). To secure your network, you need to encrypt it.

The process varies from router to router, so read your manual for the specifics. Encrypting the network typically involves:

1. **Log into your router.**

   You need to access your router's setup screen. To do so, log into the router by typing its numerical *IP* (Internet Protocol) address into the address bar of your web browser (such as Internet Explorer or Firefox). The IP address is usually `198.168.0.1` or `198.168.1.1` (but it's best to check the manual).

   Before you can log in you may be prompted for the router's username and password (this is different to the password you'll set to protect the wireless network). The factory-set login for many routers is the username 'admin', and a password of simply 'password', but again, check your manual. (Make sure you change this factory setting later to something hard to guess.)

2. **Choose the security encryption method.**

   Next, you set up a password for your wireless network. Figure 7-2 illustrates the Netgear setup screen, which has a section called Wireless Settings. Under the section entitled Security Options, a number of encryption methods are listed; we recommend WPA2-PSK (see 'Technical Stuff', below, for more on encryption methods). Don't choose WEP (Wired Equivalent Privacy), because this is an older and less secure connection method. Under 'WPA2-PSK Security Encryption' is a section for a Network Key (8 to 63 characters). This network key is your password. Type something in the box that's hard to guess (see 'Picking passwords that are hard to guess', later in this chapter) and click Apply.

You also see the term SSID in your router settings; this stands for Service Set Identifier and is a name you give your wireless network to distinguish it from any others nearby. Bear in mind that this name will be publicly broadcast to anyone in range. You can hide the broadcasting of this name so that any device wanting to connect to your network must also type in the SSID as well as the network password.

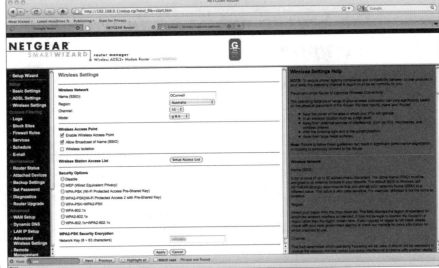

Figure 7-2:
The Netgear router settings let you set a password for your wireless network.

3. **Test the connection.**

   From now on, any device that wants to connect to your wireless network will be prompted to type in the required password.

4. **Get even more secure.**

   Large enterprises don't rely on WPA2-PSK alone, but it's definitely a solid start for a home business. Other relatively easy ways exist to further restrict access to your network, such as restricting the range of the wireless network and only allowing access to pre-approved devices by entering their Media Access Control (MAC) addresses, which are often located on the devices themselves. Read your manual for specifics.

WPA2-PSK stands for Wi-Fi Protected Access 2 – Pre-Shared Key. Without getting into great detail, this method is a far more secure way for home and small office users to protect their network. Hackers wanting to break the encryption of your network won't be able to keep up because the encryption keys used to authenticate devices are constantly changing.

Using Public Keys to Provide Security

Eavesdrop on any teenage conversation and you'll often be left with no doubt that different segments of society use code words that only their members can understand. Even computers use encoding and decoding to protect information they exchange on the Internet. The schemes used online are far more complex and subtle than the slang used by kids, however. This section describes the security method that's used most widely on the Internet, and the one you're likely to use yourself: Secure Sockets Layer (SSL) encryption.

The keys to public-key/private-key encryption

Terms like *SSL* and *encryption* may make you want to reach for the remote, but don't be too quick to switch channels. SSL makes it safer to do business online and boosts the trust of potential customers. And anything that makes shoppers more likely to spend money online is something you need to know about.

The term *encryption* refers to the process of encoding data, especially sensitive data, such as credit-card numbers. Information is encrypted by means of complex mathematical formulas called *algorithms*. Such a formula may transform a simple-looking bit of information into a huge block of seemingly incomprehensible numbers, letters and characters. Only someone who has the right formula, called a *key*, which is itself a complex mass of encoded data, can decode the gobbledygook.

Here's a very simple example. Suppose that your credit-card number is 12345, and you encode it by using an encryption formula into something like the following: 1aFgHx203gX4gLu5cy. The algorithm that generated this encrypted information may say something like: 'Take the first number, multiply it by some numeral and then add some letters to it. Then take the second number, divide it by x and add y characters to the result', and so on. (In reality, the formulas are far more complex than this example, which is why you usually have to pay a licence fee to use them. But you get the general idea.) Someone who has the same formula can run it in reverse, so to speak, in order to decrypt the encoded number and obtain the original number, 12345.

In practice, the encoded numbers that are generated by encryption routines and transmitted on the Internet are very large. They vary in size depending on the relative strength (or uncrackability) of the security method being used. Some methods generate keys that consist of 256 bits of data; a *data bit* is a single unit of digital information. These formulas are called *256-bit keys*.

Encryption is the cornerstone of security on the Internet. The most widely used security schemes, such as the Secure Sockets Layer protocol (SSL), the Secure Electronic Transactions protocol (SET) and Pretty Good Privacy (PGP), all use some form of encryption.

With some security methods, the party that sends the data and the party that receives it both use the same key (this method is called *symmetrical encryption*). This approach isn't considered as secure as an asymmetrical encryption method, such as public-key encryption, however. In public-key encryption, the originating party obtains a licence to use a security method. As part of the licence, you use the encryption algorithm to generate your own private key. You never share this key with anyone. However, you use the private key to create a separate public key. This public key goes out to visitors who connect to a secure area of your website. As soon as they have your public key, users can encode sensitive information and return it to you. Only you can decode the data – by using your secret, private key.

Getting a certificate without going to school

On the Internet how do you know that people are who they say they are when all you have to go on is a URL or an email address? The solution in the online world is to obtain a personal certificate that you can send to website visitors or append to your email messages.

How certificates work

A *certificate*, which is also sometimes called a Digital ID, is an electronic document issued by a certification authority. The certificate contains the owner's personal information as well as a public key that can be exchanged with others online. The public key is generated by the owner's private key, which the owner obtains during the process of applying for the certificate.

In issuing the certificate, the certification authority takes responsibility for saying that the owner of the document is the same as the person actually identified on the certificate. Although the public key helps establish the owner's identity, certificates do require you to put a level of trust in the agency that issues it.

A certificate helps both you and your customers. It assures your customers that you're the person you say you are, plus it protects your email communications by enabling you to encrypt them.

Obtaining a certificate from VeriSign

Considering how important a role certificates play in online security, it's remarkably easy to obtain one. You do so by applying and paying a licensing fee to a certification authority. One of the most popular certification authorities is VeriSign, which was sold to Symantec (maker of Norton security products) in August 2010 (www.verisign.co.uk). The scheme lets you apply for a range of SSL certificates that range in price from £259 for a basic one-year licence, to several thousands of pounds for more complicated packages.

A VeriSign Secure Site certificate, which you can use to authenticate yourself in emails, news and other interactions on the Net, costs £259 plus VAT for one year, but you can get a better deal signing up for longer terms (it's £399 for two years).

VeriSign also lets you try out a free certificate for secure e-mail IDs for 60 days (usually $19.95 or £12.30 per year). You can use this Digital ID to send encrypted emails and to let your recipients know that any email you send out really is from you. For more, see www.verisign.co.uk/authentication/individual-authentication/digital-id and click 'Buy Now'; you'll be able to select whether you want the free trial after choosing your web browser from the list on the next page.

Keeping Other Noses Out of Your Business

Encryption isn't just for big businesses. Individuals who want to maintain their privacy, even while navigating the wilds of the Internet, can install special software or modify their existing email programs in order to encode their online communications. You may not need to use software like this, but if you deal in sensitive data, then it's a must.

Encryption software for the rest of us

PGP (Pretty Good Privacy), a popular encryption program, has been around about as long as the web itself. Like VeriSign, it was acquired by Symantec in 2010. Symantec paid a cool £185 million in cash for PGP, which illustrates how influential it's been over the years. PGP lets you protect the privacy of your email messages and file attachments by encrypting them so that only those with the proper authority can decipher the information. You can also digitally sign the messages and files you exchange, which assures the recipient that the messages come from you and that no one has tampered with the information. You can even encrypt files on your own computer.

PGP Personal Desktop (www.pgp.com/products/desktop/index.html) is a personal encryption program. PGP offers a range of *plug-ins*, applications that work with other programs to provide added functionality. You can integrate the program with popular email programs such as Microsoft Outlook.

In order to use PGP Personal Desktop, the first step is to obtain and install the program. For a price list or more information about the 30-day free trial, go to the website at www.pgp.com. After you install the program, you can use it to generate your own private-key/public-key pair. After you create a key pair, you can begin exchanging encrypted email messages with other PGP users. To do so, you need to obtain a copy of their public keys, and they need a copy of your public key. Because public keys are just blocks of text, trading keys with someone is really quite easy. You can include your public key in an email message, copy it to a file or post it on a public-key server where anyone can get a copy at any time.

After you have a copy of someone's public key, you can add it to your *public keyring*, which is a file on your own computer. Then you can begin to exchange encrypted and signed messages with that individual. If you're using an email application supported by the PGP plug-ins, you can encrypt and sign your messages by selecting the appropriate options from your application's toolbar. If your email program doesn't have a plug-in, you can copy your email message to your computer's Clipboard and encrypt it there by using PGP built-in functions. See the PGP User's Guide files for more specific instructions.

You can use your existing software, such as Microsoft Outlook, to encrypt your mail messages using your Digital ID (such as the one offered by VeriSign; see the previous section), rather than have to install a separate program such as PGP. For detailed instructions on how to use your Digital ID with Outlook 2010, see the support document at office.microsoft.com/en-gb/outlook-help/get-a-digital-id-HP010355070.aspx.

Picking passwords that are hard to guess

You put a lot of effort into picking the names of your kids and pets, and now you get to choose passwords. But the point of creating a password is to make it difficult for thieves to figure out what it is. That is true whether you're protecting your own computer, downloading software, subscribing to an online publication or applying for a certificate (as we explain earlier in this chapter).

One method for choosing a password is to take a familiar phrase and then use the first letter of each word to form the basis of a password. For example, the old phrase 'Every Good Boy Deserves Fruit' would be EGBDF. Then, mix uppercase and lowercase, add punctuation and you wind up with eGb[d]f. If you *really* want to make a password that's hard to crack, add some numerals as well, such as the last two digits of the year you were born: eGb[d]f48.

Whatever you do, follow these tips for effective password etiquette:

>   ✔ **Don't use passwords that are in a dictionary.** It takes time but not much effort for hackers to run a program that tries every word in an online dictionary as your password. So if it's in the dictionary, hackers will eventually discover it.

✔ **Don't use the same password at more than one site.** It's a pain to remember more than one password, not to mention keeping track of which goes with what. Plus, you tend to accumulate lots of different passwords after you've been online for a while. But if you use the same password for each purpose and your password to one site on the Internet is compromised, all your password-protected accounts are in jeopardy.

✔ **Use at least six characters:** The more letters in your password, the more difficult you make the life of the code-crackers.

When it comes to passwords, duplication isn't only boring but also dangerous. It's especially important not to reuse, say, the password you use to get into your bank or PayPal account as you would to log into your Facebook or Twitter account. If a hacker discovers your password on Facebook, he could use it to hijack your email account and discover a lot of personal information that you find is no longer personal.

Microsoft thinks that a good password should really be 14 characters long. In reality this isn't always possible! You can check the strength of your password using Microsoft's (extremely stringent) password checker. The 'Strength' bar increases the stronger your password is. Your password isn't transmitted over the Internet on this site and everything is validated on your computer. We were surprised to discover just how weak Microsoft thinks some of our passwords actually are, because they didn't quite reach the 14-character mark! Have a look at Microsoft's password checker at `https://www.microsoft.com/protect/fraud/passwords/checker.aspx?WT.mc_id=Site_Link` and read Microsoft's password tips at `www.microsoft.com/protect/fraud/passwords/create.aspx`.

A mouthful of protection with authentication

Authentication is a fun word to try to say quickly ten times in a row, and it's also another common security technique used on the web. This measure simply involves assigning approved users an official username and password that they must enter before gaining access to a protected network, computer or directory.

Most web servers allow you to set up areas of your website to be protected by username and password. Not all web hosts allow this, however, because it requires setting up and maintaining a special password file and storing the file in a special location on the computer that holds the web server software. If you need to make some content on your business site (such as sensitive financial information) available only to registered users, talk to your web host to see whether setting up a password-protected area is possible.

Chapter 8

Monitoring and Improving Your Business

*O*ne of the many advantages of doing business online is the ease with which you can shift your shop's focus. With a bricks-and-mortar outlet, changing the business's name, address or physical appearance can be labour-intensive and expensive. On the web, however, you can rebuild your shop's *front door* (your home page) in a matter of minutes, and, in theory, you can revamp your sales catalogue in under an hour.

Because making changes to your website is relatively easy, you have no excuse for not making regular improvements and updates to what you're offering. Giving the shop an overhaul doesn't just mean changing the colours or the layout on your website, which are the parts of your operation that customers notice. It also means jazzing up back-office functions that customers don't see, such as inventory management, invoices, labels, packing and shipping. You can also monitor how well your website is at keeping visitors interested in your site by using free website tracking tools. Just a few subtle improvements to the structure and content of your site can not only result in more people buying your product or using your service, but also helps it appear higher in search engine results pages and encourage more people to click on *your* website before anyone else's.

This chapter examines different ways to test, check and revise your website based on its current performance so that you can boost your revenue and increase sales as well as make your website more usable.

Bolstering Your Infrastructure

Every business has its foundations – some elements that give it a presence in the marketplace or in the place where it's physically located. For a traditional, bricks-and-mortar business this foundation may be an address or phone number, or the building in which the merchandise is presented and the employees work. That's how the post office gets mail to the business, and how the customers find the stuff you want to sell.

For an online business, your infrastructure is made up of the domain name that forms your web address, and the web server that presents your website files – which, in turn, present the merchandise you have for sale. Your server makes your site available, and your domain name, or URL, gives your customers a way to find you: together, they're the equivalent of your high street address and the physical space you rent. Over time, you may have to change your domain name – say, if customers complain that your site is too hard to find or your URL is too long. You may also need to find a new web server in order to keep your business running efficiently if any of the following occur:

- ✔ Your pages slow down.
- ✔ Customers complain that your forms don't work.
- ✔ You run out of storage space on your server, and your host wants to charge you armfuls of cash for more space.
- ✔ You receive too many visitors to your site, causing you to go over your allocated *bandwidth* or data transfer limit. You need to make other regular upgrades to your domain and/or your web server, as we describe in the following sections.

Renewing your domain name

As we explain in Chapter 3, you have a choice of two different types of domain names: one that's relatively short (for example, mynewebusiness.co.uk) and one that's long-winded and difficult to recall off the top of your head (myInternetprovider.co.uk/mynewebusiness). Even though the first type of domain name is obviously preferable, some individuals still start with the longer one when creating their first website. They get a certain amount of web server space along with their monthly access account from their Internet Service Provider (ISP). (BT Business, for instance, gives you 50 megabytes of free web space and TalkTalk gives you 14 megabytes.) These individuals' natural inclination is to use the directory space they're given (which has a long URL like the latter example) just to get the site started. Does this sound like you? There's nothing wrong with doing things the easiest way possible when you're a beginner, but be aware that your businesses will evolve as it grows. Before long, you'll need to find a domain name that more accurately fits your business or is easier to remember. Not only that, but you'll quickly find yourself running out of web space, or find it a pain to make sweeping changes to your website without a content publishing system or online sales catalogue in place.

Making your own name a domain

Even if you don't make it active right away, it's a good idea to lock up a name to give you the option of using it in the future. For example, creating a personal website may well still be on your to-do list. But if your name is Joe Bloggs, you may want to purchase the domain name `joebloggs.co.uk` for future use. If you don't, you may eventually have to deal with cyber squatters – the scourge of domain name buyers.

Cyber squatters are businesses that make money by buying up lots of domain names, knowing that at some point in the future, someone will want the domain name enough to buy it at a premium price. If your ideal domain name is owned by a cyber squatter or by another business, you may have to come up with a variation on your original name. When Greg was looking for domain names, for example, he was unable to buy `Holden.com` because a car manufacturer in Australia was already using it. However, he was lucky enough to find `gregholden.com` and snapped it up straight away – even though, at the time, he didn't have a home page of his own. Ad when Kim registered `kimgilmour.com` back in 2000, she didn't use it right away, but kept it 'parked' just in case anyone else should try to claim it.

You should be doing the same for your own name or your business's name right now. In July 2011, when News International shut down the *News of the World* after the phone hacking scandal, there was great speculation that it would launch a Sunday version of The Sun newspaper. Why? A quick look online reveals that News International Newspapers has taken control of the domains, `thesunonsunday.co.uk` and `sunonsunday.co.uk`.

In fact, if you're still thinking up your business's name, you should check that the URL is available before you get too attached to your ideas! Go to `www.whois.net` to see if someone's registered a .com, .net. or .org domain, and `www.nic.uk` for .uk domains.

Most domain name companies offer free *web forwarding*, a way to redirect visitors to your current website if they type in your URL. So if Joe Bloggs is still using the free space from his ISP, visitors could be redirected there by typing `www.joebloggs.co.uk`.

Another benefit of making your own name (or your business) a domain name is that you can use it to send and receive email, without having to rely on the email address provided by your ISP. So Joe Bloggs could use `joe@joebloggs.co.uk` for his email address by setting up a mailbox with the company that hosts his website. That way, if he changes his ISP in the future, he needn't worry about informing everyone of his change of address. You can also check email via web-based services like Gmail and Hotmail, so you can check it from anywhere you like!

Deciding which top-level domain name to use

Where does a business like yours get the easy-to-remember addresses you need? You purchase them from one of the approved domain name registrars. A *registrar* is a business that has been designated as having the responsibility for keeping track of the names registered in one of the top-level domains. Originally, six domains existed, but as .com, .co.uk and others became crowded, alternatives were eventually approved. The total list of domains is already bewildering enough, so we include a scaled down version of what currently exists in Table 8-1.

A *top-level domain* (TLD) is one of the primary categories into which addresses on the Internet are divided. It's the part of a domain name that comes after the dot, such as com in .com. A *domain name* includes the part that comes before the dot, such as wiley in wiley.co.uk. A fully qualified domain name includes the host name – for example, www.wiley.com or bbc.co.uk.

You can typically register a *generic* TLD (gTLD) worldwide, although some restrictions on their use exist (for example, only bona fide businesses can use .biz). A *country code* TLD (ccTLD) is the domain name associated with a country, such as .uk for the United Kingdom or .it for Italy. Registration restrictions apply for some countries, and others, like Tuvalu (.tv), have seen ccTLDs as a source of national income! A company might use a ccTLD to create unconventional domain names or very short, easy-to-remember ones. The URL-shortening service, bit.ly, which condenses long email addresses into short, easy-to-link-to ones, uses Libya's ccTLD.

Some top-level domain names aren't officially recognised by ICANN, the organisation that oversees the Internet. One such example is uk.com. Domain registry CentralNIC owns the uk in uk.com, and sells off what's technically second level domain names with the .uk.com at the end, such as music band Radiohead's online merchandise store found at www.waste.uk.com. CentralNIC also owns us.com and eu.com.

Table 8-1	Top-level Domain Names		
Domain Name	**Primary Use**	**In Original Six Domains?**	**Good for Online Businesses?**
.biz	Businesses	No	Yes, but still far less popular than .com or .co.uk
.com	Companies or individuals involved in commerce	Yes	Yes

Domain Name	Primary Use	In Original Six Domains?	Good for Online Businesses?
`.coop`	Co-operatives, such as the Co-operative supermarket at www. co-operative.coop	No	No, unless you are an eligible co-operative
`.co.uk`	Same as above, but for business located in the UK	No	Yes
`.eu`	Companies or individuals in Europe	No	Yes, if you're a Europe-wide company
`.gov.uk`	Government agencies	Yes	No
`.info`	Sites that provide information about you, your ideas or your organisation	No	Yes
`.name`	Any individual	No	No
`.net`	Network providers	Yes	Potentially
`.org`	Not-for-profit organisations or ventures	Yes	No
`.pro`	Licensed professionals	No	Potentially
`.travel`	Those in the travel and tourism industry	No	Potentially, if your business is eligible; bed and breakfasts, restaurants and car hire operators can register

Some of the newer domain names, of course, haven't really taken off. They were created in order to provide alternatives for organisations that couldn't find names in the original domains. In reality, big companies and other organisations are forced to keep buying up domain names to prevent others from trading on their good name.

A perfect example of why this is necessary occurred when Pricewaterhouse-Coopers, an accountancy firm, changed the name of its consulting arm to Monday. To spread the word, it bought the domain name www.introducing monday.com. It didn't buy the .co.uk equivalent, however, which was promptly snapped up by a group of tricksters with too much time on their hands. They created a website mocking the new name, a fact that helped to destroy the rebrand.

Having said that, one or two of the newer domains have gathered popularity. In particular, the .info name has taken off. According to its registry service, Afilias (www.afilias.info), it's the sixth largest domain on the Internet, with around half a million sites. Because virtually every business needs to put information about itself online, the .info domain is a good alternative if your first-choice domains aren't available.

And, with the new TLDs poised to revolutionise the way we access websites, the opportunities are virtually endless.

Certain domains are restricted only to particular types of individuals or organisations. For example, .gov.uk is restricted to government-funded groups, and .org.uk is restricted to noncommercial organisations, such as lobbies, trade unions and so on. In cases where a screening process isn't in place to ensure you're a legitimate and relevant business, these restrictions aren't observed very strictly. The .net domain, which was originally intended for network service providers such as ISPs and web hosts, is commonly used by businesses that can't find their ideal name in the .com or .co.uk domains, for example. You aren't limited to one domain, either.

Registering domain names related to yours

Even if you already have a domain name, paying a nominal fee to lock up a related name makes sense. That way, other businesses or cyber squatters can't attempt to register a domain that's like yours and possibly steal some of your visits. For example, Kim owns www.kimgilmour.com, but not www.kimgilmour.co.uk. To go about registering such a domain, follow these steps:

1. **Start up your web browser and go to a recognised domain name provider, such as Nominet, Easyspace, Ukreg, 123-reg or Freeparking. co.uk. You aren't restricted to UK registrars, either – plenty exist, such as the US-based AletiaNIC.com.**

   The home page for your choice opens.

2. **All domain name providers allow you to check whether your domain name is available, so type the name in the space provided and click Go.**

   In most cases, you see a screen saying 'Yes, it's available' or 'No, it's not'.

   If the domain name isn't available, the provider should offer alternative TLDs. If not, simply search again.

   If your domain is available, then snap it up as quickly as possible! Providers accept debit and credit cards, and domains vary in price from around £8 to around £25, depending on whether they're national (.co.uk) or international (.com). You usually pay less if you register your domain for a number of years at a time.

Most organisations that sell domain names also offer servicing such as hosting and design. If you're just starting out and are keen to get going with your website then give these services some thought; if not, ignore them.

Nominet may be the best-known registrar, but it's not the least expensive. You save money by shopping around for domain name registrars. A simple search using the phrase 'domain names' can turn up hundreds of options. A word of warning, though: mega-cheap deals are usually not all they seem. Make sure you have true control of your domain name, and that you'll be able to link your domain name to your chosen web hosting company's servers. Some rock-bottom domain name deals come with a catch in the small print: they tie you into using their own hosting services for a while. This can restrict you further down the line if you aren't happy with their offerings – much like tying yourself into an 18-month broadband or phone contract, but with far more severe consequences.

Finding a new web server

You should always consider the option of finding a new web host if you aren't happy with the one you have (as we mentioned in the previous section, make sure you have the ability to transfer your domain to your new web host). Chances are you're on a *shared* server that shares space with lots of other individuals and websites. If some of the organisations that share space on your server start streaming audio or video or experience heavy traffic, the performance of your website will likely suffer. You may even experience website downtime too. In either case, you should arrange with your hosting service to find a better web server to house your site or find another host altogether.

And although you may be happy accepting e-commerce payments via your website by redirecting people to PayPal or a payment service provider like WorldPay or Paypoint.net, things may get more complex if you decide to host all secure transaction files on your own website. In many cases, this may not be technically possible if you're sharing your computer with others (for more on accepting payments, see Chapter 11).

One upgrade you may consider is renting a *dedicated server* – a computer on which yours is the only website. This option is far more expensive than a shared hosting account, but after you've developed a customer base and have the resources, it may be worth it. Also consider the following factors that you may find with another host:

- ✔ **Data transfer or bandwidth capability:** The amount of data, in gigabytes, megabytes or kilobytes, of information that you're allowed to transfer each month before you're charged an additional fee. Successful e-commerce sites can quickly pile up thousands of page views per month, and if you go over your limit, you can get a shock when your bill arrives.

- ✔ **Marketing services:** Some web hosting services help you advertise your online business. For example, Easyspace (www.easyspace.com) offers business directory listings and search engine optimisation to improve your business's marketing reach.

✔ **Technical support:** When you're just starting an online business, you'll probably have questions you just can't answer or problems you can't solve on your own. Therefore, you should choose a host that can provide you with round-the-clock tech support.

Another option you have open to you is setting up your own web server using your broadband Internet connection. This option gives you total control over the management of your website. That sounds really nice, but keep in mind that it also means that if something goes wrong, it's your responsibility to get things up and running again. If you're ambitious and technically able (or know someone who is), you should consider the popular (not to mention free) web server program Apache (www.apache.org). You may want to consider an ISP that specialises in business services, such as BT or Zen.

Setting up and running a website in this way isn't for beginners. If your kids unplug or crash the computer on which your website is running, your business goes offline, which can cost you money. If your computer runs slowly or doesn't have enough memory, your site's performance may suffer. It's generally best for beginners to leave the hosting to professionals. Web hosts have the ability to purchase and maintain the best hardware available and have technicians on call to solve problems round the clock. If you leave the hosting to someone else, you have more time to focus on essentials such as building inventory, maintaining the content on your site and providing good customer service.

Performing Basic Web Housekeeping

To be better prepared to maintain and improve your website, you should visit it yourself on a regular basis. In fact, you should be the first one to view your pages when they go online; after that, you need to revisit as often as you can to make sure that your photos display correctly and that your links take you where you want them to go. We offer other helpful tips in the following sections.

All web browsers aren't created equally in the way that they handle colours, fonts and other web page elements. Be sure to visit your site by using different browsers in order to confirm that things work the way you want in all cases. At the very least, check your site with the two market leaders Microsoft Internet Explorer and Mozilla Firefox (www.mozilla.com); other popular browsers include Safari (www.apple.com/safari), Google Chrome (www.google.com/chrome) and Opera (www.opera.com). Another good idea is to ask your friends or family to take a look at your website and suggest improvements or amendments.

Microsoft's Internet Explorer 6 (IE6) is around ten years old, and the company is desperate to get people to stop using this unstable and product – we're already up to version 9. It wants to get IE6 usage down to 1 per cent, but it's currently still hovering at 10 per cent (33 per cent of Chinese still use it; and even in the UK just over 2 per cent are still on it). Microsoft has launched a special website that "counts down" the percentage of IE6 users. You can find it at `www.ie6count down.com` and help spread the word about shifting people off this browser.

Checking the technical mistakes

Your website might appear lovely on the outside, but does it pass the rigorous standards of the World Wide Web Consortium? This body, known as W3C, is responsible for releasing guidelines that help technical bods ensure that a website's structure, or its *information architecture*, is up to scratch. You can find a free W3C checker on the W3C website, `www.w3.org`. You simply type the URL of your website into the validator or, if it's not yet live on the web, you can upload the HTML file. The validator has helped Kim detect several problems on her London Photos blog (`www.londonphotos.org`). For example, the small, square picture (known as a favicon) that appears next to the web address wasn't showing up and Kim had no idea why until the W3C validator detected that she had been using an incorrect quotation mark in some of her code.

Try it yourself at `http://validator.w3.org` (you don't have to use your own website; you can use anyone else's). If your site passes muster, then you can display a W3C logo on your site that links to the validation page. We recommend following W3C standards as closely as possible, but please don't take it to heart if the validator finds more errors than you were expecting – it's not at all forgiving, and a lot of time you can ignore some of the so-called 'errors' in practice. When we checked, Amazon's website at `www.amazon.co.uk` had 591 'errors', yet it's one of the biggest sites in the world and has millions of happy customers! Check with your technical expert if you're unsure.

Making sure that your site is organised

One of the basic principles of e-commerce is that products must be easy to find. The way you organise your website defines whether customers find your products easily or get caught up in an impromptu game of hide and seek. The people who make a living writing about and designing websites call this *usability*. As long as the web has existed, experts have been studying what makes a website usable. Most agree on the following essential characteristics:

- ✔ **Keep it logical.** Create an organised path through your site that leads to your shopping trolley and checkout area.

- ✔ **Keep it simple.** Each one of your web pages should do one thing and one thing only.

- ✔ **Keep it searchable.** Shoppers who are in a hurry want to jump past all your sales categories, enter a product name in a search box and go straight to a page of search results that satisfy their enquiry. Give them the chance to do it.

✔ **Keep it navigable.** The best websites offer plenty of points at which users can return to the home page, check out or navigate back to a broad category.

You can add a search box to your site and have your pages indexed by a service from Google, Yahoo! or Bing. For more, see the step-by-step instructions in the section 'Ensuring that your site is searchable', later in this chapter, on how to add a search box to your website using Google.

Make sure that your site has a logical page flow. How many web pages do your customers have to click through before making their purchases? The general rule 'the fewer, the better' applies. Your goal is to lead shoppers into your site and then encourage them to search through your sales catalogue.

Adding navigational links

Another reason to review your e-commerce website is to evaluate the number of navigational buttons or other links you give your visitors. The most common options are a row of buttons or links across the top of the page and a column along the left side of the page. These spots are the most obvious places to put such links, but are by no means the only types of navigational aids you can add. Your goal should be to provide three types of links when the customer is viewing a sales item:

✔ Links that make it easy to 'back out' of the category the customer is in by following links to the previous level

✔ A link to your site's home page

✔ Links to other parts of your site so that shoppers don't need to return to the home page continually when they want to explore new parts of your site

The usability company Webcredible (www.webcredible.co.uk) releases an annual report on how well the UK's top 20 high street brands translate to the web. One of the best in 2010, receiving a score of 90 per cent, was the children's toy retailer Early Learning Centre. John Lewis also scored highly, with 91 per cent. As you can see in Figure 8-1, its website shows a range of useful links that appear on a catalogue page. Hover over any link and you see a range of sub-categories appear in a drop-down menu. Click through to any of these and you see links appear to related items and to other categories within the site.

Make a map of your website

When it comes to your e-commerce website, a *site map* can help you make your site easier to navigate for both humans and the search engine robots that index your site. It provides a snapshot of your website contents at a glance.

A traditional site map is a diagram that graphically depicts all the pages in the site and how they connect to one another. You don't need to provide a map if your site is small (say, only a few pages), but it can help if your site has lots of different areas to explore. Two main types of site map exist:

✔ The traditional one that is visible to your human visitors and created in HTML.

✔ The XML site map: a technical site map only visible by the major search engine robots, to help them understand your site's structure and index it better.

You can find a free online site map generator at www.xml-sitemaps.com that creates both HTML and XML site maps. It offers a paid-for version for more complex websites.

Keep in mind that you don't have to invest in a fancy (and expensive) software program in order to create a site map. You can also create one the old-fashioned way, using a pencil and paper. Or you can draw boxes and arrows, using a computer graphics program you're familiar with. The point is that your site map can be a useful design tool for organising the documents within your site.

Although not everyone clicks on an HTML site map, they give a great overview of what's on your site. Check out Google's HTML site map at: www.google.com/sitemap.html. Did you know that so much content lurks behind its simple home page?

Figure 8-1:
Highly visible links show the customer exactly what's on offer.

John Lewis © 2011

Ensuring that your site is searchable

The single most useful type of navigational aid is a *search box* – a text box into which visitors enter keywords to search your catalogue by product name or number. Here again, you have different options for adding such a box to your site:

✔ **The hard way:** You create a web page with a text box. You write a script that processes the data submitted by visitors. The server that hosts your site needs to be able to process such scripts. Usually, this require-ment means the server has to have the programming language present.

For example, if a script is written in the programming language Perl, the host needs to have Perl running on the server. Not all hosts allow the execu-tion of scripts on their servers, however; check with yours to make sure.

✔ **The less hard way:** You create a web page with a text box, but you borrow a script so that you don't have to write your own. You can use the popular Simple Search form at Matt's Script Archive (`www.script archive.com`).

✔ **The plug-in way:** You use a content publishing system, such as Wordpress, and install an add-on that lets you place your own searchable site index onto your site.

✔ **The easy way:** You sign up with a service that indexes your site – in other words, scours your web pages and records their contents – and provides you with a search box that you can add to your site.

✔ **The alternative way:** You get your website designed and built for you by a professional company, at a cost. In your brief to the company, you stipulate that you'd like users to search through your products. They'll do the rest for you.

Because the 'easy way' is the one that doesn't require any programming and is easiest for beginners, we describe it in more detail. Services that make other people's websites searchable usually provide two options. One is free, but the results that appear when someone searches your site have advertisements displayed as well. The other isn't free, but the search results *are* ad-free. These days, shoppers are so accustomed to seeing ads displayed all over the web that they probably won't be put off if some appear in your search results. So we wouldn't be reluctant to choose the free search option if it's available, and upgrade to a paid-for version later down the line after the ball gets rolling.

Google (as well as Yahoo! and Bing) make it easy to place a search box on a website, either on a free, ad-supported basis or on a subscription basis. Google's paid-for service (at `www.google.com/sitesearch`) looks a lot more professional, because the results can be woven seamlessly into your site on an ad-free basis. You pay $250 (£155) for up to 50,000 search queries a year, which won't break the bank and is ideal for small businesses. But the free version, Google Custom Search, is still hugely popular and highly effec-tive, and lets you create your very own mini-search engine.

Go to Google Custom Search's home page at www.google.com/cse. You'll need to log into the Custom Search Engine page using your Google Account details. If you already have a Gmail address or use any other Google service such as Blogger or YouTube, then you can use these credentials to log in. Otherwise, go to 'Create an account now' and follow the process to create a Google account (it's free). Next, follow these steps to add a custom search box to your site:

1. **Describe and define your search engine.**

   Enter a name for your search engine, such as Kim's Portfolio. Enter the URLs of the sites to search (you'll probably only have the one). Entering youronlinebusiness.co.uk/*, with the asterisk after the / and without the www. indexes all pages on that site. You can narrow this down; click 'Learn more' to find out how.

2. **Choose 'Standard Edition', which is the free, ad-supported version.**

   You can always upgrade later.

3. **Read and agree the Terms of Service, tick the box and click 'Next'.**

4. **Choose a look and feel.**

   Select a layout for your results pages that most closely resembles your website. You can click 'Customise' to then play around with the colour scheme and font selection.

5. **Test your search engine.**

   Under 'Try your search engine' you can see your Google Custom Search in action. Type in a keyword or two and see your results appear like magic! When you're happy, click 'Next'.

6. **Get the code.**

   A page appears with the Custom Search element code. You place this code in the page where you want your search box to appear. To copy the code, place the mouse pointer in the box and press Ctrl+C. But wait! You can still make refinements.

7. **Customise look and feel.**

   To further customise your search box's look and feel, access the Custom Search control panel. Go back to www.google.com/cse/ and click 'Manage my current search engines'. Next to your search engine, click 'Control panel'. Here you find many more options to refine the search engine you just created.

   On the left-hand side, you see plenty of options to further enhance your search results. Click 'Look and feel' to change your search result page layout to either full-width, compact or two-column results.

8. ***Now* get the code.**

   Click 'Get code' on the left and now you can paste the code into your chosen page, as we describe in Step 6. In Figure 8-2, you see the how the search box looks on Kim's website.

Figure 8-2:
Free site search services index your website contents and provide you with a searchable text box.

Do a search on your page to see how the service works. As you can see from Figure 8-3, ads are included in a search of Sean McManus's website. But because Kim searched for the term *eBay*, the ads are at least related to the topic – in other words, the ads are keyword-based.

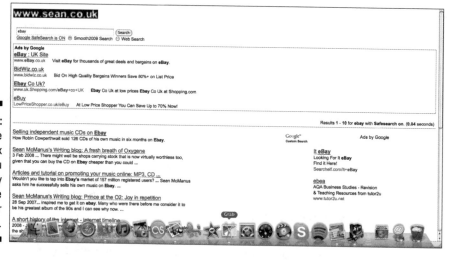

Figure 8-3:
A free search box requires you to display Google-type ads in your results.

Taking your site for a test run

After you've enhanced your website with navigational aids, search boxes and other changes, you need to visit it yourself to make sure that everything works the way you want. You not only need to make sure that your site creates a good visual impression, but also watch out for any problems you have to undo, such as:

- Background colours that are too similar to the colour of your body text and that make it hard to read
- Pages that are overcrowded, with insufficient room between columns or between images and text
- Errors in spelling or grammar
- Type that's too small that older viewers can't easily read
- Copyright notices or 'This site was last updated on . . .' messages that are old and out of date
- Factual statements that are no longer accurate
- Broken links
- Images that aren't cropped closely enough, which makes them bigger in file size than they need to be (which, in turn, makes them appear on screen too slowly)

Always reduce the dimensions of your images in your image-editing program before uploading them to your website. Don't make the mistake of uploading a massive, full-resolution image and simply reducing the dimensions you want it displayed at in your HTML. The large image won't go away – it'll display smaller, but will take a long time to load. It won't look any better, either.

It makes sense to perform such evaluations when you change your site. But you should test things whenever you move files from your computer to your web server. In order to know how to best make improvements, it's important to continue to test and make evaluations.

If you want an entertaining rundown of bad web design features to avoid on your own site, visit Web Pages That Suck (www.webpagesthatsuck.com). Author Vincent Flanders includes a feature called Mystery Meat Navigation that shows how *not* to guide visitors through your website.

It's easy to verify your website: Kim did it herself in a matter of minutes. Simply upload a small file to your web space containing a unique code and Google will know it's yours. It may take a little while for the statistics to roll in, but once they do, it provides an intriguing look into the mechanisms of the search world. For even more information about your visitors, Google Analytics is essential (www.google.com/analytics). We talk more about both these amazing (and did we mention free?) resources in Chapter 13.

Be an instant webmaster

A few years ago, the word *webmaster* might have conjured up images of a nerdy fellow sitting up the back scrawling through and tinkering with thousands of lines of computer code. But these days, you don't need to be a tech-head to know how to conquer the search engines and have visitors clamouring to knock on your business's virtual doors before anyone else's. You can do it for free, with a couple of mouse clicks. Think of Google Webmaster Tools (www.google.com/webmasters/tools) as a way of tuning up your site without the hard work (that might come later, depending on what needs fixing). Google Webmaster Tools informs you of any errors such as broken links, and you can see who links to your site, discover how many people click through to your site after it appears in Google's search engine results pages and much more.

Managing Goods and Services

Shoppers on the web are continually in search of The New: the next new product, the latest price reduction, the latest must-know information and up-to-the-minute headlines. As a provider of content, whether in the form of words or images or products for sale, your job is to manage that content to keep it fresh and available. You also need to replenish stock as it's purchased, handle returns and deal with shipping options.

Sourcing goods

Sourcing is a fancy term for buying items at a really low price so that you can sell them for a profit. For a small business just starting out on the Internet, sourcing isn't an easy prospect. Lots of online businesses advertise themselves as wholesale sellers. Many say they'll *drop-ship* their merchandise – in other words, ship what's purchased directly from their wholesale facility so that you never actually have to handle them and may never see them.

Sound too good to be true? In some cases, it is, and you should always exercise a healthy dose of caution when you're looking for wholesale suppliers. The eBay sellers we've talked to who have faithful, reliable wholesalers guard the identities of those suppliers jealously. They usually find such suppliers only by word of mouth: rather than answering an ad or visiting a website, they ask someone who knows someone who . . . you get the idea.

If you aren't in the business of selling goods or services that you manufacture yourself, you need to find a steady stream of merchandise that you can sell online. Your goal is to find a wholesaler who can supply you with good-quality items at rock-bottom prices; you can mark up the prices and make a profit while keeping the prices low enough to make them attractive. Generally, the best wholesale items are small objects that you can pack and ship inexpensively. On eBay, things like cheap watches, t-shirts, jewellery and other small gift items are commonly sold by PowerSellers, along with the occasional antique or collectible. Here are a few general rules for finding items you can sell:

- ✔ **Try them out yourself.** Purchase a few items yourself to start with or ask the wholesaler for samples. (Resist any attempts by the wholesaler to sell you, say, 10,000 items at a supposedly dirt-cheap price straight off the bat.) Take a few of the items for a test drive. It's easier to convince others to buy what you like yourself.

- ✔ **Try to sell many small, low-priced items rather than a few large ones.** Instead of computers or printers, consider selling computer memory chips or printer ink cartridges, for example.

- ✔ **Ask for references.** Talk to businesspeople who've already worked with the supplier. Ask how reliable the supplier is and whether the prices are prone to fluctuate.

When looking for merchandise to sell, try to build on your own hobbies and interests. If you collect model cars, try to develop a sideline selling parts, paints and components online. You'll find the process more enjoyable when you're dealing in things you love and know well.

Handling returns

Any organisation doing business in the UK has to comply with local legislation, right? Under the Distance Selling Regulations, businesses must offer a seven-day cooling off period so buyers can return unwanted, unused items (with some exceptions). All they need to do is inform you in writing, including email, of their intention to return the item, and you must give them a refund. Unless it's stipulated in the contract, you need to cover the delivery costs too. The cooling off period usually applies seven working days after the goods have been delivered to the customer. For more, see Chapter 14 and search for Distance Selling Regulations at www.businesslink.co.uk.

The Distance Selling Regulations also apply if you operate as a business and sell on eBay. Even if you're only an occasional private seller, you should accept returns, if only because many of the most experienced and successful sellers do too.

Adding shipping rates

As part of creating a usable e-commerce catalogue, you need to provide customers with shipping costs for your merchandise. Shipping rates can be difficult to calculate. They depend on your own geographic location as well as the location where you're planning to ship. If you're a small-scale operation and you process each transaction manually, you may want to ship everything a standard way (for example, via Royal Mail). Then you can keep a copy of your shipper's charges with you and calculate each package's shipping cost individually.

Maintaining inventory

Shoppers on the web want things to happen instantly. If they discover that you've run out of an item they want, they're likely to switch to another online business instead of waiting for you to restock your shop. With that in mind, obey the basic principle of planning to be successful: instead of ordering the bare minimum of this or that item, make sure that you have enough to spare. In other words, too much inventory initially is better than running out early (but you don't want to go overboard and end up with a room full of 4,000 green toilet roll holders).

Rely on software or management services to help you keep track of what you have. If you feel at ease working with databases, record your initial inventory in an Excel spreadsheet from Microsoft. This step forces you to record each sale manually in the database so that you know how many items are left. You can connect your sales catalogue to your database. For example, the accounting software QuickBooks can be linked to your shopping cart. Such a setup can update the database on the fly as sales are made. But you may need to hire someone with web programming experience to set the system up for you and make sure it actually works with the shopping cart you're using.

If you sign up with a sales management provider like Marketworks (www. marketworks.com/uk), inventory is tracked for you automatically. Marketworks is popular with eBay.co.uk auction sellers, but there's no reason why you can't establish an account with back-end functions such as payment, invoices and inventory management for any online business. Whether you do the work yourself or hire an outside service, you have to be able to answer basic questions such as

- **When should you reorder?** Points in your business cycle at which you automatically reorder supplies (when you get down to two or three items left, for example).

- **How many do you have in stock right now?** You need to forecast not only for everyday demand but also in case a product gets hot or the holiday season brings about a dramatic increase in orders. Know when stuff will be in demand (sunglasses in summer, for example) and buy accordingly.

An e-commerce hosting service may also be able to help you with questions that go beyond the basics, such as the past purchasing history of customers. Knowing what customers have purchased in the past means you can suggest additional items your customers may want. But in the early stages, make sure that you have a small cushion of additional inventory – you don't want demand to outstrip supply early on – that may dent your reputation just when you're trying to establish a good one!

Part III
Running and Promoting Your Online Business

'We only started our eBay business, webuyoldmasters.co.uk, this morning and the response has been amazing.'

In this part . . .

Going into business doesn't mean going it alone. For one thing, you don't necessarily want to quit your day job right away. You aren't ready to start making money online 24/7 and maintain the infrastructure that goes with an online business. Signing up with a well-known hosting service is like renting office space in a mall, except that in this case, your virtual landlord gives you a jump-start. In this part, you discover how to start making money with the help of online business stalwarts such as eBay. You also discover how to accept payments, provide top-notch service, and get on the radar of search engines.

Chapter 9

Easing the Shopping Experience

· ·

In This Chapter

▶ Understanding the purchasing needs of online consumers

▶ Obtaining technical help and support from your web host

▶ Choosing one of the major e-commerce hosting services

▶ Evaluating the performance of your website

▶ Gaining benefits by working with cloud-based services

· ·

*N*othing can compare to the emotional thrill you feel when you start your own new business and get it online. Nothing, that is, but the real excitement of getting paid for what you do. A pat on the back is nice, but it's even better to receive the proverbial cheque in the mail or have funds transferred to your business account.

When you're in an online business, financial transactions involve two important elements. First, you must take more care than a bricks-and-mortar shopkeeper to reassure customers (and make sure that they pay you promptly). You also need to protect your money. It's nice to know that, because e-commerce has been around for a few years, you have your choice of experts, services, and online tools that make your job easier. Even though independence may be one of the factors that you like most about running your own online business, you have plenty of demands on your time, and getting help is a sensible idea.

For example, the technical side of starting up a site doesn't have to be your concern. You don't have to spend years studying to be a programmer. Plenty of gizmos are available to help you create web pages, make links, keep your books and do other tasks online.

Time is on your side in this case because the range of software 'shortcuts' is becoming larger and more user friendly. You can create forms that process data and send it to you. You can keep track of your business expenses online, create banner ads and animations, hold video conferences and more. In this chapter, we suggest practices that reduce your business time-to-market as well as ways to share information more efficiently. Every hour you save by taking advantage of these services is an hour you can spend on another part of your business, or perhaps even relaxing.

Here's a short list of what you need to do to be a successful e-commerce businessperson: set up the right atmosphere for making purchases, provide options for payment and keep sensitive information private. Oh, and don't forget that your main goal is to get goods to the customer safely and on time.

Attracting and Keeping Online Customers

You've heard it before, but we can't emphasise enough the importance of understanding the needs and habits of online shoppers and doing your best to address them. When it comes to e-commerce, a direct correlation exists between meeting the needs of your customers and having a healthy balance in your bank account.

See your merchandise

Customers may end up buying an item in a brick-and-mortar shop, but chances are that they saw it online first. In fact, they often aren't interested until they read a detailed description and reviews. More and more shoppers are assuming that legitimate shops have a website and an online sales catalogue. Actually, these days a person is more likely to research a product online, go into a shop to see how it looks in person and then go back online to buy it because it's cheaper.

'It's not enough to just say we have this or that product line for sale. Until we actually add an individual item to our online shop, with pictures and prices, we won't sell it,' says Ernie Preston, who helped create an 84,000-item online catalogue for a bricks-and-mortar tool company. 'As soon as you put it in your online catalogue, you'll get a call about it. Shopping on the web is the convenience factor that people want.'

Don't hesitate to post as many items as possible on your online catalogue and don't scrimp on the amount of detail that you include about each item. Two great examples are clothing retailer Next (www.next.co.uk) and Pixmania (www.pixmania.co.uk). The first site is great because you can see exactly what you're getting (in different colours, at different angles and in great detail because you can zoom right in on the item), and the second site offers splendid descriptions of the stuff you're looking for. For more and more businesses, having an online catalogue is becoming an integral, not peripheral, part of their identity.

Tell me that the price is right, right now

Customers may have a lot of questions to ask you, but what they want to know first and foremost is how much an item costs. Be sure to put the cost right next to the item that you're presenting and indicate if this doesn't include value-added tax (VAT). Searching through a price list will lose the competitive edge of speed and convenience, which is what web shoppers want most. They don't have the patience to click through several pages. Chances are that they're comparison shopping and in a hurry.

The rise of price comparison websites like Kelkoo.co.uk, Confused.com and PriceRunner.co.uk has changed the way people shop. They can check out the cheapest price for almost any product. Leave out the price, or make it hard to find, and your customers will leave your website in droves.

TIP

Microsoft Office, the widely used suite of applications that includes Word, Excel and PowerPoint, gives you access to media libraries that help highlight sales items. Simply download the image that suits your business. Figure 9-1 shows an example of some of the many graphics in the Microsoft Office image library found at `http://office.microsoft.com/en-gb/images`.

Figure 9-1:
Use graphics to call attention to the information your customer wants the most: the price.

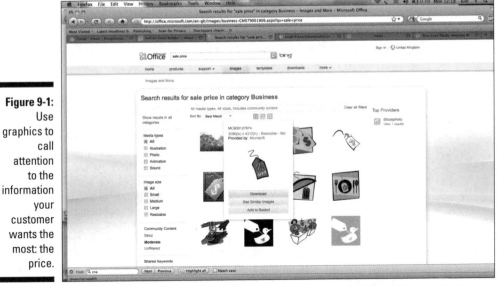

Show me that I can trust you!

Trust is the foundation on which every good relationship is built, and building trust is especially important for an online business. Despite e-commerce's maturity in recent years, plenty of customers still have fears:

> ✔ How do I know that someone won't intercept my name, phone number or credit card information and use the data to make unauthorised purchases?

✔ How can I be sure that your online business will actually ship me what I order and not 'take the money and run'?

✔ Can I count on you not to sell my personal information to other businesses that will flood me with unwanted emails?

How do you build trust online? If you run an eBay.co.uk shop, you have the advantage of being able to display a feedback rating, and customers can look up comments left on the site by previous customers. If you're not on eBay.co.uk, the best way to reassure people is to publish comments from satisfied customers. If you're really savvy, you'll have generated some press coverage (local usually, but national/international if you're very good), and the fact that you've been profiled by a newspaper or website adds to your legitimacy. Failing that, you need to state your policies clearly and often. Don't overdo it, though. Constantly reiterating that you'll keep information safe and that you honestly really, really will send customers their purchased goods will arouse suspicion rather than trust. If you plan to accept credit card orders, use a trusted payment service provider and make sure any software installed on your site is secure.

Give me the essentials; show me the products

Remember that one of the big advantages of operating a business online is space. You have plenty of room in which to provide full descriptions of your sale items. Be clever with your descriptions, however, and try not to bore people. Remember that people stick on a web page for a few moments unless something grabs them, so make your words jump out of the screen. Whatever you do, don't bang on about how great your products are and don't tell people stuff they already know. Customers (and people in general) hate being patronised. Here are some suggestions of how to provide information that your customer may want:

✔ If you sell clothing, include a page with size and measurement charts, display plenty of photos and use a model (a person or a dummy) to model the clothes. People like to see how things fit, and they can't do that if you display clothes folded up. Sites like Marks & Spencer and Next include size comparison charts to cater for their international customers. Look also at designer fashion website Net-a-Porter (www.net-a-porter.com) for examples of how you can use video to show off a product.

✔ If you sell food, provide weights, ingredients and nutritional information. More importantly, be very clear about what customers actually get for their money. Don't just say hamper – £35. Give some pertinent details about what goes in it!

✔ If you sell web design, artwork, calligraphy, poetry or anything else that needs to 'be seen', provide samples of your work, links to web pages you've created and testimonials from satisfied clients. Those into arts and crafts could consider peddling one-off designs on a ready-made marketplace like Etsy (www.etsy.com).

✔ If you're a musician, publish a link to a short sound file of your work or direct people to your Facebook or MySpace profile where people can listen to your tracks. Even better, link to a YouTube video of yourself playing your music.

Don't be reluctant to tell people ways that your products and services are better than others. Estate agents and auctioneers are very good at selling the quality of the things they're marketing. Check out www.foxtons.com and www.sothebys.co.uk for examples of how businesses play up their products.

Looking for a Good Web Host: The Lowdown

Time and again, we hear successful entrepreneurs extol the virtues of the companies that enable their businesses to go online. Why all the praise? Some web hosting services go beyond the basic tasks of providing space on a web server and keeping the server functioning smoothly.

Finding the right hosting company is one of the most important parts of building an online website that works. Whether you're building the site yourself, or getting a professional to do it, it's worth snooping for recommendations and referrals. Choosing a host that no one has recommended is unwise. No matter what type of website you run, you'll be handing over a substantial amount of money to your host – so make sure that the company is worth it.

See Chapter 3 for some more information on what you should look for in a host.

Before you sign up with a host, check out customer service options. Specifically, find out when service staff are available by telephone. Also ask whether telephone support costs extra. If you're working alone and don't have a technical person you can call, being able to speak to a technical support person about a problem you're encountering on your site can be invaluable.

It may seem surprising to think of your web host as one of the reasons for your success. After all, you do most of the work. At the most basic level, a hosting service is just a company that provides you with space on a server. You call them only when you have a problem or a billing question. At least, that's how most people look at their web host.

But the relationship with your host can go deeper than that, if you pay for the privilege. For example, FastHosts (www.fasthosts.co.uk) comes in for a lot of praise from novices and experts alike. It was created by an entrepreneur during the height of the dotcom boom when hosting companies were charging a fortune for their services. FastHosts strives to be cost-effective but reliable – and on the whole, it has achieved that goal. Basic hosting packages start at just £5.99 a month including VAT. For all hosting products you get unlimited bandwidth (traffic) no matter how successful your site becomes, so you won't ever need to pay more for this. But if you do invest a little extra (between £10.79 and £15.99 a month), you can command extra services that rise above standard deals:

- ✔ **Load balancing:** Basically, this feature means your website will almost certainly never go down. Because it's hosted across numerous servers, if one suffers a blip, then another one will seamlessly take over.

- ✔ **TrafficDriver:** FastHosts makes extra effort to get your website to the top of the world's most popular search engines, such as Google and Yahoo!.

- ✔ **Advanced password protection:** This feature helps if you run a membership-based organisation or if you want to confirm your service to a few paying customers. The passwords and logins are stored in a directory where you can add or delete at will.

- ✔ **Thirty-day money back guarantee:** This one is a very nice extra. If you're not totally happy with the service (and Dan reckons you probably will be), you can get your money back without quibble. Setup is free, and you can activate your account just about instantly.

Don't get locked in to a two- or three-year contract with a web host. Go month to month or sign a one-year contract. Even if you're initially happy with your host, a shorter contract gives you a chance to back out and go elsewhere if the company takes a turn for the worse or your needs change.

Domain name registration

People frequently get confused when Greg tries to explain how to register a domain name and how to 'point' the name at the server that hosts their websites. Your host usually also doubles up as a domain name registrar: the host provides a service that enables anyone to purchase the rights to use a domain name for one, two or more years. It's a kind of one-stop shopping: you can set up your domain name and, if the same company hosts your site, you can easily have the name associated with your site instead of having to go through an extra step or two of pointing the name at the server that holds your site.

But in order to avoid tying yourself to a hosting contract (see the previous section for more on this), you can purchase your domain name from a separate registrar rather than use your host's services. If you don't like your host but also bought your domain name from them, you might need to pay a maintenance fee if you want to move to a new registrar.

Kim registers all her domains through a company called Free Parking (www. freeparking.co.uk). Its website has changed little since Kim first used it in 2000 and they aren't the cheapest, but it's very convenient to manage all her domains through them and point them to new hosts whenever she feels like a change.

By *pointing* your domain name at your server, we mean the following: you purchase the rights to a domain name from a registrar. You then need to associate the name with your website so that when people connect to your site, they won't have to enter a long number called an IP (Internet Protocol) address, such as 76.345.23.10. Instead, they'll enter www.mybusiness.co.uk. To do so, you follow these steps (we're assuming your domain name registrar and your web host are separate companies; if not the process is simpler):

1. **Tell your web host the domain name you want associated with your website (www.yourbusiness.co.uk).**

   Your web host enters your domain details into the domain name system (DNS) and associates it with your website.

2. **Ask your web host for the information you need to give your registrar.**

   Typically, this includes your host's IP addresses (the addresses associated with your host servers). You need this information so your domain name can be matched up to your website. Also ask them for the website's *primary* and *secondary* name servers. These usually take the form ns.yourhost.com and ns2.yourhost.com.

3. **Log in to your registrar's website to assign your domain to your host.**

   You should see fields to maintain your domain name's DNS records. In the fields provided, enter the IP addresses provided by your host (usually in the A-record or address record field) as well as the name servers.

4. **Wait 24 to 72 hours for the records to update as they propagate across the Internet's domain name system.**

That's basically all there is to it. A few technical configurations exist, such as making sure that people who don't type in the www before your website name are still redirected, and 'locking' your domain to prevent anyone from hijacking it. Your registrar should have all the information you need about this and other issues.

When you're registering your site, you need to enter your contact details. This means your personal details including your name, address, email and phone number are accessible when people look up the details behind your domain name on sites like www.whois.net or www.whois.domaintools.com. The best thing to do is list your business details when buying your domain – not your personal telephone number!

Catalogue creators

Some of the biggest web hosts give you software that enables you to create an online sales catalogue by using your web browser. In other words, you don't have to purchase a web design program, figure out how to use it and create your pages from scratch.

On the downside, many of the host-provided catalogue creation tools are proprietary products and don't necessarily give you the ultimate control over how your pages look. You might be able to customise the HTML to some extent, but this might cost extra. On the plus side, however, if you have no interest in web design and don't want to pay a designer, you can use one of these tools to save time and money by getting your pages online quickly all by yourself.

Database connectivity

If you plan on selling only 5, 10 or even 20 or so items at a time, your e-commerce site can be a *static* site, which means that every time a customer makes a sale, you have to manually adjust inventory. A static site also requires you to update descriptions and revise shipping charges or other details by hand, one web page at a time.

In contrast, a *dynamic* e-commerce site presents catalogue sales items 'on the hoof' (dynamically) by connecting to a database whenever a customer requests a web page. Suppose, for example, that a customer clicks a link for shoes. On a dynamic site, the customer sees a selection of footwear gathered instantly from the database server that's connected to the website. The web page data is live and up to date because it's created every time the customer makes a request. For more on dynamic pages and how they can help your business, see Chapter 3.

If you need to create a dynamic website, another factor in choosing a web host is whether it supports the web page and database software that you want to use. If you want to use a database program such as MySQL, for example, you want a web host that allows you to create MySQL databases.

Payment plans

Handling real-time online transactions is one of the most daunting of all e-commerce tasks. Some web hosts can facilitate the process of obtaining a merchant account and processing credit card purchases made online. FastHosts.co.uk, for one, says you can make direct payments into your UK account at no extra cost.

BT eShop (`http://business.bt.com/domains-and-web-hosting/web-hosting/eshop/`), one of the longest-established web hosts, has a hosting plan especially for business beginners hoping to set up e-commerce websites. The service is incredibly simple and costs only £25 a month plus VAT (with no setup fees) for a fully functioning e-commerce site and two domain names. Of course, for this money, you're not going to set the world on fire with your design or functionality – but it's perfect for a part-time or hobby business. An 'elite' version of the service, which lets you add features like a blog or forum and allows up to 10,000 product listings, costs £45 a month plus VAT. After you've designed and built your website from one of 300 templates, you're able to add up to 2,000 different products to sell.

BT has recently done a deal with SagePay so you can use this payment platform on your site. eShop is also compatible with a range of other payment systems like PayPal, WorldPay and more that you can integrate through its website.

In any case, you still have to set up your website, catalogue and shopping trolley pages, and you still have to ship out your items and answer your customers' questions. But having your web host provide you with the sales and payment tools, along with the availability to answer your questions, removes part of the burden.

Seeing What Social Media Can Do for Your Business

The prevalence of social networking sites like Twitter and Facebook means that advising companies on how they can use these sites to boost their bottom lines is big business. You can tap into social media through targeted advertising, or by using the sites to create pages dedicated to promoting your products and then cultivating a fan base. Because trends on social networks spread like wildfire, you don't need to build up a huge following to suddenly get more people 'liking' your page on Facebook, 'retweeting' you on Twitter or 'following' you on YouTube. But in order to get those interactions, you do need to be providing people with something worth responding to!

The key is *not* to just plonk your business onto Twitter and Facebook and start going on about how wonderful you and your products or services are, but to have a coherent marketing plan in place and connect with your followers.

Graham Cluley, technology consultant at the anti-virus software company Sophos, has built up a reputation as a prominent media spokesperson on security-related issues. He posts frequently to his Twitter page at www.twitter.com/gcluley, linking to articles related to security glitches and scam alerts. He also maintains a more detailed security blog on the Sophos website. This is an example of a company using social media to build up brand awareness while also delivering genuinely useful information from an approachable, well-known person in the industry.

In Chapter 4 we discuss detailed, step-by-step ways in which you can use social media to add value to your business, and include a case study outlining the benefits of using the new generation of web tools to build interest and momentum in a product.

Boosting Business through Efficient Communication

In the earlier sections of this chapter, we show you how your web host can help you create catalogues, process payments, obtain domain names and perform other business tasks. However, sometimes the tasks that aren't directly related to marketing and sales can actually enable you to improve your profit margin by giving you more time to do marketing and sales. If you can use the Internet to communicate with vendors, co-workers and other business partners, you increase efficiency, which, in turn, enables you to take care of business.

Efficiency involves getting everyone on the same page and working together, if not at the same time, at least at the *right* time.

Plenty of collaborative software (also known as groupware) and services give you the right tools to take care of business. Email is the most obvious example, but other things that fall under this banner include sharing Word, Excel and PowerPoint documents using the Google Cloud Connect plugin for Microsoft Office (http://tools.google.com/dlpage/cloudconnect); collaborative brainstorming and mind-mapping with MindMeister (www.mindmeister.com); shared to-do lists with Tada List (www.tadalist.com) or TaskBin (www.taskbin.com); and video chat and video conferencing with Skype (www.skype.com). You can also categorise under groupware things such as a calendar, an address book, a to-do list and email, so that members of a workgroup can co-ordinate their schedules.

Figure 9-2 shows how Google Cloud Connect (currently only available for Windows) lets people share and collectively edit Microsoft Office documents. Google hosts your files and keeps track of revisions. For more on cloud computing, see the section 'Outsourcing Your Business Needs', later in this chapter.

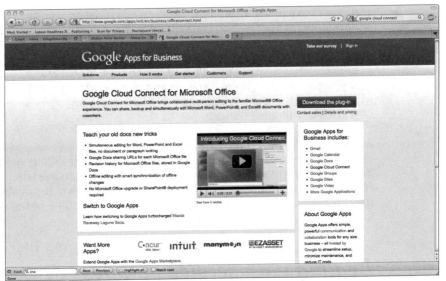

Figure 9-2:
Google Cloud Connect lets multiple people share and edit documents. It works offline, too – when you're back online, changes you've made are synced to Google's servers.

Making Sure That Your Website Is Up to Scratch

It's tempting to just get your website online and then forget about it. It's up to your hosting service to monitor traffic and make sure that everything's up and running. That's their job, right?

It *is* their job, to be sure, but unless you keep an eye on your site and its availability to your customers, you may not be aware of technical problems that can scare potential business away. If your site is offline periodically or your server crashes or works slowly, it doesn't just waste your customers' time – it can cut into your sales directly. Luckily, some shortcuts help you monitor your website, and they don't take a lot of time and effort or technical know-how.

Using software to monitor performance

A number of programs are available for anywhere up to a few hundred pounds that continually keep an eye on your website and notify you of any problems. Such programs take effort to install. But the effort required to get them up and running has a big benefit – you know about setbacks at least as soon as your customers do, if not before.

You don't have to install your own software in order to monitor your website's performance, of course. You can sign up with a company that offers such monitoring as a service. In this case, you use the company's software, which resides on its computers, not yours. For example, Site Confidence (www. siteconfidence.com) provides an online service that checks your site's logins, search facility, upload speeds and email servers periodically to see whether everything is working correctly. The company offers several levels of service to suit most budgets.

Another company that provides this service is Pingdom (www.pingdom. com), which costs £6 for a basic setup of up to five sites. Pingdom frequently 'pings' your site at server locations around the world to see whether they respond. You get a text message if your website is down. It can also tell you the error message it received and how long any downtime lasted (see the following section on what to do when this happens).

Dealing with service outages

Ideally, your web host provides a page on its website that keeps track of its network status and records any recent problems. One site monitoring notification (from a program you install yourself or one that you 'rent' as a service from a cloud provider – see the next section 'Outsourcing Your Business Needs') probably shouldn't be cause for concern. However, when you receive a series of notifications, call your web hosting service and talk to its technical staff. Be courteous, but specific. Tell technical support exactly what the problems are/were. You may even want to print the reports you receive so that you can be aware of the exact nature of the problems. Web hosts can no longer excuse regular service outages; plenty of service providers out there promise that your site will almost never go down. To avoid these problems, go for a host that has good track record and a long list of satisfied customers.

If the problem with your site is a slow response to requests from web browsers rather than a complete outage, the problem may be that your server is slow because you're sharing it with other websites. Consider moving from shared hosting to a different option. In *colocation*, you purchase the server on which your files reside, but the machine is located at your web host's facility rather than at your own location. Your site is the only one on your machine. You also get the reliability of the host's technical support and high-speed Internet connection.

If you really need bandwidth, consider a *dedicated server*. In this case, you rent space on a machine that's dedicated to serving your site. This arrangement is far more expensive than sharing a web server, and you should choose it only if the number of visits to your site at any one time becomes too great for a shared server to handle. You know a shared server is becoming overtaxed if your site is slow to load. Discuss the situation with your host to see whether a move to a dedicated server makes sense.

Outsourcing Your Business Needs

One of the most effective ways to save time and money doing business online is to let someone else install and maintain the computer software that you use. *Outsourcing* is now a common method of business, but in terms of e-commerce, it refers to the practice of using an online service to perform various tasks for you, such as web hosting, form creation, data storage, applications or financial record-keeping rather than installing software and running it on your own computer. Outsourcing isn't anything mysterious, however: it simply refers to the practice of having an outside company provide services for your business.

Companies that provide web-based services on an outsourced basis are known as *cloud providers* to mainstream folk, but you might also hear the term *software as a service* (SaaS) or *application service provider* (ASP) being bandied about. Essentially, all three terms mean the same thing – they all refer to a company that makes business or other applications available on the web. You and your colleagues can then use those applications with your web browser instead of having to purchase and install special software. The latter two terms are (in Internet terms) old-fashioned and originate from the larger corporate companies that first offered hosted solutions; which were often far costlier than the many cheap or free products available today.

You're probably already using cloud services in everyday life. For example, if Google stores all your mail with none of it sitting on your home machine, then you're using Google as a cloud provider for your messaging. Or if you create a web shop page on eBay.co.uk by filling out a form and choosing a design, eBay provides the cloud computing service.

Google provides plenty of cloud-based services through Google Apps (www.google.com/apps/intl/en/business) and Amazon has been in on the act for a few years (see the sidebar 'Amazon Web Services', later in this chapter).

Another advantage of cloud computing is collaboration. You don't have to be in the same place as a colleague to work on a document together. Microsoft Office Web Apps lets you edit Word documents, PowerPoint presentations, spreadsheets and OneNote notebooks all from the comfort of your web browser.

You can either use cloud computing from the ground up if your business is new, or integrate it with your existing infrastructure.

How cloud services can help your company

Amazon Web Services (see the sidebar later in this chapter) uses a great analogy to describe cloud computing; likening it to the energy grid. 'When companies were freed from having to create their own electricity, they were able to focus on the core competencies of their line of business and the needs of their customers,' it says. In much the same way, cloud computing lets businesses concentrate on their business rather than things like 'compute power, storage, databases, messaging and other building block services'.

In the past five years, cloud services have matured immensely to the point where many rely on them to manage a huge part of their businesses. One of the biggest providers is Salesforce.com, which provides cloud computing services to 100,000 customers big and small – but plenty of alternatives exist too. Some of the most popular ways in which cloud services can help your business include:

- **Payroll and administration:** Intuit Online Payroll (formerly Paycycle) provides an easy-to-operate web-based payroll solution, aimed specifically at people like you. It integrates with Intuit QuickBooks so you can export employee and contractor data to your accounting software and it takes just a couple of minutes to make a payment. Like with most services of this type, the cost depends on how many people you employ. An online calculator gives you the pricing structure – see www.paycycle.com for more.

- **File storage and bandwidth:** By using the massive resources of a huge cloud computing provider you can store images from your vast catalogue, along with videos and other multimedia files. Should your business get immensely popular, your current hosting plan may not be enough to suit your needs – but storage in the cloud could be cheaper than upgrading to a different plan. No end of providers are available and you typically only pay for the capacity you use.

- **Email marketing campaigns:** In Chapter 12, we discuss how email marketing provider VerticalResponse can help you create email templates from scratch and monitor email marketing campaigns. You control everything from within your web browser – you can save newsletters, create new ones, design templates and manage email lists.

- **Online form creation:** FormSite.com (www.formsite.com) is a leader in creating a variety of forms that can help online shoppers provide such essential functions as subscribing to newsletters or other publications, asking for information about your goods and services, or providing you with shipping or billing information. The sample bed and breakfast reservation form shown in Figure 9-3 asks for the guest's name and address as well as particulars about dates and room type.

- **Marketing and survey data gathering online:** LeadMaster (www.leadmaster.com) calls itself an 'online lead management system'. You store your customer information with LeadMaster, and LeadMaster provides you with an online database that you can access any time with your web browser. It enables you to develop mailing lists based on your customer database. You can use LeadMaster's online tools to do sales forecasting and develop surveys that give you a better idea of what your customers need and want.

Figure 9-3:
A cloud
provider like
FormSite.
com lets
you create
a database-
backed web
page fea-
ture, such as
a feedback
form, with-
out having
to purchase,
install and
master a
database
program.

- ✔ **Collaboration:** Google Apps and Microsoft Office Web Apps let you and your colleagues review, edit and access documents from within a central-ised location, saving on the technical trouble of networking storage sys-tems and having to physically be in the same office to view documents.

- ✔ **Website monitoring:** Services provided by companies like Pingdom.com (see the earlier section 'Using software to monitor performance') make sure your site is still up and running. You don't want to lose any busi-ness through downtime!

- ✔ **Content management:** You can update your website using a content management system installed on your website server, but other providers make this possible while hosting the whole shebang on their own serv-ers instead. Adobe Business Catalyst is one product that lets you operate your entire e-commerce site in the cloud – you access all your design elements from within a web browser. Create forms, design templates, manage customer databases, set up an online shop and more. Adobe claims you only need 41 seconds of your time to sign up and try out the service, which at the time of writing costs around £5.50 a month for a starter plan to around £24 a month for a pro service (you'll be billed in US dollars). To compare plans and features go to www.businesscatalyst.com, whose homepage is shown in Figure 9-4.

Although cloud service providers can help you in many ways, they require research, interviewing, contract review and an ongoing commitment on your part. When does the extra effort make sense? We illustrate the potential pluses and minuses of the cloud in Table 9-1.

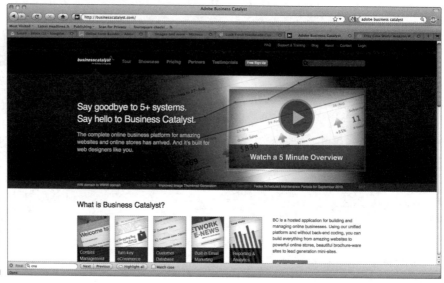

Figure 9-4:
Adobe
Business
Catalyst lets
you set
up your
entire website
from within
your web
browser– no
programming
experience
required.

Table 9-1	Cloud Computing Benefits and Risks
Pros	*Cons*
Time-saving: Cloud computing is convenient as you can access it from anywhere. Saving time can save you money in the long run.	**Lack of customisation:** You rely on the cloud service provider's way of doing things.
Saves on staff: Small businesses can't afford to fork out for a dedicated IT support person. Cloud computing means someone else handles the day-to-day technical issues – and is also at the other end of the phone if you ever do need help.	**You need to be online:** Everyone is online in some form or another nowadays, but if your Internet connection is down or if you're on holidays in remote Scotland and your smartphone can't get reception, then you won't be able to access the latest business information in the cloud.
Better customer service: By outsourcing scheduling or other functions, businesses give customers more options for interacting with them online. Customers don't have to call or email the company; in the case of online scheduling, customers can schedule or cancel appointments by accessing the company's online calendar.	**Loss of 'control':** Although cloud providers will take considerable care to manage your data, you need to be comfortable with leaving a large chunk of your business information with them – emails, memos, personal customer details and sensitive marketing details are just a few of the things they could be storing and managing. That said, it's just as easy for a laptop containing all this information to be stolen.

Pros	*Cons*
Greater website functionality: Cloud services enable your site to provide better service to your customers and allow you to get more work done.	**Cloud providers face stiff competition:** The market is very crowded and several providers have failed in recent years. Make sure that the companies you sign agreements with will be around for a while by talking to current customers and reviewing CVs of senior staff and key employees. Scan the web for any press releases or articles that serve as warning signs about the provider's financial health.
Expanded scope: You don't have to become proficient in subjects that aren't part of your core business or expertise.	**Security risks:** The moment you hand over your business data to another online firm or give outside companies access to your internal network, you risk theft of data or virus infections from hackers. Make sure that the cloud providers you work with have a good track record and use encryption and other Internet security measures. (See Chapter 7 for more on website security.)
Scalable: As your business grows, you don't need to invest in costly infrastructure or expensive software upgrades. This is all handled for you in the cloud, which adapts as your business grows.	**Potential downtime:** Although cloud providers go out of their way to provide 24/7 uptime, their servers or their network could still go down – the Internet phone service Skype was down for a number of days in late 2010 due to a technical glitch, causing thousands of (paying) businesses across the globe headaches and lost opportunities in sales because they were unable to log on and make and receive calls.
Tap into social media: You can use mainstream tools like Facebook to gain insight into your customers. By setting up a Facebook page dedicated wholly to your company, you can see exactly where they come from, as well as other key demographics, which can help you understand your customers.	**Confusing pricing structures:** No real 'standard' pricing structure exists with cloud providers. Some are free, some have a monthly fee, others depend on data usage, some charge per user. A bit of a learning curve exists.

Outsourcing not only improves your company's bottom line, but also helps you convey your message to potential customers that you may never reach otherwise.

Amazon Web Services

Amazon's known for selling books and other stuff, right? Well, yes, but you may not know that Amazon also offers a whole range of hosted cloud-based services to help make life easier for countless businesses across the globe (particularly technology startups who want a powerful environment where they can test their great ideas).

You need technical knowhow to get to grips with Amazon Web Services (AWS) and it's not designed for everyone. But we think it's worth mentioning how far AWS reaches across the globe. All kinds of businesses that want to tap into Amazon's immense computing and storage resources use AWS.

Although the services are more than what a typical reader of this book will need (at least initially) AWS does cater for businesses of all sizes and offers a generous free usage tier. You only pay for what resources you use, without having to fork out any money upfront (you need a credit card to register but you can cancel at any time).

Many big-name sites use AWS to host images, deliver streaming content and send emails across Amazon's servers. Famously, AWS used to host content from WikiLeaks but decided to stop doing so in December 2010 after claiming Wikileaks contravened its terms of service by uploading documentation it didn't own. Some of the services it can offer include:

- ✔ **Amazon Simple Storage Service (S3):** A convenient way to store data such as images. Also suitable for backing up crucial information.

- ✔ **Amazon Elastic Compute Cloud:** With this service, you rent servers to act as virtual machines in the cloud. Using a pay-as-you-go method, you can place any application of your choosing on Amazon servers. Games company Playfish, popular for its Restaurant City social game, grew from 22 million users to 55 million in 2009. It was able to handle the increase in popularity by taking advantage of Amazon's scalable capacity.

- ✔ **Amazon Auto Scaling:** You can specify when you want server capacity to go up or down depending on predicted usage spikes. For example, in the run-up to Christmas, you might expect triple the usual capacity.

- ✔ **Elastic Load Balancing:** By putting your website across several servers and sharing the load, you reduce the risk of downtime.

- ✔ **CloudFront:** Amazon can deliver streaming content and hosts your data at locations across the globe. It taps into the data you store using S3.

Many more ways exist in which AWS can manage business applications. For more information, including a more comprehensive list of products, go to Amazon Web Services at `http://aws.amazon.com`.

A good place to find out more about the latest up-and-coming companies – cloud or not – is Mashable (`www.mashable.com`), which features the best in social apps and cloud-based tools. Another is ReadWriteWeb's cloud computing channel at `www.readwriteweb.com/cloud`. Searching Google News or Yahoo! news for a company you're interested in is worth a go. If you don't find any positive mention of the company in the press, then it's probably not well-established enough for you to take a chance on.

The Business Link website provides some handy, commonsense advice about what to look for in a cloud provider. Go to `www.businesslink.gov.uk` and search for *cloud computing*.

Before you sign on the dotted line . . .

Make sure you try out the software before committing yourself. All good cloud providers give you an opportunity to try their product out first. You usually need to sign a contract to keep using the service or at least provide a credit card to keep up the monthly payments. This step is the time to slow down and read the fine print. Is there an annual commitment? Or can you pay monthly? If it's a pay-as-you-go setup, what are the actual rate cards if you happen to use up a lot of storage space or bandwidth?

Don't rush, even if you're experiencing the time-to-productivity pressures, merger upheavals or lack of IT resources that drive many companies to outsource. In the following list, we present some suggestions to help you get the service you should be getting:

- **Understand pricing schemes.** Does the cloud provider charge per user account? Or does it depend on data usage? Is there a flat monthly fee? Google Apps charges £30 per user, which includes 25GB of storage space for every user.

- **Pin down startup fees.** How much does it cost to set up? Does the price include any customisation that may be required?

- **Don't accept just any SLA.** Obtaining a *service level agreement* (SLA), a document that spells out what services you expect a cloud provider (or other vendor) to provide, is essential. Google Apps has a 99.9 per cent SLA. But regard the SLA as a dynamic document. Think of SLA as standing for Stop, Look and Adjust.

- **Avoid 'gotcha' fees.** One disadvantage with cloud providers is the inconsistent, non-standard pricing arrangements. Some of the big hidden costs involve personalising or customising the service to adapt to legacy systems. Here are some questions you can ask in order to avoid wincing at 'gotchas' when you open up the bill from your cloud provider:

  - Is there an additional cost for customising or personalising the application?

  - Does it cost extra to back up my company's data and recover it if one of my computers goes down?

  - Is help desk support included in my monthly fee, or will you charge me every time I call with a question or problem?

✔ **Make sure that you have security.** Having information reside on some-one else's system is a double-edged sword. Putting this data on the web makes it accessible from anywhere. But some huge security risks are associated with transmitting your information across the wide-open spaces of the Net. Make sure that your provider takes adequate security measures to protect your data by asking informed questions, such as:

- Is my data protected by SSL encryption?

- Do you run a virtual private network?

- How often do you back up your customers' data?

If the answer to any of these questions seems inadequate, move on to the next provider – plenty are out there, and competition among them is fierce. So right now at least, it's a buyer's market, and you should be able to get what you want.

Chapter 10

Running a Business on eBay.co.uk

*T*hroughout the credit crunch, one marketplace has remained a strong, reliable presence for those wanting to grab a bargain or make a bit of extra cash. As you probably know, it's eBay – and chances are you've bought or sold some things yourself at the world's most popular auction site.

A difference exists, though, between selling occasionally in order to make a few extra quid and doing what thousands have already done: selling on eBay.co.uk as a means of self-employment. For the lucky ones, eBay is truly a lucrative opportunity. The marketplace has defied the odds, churning out a tenfold increase in £1 million businesses trading via the site since 2007, rising to more than 100 by 2010. Of the 66 businesses that enjoyed £1 million turnover in 2009, only 8 experienced a dip in revenue.

In the UK alone eBay has 160,000 registered businesses using the site to reach a global audience. It's a full time job for many, while countless others sell through the auction site on a permanent part-time basis to earn a little sideline cash. Whatever the reason, you can't overlook eBay.co.uk as a way to get a first business off the ground. With eBay, you don't necessarily have to create a website, develop your own shopping trolley or become a credit-card merchant: the auction site itself handles each of those essential tasks for you. But that doesn't mean that developing your own eBay business is easy. It takes hard work and commitment, combined with the important business strategies we describe in this chapter. For a more in-depth assessment of starting and running a business on eBay.co.uk, check out Kim's co-authored book *eBay.co.uk Business All-in-one For Dummies* (Wiley, 2009).

Running a business on eBay.co.uk doesn't necessarily mean that you depend on eBay as the sole source of your income. You may sell on eBay.co.uk part-time for some supplementary income each month. This chapter assumes that you want to sell regularly on eBay and build up a system for successful sales that can provide you with extra money, bill-paying money or 'fun money'.

Understanding eBay.co.uk Selling Formats

In any contest, you have to know the ground rules. Anyone who's held a garage sale knows the ground rules for making a person-to-person sale. eBay has long been famous for its auctions, but over the past few years it's shifted its focus to fixed-priced items sold through the site. And for business sellers who choose to open a customisable eBay shop, listing large lots of fixed-price items at once is now more cost effective.

eBay.co.uk still hasn't abandoned its auction roots and continues to give its members many different ways to sell, and each sales format has its own set of rules and procedures. It pays to know something about the different sales so that you can choose the right format for the item or items you have.

This section assumes that you have some basic knowledge of eBay.co.uk and that you've at least shopped for a few items and possibly won some auctions.

When it comes to putting items up for sale, eBay gets more complicated. You've got the following sales options:

- **Standard auctions:** This is the most basic eBay auction. You put an item up for sale, and you specify a starting bid (usually a low amount because you want to generate interest in your item). If you don't have a reserve price, the highest bidder at the end of the sale wins (if there is a highest bidder). Standard auctions and other auctions on eBay can last three, five, seven or ten days. The ending time is precise: if you list something at 10:09 a.m. on a Sunday and you choose a seven-day format, the sale then ends at 10:09 a.m. the following Sunday.

- **Reserve auctions:** A *reserve price* is a price you specify as a minimum in order for a purchase to be successful. Any bids placed on the item being offered must be met or exceeded; otherwise, when the sale ends the seller isn't obligated to sell the item. You know whether a reserve price is present by the message Reserve Not Yet Met next to the current high bid. When a bid is received that exceeds the reserve, this message changes to Reserve Met. The reserve price is concealed until the reserve is met (unless you choose to mention it in your listing description).

- **Fixed-price Buy It Now sales:** A Buy It Now price is a fixed price that the seller specifies. The seller specifies that you can purchase the item for, say, £10.99; you click the Buy It Now button, agree to pay £10.99 plus postage and packing if applicable and you instantly win the item. You find fixed price items in all eBay.co.uk shops and individual sellers can also list Buy It Now items.

- **Auction format with Buy It Now option:** You can offer Buy It Now prices in conjunction with standard or reserve auctions. In other words, even though bidders can place bids on the item, if someone agrees to pay the fixed price, the item is immediately sold and the sale ends. If a Buy It Now price is offered in conjunction with a standard auction, the Buy It Now price is available until someone placed the first bid; then the Buy It Now price disappears. If a Buy It Now price is offered in conjunction with a reserve auction, the Buy It Now price is available until the reserve price is met. After the Buy It Now price disappears, the item is available to the highest bidder.

Those are the basic types of sales. You can also sell cars on eBay.co.uk Motors or even your home (check out `property.shop.ebay.co.uk`). By knowing how eBay.co.uk sales work and following the rules competently, you'll gradually develop a good reputation on the auction site.

How you sell is important, but the question of exactly *what* you should sell is one you should resolve well before you start your eBay.co.uk business, just like in any business. Sell something you love, something you don't mind spending hours shopping for, photographing, describing and eventually packing up and shipping. Sell something that has a niche market of enthusiastic collectors or other customers. More importantly, sell something that *isn't already there* or for which clearly a lot of demand exists. Do some research on eBay.co.uk to make sure that a thousand people aren't already peddling the same things you hope to make available.

Building a Good Reputation

In order to run a business on eBay.co.uk, you need to have a steady flow of repeat customers. Customer loyalty comes primarily from the trust that's produced by developing a good reputation. eBay.co.uk's feedback system is the best indicator of how trustworthy and responsive a seller is because past performance is a good indication of the kind of service a customer can expect in the future. Along with deciding what you want to sell and whether you want to sell on eBay.co.uk on a part- or full-time basis, you need to have the development of a good reputation as one of your primary goals.

Feedback, feedback, feedback!

eBay's success is due in large measure to the network of trust it has established among its millions of members. The feedback system, in which members leave positive, negative or neutral comments for the people with whom they've conducted (or tried to conduct) transactions, is the foundation for that trust. The system rewards users who accumulate significant numbers of positive feedback comments and penalises those who have low or negative feedback numbers. By taking advantage of the feedback system, you can realise the highest possible profit on your online sales and help get your online business off the ground.

Customer service levels are also paramount and when buyers leave feedback they also have the opportunity to rate sellers out of five stars on four important criteria: Item as Described, Communication, Dispatch time and P&P Charges. Buyer ratings are averaged to give the seller a Detailed Seller Rating (DSR) score.

There probably aren't any scientific studies of how feedback numbers affect sales, but we've heard anecdotally from sellers that their sales figures increase when their feedback levels hit a certain number. The number varies, but it appears to be in the hundreds – perhaps 300 or so. The inference is that prospective buyers place more trust in sellers who have higher feedback numbers because they have more experience and are presumably more trustworthy. Those who have PowerSeller status, denoted by the PowerSeller icon, are even more trustworthy (see the 'Striving for PowerSeller status' section, later in this chapter).

Developing a schedule

One thing that can boost your reputation above all else on eBay.co.uk is timeliness. If you respond to email enquiries within a few hours, or at most a day or two, and if you can ship out merchandise quickly, you're virtually guaranteed to have satisfied customers who leave you positive feedback. The way to achieve timely response is to observe a work schedule.

It's tedious and time consuming to take and retake photos, edit those photos, get sales descriptions online and do the packing and shipping that's required at the end of a sale. The only way to come up with a sufficient number of sales every week is to come up with a system. And a big part of coming up with a system is developing a weekly schedule that spells out when you need to do all your eBaying. Table 10-1 displays a possible schedule.

Table 10-1	eBay Business Schedule	
Day of Week	*First Activity*	*Second Activity (optional)*
Sunday	Get seven-day sales online	Send end-of-sale invoices
Monday	Packing	Emails
Tuesday	Shipping	Emails
Wednesday	Plan car boot sales	Take photos
Thursday	Go to car boot sales	Prepare descriptions
Friday	More sales	Prepare descriptions
Saturday	Respond to buyer enquiries	Get some sales online

You'll notice that something is conspicuously missing from this proposed schedule: a day of rest. You can certainly work in such a day on Sunday (or whatever day you prefer). If you sell on eBay.co.uk part time, you can probably take much of the weekend off. But most full-time sellers (and full-time self-employed people in general) will tell you that it's difficult to find a day off, especially when it's so important to respond to customer emails within a day or two of their receipt. You don't have to do everything all by yourself, however. You can hire full- or part-time help, which can free up time for family responsibilities.

In the UK after you sell items intending to make a profit on eBay you're considered a business – not just by eBay, but by the tax authorities. So be sure to change your personal eBay account to a business one as soon as possible. Go to `pages.ebay.co.uk/services/registration/businesslanding.html` to start the new business account registration process. Don't worry, you'll keep all the positive feedback you've accumulated!

Sharing your expertise

One of the best ways to build your reputation on eBay.co.uk is to contribute to the eBay community and tell people about yourself and your interests. You can do this in a number of ways:

- ✔ **About Me page:** eBay lets members create this free, customisable page to tell people about who they are. An About Me page can be simple; it can contain links to your eBay shop and your eBay auction sales. See the following section for more information.

- ✔ **My World page:** You can add a personal description explaining why you're a reputable seller, photographs, links to your items for sale and much more here. It takes only a few minutes to edit your My World page (not much longer than filling out the Sell Your Item form to get a sale online, in fact). If you want to include a photo, you should take a digital image and edit it in an image-editing program, such as Paint Shop Pro or Photoshop, just as you would any other image. Figure 10-1 shows what Kim's My World page looks like.

- ✔ **Join the eBay community:** eBay has a huge network of members sharing their expertise with each other through discussion boards, groups and video tutorials. You can even write tutorials and guides to buying and selling on eBay.

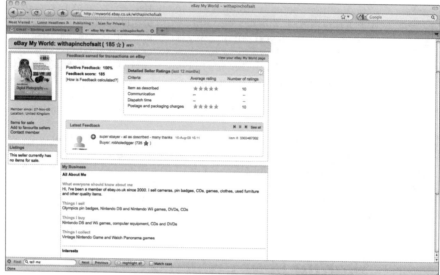

Figure 10-1:
A descriptive, friendly My World page gives buyers confidence.

Creating an About Me page

When you create an About Me page, a special 'Me' logo appears next to your eBay username. Potential buyers can click on this to read more about you. You don't need to know anything technical to create an About Me page, but you can make it look less plain using HyperText Markup Language (HTML), the markup language used to specify how to format a web page (for more on HTML, see Chapter 5), and by linking to external images.

When you've decided what you want to say on your About Me page:

1. **Click My eBay on the navigation bar at the top of virtually any eBay.co.uk page.**

   A login page appears.

2. **Type your User ID and password and click Sign In.**

   The My eBay page appears.

3. **Click the Account tab that appears on the top of the My eBay section.**

   The My eBay Account: Personal Information page appears.

4. **Scroll down to the About Me page section and click Edit.**

   For security reasons, you may need to log in again. The About Me page appears.

5. **Look toward the bottom of the page and click Create Your Page (if you already have one, you see the button to Edit Your Page.**

   The Choose Page Creation Option page appears.

6. **Leave the Use Our Easy Step-By-Step Process option selected and click Continue.**

   The About Me: Enter Page Content page appears.

7. **As indicated on the page, type a title and paragraphs for your page (HTML is allowed). Add photos if you wish by browsing to their location on your computer, or enter the URL for the photo in the Your Web Hosting tab. You can also show links to your recent eBay activity and type links to favourite pages and your own web page if you have one. When you're done, click Continue.**

   The Preview and Submit page appears, as shown in Figure 10-2.

8. **Choose one of three possible layouts for your page and preview your page content in the bottom half of the page. When you're finished, click Submit.**

   Your page goes online.

Like any web page, you can change your About Me page at any time by following the preceding steps.

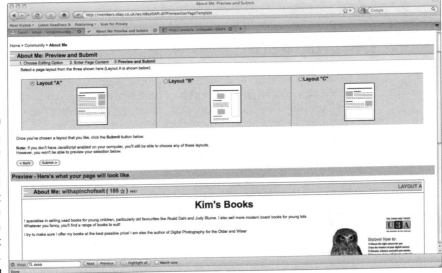

Figure 10-2: Take a few minutes to proofread your About Me page before you post it online.

Another way to build a good reputation as a seller is to participate actively in eBay's discussion boards. Pay special attention to boards that pertain to the type of merchandise you buy and sell. Responding to questions from new users and offering advice based on your experience can boost your standing within the user community. If you're a stamp collector and dealer, why not voice your opinions about the latest trends, give advice to budding collectors and share stories about your treasured collection?

Preparing Sales Descriptions That Sell

How do you actually go about selling on eBay.co.uk? The process is similar to other forms of e-commerce: you select merchandise, take photos, type descriptions and put the descriptions online in a catalogue.

But some critical differences exist as well. You don't always have to specify a fixed price on eBay.co.uk; you can set a starting bid and see how much the market will bear. All sales descriptions aren't created equal, however. Many sellers would argue that clear, sharp photos are the most important part of a description and that if you show the item in its best light it practically sells itself. We're of the opinion that a good heading and descriptions that include critical keywords are just as important as good photos. You can best discover the art of creating descriptions by inspecting other people's sales listings and seeing how much the items sold for; we describe the essentials in the following sections.

Details, details

The primary way of getting your sales online is eBay.co.uk's Sell Your Item form. You can access this form at any time by hovering your mouse pointer over Sell on the eBay navigation bar, which appears at the top of any page on the eBay.co.uk website, and then click Sell Your Item. The Sell Your Item form is easy to use, so we don't take you through every little option. In this section, however, we do point out a few features you may overlook and that can help you get more attention for your sales.

The Sell Your Item form is by no means the only way to get eBay sales online. It can get tedious and time consuming spending time listing items one by one. Many full- or part-time businesspeople use special software that allows them to upload multiple images at once or schedule multiple sales so they all start and end at the same time. The software saves your listing descriptions for another day, so you won't need to enter everything in again from scratch. Popular third-party listing management tools include ChannelAdvisor's Basic and Premium Marketplaces (see more at www.channeladvisor.com) and Andale, owned by US company Vendio, at uk.andale.com. In addition, eBay offers two programs you may find helpful:

- ✔ **Turbo Lister** (`pages.ebay.co.uk/turbo_lister/index.html`), which is free, lets sellers list and edit items in bulk and design templates that they can use to add graphic interest to their sales descriptions.

- ✔ **Selling Manager** (`pages.ebay.co.uk/selling_manager/index.html`), a monthly subscription service, is sales and management software. It provides you with convenient lists that let you track what you have up for sale, which sales have ended, which items have been purchased and what tasks you have yet to do – for example, sending emails to winning bidders or relisting items that didn't sell the first time.

Choosing a second category

One of the first things you do in the Sell Your Item form is to choose a sales category in which to list your item. We recommend using the search box at the top of the Select a Category page. Enter a keyword and click Search. You're presented with a detailed list of sales categories on the left-hand side of the page. The best thing about the list is that it's ranked in order of the ones that are most likely to sell items matching your desired keywords. The categories near the top of the list are the ones to choose.

We also recommend paying an extra few pence or so (when you choose a second category, your listing fee doubles) and listing the item in a second category – especially if the second category is closely related to the first.

Focusing on your auction heading

The heading of an eBay sales description is the set of six or seven words that appears in a set of search results or in a set of listings in a category. In other words, it's the set of words that a potential customer initially sees when she's deciding whether to investigate a sale and possibly bid on it. Keep your heading short and specific. Include dates, colours or model numbers if applicable. Potential buyers typically only search for an item by the title listing – not its description as well – so make sure these descriptive *keywords* are concise and relevant. If a buyer can find your item, she can then follow through with its purchase. To stand out from the crowd, you can try to pick just one keyword that may attract a buyer, such as *rare*, *hard-to-find*, *mint*, *new* or something similar.

Choosing a good ending time for your sale

With eBay sales, it's not the starting time that counts but the ending time that makes a difference. The more attention you can get at the end of a sale, the more likely you are to make a profit. Most sales get attention on weekends, when the majority of shoppers aren't working. Optimal times are Saturday or Sunday afternoons and Sunday evenings. You could list a ten-day auction on a Thursday. That way you get one weekend of people browsing and following your item, and another weekend for the bids to flood in.

Of course, bidders can come from all over the world, and what's early afternoon on a Sunday morning in London is the middle of the night in Australia.

But don't worry too much about such distinctions: pick an ending time that's convenient for eBay.co.uk shoppers in your own country to be present – not in the middle of a work day, but on the weekend.

To keep delivery costs down, you can specify that you'll only accept bids from people within the UK. Don't worry about getting your item seen by everybody in the world!

Adding keywords

Although most people on eBay search by listing title only, it's important to provide a thorough, accurate description in the body of the listing because enthusiastic buyers also do advanced searches based on item descriptions. You don't have to make the description overly lengthy.

The description is where you can show off your sales prowess. Providing factual information that highlights all the great things about your item – while not ignoring the teeth marks on the playpen or the small crack on the underside of the elephant carving – gets the bids rolling in.

In your title and description, think of all the terms that someone would use when looking for your item and add as many of those keywords to the title and to the body of the description as you can. If you're selling an electric drill, for example, use keywords such as *cordless, electric, drill, Black & Decker* or anything else a likely buyer may enter.

Upgrading your listings

Near the end of the Sell Your Item form, you get the option to specify whether you want to upgrade your listings. *Upgrade*, in this case, means adding graphic highlights to help your listing stand out from those around it, either in search results or on category pages. We list some of the major upgrade options in Table 10-2 along with their costs (which are subject to change and refer to individual sellers, not). For a more comprehensive listing, including advanced advertising options for those making a serious income from eBay, see pages.ebay.co.uk/help/sell/promoting_ov.html.

Table 10-2	Listing Upgrades	
Upgrade	*Description*	*Cost*
Gallery	A thumbnail image appears next to auction title.	Free
Gallery Plus	A Gallery image appears in a Featured Items area at the top of Gallery pages.	95p for a 3, 5, 7 and 10 day auction and Buy It Now, or £2.85 for 30 day Buy It Now only

Upgrade	Description	Cost
Item subtitle	A line of descriptive information is listed underneath the item title. Buyers see this before clicking through to your listing.	35p for a 3, 5, 7 and 10 day auction and Buy It Now, or £1.05 for Buy It Now only
Scheduled listing	Start your listing at a particular time so it ends during a busy period (see 'Tip', below).	6p
Listing designer	Add a theme to your listing to make it look pretty. Not a necessary inclusion, but may be worth it if you're after a more professional look and feel. Fees are not charged if using Turbo Lister or Selling Manager Pro at the time of listing.	7p for a 3, 5, 7 and 10 day auction and Buy It Now, or 21p for 30 day Buy It Now only

In eBay's early days, if you wanted a sale to end at a particular time (say, 7 p.m. on a Sunday, when lots of bidders are online), you had to physically be present to create the description at a certain time. For example, if you wanted such a sale to last seven days, you had to list it at precisely 7 p.m. the preceding Sunday. Now, you don't have to be physically present exactly a week, five days, three days or one day before you want your sale to end: you can specify an ending time when you fill out the Sell Your Item form (it costs 6p).

Understanding the fees

Although it's free to register for an account on eBay.co.uk and free to fill out the Sell Your Item form, eBay typically charges you an Insertion Fee when you actually put an item up for sale. Insertion fees vary depending on the starting price of the auction and whether you're a private seller, business seller or shop owner (for more on shops, see 'Opening an eBay.co.uk shop', further on in this chapter). For example, listing most items with a starting price from 1p to 99p is free for private sellers and 10p for business sellers. Listing media such as books and DVDs is also free for private sellers, but costs 5p for business sellers.

A Final Value Fee is also charged at the end of the auction or fixed price listing, and this amount gets very complicated, particularly for business sellers (so you may want to grab a strong drink before trying to figure it out). Not only does this fee depend on the final sale price, but it also depends on the type of item sold. Thankfully, eBay works it all out automatically for you at the end of the sale.

For a business seller, selling media such as a DVD incurs a Final Value Fee of 9 per cent of the closing balance. Simple. But if you sell a technology item such as an MP3 player for £35, the Final Value Fee is 5.25 per cent of the initial £29.99 (£1.57) plus 3 per cent of the remaining balance of the final selling price. For a greater-value technology item, such as a television sold for £700, it's 5.25 per cent of the initial £29.99, plus 3 per cent of the £30–£99.99 (£2.10), plus 2.5 per cent of the initial £100–£199.99 (£2.50) plus 2 per cent of the initial £200–£299.99 (£2) plus 1.5 per cent of the initial £300–£599.99 (£4.50) plus 1 per cent of the remaining balance of the final selling price. Prices vary yet again for other types of items sold.

Phew, we told you it was complicated! For a detailed explanation of the formula used to calculate fees, see `pages.ebay.co.uk/help/sell/fees.html`.

Including clear images

No matter how well written your auction's headings and description, all your work can quickly be undone by digital images that are dark, blurry or slow to load because they're too large in either physical or file size. The same principles that you use when capturing digital images for your e-commerce website apply to images on eBay.co.uk:

- Make sure that you have clear, even lighting (consider taking your photos outdoors).
- Use your camera's auto-focus setting.
- Crop your images so that they focus on the merchandise being sold, not on a piece of fluff on the floor or someone hovering in the background.
- Keep the file size small by adjusting the resolution with your digital camera or your image editing software – but don't compromise on image quality.

Some aspects to posting images along with auction descriptions are unique to eBay:

- **Image hosting:** If you run a business on eBay.co.uk and have dozens, or even hundreds, of sales items online at any one time, you can potentially have hundreds of image files to upload and store on a server. If you use eBay Picture Services as your photo host, the first image for each sale is free. Each subsequent image costs 12p (or 36p for 30-day Buy It Now listings). Finding an economical photo hosting service, such as Auctionpix (`www.auctionpix.co.uk`) or Auctiva (`www.auctiva.com`) is worthwhile. You can also use your own web space to host your images and link to their location. For more on web hosting see Chapter 3.

- **Close-ups:** If what you're selling has important details such as brand names, dates and maker's marks, you need to have a camera that has *macro capability* – that is, the ability to get clear close-ups. Virtually all digital cameras have a macro setting, but it can be tricky to hold the camera still enough to get a clear image (you may need to mount the camera on a tripod).

- **Multiple images:** You'll never hear an eBay shopper complaining that you included too many images with your auction listings. As long as you have the time and patience and an affordable image host, you can include five, six or more views of your item (for big, complex objects such as cars and motorbikes, multiple images are especially important).

Be sure to crop and adjust the brightness and contrast of your images after you take them, using a program such as Corel Paint Shop Pro (www.corel.com) or Adobe Photoshop Elements (www.adobe.com). Basic image-editing tools are also available for free by downloading programs such as Google's Picasa (picasaweb.google.com) and Windows Live Photo Gallery, which comes with Windows 7 and is also available for earlier versions of Windows at the Microsoft website (www.microsoft.com).

If you want to find out more about creating sales descriptions (and practically every aspect of buying or selling on eBay.co.uk, for that matter), take a look at Dan's book, *Starting a Business on eBay.co.uk For Dummies* (Wiley, 2006) or Kim's book *eBay.co.uk Business All-in-One For Dummies* (Wiley, 2009).

Accepting PayPal

It may seem like payments are the most nerve-wracking part of a transaction on eBay.co.uk. They have been, in the past, but as time goes on eBay provides more safeguards for its customers. These days, most buyers pay using PayPal and in fact eBay now requires that you offer PayPal as a payment option for most items. PayPal is secure and simple and offers sellers protection in most cases, but in practice you'll still need to meet certain requirements in order to be eligible for its Seller Protection programme. This protects sellers from the possibility of a *chargeback* – this is when the buyer automatically requests a refund from PayPal after noticing that the item wasn't as described, never arrived or wasn't authorised by the account holder. The latter happens in cases of fraud.

According to PayPal's terms and conditions, to be eligible for Seller Protection you must meet these conditions:

- ✔ You must have a registered UK PayPal account.
- ✔ You must be selling a physical item that can be posted.
- ✔ The item must be marked as eligible for Seller Protection under the account Transaction Details page.
- ✔ You must post the item to the address marked on the Transaction Details page.
- ✔ In order to be protected for unauthorised payments, you *must* have proof of postage for your item (a receipt isn't enough; you need to get a form stamped by the post office). If a buyer claims she never received your item, you need proof of receipt dated within seven calendar days after receiving payment (so use Special Delivery, where the recipient has to sign for the item).

Seller beware!

When Kim decided to sell her 32-inch LCD television on eBay, she painstakingly photographed it, provided details of the model and purchase date, and gave buyers the option to collect it for free from her home in North London or pay an extra £20 for a courier service. She listed the item as an auction with a Buy It Now option of £280, and by the end of the day, someone with a feedback of 82 committed to purchase it under Buy It Now.

The buyer sent a message asking Kim to call him on a mobile number to arrange a collection time. Kim called the buyer that evening, but immediately she had her suspicions when the man on the other end asked her for her username so he could pay with PayPal. Anyone with a feedback of 82 should know if you go into My eBay, all your transactions are listed clear as day and you can click right through to the PayPal site in order to pay. No one needs to note down anyone's username. The buyer then made the excuse that he'd 'bought several TVs' that day so was confused about which sale was which!

Kim asked the man's name and he replied, 'I am Mr Greenaway' – the account username included the name 'greenaway' but the man didn't want to give Kim his first name. She also got worried when she noticed that the real name listed on the account didn't include the name 'greenaway' at all. When Kim queried the discrepancy, the man said he shared the account with his brother!

The buyer was keen to pick up the TV right away, and said he would pay for the item in 15 minutes using PayPal. The fact he wanted the TV so quickly sounded suspicious. An hour passed, and no payment had gone into Kim's PayPal account. It was almost 9 p.m. Kim sent a reminder text to the man who texted back saying, 'Just paid and my driver is on his way to collect the TV.'

After the words 'my driver', alarm bells began ringing. Why would he need a driver? And at this hour? Kim called the man, who didn't answer, and she left him a voicemail saying she wanted to cancel the sale because she wasn't comfortable about it. Kim then turned off all the lights and made sure the door was locked – thankfully no one turned up!

Her eBay account finally indicated that the item had been paid for using PayPal, but when Kim logged into PayPal she saw the words 'Unauthorised claim'. PayPal was withholding the funds because it automatically had its suspicions. Kim frantically logged on to eBay live chat and spoke with a representative who confirmed that a 'problem' existed with the PayPal account and advised Kim not to proceed with the sale. Hours later, the eBay account was deemed to have been compromised (a fraudster had obtained the login details), and the eBay listing and final value fee charges were refunded to Kim's account.

Also, the programme doesn't apply for items picked up in person, so you might want to make sure someone's paying in cash – read Kim's close shave experience with an eBay fraudster in the nearby sidebar 'Seller beware!' for more about this.

You have other protections as a seller: if someone doesn't respond, you can relist your item; if someone's cheque bounces, you don't lose out on your sales item because you held on to it during the process of the cheque clearing process.

As an eBay.co.uk seller, you should accept the basic forms of payment. A PayPal account covers most of your customers, but some will want to pay by other means such as cheque or card. You can enable your customers to pay with a credit card, either by using your merchant credit-card account if you have one (see Chapter 11), or by using one of a handful of popular electronic payment services such as NoChex (www.nochex.com), Sagepay (www.sagepay.com) or WorldPay (www.rbsworldpay.com).

In the case of PayPal, you're charged a nominal fee (1.4 to 3.4 per cent of the amount plus a 20p fee) when a buyer transfers money electronically to your account. Those receiving more than £1,500 per month are eligible for lower merchant rates depending on sales volume from the previous calendar month.

Never accept other forms of payment from buyers such as Western Union transfers. Occasionally, a buyer insists on sending you cash in an envelope; you should insist, in turn, that the buyer sends a postal order instead.

Providing Good Customer Service

When you make the decision to sell on eBay.co.uk on a regular basis, you need to develop a good reputation. Earlier in this chapter, we outline ways that you can do that. But one of the best ways to achieve this goal – providing a high level of customer service to your buyers – is an issue that warrants a separate discussion. The single best way to do give great customer service is to be responsive to email enquiries of all sorts. Good customer service means checking your email a few times a day and spending lots of time responding to your customers' questions. If you take days to get back to someone who asks you about the colour or the condition of an item you have for sale, it may just be too late for that person to bid. And a slow response to a high bidder or buyer after the sale can make the buyer nervous and result in neutral feedback – not a complaint about fraud or dishonesty, but a note about below-par service. Such feedback is as bad as a negative comment on eBay.co.uk.

Setting terms of sale

Getting back to people quickly and communicating clearly and with courtesy is part of good customer service. When you receive enquiries, you should always thank prospective customers for approaching you and considering the sale; even if they don't end up placing bids, you've spread goodwill, which hopefully you'll get back.

Another way to be good to your customers is to be clear about how you plan to ship your merchandise and how much it will cost. When you fill out the Sell Your Item form (which we discuss in the earlier section, 'Details, details'), you must specify either an *actual shipping cost* (a cost based on weight and the buyer's residence) or a *flat shipping fee* (a shipping fee you charge for all your items).

If you haven't used eBay in a while, be aware that rules around postage and packing charges have changed. You always need to specify how much you'll post your item for domestically before you sell, and maximum postage charges exist for certain items (for DVDs it's £1, for example). eBay encourages sellers to offer free postage and packing whenever they can to attract more buyers. See `pages.ebay.co.uk/help/sell/maximumPP_FAQ.html` for more.

Packing and shipping safely

One of the aspects of selling on eBay that's often overlooked (not by *buyers*) is the practice of packing and shipping. After sending payment for something, buyers often wait on tenterhooks, expecting to receive their items while dreading the prospect of an unresponsive seller who neglects to ship what they've purchased.

Besides the danger of fraud, the danger exists that the item you send will be damaged in transit. Be sure to use sturdy boxes when you ship and to adequately cushion your merchandise within those boxes. We've received boxes from sellers who stuffed the insides with bubble wrap and newspaper, and we were happy for the trouble. If you're shipping something particularly fragile, consider double-boxing it: put it in a box, place the box in a larger one and put cushioning material between the two. Your customers will be pleased to receive the merchandise undamaged, and you'll get good feedback as a result.

Place a thank-you note, business card or even a small gift inside the box with your shipment. This gesture reminds buyers that you're a trustworthy seller and lets them know how to get in touch with you in the future.

Moving from Auctioneer to eBay.co.uk Businessperson

Few eBay.co.uk sellers start out proclaiming, 'I'm going to be a PowerSeller, and I'm going to sell full-time on eBay for a living!' Rather, they typically start out on a whim. They find an object lying around in a box, in the loft or on a shelf, and they wonder: will anyone pay money for this? Other sellers are existing businesses who join eBay.co.uk to earn some extra cash, many of whom soon realise it's not just a supplement but an essential component of their business.

For example, take Nick Talley, who runs the phenomenally popular eBay.co.uk shop iPosters (`stores.ebay.co.uk/iposters-Poster-and-Print-Shop`). He gave up his courier business after 16 years because of rising bills and set up a website called `www.pop-culture.biz`. Like many people he thought eBay.co.uk would provide a useful second source of income, but around 60,000 sales later and with 'Top-rated seller' status, Nick is pulling in some very useful profits. Nick says, 'Good old-fashioned customer service, as well as in-demand products and a well-designed site, are the most essential components of any online business. But on eBay.co.uk, which brings together so many sellers in one place, this matters more than ever.'

Opening an eBay.co.uk shop

An *eBay.co.uk shop* is a website within eBay's own voluminous web empire. It's a place where sellers can post items for sale at fixed prices and it's an increasingly popular part of eBay's virtually infinite marketplace. The great advantage of having a shop is that it enables a seller to keep merchandise available for purchase for 30, 60, 90 or even an unlimited number of days at a time.

You can choose from different 'tiers' of shop – Basic (£14.99 per month), Featured (£49.99 per month) and Anchor (£349.99 per month). The latter two tiers are only available for registered business sellers and you need to retain a high quality of customer service.

Anchored and Featured shops' monthly fees seem high – but for high-volume sellers, the benefits are in the low insertion fees: for a Featured shop it costs just 5p to list an item, and you only pay one fee to list multiple identical items in the same listing (so if you're selling 200 of the same type of necklace, you only pay 5p). For an Anchored shop, it costs just 1p to list an item and for a Basic shop, 20p (10p for media products). However, most people find that the Basic shop is more cost-effective – at least to start off with – because they don't have a huge variety of items for sale.

eBay shops give customers another way to buy from you, and can significantly increase your sales too. eBay frequently claims that eBay shops bring an average 25 per cent increase in overall sales after the first three months of trading. (Kimberly King, a US-based PowerSeller we profile later in this chapter, says her shop accounts for perhaps 55 to 60 per cent of her sales.)

eBay.co.uk's own Shop Toolkit section is well worth a look. It describes how you can set up your shop, make it look good, offer discounts, sell effectively and get it picked up by major search engines.

For more on eBay Shops and getting your shop noticed, check out the following link: `pages.ebay.co.uk/storefronts/seller-landing.html`.

Striving for PowerSeller status

PowerSellers are eBay.co.uk's elite. Those members who have the coveted icon next to their names feel justifiably proud of their accomplishments. They've met the stringent requirements for PowerSellers, which emphasise consistent sales, a high and regular number of completed sales and excellent customer service. Moving from occasional seller to PowerSeller is a substantial change. PowerSellers also come in different levels and flavours, such as Top-rated Seller, Standard and Above Average, but all need to meet basic requirements including:

✔ At least 100 unique feedback results – 98 per cent of which are positive

✔ A minimum of 100 transactions and £2000 of sales in the last 12 months

✔ A good standing record – achieved by complying with eBay listing policies

✔ A Detailed Seller Ratings (DSR) score of 4.60 or more

✔ A maximum of 1 per cent or three opened cases (0.5 per cent or two opened cases for Top-rated Sellers) and a maximum 0.3 per cent or two cases that closed without resolution

The PowerSeller programme isn't just something you apply for. eBay.co.uk reviews your sales statistics and invites you to join the programme when you've met the requirements. You can find out more about the requirements and benefits of the PowerSeller programme at pages.ebay.co.uk/services/buyandsell/powerseller/benefits.html.

In return for the hard work required to meet these standards, PowerSellers do get a number of benefits in addition to the icon. These include Final Value Fee discounts, priority email and phone support, a special discussion board just for PowerSellers and higher priority in search listings.

You are strictly forbidden from using the PowerSeller logo or refer to your PowerSeller status on listing descriptions, in templates, on About Me pages or in eBay Shop pages. Only the PowerSeller badge identifies you as a top seller. You won't be allowed to list a product that breaches this policy. See http://pages.ebay.co.uk/help/policies/selling-practices.html for more.

For more on the PowerSeller programme, see: pages.ebay.co.uk/services/buyandsell/powersellers.html.

Finding lots of merchandise to sell

Moving up to PowerSeller status means an ongoing commitment to conducting a large number of sales, responding quickly to customers and shipping efficiently. It also means finding a steady and reliable stream of merchandise to sell. When you need to get 50 or more items up for sale each week, car boot sales quickly become impractical for all but the most dedicated. Many PowerSellers manage to find sufficient stock by heading to antiques fairs and car bootathons in teams, showing up in the pre-dawn hours and queuing up, and then buying as many things as they can grab. Others find a wholesale supplier who can provide them with low-cost items, such as figurines, clothes or holiday decorations, in bulk.

Finding a wholesale supplier

All the PowerSellers we've spoken to in recent years assure us that finding a reputable, reliable wholesaler isn't easy. They urge other sellers to do their homework by getting references and talking to satisfied customers. Many wholesalers are primarily interested in taking sellers' money and not providing good service, they say. Often, finding wholesalers is a matter of word of mouth: you ask someone who knows someone, and so on. Kimberly King (the seller we profile in the 'PowerSeller keeps sales going with a little help from her friends' sidebar) used connections left over from her former management position at a herbal tea company to find a supplier. She cautions:

> You're not going to find someone on eBay who is going to tell you their wholesaler. They're too valuable. My advice is to make sure to call and check out references; do everything you can to find out everything about a company. Some force you to make an initial order of maybe £500 minimum up front, knowing when you see the product you'll never order it again.

PowerSeller keeps sales going with a little help from her friends

PowerSeller status is something that many eBay sellers strive for, and Kimberly King is no exception. After she started selling on a regular basis, she decided to try for the coveted icon. 'When I realised that I could do this, I had to do a little more research about what I was selling,' she says. 'Having not been in sales before, I found that there are some strategies you have to follow and some things you have to hunt for, like a wholesale supplier.'

Having a steady stream of merchandise to buy at wholesale and then resell on eBay.co.uk is important for PowerSellers. They're required to maintain the very best in customer service in order to keep their PowerSeller icon and sell at least £2,000 worth of merchandise a year. This requirement does put some pressure on

a seller, King says. 'I do put some pressure on myself to keep my PowerSeller status. I feel I have to list a certain number of items and be available for people constantly. You have more people you are helping and working with.'

A housewife and mother, King has to fit her eBay activities in between errands, childcare and many other responsibilities. Still, she manages to spend as much as six hours on the auction site each day. This is the level of commitment required from eBay.co.uk's top sellers too – you can't just dip in and out! She takes her own photos of each of her sales items even though her wholesaler has offered stock photos because, she says, shoppers need to see exactly what they're buying. 'Right now I am striving to list ten sales online per day. It's

(continued)

(continued)

hard to remember to do this yourself, so some other sellers and I have decided to be 'listing buddies'. We remind each other every day that we need to keep up our quota; that way, we're accountable to someone.'

Having items up for sale for a month or more at a time helps King maintain her PowerSeller sales quotas. 'If one of my kids is home from school sick and I can't do something that week, I have those sales in my store. It's not like I completely left eBay that week.'

One of the best sources of support and help has been the member-created discussion forums called eBay Groups. 'When you find something, you can post a message on one group asking, "Hey I found this neat thing at a garage sale, does anyone know what this is?"' King says. 'Those discussion boards have been so helpful

because you get information from really knowledgeable sellers.'

A good UK example of a dedicated PowerSeller who can compete with the high street is Online4baby, a Top-rated shop that turns over more than £4 million a year – more than double what it made in 2007 (`stores.ebay.co.uk/online4baby`). The business, established by Warren Blayds, sells fixed-price items such as pushchairs, baby monitors, cots, rockers, swings, changing accessories, car seats and much more. With a positive feedback score of more than 173,000, the business is big enough to employ a sales team. As you can see from the figure, the shop's About Me page is indeed very snazzy but also provides clear information about the company's history, reputation and range of products.

Chapter 11

Accepting Payments

· ·

In This Chapter

▶ Anticipating your online customers' purchasing needs

▶ Applying for credit card merchant status

▶ Finding shortcuts to processing credit card data

▶ Providing shoppers with electronic purchasing systems

▶ Delivering your products and services

· ·

*S*tarting up a new business and getting it online is exciting, but believe us, the real excitement occurs when you get paid for what you do. Nothing boosts your confidence and tells you that your hard work is paying off like receiving the proverbial cheque in the post.

The immediacy and interactivity of selling and promoting yourself online applies to receiving payments too. You can get paid with just a few mouse clicks and some important data entered on your customer's keyboard. But completing an electronic commerce (*e-commerce*, for short) transaction isn't the same as getting paid in a traditional retail store. The customer can't personally hand you cash or a cheque. Or, if a credit card is involved, you can't verify the user's identity through a signature or photo ID.

In order to get paid promptly and reliably online, you have to go through some extra steps to make the customer feel secure – not to mention protect yourself too. Successful e-commerce is about setting up the right atmosphere for making purchases, providing options for payment and keeping sensitive information private. It's also about making sure that the goods get to the customer safely and on time. In this chapter, we describe ways in which you can implement these essential online business strategies.

Sealing the Deal: The Options

As anyone who sells online knows, the point at which payment transfers is one of the most eagerly awaited stages of the transaction. It's also one of the stages that's likely to produce the most anxiety. Customers and merchants who are used to dealing with one another face to face and who are accustomed to personally handing over identification and credit cards suddenly feel lost. On the web, they can't see the person they're dealing with.

Despite the ubiquity of online shopping, some customers are still uncertain about paying for something bought over the Internet. And with all the scare stories about fraud, it can still be nerve-wracking for merchants like you, who want to make sure that cheques don't bounce and that customers aren't making purchases with stolen credit cards.

Your goal, in giving your customers the ability to provide payments online, should be to accomplish the following:

- ✔ **Give the customer options.** Online shoppers like to feel that they have some degree of control. Give them a choice of payment alternatives: phone, cheque and credit/debit cards are the main ones.

- ✔ **Keep their credit card numbers secure.** You can do this in two ways. Either pay an extra fee to your web host in order to have your customers submit their credit card numbers or other personal information to a secure server – a server that uses Secure Sockets Layer (SSL) encryption to render data unreadable if stolen. The alternative is to use a third-party payment service provider to securely process and handle the customer data for you.

- ✔ **Make payment convenient.** Shoppers on the web are in a hurry. Give them the web page forms and the phone numbers they need so that they can complete a purchase in a matter of seconds. Give them the option of making a purchase *without* having to register on your website.

Though the goals are the same, the options are different if you sell on eBay. co.uk or on a website other than eBay's (see Chapter 10). If you sell on eBay. co.uk, either through an auction or an eBay shop, you can take advantage of eBay's fraud protection measures: a feedback system that rewards honesty, fraud insurance, investigations staff and the threat of suspension. These safeguards mean that accepting personal cheques or postal orders from buyers is feasible. If you don't receive the cleared funds, you don't ship.

On the web, you don't have a feedback system or an investigations squad to ferret out dishonest buyers. You can accept cheques or postal orders, but credit or debit cards are the safest and quickest option, and accordingly, they're what buyers expect. It's up to you to verify the buyer's identity as best you can in order to minimise fraud.

Knowing How Online Transactions Work

When customers want to buy something they've seen in your online store, they follow a number of steps in the process. The technicalities may differ depending on whether you're hosting the entire process on your own website or getting another company to handle it on your behalf, but the general principles remain the same.

1. **The customer browses the items you have for sale in your online store and adds them to a shopping trolley (or cart) by clicking a Buy or Add to Cart button or similar. When he's ready, the customer clicks a Checkout button.**

2. **After verifying the total price including any shipping costs, the customer enters his credit card and billing details via a secure form that encrypts his information, preventing it from being intercepted. He then clicks a button such as 'submit order' or similar.**

3. **The encrypted data is then sent to a payment gateway, a means of transmitting the credit card details to a payment service provider.**

4. **A payment service provider authenticates the order and verifies credit card details with your bank, which passes the details on to the customer's card issuer to check that the transaction isn't dodgy. Often, the payment service provider also does additional fraud checks. When all is well, everything passes back through the gateway and the customer receives on-screen confirmation that the transaction is complete. Payment service providers also often provide the payment gateway mechanism we describe in step 3.**

5. **Within a few working days, the money should clear and you're credited for the transaction, minus processing fees.**

After the customer submits the order, the payment approval process (steps 2 to 4) only takes a number of seconds!

Enabling Credit Card Purchases

Having the ability to accept and process credit card transactions makes it especially easy for your customers to follow the impulse to buy something from you. You stand to generate a lot more sales than you would otherwise.

Thanks to companies like PayPal, the web has made it easy for anyone to accept payments via their website, even without prior bank approval. With PayPal, it takes just a few minutes to display a Buy Now button on your website under an item for sale, provided you already have a PayPal account. All you do is insert a few lines of code into your web page (PayPal provides you with the appropriate information). Anyone with a PayPal account or a credit card can then start buying items via your site (they'll be briefly redirected to PayPal in order to complete the transaction).

However, if your business operates (or anticipates) a regular turnover of several thousand pounds a month, you may find it far more flexible as your business moves forward to obtain an *Internet merchant account* through your bank or via another online provider. This is a special account that lets your bank settle the credit card orders that you receive. Start-up costs may initially be higher, but transactional fees could be cheaper in the long run, depending on your sales volume. And the big bonus is, it usually takes less time for the money to get to you because funds are deposited directly into your account, rather than initially being held by PayPal. Effectively, this makes bookkeeping easier to manage.

Don't get us wrong, we love PayPal and the efforts it has made to combat fraud and make online purchasing a breeze for shoppers around the world. And we still recommend offering PayPal as a payment option for customers, particularly if you already have an eBay shop. But it's worth exploring the other options out there. We don't want to discourage you from becoming credit card ready by any means, but you need to be aware of the steps (and the expenses) involved, many of which may not occur to you when you're just starting out. For example, you may not be aware of one or more of the following:

- **Merchant account approval:** You have to apply and be approved for a merchant account. If you work through a traditional bank, approval can take days or weeks. However, a number of online businesses are providing hot competition, which includes streamlining the application process. These quick set-up solutions are also suitable for companies with lower turnovers or for ones that aren't established enough to be approved by a traditional bank.

- **Payment gateway:** This is the secure means by which credit card details are transmitted from your website and over the Internet to your bank. If the gateway is weaved into your own website, then your technical bod can set it up for you. But to save yourself the technical complexities, upfront cost and the hassle of managing card details, you may opt for a payment service provider (see the next bullet) that can host the entire transactional process – including the payment gateway. WorldPay (www.worldpay.com), Sagepay (www.sagepay.com) and Paypoint.net (www.paypoint.net) are examples of companies that provide such a service. For more, see 'Setting up a merchant account', later in the chapter.

- **Payment service provider:** Your merchant account handles the banking side for you, while a payment service provider (PSP), approved or operated by your bank, acts like a virtual till or swipe card, collecting and checking credit card details before passing them on to your bank.

- **Setup fees:** Fees can be high but they vary widely, and it pays to shop around. Some banks charge a merchant setup fee (up to a couple of hundred pounds). On the other hand, some online companies such as Paypoint.net (www.paypoint.net) charge a monthly fee starting from £15, and others, like Nochex (www.nochex.com), charge only a nominal fee of £50.

- **Usage rates:** All banks and merchant account companies (PayPal included) charge a *usage fee*. Typically, this fee ranges from 1 to 6 per cent of each transaction. Plus, you may have to pay a monthly premium charge to the bank or payment service provider. Nochex asks for £50 upfront and then charges you 2.9 per cent plus 20p per transaction. However, if you sell regularly, you pay no monthly fee, and the charges come down.

✔ **PCI compliance:** UK businesses, like others around the world, need to comply with the Payment Card Industry Data Security Standard (PCI DSS). This is a global standard supported by credit card providers and banks, designed to combat credit card fraud. It requires businesses to declare they are securely processing transactions and safely handling customer data by following several main principles. Small businesses need to verify that they are compliant by filling in a self-assessment form from www.pcisecuritystandards.org (the site also answers all your questions about PCI compliance). Those who don't comply risk being fined or having payments blocked. But don't worry: as a small business, you'll most likely be passing the entire payment process to a payment service provider who's already PCI DSS compliant, which makes life a lot easier (see 'Exploring Online Payment Systems', later in the chapter). The e-commerce software provider Actinic has a handy FAQ about PCI DSS compliance at: www.actinic.co.uk/ecommerce-software-for-businesses/services/online-card-payments/pci-dss-compliance.html.

You must watch out for credit card fraud, where criminals use stolen numbers to make purchases. You, the merchant – not the issuing bank – end up being liable for most of the fictitious transactions. Thankfully, payment service providers can detect fraud using automated processes, but many merchants still manually double-check that things aren't looking dodgy. For more information, see the later section, 'Verifying credit card data'.

Setting up a merchant account

The good news is that getting merchant status is relatively easy, because banks have come to accept the notion that businesses don't have to have an actual, physical shop front in order to be successful. Getting a merchant account approved, however, still takes time, and of course you have to pay for the privilege. Banks look more favourably on companies that have been in business for several years and have a proven track record, but they see the benefits of taking on newbies too.

That's why it's important that you have a solid business plan and realistic goals about where your business is going before you apply to your bank for a merchant account. Banks favour people who can provide good business records proving that they're a viable, moneymaking concern. They're also more likely to approve your application if you already have a merchant account for old-school offline transactions because it can be easily tied into this account.

Traditional banks are reliable and experienced. The newer web-based companies that specialise in giving online businesses merchant account status welcome new businesses and give you wider options and cost savings. Plenty have been around for a while – although they haven't been around as long as traditional banks have. Do your research into how reliable they are before taking the plunge. The list of merchant account providers is growing so long that knowing which company to choose is difficult. You may want to investigate what other well-established online businesses are already using.

Although it's far more professional to set up an Internet merchant account with your bank, many payment service providers can help you get up and running with an online store *without* you having to set up a bank-approved Internet merchant account.

We mentioned PayPal. And Paypoint.net offers merchants an option to redirect customers to a customised online store and payment page fully hosted by Paypoint.net and it takes responsibility for the Internet merchant account – a much cheaper and simpler option as you won't be holding any of the customer data on your own website. For sites with larger transactional volumes, PayPoint. net gives you the option to tie its payment gateway in with your existing Internet merchant account and host the whole shebang on your site for total control. Online gadget retailer Firebox.com uses Paypoint.net to set up and process its credit card transactions. Firebox.com is a popular site, and it integrates Paypoint.net's payment processing system into its own website so that it can keep customers on Firebox.com throughout the transactional process.

Another long-established example of a company that gives you flexible payment options is WorldPay. You can either use your own bank's Internet merchant account and combine it with WorldPay's payment gateway, or apply for an Internet merchant account via WorldPay.

We recommend visiting Business Link's website (www.businesslink.gov. uk), which provides you with a solid overview of what's required to obtain a merchant account and accept online payments.

For merchant accounts, be sure to ask about the monthly rate that the bank charges for Internet-based transactions before you apply. Compare the rate for online transactions to the rate for conventional 'card-swipe' purchases. Most banks and credit card processing companies charge 1 to 2 extra percentage points for online sales.

Finding a secure server

A *secure server* is a server that uses some form of encryption, such as Secure Sockets Layer, which we describe in Chapter 7, to protect data that you receive over the Internet. Customers know that they've entered a secure area when the security key or lock icon at the bottom of the browser window is locked shut.

If you plan to receive credit card payments through a gateway on your own site rather than outsource the process to a third-party, you definitely want to find a web-hosting service that protects the area of your online business that serves as the online store. In literal terms, you need secure server software protecting the directory on your site that is to receive customer-sent forms. Water-tight security should be a given by now, but it's always good to make sure that your customers will be protected. Ask your host (or hosts you're considering) whether any extra charges apply.

It's likely, too, that you'll need to have a *dedicated* web server to accept payments online in this manner, rather than web space that's shared among other sites. This could add thousands to the cost of your website. For more on this see Chapter 3.

If you aren't sure about whether to host the entire credit card process on your own website, then don't. Use a third-party payment processing service instead. Just make sure you choose a setup that allows you to move to a fully-hosted solution in the future with minimal technical pain, should you want to.

Processing and verifying credit card data

Your payment systems should automatically process customer credit card orders for you. They compare the shipping and billing addresses to help make sure that the purchaser is the person who actually owns the card and not someone trying to use a stolen credit card number. If everything checks out with the card provider, your payment systems transmit the information directly to the bank so it can process your funds.

Unfortunately, people are out there who try to use credit card numbers that don't belong to them. The anonymity of the web and the ability to shop anywhere in the world, combined with the ability to place orders immediately, can facilitate fraudulent orders, just as it can benefit legitimate ones.

When Kim did some undercover investigating for a computing magazine, she managed to access a marketplace where organised criminals were selling thousands of British, American, Canadian and Australian credit card details for around $2 each. It's likely that hackers obtained these details through compromised computers. Although Kim only browsed the forum, it was a revelation into another world. 'Top' sellers were rated by buyers; based on the 'quality' of the stolen credit card details – just like on an auction site!

Protecting yourself against credit card fraud is essential. Always check the billing address against the shipping address. If the two addresses are thousands of miles apart, contact the purchaser by phone to verify that the transaction is legit. Even if it is, the purchaser will appreciate your taking the time to verify the transaction.

Anything Left-Handed (www.anythinglefthanded.co.uk), the online store that we profile in Chapter 1, uses several online fraud detection techniques to be doubly sure that orders are legit. According to owner Keith Milsom, 'We use online fraud detection through our merchant accounts and payment system. Once orders are downloaded, we also get off-line credit checking by referring all orders to The 3rd Man service (www.the3rdman.co.uk). On top of that, we manually review all orders to make sure they are not unusual – odd combinations of high-value products, orders for delivery to different countries from the credit card and high value orders with courier delivery.'

You can use software to help check addresses. Here are three programs that perform this service:

Keeping the business well-oiled

In August 2009, award-winning entrepreneur Julia Hunter hit upon the idea of making truly waterproof cushion covers that can be kept outside – and so Oily Rag® was born (www.oilyragfabrics.co.uk). After a few months of hard work, she patented a top-secret technique that makes her oilcloth fabrics and wool fillings resistant to mould and mildew, and also developed a way to seal the seams and keep the rain out of them. By April 2010, her business was live and on the web.

Not only did Julia have to research how to develop her innovative product, but she also had to learn all about the world of online business and working with web designers! She has been lucky enough to go on several government-funded courses, and her efforts paid off after the Suffolk Chamber of Commerce gave Oily Rag the Best Start-up Business award in December 2010. Here, she explains the payment side of the website:

Q. How do you process credit card orders?

A. I have a merchant account and it was important to me to be seen from the outset as a professional company, not just running a business as a hobby, [although] I do have a PayPal account myself. Also, with people's worries about PCI compliance I wanted to dispel any questions about security issues from people's minds.

Q. How difficult was it to integrate the payment system into your shopping trolley software, CubeCart?

A. Decide on your payment methods early, as some design software does not work as well with some payment systems. My web designer integrated the merchant system into CubeCart (www.cubecart.com) and I think you need to be sure that this is done properly. I am not a computer geek, and it is best to know when to get help. The crucial thing is to have complete control over your website by being able to content manage your site.

Q. Do you ship your goods yourself or use someone?

A. I have all my goods delivered to me, where I then coordinate the shipping with my courier.

Q. How is the online side of the business going now?

A. I think anybody who sets up their own business should be applauded. It is not the easy answer for a work/life/family balance. The amount of hours I have invested into getting the business up and running would be scary if I worked it out. However, moving forward, I anticipate the online shop giving me greater flexibility in terms of my working hours. The nicest part is when you have been out for the day and return to find you have a stack of orders!

✔ CapScan (`www.capscan.com/products.htm`)

✔ WorldPay fraud screening (`www.worldpay.com`)

✔ QAS, part of credit reporting company Experian (`www.qas.co.uk/products`)

Automatic credit card processing works so fast that your customer's credit card can be charged immediately, whether or not you have an item in stock. If a client receives a bill and is still waiting for an item that's on back order, he can get very unhappy. For this reason, some business owners choose not to use automatic credit card processing. However, tying your inventory in with your shopping trolley software solves this problem, because items can be flagged as 'out of stock'. See the section 'Shopping trolley software', later in the chapter.

Exploring Online Payment Systems

A number of organisations, like the ones we mention in the earlier 'Setting up a merchant account' section, have devised ways to make e-commerce secure and convenient for shoppers and merchants alike. These organisations all help you complete credit card purchases in one form or another, either managing everything from shopping cart to order processing, or bits of the process.

To set up a shop and accept payments on your website, some technical configuration may need to take place and the degree of technical configuration varies. If you're unsure, this is definitely an area where paying a consultant to get your business set up saves time and headaches and gets your new transaction feature online more efficiently than if you tackle it yourself. Costs can also vary wildly too, so get some independent advice. Which payment system and shopping trolley software is right for you? That depends on what you want to sell online and your budget. If you're providing articles, reports, music or other content that you want people to pay a nominal fee to access, something like PayPal or Google Checkout might be the route to go. The important things are to provide customers with easy options for submitting payment and to make the process as painless as possible for them.

Shopping trolley software

When you go to the supermarket or another retail outlet, you pick goodies off the shelves and put them in a shopping trolley. When you go to the cash till to pay for what you've selected, you empty the trolley and present your goods to the cashier.

Chargebacks explained

A chargeback is what happens when a credit card holder disputes a transaction and files a refund claim with the issuing bank, asking it to reverse the payment. Be prepared for this to happen now and again; this is part of the territory when accepting credit card payments on your website.

When a chargeback happens, you're responsible for paying your bank for the loss incurred – and your bank also charges an additional chargeback fee (these vary; you may be required to reserve funds with your bank as security for chargebacks).

Chargebacks typically happen when a card was used fraudulently, which is why it's so important to have the fraud checks we describe in the earlier section 'Processing and verifying credit card data' in place. Other reasons for chargebacks include when buyers claim an item was never received, or if goods were not as described.

In the case of fraudulent claims, you can help protect yourself if you take an extra security measure. In order to reduce so-called 'card not present' fraud, Mastercard and Visa introduced an additional layer of authentication called 3D Secure. Visa calls its 3D Secure scheme 'Verified by Visa' while MasterCard calls theirs 'MasterCard SecureCode'. When buyers make a purchase from a participating site or a payment service provider such as WorldPay which uses 3D Secure technology, they're prompted to enter a password after submitting credit card details. Think of it as an online version of chip and pin.

Barclays Bank has a useful web page about chargebacks and what they mean for merchants. See www.barclaycard.co.uk/business/existing-customers/chargebacks/.

Shopping trolley software (sometimes called 'shopping cart' software) performs the same functions on an e-commerce site. Such software sets up a system that allows online shoppers to select items displayed for sale. The selections are held in a virtual shopping trolley that 'remembers' what the shopper has selected before checking out.

Shopping trolley programs can be pretty technical for nonprogrammers to set up, but if you're ambitious and want to try it, you can download and install one of two popular free programs: osCommerce (www.oscommerce.com) or ZenCart (www.zencart.com). You can also try off-the-shelf software like Actinic (www.actinic.co.uk) and CubeCart (www.cubecart.co.uk) on your website.

Whatever route you choose, always go for shopping trolley software that can integrate with your website and payment gateway. For example, osCommerce works with PayPal and Paypoint.net and other add-ons are available.

You can sign up with a web host that provides you with shopping trolley software as part of its services too, like 1&1 (www.1and1.co.uk), but do check how flexible their software allows you to be.

Payment systems

The following sections outline some of the main payment systems you can use.

PayPal

PayPal was one of the first online businesses to hit on the clever idea of giving business owners a way to accept credit and debit card payments from customers without having to apply for a merchant account, download software, apply for online payment processing or some combination of these steps.

PayPal functions as a sort of financial middleman, debiting buyers' accounts and crediting the accounts of sellers – and, along the way, exacting a fee for its services, which it charges to the merchant receiving the payment. The accounts involved can be credit card accounts, current accounts or accounts held at PayPal into which members directly deposit funds. In other words, the person making the payment sets up an account with PayPal by identifying which account (bank account, credit card or debit card, for example) a payment is to be taken from. The merchant also has a PayPal account and has identified which debit or credit card or bank account is to receive payments. PayPal handles the virtual 'card swipe' and verification of customer information; the customer can pay with a credit card without the merchant having to set up a merchant account.

PayPal is best known as a way to pay for items purchased on eBay. eBay, in fact, owns PayPal. But the service is regularly used to process payments both on and off the auction site. If you want to sell items (including through your website), you sign up for a PayPal Business or Premier account. You get a PayPal button that you add to your auction listing or sales web page. The customer clicks the button to transfer the payment from his PayPal account to yours, and you're charged a transaction fee.

Setting up a PayPal account is free. The big advantage with using a PayPal account is that customers don't need to enter their credit card details every time they shop online because PayPal stores them on its own servers. All they need to go is log in to PayPal with their email address and password.

The nice thing about using PayPal is that the system enables you to accept payments through your website without having to obtain a merchant account. Customers don't need to be a PayPal user either, as they can choose to enter credit card details through the PayPal interface – but chances are those who buy or sell on eBay already have one. The thing to remember is that both you and your customers place a high level of trust in PayPal to handle your money. If a problem with fraud arises, PayPal will investigate it – hopefully. Some former PayPal users detest PayPal due to what they describe as a lack of responsiveness, and they describe their unhappiness in great detail on sites like www. paypalsucks.com. You should be aware of such complaints in order to have the full picture about PayPal and anticipate problems before they arise.

For more on the PayPal Business products, see www.paypal.co.uk and click on the 'Business' tab or go to https://www.paypal-business.co.uk (note the secure 's'). Setting up a PayPal Business account is free, but if you want to use their more complete payment solutions, it could cost an extra £20 a month. For example, PayPal's website Payments Pro lets you fully customise the payment page hosted by PayPal so that it reflects the look and feel of your website. You can also easily download sales reports, search transactions, conduct additional fraud checks and have access to phone support.

Actinic

Actinic is British multi-award-winning payment software that can help you build a payment platform for any type of business, but it specialises in small and medium-sized enterprises. Actinic has been around since 1996, and provides a broad range of shopping cart software to suit different types of businesses. The entry-level service, Actinic Express, operates online and lets you choose from a number of ready-made designs for your shop. Actinic hosts the payment page and it can integrate with payment systems such as Google Checkout (see below).

The company's other products, Actinic Catalog, Actinic Business and Actinic Business Plus, are desktop software solutions that are easier to customise and give you more control over the design of your online shop. They can also integrate into inventory systems and product databases, allowing you to keep track of what's in stock and letting customers conduct searches of your available products via your website.

For comprehensive explanations of its products, current prices and some handy guides on how to get started, see Actinic's website at www.actinic.co.uk. Much of the information is relevant even to those who don't choose to use Actinic products.

Paypoint.net

We discuss PayPoint.net and its benefits in the section 'Setting up a merchant account', earlier in this chapter. The website has some thorough explanations of how its service works and the options available depending on how much you want Paypoint.net involved in the payment process. The company is part of the nationwide network that facilities bill transactions that you see in your local grocery store or off licence, so it's pretty well established. The online trading part of the business was established when Paypoint.net acquired SECPay and Metacharge a few years back. Paypoint.net can help you set up an Internet merchant account without getting direct approval from your bank if you so choose.

Sage Pay

This online payment provider's motto is to 'keep money moving'. It services around 30,000 UK businesses and claims to be the UK and Ireland's largest independent payment service provider. Subscriptions start at £20 per month. You can also apply for a Sage Pay merchant account, which could get you up and running in no time.

For comprehensive fact sheets, help files and explanations of services available check out www.sagepay.com.

Google Checkout

Google Checkout lets merchants in the US and UK create an online store and begin accepting payments via credit or debit card in much the same way as PayPal does. Buyers who have a Google Checkout account can securely store their shipping and credit card information with Google, saving you the hassle of having to manage and process the data – and it saves buyers having to type it out too. They can also track purchases made from other Google Checkout-enabled stores.

Integrating Google Checkout into your website can be as easy as entering lines of code into the relevant web page so that a Buy Now button appears under your item – a breeze if you only sell a few lines of items. There's also a nifty Google tool that lets you create a store in minutes by listing your products in a Google spreadsheet and embedding the gadget into your blog or website.

See the demo store in action in Figure 11-1 and at http://checkout. google.com/seller/gsc/v2/demo/index.html.

Alternatively, if you have a fully-fledged shopping cart supported by Google Checkout, the integration work has been done for you. Partners include ChannelAdvisor (www.channeladvisor.com) and Actinic (see the earlier section on this company). Check out (excuse the pun) http://checkout. google.com/seller/?hl=en&gl=GB for more details on the latest fees, integration help and anti-fraud information.

Figure 11-1: Google lets you create a store in minutes and accept credit card payments.

©2011 Google

Fulfilling Your Online Orders

Being on the Internet can help when it comes to the final step in the e-commerce dance: order fulfilment. *Fulfilment* refers to what happens after a sale is made. Typical fulfilment tasks include the following:

- ✔ Packing up the merchandise
- ✔ Shipping the merchandise
- ✔ Solving delivery problems or answering questions about orders that haven't reached their destinations
- ✔ Sending out bills
- ✔ Following up to see whether the customer is satisfied

Order fulfilment may seem like the least exciting part of running a business, online or otherwise. But from your customer's point of view, it's the most important business activity of all.

At your end, you must always retain proof of postage in case of any disputes and use a trackable, recorded delivery service whenever possible for peace of mind. The following sections suggest how you can use your presence online to help reduce any anxiety your customers may feel about receiving what they ordered.

The back-end (known as *back office*) part of your online business is where order fulfilment comes in. If you have a database in which you record customer orders, link it to your website so that your customers can track orders. Your shopping cart software can help with this process.

Provide links to shipping services

One advantage of being online is that you can help customers track packages after shipment. The Royal Mail online order-tracking feature, shown in Figure 11-2, gets thousands of requests each day. If you use Royal Mail, provide customers with their parcel's tracking number and a link to the Royal Mail website at www.royalmail.com.

The other shipping services have also created their own online tracking systems. You can link to these sites, too:

- ✔ United Parcel Service (www.ups.com/gb)
- ✔ Royal Mail (www.royalmail.co.uk)
- ✔ DHL (www.dhl.co.uk)

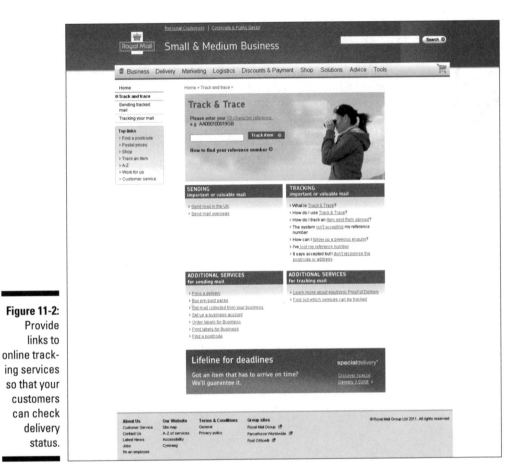

Figure 11-2:
Provide
links to
online track-
ing services
so that your
customers
can check
delivery
status.

Present shipping options clearly

In order fulfilment, as in receiving payment, it pays to present your clients with as many options as possible and to explain the options in detail. Because you're online, you can provide your customers with as much shipping informa-tion as they can stand. Web surfers are knowledge hounds – they can never get enough data, whether it's related to shipping or other parts of your business.

When it comes to shipping, be sure to describe the options, the cost of each and how long each takes. Here are more specific suggestions:

✔ **Compare shipping costs.** Don't settle for a shipping provider until you've done the rounds and assessed who's the most reliable for the least cost.

✔ **Make sure that you can track.** Pick a service that lets you track your package's shipping status.

   ✔ **Be able to confirm receipt.** A confirmation helps everyone's peace
     of mind.

As you're shipping goods from your website rather than selling face-to-face,
you're obliged to adhere to the UK's Distance Selling Regulations. Unless
stated otherwise, goods must be shipped within 30 days of purchase, and
there's a 7 working-day cooling off period which means customers are allowed
to change their minds if they aren't happy. This cooling-off period doesn't
apply to auction goods on eBay, but it *does* apply for fixed-price goods sold
by registered businesses on eBay. See www.businesslink.gov.uk and
Chapter 14 for more.

Chapter 12

Service with a Virtual Smile

*I*t's only human nature: customers often wait until the last minute to request a gift or other item for a specific occasion, and that leads to an emergency for you. It may not seem fair, but a delay in responding to your customers can lead to lost business. These days, everything seems to be instant, from your porridge to your broadband connection. We take it for granted that shops no longer close on a Sunday and that they'll be open late into the evening for our convenience. Many shoppers still like to spend hours milling around the shopping centre, browsing and lunching at their leisure. But chances are that your customers are coming to you in the first place to save time as well as money. And they expect to get what they want – and fast.

Customer service is one area in which small, entrepreneurial businesses can outshine brick-and-mortar high street shops – and even larger online competitors. It doesn't matter whether you're competing in online music, retail or any other sort of trading. Simple yet powerful tools such as email and contact forms, coupled with the new generation of social media that gets you closer to your customer than ever before, give you a powerful advantage when it comes to retaining customers and building loyalty.

What constitutes good online customer service, particularly for a new business that has only one or two employees? Dealing with them on a personal, one-to-one basis is, of course, important. But being responsive and available is only part of the picture. This chapter presents ways to succeed with the other essential components: providing information, communicating effectively and enabling your clientele to talk back to you online.

The Best Customer Is an Informed Customer

In a manner of speaking, satisfaction is all about managing people's expectations. If you give your customers what they're expecting or even a little bit more, they'll be happy. But how do you go about setting their level of expectation in the first place? Communication is the key. The more information you can provide up front, the fewer phone queries or complaints you'll receive later. Printed pamphlets and brochures have traditionally described products and services at length. But online is now the way to go.

Say that you're talking about a 1,000-word description of your new company and your products and/or services. If that text were formatted to fit on a 4-x-9-inch foldout brochure, the contents would cover several panels and cost an arm and a leg to print enough copies to make it worthwhile.

On the other hand, if you condense those 1,000 words into a succinct 250-word description of your business and put it on your website, its file size would be absolutely negligible and would cost you virtually nothing. The same applies if you distribute your content to a number of subscribers in the form of an email newsletter. In either case, you need pay only a little to publish the information.

And online publishing has the advantage of easier updating. When you add new products or services or even when you want a different approach, changing the contents or the look takes only a little time and effort.

Why FAQs are frequently used

It may not be the most elegant of concepts, but it has worked for an infinite number of online businesspeople and it'll work for you. A set of *frequently asked questions* (FAQs) is a familiar feature on many online business sites – so familiar, in fact, that many people expect to find a FAQ page on every business site.

Even the format of FAQ pages is pretty similar from site to site, and this predictability is itself an asset. FAQ pages are generally presented in Q-and-A format, with topics appearing in the form of questions that have been asked by other customers or that have been made up to resemble real questions. Each question has a brief answer that provides essential information about the business. But just because we're continually touting communication doesn't mean we want you to bore your potential customers with endless words that don't apply to their interests. To keep your FAQ page from getting too long, we recommend that you list all the questions at the top of the page. This way, by clicking a hyperlinked item in the list, the reader jumps to the spot down the page where you present the question that relates to them and its answer in detail. (Another way to do it is to 'hide' the answer under the question using Javascript. When someone clicks the question link, the answer is revealed below.)

Just having a FAQ page isn't enough. Make sure that yours is easy to use and comprehensive. Clarity and accessibility are both essential factors in a successful website, and your FAQ section should reflect these qualities. Check out the examples at `www.noupe.com/how-tos/faq-pages-best-practices-examples.html`.

Some FAQs have a search box next to them, so if people can't find what they're looking for straight away, they can type their query in the box.

Sure, you can compose a FAQ page off the top of your head, but sometimes getting a different perspective helps. Invite visitors, customers, friends and family to come up with questions about your business. You may want to include questions on some of the following topics:

- **Contact information:** If I need to reach you in a hurry by email, post or phone, how do I do that? Are you available only at certain hours?

- **Instructions:** What if I need more detailed instructions on how to use your products or services? Where can I find them?

- **Service:** What do I do if the merchandise doesn't work for some reason or breaks? Do you have a returns policy?

- **Value-added tax (VAT):** Is VAT added to the cost I see on-screen?

- **Shipping and returns:** What are my shipping options? What if I want to return an item?

Writing an email newsletter

You may define yourself as an online businessperson, not a newsletter editor. But sharing information with customers and potential customers through an email newsletter is a great way to build credibility for yourself and your business.

For added customer service (not to mention a touch of self-promotion), consider emailing out a regular publication to your customers, say once a fortnight or once a month, that you send out to a mailing list. Your mailing list could begin with customers and prospective customers who visit your website and indicate that they want to subscribe. Alternatively, they could agree to sign up to your newsletter when they buy something from your site.

Although it's easy to send an email out *en masse* to customers using your regular email program, this isn't practical when your customer base grows. You'd also need to remember to hide your recipients' email addresses from each other and manually sort out which of your customers has agreed to receive communications or not. Plenty of web-based email marketing services help you create and manage timely, professional-looking emails. You needn't be a technical genius to craft them, either, because pre-designed templates are available.

Newsletters are a key part of your business's promotional efforts – they come under the email marketing umbrella (we explain more about the power of email in Chapter 9). Essentially, you can use your emails to track whether people are responding to your emails, advertise a new service, target a particular customer base (if you sell sweets, someone who recently bought some might be interested in buying ones from the same maker), personalise messages so that customers' names appears on emails and so on.

Writing your newsletter

The fun part is to name your newsletter and assemble content that you want to include. Take a look at this suggested checklist on what to include in your newsletter:

1. **Create a newsletter, usually formatted in rich text HTML.**

   Most people send out newsletters using HTML these days (see Chapter 5 for more on this format) and include graphics and layout that echoes your business brand and logo. Images are pulled from your website server, rather than included in the body of your email. Many email programs including Hotmail, Yahoo! and Gmail block images in emails by default for security and privacy reasons, so make sure any email newsletter you send makes sense without images turned on. You can choose to send a plain-text newsletter (gossip website Popbitch still sends old-fashioned, 1994-era emails to its subscribers every week).

2. **Keep subject lines to the point.**

   People are busy and only have time to scan their inboxes. They won't open an email without a call to action – and don't forget to mention your company name in the sender field or subject line, otherwise people will think your email is spam.

3. **Keep it friendly.**

   In the body of your email, write as if you were addressing an individual rather than an entire block of customers. Keep the tone personal, yet still appropriate for the nature of your business.

4. **Ask for a second, third and even a fourth opinion.**

   The beauty of the web is that you can easily fix the odd typo or broken link with minimal fuss. But after you've sent out thousands of emails, that's it. You can't retract them, or amend the misspelling of your company name or the link that takes you to the wrong website. The emails have already hit people's inboxes – and people will start responding within seconds. So, always get your newsletter proofread by a few other people and get them to double-check any links.

5. **Provide full company details and an unsubscribe link.**

   Don't forget to provide all your details in the footer of your message. Include the company name and address and, if applicable, the registration number and VAT number. Also give the opportunity for subscribers to unsubscribe. (Most email marketing programs generally automatically include such a link at the bottom of the email template.)

In order to comply with the UK's privacy and e-commerce regulations, always give customers an opportunity to unsubscribe from receiving further communications. You can download a privacy checklist for your business at www. ico.gov.uk.

Using VerticalResponse to send an email newsletter

Many email marketing services are available and you can have a play around with several of them before you commit to paying for their services. One we like, which offers a 28-day free trial, is VerticalResponse (www.verticalresponse. com). It's what Sean McManus (www.sean.co.uk) uses for his regular newsletter. Features are far too numerous to outline here, but include the ability to track the success of your emails. Prices vary but per-unit costs decrease if you buy email credits in bulk. For a pay-as-you-go plan, you're looking at paying around $15 (around £9) for 1,000 email credits. This decreases to $7.50 (around £4.50) per thousand if you buy 100,000 to 500,000 email credits at once. Alternatively, you can send as many emails to your recipients as you want for a monthly fee ($10 or £6.20 a month for up to 500 email addresses, rising to $240 or £150 for 25,001 to 40,000 email addresses). Figure 12-1 shows the VerticalResponse home page.

With VerticalResponse, you can create newsletters (and other marketing messages) in one of four ways:

Figure 12-1: Vertical-Response is ideal for small-to-medium businesses who want to keep in touch with their customers.

✔ **The email wizard:** This is the easiest method. It lets you choose from dozens of customisable, professional-looking templates. You can link images into your text, add snippets of information, customise headings, add a logo and more, simply by dragging and dropping elements into the layout screen and typing your text in the boxes. Figure 12-2 shows the VerticalResponse email wizard in action.

✔ **Freeform HTML support:** If your newsletter is already designed in HTML, simply copy the code and paste it in.

✔ **Plain text:** Just type plain text without any pictures or logos.

✔ **Email canvas:** Format your newsletter using a WYSIWYG (pronounced wizzy-wig; What You See Is What You Get) editor. This works in a similar way to how you'd format pages using a word processing program or blogging tool. Best if you want to create both a rich-text HTML and a plain-text version of your newsletter.

Signing up to the trial only takes a minute. Go to www.verticalresponse. com and enter your contact details, including a chosen password. No credit card is necessary. VerticalResponse emails you an activation link; click this to verify your account and start using the service.

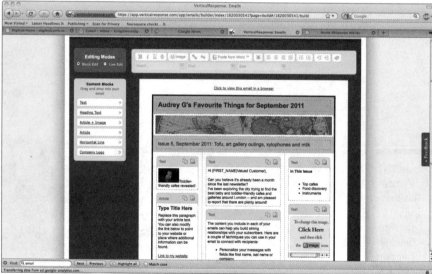

Figure 12-2: No technical experience is required with Vertical-Response's easy-to-use email creation wizard.

Mixing bricks and clicks

If you operate a bricks-and-mortar business as well as a web-based business, you have additional opportunities to get feedback from your shoppers. Take advantage of the fact that you meet customers personally on a regular basis and ask them for opinions and suggestions that can help you operate a more effective website too. (See 'Getting up close with comic fans', later in this chapter, for a case study on how one business drums up customer loyalty.) When your customers are in the checkout line (the real one with the cash till, not your online shopping trolley), ask them to fill out a questionnaire about your website. Consider asking questions like the following:

- ✔ Have you visited this shop's website? Are you familiar with it?

- ✔ Would you visit the website more often if you knew there were products or content there that you couldn't find in our physical location?

- ✔ Can you suggest some types of merchandise, or special sales, you'd like to see on the website?

Including your site's URL on all the printed literature in your shop is a good idea. The feedback system works both ways, of course: you can ask online customers for suggestions of how to run your bricks-and-mortar shop better, and what types of merchandise they'd like to see on your real as opposed to your 'virtual' shelves.

Helping Customers Reach You

Your customers need to believe that they'll get attention no matter what time of day or night, particularly as your website will always be up and running even when you're fast asleep. Of course, you don't have to promise to be available 24/7 to your customers in the flesh, but you can include a wealth of contact information on your site. Be sure to include a phone number as well as your email address. You could consider including a contact form on your website (see 'Creating forms that aren't formidable', later in this chapter) so that customers can reach you just by typing a message in a box and clicking Send.

Most web hosting services (such as the types of hosts that we describe in Chapter 3) give you more than one email inbox as part of your account. So it may be helpful to set up more than one email address. One address can be for people to communicate with you personally, and the other can be where people go for general information or customer support. You can also set up email addresses that respond to messages or purchases by automatically sending a message in response. (See the 'Automatic email responses' section, later in this chapter.)

Even though you probably won't meet many of your customers in person, you need to provide them with a human connection. Keep your site as personal and friendly as possible. A contact page is a good place to provide some brief biographical information about the people visitors can contact, namely you and any employees or partners in your company.

Not putting your contact information on a separate web page has some advantages, of course. Doing so makes your patrons have to wait a few seconds to access it. If your contact data is simple and your site consists only of a few pages, by all means put it right on your home page.

Going upscale with your email

These days, nearly everyone has an email account – it only takes a minute to set one up with a web-based email service. But when you're an online businessperson, you need to know more about the features of email than just how to share a joke or exchange a recipe. The more you discover about the finer technical points of email, the better you're able to meet the needs of your clients. The following sections suggest ways to go beyond simply sending and receiving email messages. For more on email marketing, see 'Writing an email newsletter', earlier in this chapter, and Chapter 9.

Automatic email responses

If a customer has just emailed you about a purchase – or she has any other query related to your business – then you can set up your email system to automatically and instantly send the customer an email acknowledging receipt of her message and indicate when she might receive a response.

You can provide automatic responses either through your own email program or through your web host's email service. If you accept payments on your website, you can also use their system to customise any confirmation emails. For instance, the online payment service WorldPay lets you tweak the confirmation email customers receive after a purchase.

Ask your web host about their email hosting features. Typically, your host assigns you an email address that takes the form info@mycompany.co.uk. In this case, someone at your hosting service configures the account so that when a visitor to your site sends a message to info@yourcompany.com, an email of your choice automatically goes out to the sender as a reply.

If the service that hosts your website does not provide this service as part of its package, you can always do it through your Outlook email software, which comes with Microsoft Office. Consult your help documentation for assistance.

Noting by quoting

When you reply to a message, the *quoted text* is automatically retained so that whoever you're responding to knows what you're replying about. How do you tell the difference between the quoted material and the body of the new email message? Commonly, email services put a greater-than (>) character in the left margin, next to each line of the quoted material.

You can choose to reply above the entire quote, or include snippets of the email, such as questions, throughout your reply (helpfully, email programs often quote text in a different colour to yours).

Attaching files

A quick and convenient way to transmit information from place to place is to attach a file to an email message. _Attaching_, which means that you send a document or file along with an email message, allows you to include material from any file to which you have access. Attached files appear as separate documents that recipients can download to their computers.

If the sender expects an attachment, then by all means include it. (Kim's busy emailing Word documents and image files every other day to her publishers at John Wiley & Sons in the course of updating this book.) However, we don't recommend including attachments on email unless absolutely necessary. Many email programs consider them a security risk because they can contain malicious software. Some workplaces even filter out certain types of attachments, or ones that are above a certain allowed size. Compressing a lengthy series of attachments by using software conserves bandwidth. Windows 7 and Mac OS X incorporate compressing (and uncompressing) files so you don't need separate software to open files like you did in the old days.

Creating a signature file that sells

One of the easiest and most useful tools for marketing on the Internet is called a signature file, or a sig file. A _signature file_ is a blurb that your system automatically appends to the bottom of your email messages and newsgroup postings. You want your signature file to tell the readers of your message something about you and your business; you can include information such as your company name and how to contact you.

Thinking about what to put in your signature file will probably take longer than creating it. Your web-based email lets you set up a signature very easily. In Gmail, go to Settings ⇨ Signature and use the built-in editor to add a rich-text message (meaning you can format the HTML to some extent and even include a URL to an image on your website). When you're done, click Save.

When composing your sig file you can press and hold down the hyphen (-) or equal (=) sign key to create a 'dividing' line that separates your signature from the body of the message, but this isn't always necessary.

As you can see in Kim's signature file in Figure 12-3, she's experimented by including a link to a small image of one of her books. If the person she sends the email to has images turned off (most likely), then this won't appear. For this reason, you should always make sure your signature file is still meaningful as plain text. When composing your signature, include such information as your name, job title, company name, email address and web address. A three- or four-line signature is the typical length.

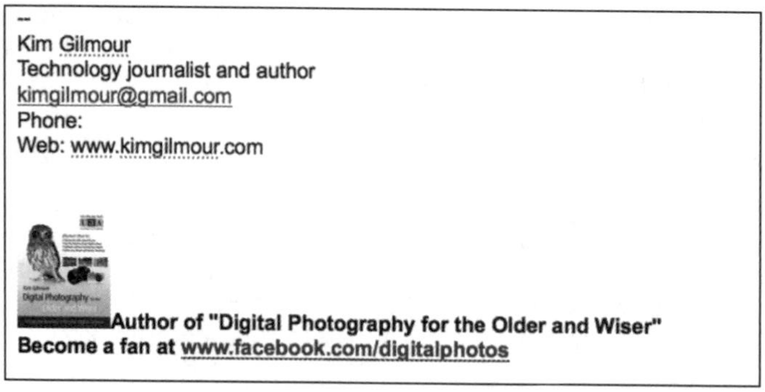

Figure 12-3:
A signature
file can
include
some simple
HTML and
a short
marketing
message.

--
Kim Gilmour
Technology journalist and author
kimgilmour@gmail.com
Phone:
Web: www.kimgilmour.com

Author of "Digital Photography for the Older and Wiser"
Become a fan at www.facebook.com/digitalphotos

Always include the URL to your business website in your signature file and be sure to include it on its own line. Why? Most email programs recognise the URL as a web page by its prefix (`http://www.`) and suffix (`.com`, `.co.uk` and so on). When your reader opens your message, the email program displays the URL as a clickable hyperlink that, when clicked, opens your web page in a web browser window.

To test your new signature file, compose a new message and it should appear in the body of the message composition window. You can compose a message by clicking before the signature and starting to type. Send a message to yourself or someone sitting next to you and check out how it looks.

Creating forms that aren't formidable

In the old days, people who heard 'here's a form to fill out' usually started to groan. Who likes to stare at a form to apply for a job or for financial aid or, even worse, to figure out how much you owe in taxes? But as an online businessperson, forms can be your best friends because they give customers a means to provide you with feedback as well as essential marketing information. Using forms, you can find out where customers live, how old they are and so on. Customers can also use forms to sound off and ask questions.

Forms can be really handy from the perspective of the customer as well. The speed of the Internet enables them to dash off information right away. They can then pretty much immediately receive a response from you that's tailored to their needs and interests.

Forms consist of two parts, only one of which is visible on a web page:

- ✔ The visible part includes the text-entry fields, buttons and tick boxes that an author creates with HTML commands.
- ✔ The part of the form that you don't see is a computer script that resides on the server that receives the page.

You can write the script in one of many languages, but these days you needn't worry too much about the programming side of forms because they're available as add-ons to content publishing platforms like Joomla, Drupal and Wordpress.

Getting the data to you

What exactly happens when customers connect to a page on your site that contains a form? First, they fill out the text-entry fields, radio buttons and other areas you've set up. When they finish, they click a button, often marked Submit, in order to transmit, or *post*, the data from the remote computer to your website.

A computer script receives the data submitted to your site and processes it so that you can read it. Depending on the form's action, the data could be emailed to you or presented in a text file in an easy-to-read format.

Most forms automatically send users to a web page that acknowledges that you've received the information and thanks them for their feedback. It's a nice touch that your customers are sure to appreciate.

Some clever businesspeople have created some really useful web content by providing a way for nonprogrammers such as you and us to create forms online. Appropriately enough, you connect to the server's website and fill out a form provided by the service in order to create your form. The form has a built-in script that processes the data and emails it to you. Services like Freedback (www.freedback.com) can help you to create a simple contact form to put on your site – see the following section for details.

Using Freedback to create a form

You can use Freedback to create a simple form for your website. The free version is supported by advertising which appears after people send you their query, but to get rid of the ads and get extra features such as automatic responders and up to ten forms, you can pay around $19 (around £12) per month. One basic ad-free form costs $9 (around £5.50) per month. You don't need technical knowledge to use Freedback, but the form creation process generates some HTML code that you need to paste into your chosen page. Just make sure you're in HTML view mode when using your web page editor or content publishing platform.

The first step in setting up a web page form is determining what information you want to receive from someone who fills out the form. Whatever program you're using to create the form then gives you options for ways to ask for the information you want. Figure 12-4 shows Freedback's home page.

Here are the steps you follow on Freedback:

1. **Go to www.freedback.com and click Sign Up.**

   Enter your name, email address and your chosen login password. An email from Freedback arrives in your inbox; click the link to verify your email address.

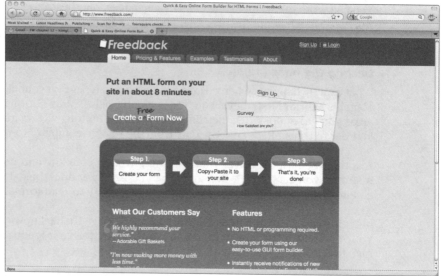

Figure 12-4:
Freedback
lets you
create
a form
for your
website in
minutes
without any
technical
effort.

2. **Start building your form.**

   Use the controls to add, delete or edit the questions you want to include in your form. To get you started, the name and email address fields are filled out but you can delete or edit these if you wish.

3. **Add a new field.**

   Click Add Question and select the type of question you want to add: a short answer, long answer, radio buttons, checkboxes, text box or a drop-down selection box. Hover your mouse pointer over these selections to see examples of what these look like in practice.

4. **Customise your question.**

   After selecting your chosen question, fill in the boxes to begin customising the form. If you're listing several options for people to tick such as, 'What kind of car do you drive?', type one 'answer' per line. If the field in the form is essential for the customer to fill in, tick the Required box. When a customer submits the form but hasn't filled in a required field, a prompt will appear.

5. **Click Save.**

   Keep adding questions until you've finished, then click Continue.

6. **Select what happens when a form is submitted.**

   If you've only chosen the free option then you can't customise this. An advertisement appears after customers send the form. Otherwise, you can upgrade to redirect customers to a web page, or have them view a thank-you message. An email reply to the customer is also an option if you upgrade.

7. **Click Continue.**

8. Add the HTML to your page.

The HTML code that you must add to your website appears. Click your mouse pointer within the window of code, then press Ctrl + A to select it and Ctrl + C to copy it. Then paste this code into the HTML of the web page you wish to include the form on by pressing Ctrl + V.

Making Customers Feel That They Belong

In the old days, people went to the market often, sometimes on a daily basis. The shopkeeper was likely to have set aside items for their consideration based on individual tastes and needs. More likely than not, the business transaction followed a discussion of families, politics and other village gossip.

Good customer service can make your customers feel like members of a community that frequent a family bakery – the community of satisfied individuals who regularly use your goods and services. In the following sections, we describe some ways to make your customers feel like members of a group, club or other organisation who return to your site on a regular basis and interact with a community of individuals with similar interests.

Putting the 'person' into personal service

How often does an employee personally greet you as you walk through the door of a shop? On the web as well as in real life, people like a prompt and personal response. Your challenge is to provide someone on your website who's available to provide live customer support.

The online auction giant eBay.co.uk has a live *chat* function, which Kim used when a fraudster tried to steal her TV by using a dodgy PayPal account. It's a very immediate sort of customer support in which individuals type messages to one another over the Internet in real time.

LivePerson (`www.liveperson.com`) provides a simple alternative that allows small businesses to provide chat-based support. LivePerson is software that enables you to see who's connected to your site at any one time and instantly lets you chat with customers, just as if you were greeting them at the front door of a bricks-and-mortar shop.

LivePerson works like this: you install the LivePerson Pro software on your own computer (not the server that runs your site). With LivePerson, you or your assistants can lead the customer through the process of making a purchase. For example, you may help show customers what individual sale items look like by sending them image files to view with their web browsers. You can try a LivePerson Pro demo on its website; at the time of writing it cost around $100 (£62) per month.

CASE STUDY

Getting up close with comic fans

David Cresswell, co-founder of the Comic Domain online store (www.comicdomain.co.uk), enjoys meeting his customers (and potential new ones) at comic conventions.

David started the site back in 2000 with his brother Steve, and it has grown from strength to strength. He embraces tools like Facebook and Twitter to keep customers satisfied. These new social networking techniques have also helped to promote his brand. 'We're certainly seeing many new customer names and a few have mentioned they found us on Facebook rather than the usual answer of Google,' he says.

The Comic Domain website includes a searchable online catalogue set up with Actinic, a blog and links to its Facebook page and Twitter feed.

Here, David explains the secrets of his success.

Q: How important is it to get to know your customers in person?

A: With all the joys of being an online-only retailer, you just can't beat meeting your customers face to face. Answering people's questions and showing them the stock has been the best retainer of customers when we attend conventions up and down the country.

Q: How do you keep a competitive edge, given that you aren't the only comic retailer out there?

A: We take pride in the service we provide. We've found that when a customer leaves us for whatever reason, they're back soon enough and have thanked us for the better customer service that we provide. We're also very knowledgeable about the product we well. So if anyone has a question, they're free to email

us or even give us a call via Skype. We've had customers who have stayed with us since day one. More than ten years later, they're still with us and we're extremely thankful. You wouldn't stay if the service was terrible.

Q: Do you operate completely online or are there offline aspects of your business?

A: At the start, Comic Domain operated purely online, but customers requested a standing order service, where we pretty much act as a personal shopper. All the customer details and communication is still handled online via email or Skype but it allows a customer to 'pop in' online and request additional titles to be added to their regular weekly, fortnightly or monthly orders. Based on turnover now, it's probably a 50/50 split of online and offline standing order sales.

The use of flyers has changed and updated with us over the years. With our online shop we can now accept special offer codewords so when we attend a comic show we can turn our flyer into a money-off voucher that the customer can use when they go home, giving them even more incentive to try our services and buy our products.

Q: Given that budgets are tight these days what are your top tips for marketing on a budget?

A: There's a lot you can do which is absolutely free, but it will require your time to sit down and lean something new. Use your marketing budget wisely and always set something aside from each promotion to give you a starting budget on your next one. Always think two steps ahead.

Not letting an ocean be a business barrier

You're probably familiar with terms such as *global village* and *international marketplace*. But how do you extend your reach into the huge overseas markets where e-commerce is just beginning to come into its own? Making sure that products are easily and objectively described with words as well as clear images and diagrams, where necessary, is becoming increasingly important. Other ways to effectively overcome language and cultural barriers exist; some are common sense and others are less obvious.

Keep in mind the fact that shoppers in many developing nations still prefer to shop with their five senses. So that foreign customers never have a question on how to proceed, providing them with implicit descriptions of the shopping process is essential. You should make information on ordering, payment, execution and support available at every step.

Take a look at overseas-based sites to see how they differ to UK ones. Kim noticed that eBay in Australia operates slightly differently to in the UK. Direct deposits into sellers' bank accounts are a very popular option and PayPal, while popular, doesn't seem as widespread.

Having a discussion area can enhance your site

Can we talk? Even Greg's pet birds like to communicate by words as well as squawks. A small business can turn its individual customers into a cohesive group by starting its own discussion group on the Internet. Discussion groups work particularly well if you're promoting a particular type of product or if you and your customers are involved in a provocative or even controversial area of interest.

Some kinds of discussion groups include:

- ✔ **A Facebook group:** You can create a Facebook page for your business that acts pretty much like an individual's Facebook page, but anyone can join and post messages, videos and photos and initiate discussion groups if you let them. The great thing is that you retain ultimate administrator control of the page and can view how many people have interacted with the various elements of your page (or delete spammy posts).

✔ **A web forum:** An online message board, often created to complement a website, that lets people post topics and respond to message *threads* (all the messages relating to a topic of conversation). You can install free software onto your website such as phpBB (provided your website is database enabled). Many hosts allow you to install popular software with just one click; otherwise you need a little technical setup knowledge. A popular paid-for option is vBulletin (www.vbulletin.com).

✔ **Other web groups:** You'll find little communities springing up all over the place. On Flickr, tens of thousands of groups are dedicated to certain photographic themes (Kim's a member of dozens of esoterically themed groups, from one showcasing people's blue and white images, to ones taken solely from a low perspective).

✔ **Blogging communities:** Regular visitors to certain blogs tend to leave comments underneath the posts. A conversation thread often starts underneath these blog posts. If you operate a blog on your website, be prepared for customers to make comments. Don't delete negative opinions; this is a good opportunity for you to apologise to customers and respond constructively to their complaints. Other people who read the blog will be able to see that you've taken the time to respond personally to something that's troubling one of your customers, and that's a good thing. These days, the web means opinions are very public and you can't control everything that people say about you on the web (unless, of course, you live in a country that has the power to censor critical comments out before they even get posted!).

In addition to online groups, many large corporations host interactive chats moderated by experts on subjects related to their areas of business. But small businesses can also hold chats, most easily by setting up a chat room on a site that hosts chat-based discussions.

Starting a Yahoo! group

These days, the web is pretty much (along with email) the most popular way to communicate and share information. That's why starting a discussion group on the web makes perfect sense. A web-based discussion group is somewhat less intimidating than others because it doesn't require a participant to use newsgroup software.

Yahoo! groups are absolutely free to set up. The service exists only on the .com version of Yahoo! and not the .co.uk one as yet, but then that's the great thing about the Internet: it's not confined by national borders. (To find out how to set up a group, just go to the FAQ page at help.yahoo.com/help/us/groups/index.html and click the How Do I Start a Group? link.) Yahoo! Groups not only enables users to exchange messages, but also communicate in real time by using chat. And as the list operator, you can send out email newsletters and other messages to your participants too.

Simply operating an online shop isn't enough. You need to present yourself as an authority in a particular area that's of interest. The discussion group needs to concern itself primarily with that topic and give participants a chance to exchange views and tips on the topic. If people have questions about your shop, they can always email you directly – they don't need a discussion group to do that.

Tracking orders

Letting people track the status of their order online isn't essential, but if your business setup allows for it, then we think it's a great added extra. After an item has been dispatched, it's courteous to send your customer an email saying so. And if you use a courier or postal service that provides customers with a tracking number (such as Royal Mail recorded delivery or DHL), you can include this on the email too. Customers can enter the tracking number on the courier's website to see where the item is.

Chapter 13

Search Engines: What You Need to Know

....

In This Chapter

▶ Analysing how search engines find your site

▶ Focusing on ways to improve your coverage on Google

▶ Optimising content so it appears higher in search engine results

▶ Tracing referrals and visits to increase revenue and customer loyalty

....

The other day, Greg took some old radios to a local repair shop. The shop has been in business for more than three decades but never seemed to be busy. This time, however, the owner told Greg he was overwhelmed with hundreds of back orders and wouldn't be able to get to Greg's jobs for several weeks. His shop had just been featured on a television show, and now people were driving long distances to bring him retro audio equipment to fix.

If you can get your business mentioned in just the right place, customers find you more easily. On the web, search engines are the most important places to get yourself listed. One of the key requirements for any business is the ability to match up your products or services with potential customers and to ensure that your company shows up in lots of search results and that your site is near the top of the first page. You do have a measure of control over the quality of your placement in search results, and this chapter describes strategies for improving it.

Search engines have created a huge industry for themselves and the search engine optimisation (SEO) businesses that feed off them. People around the world lodge billions of search enquiries every month, which lead to billions of results. You can see why your website can easily get lost in the jumble of businesses that are vying for attention.

SEO is actually something you and your web designers should be thinking about *before* you write the content for your site, because going back and tweaking things later is harder. But don't worry if your site is already up and running. We know plenty of ways to monitor how well pages are working for you (or not), and this chapter helps you fix things accordingly. Besides, SEO isn't something you just walk away from: it's an ongoing process. The web is constantly changing and new competition is always on the horizon, so you need to be on the ball. For even more in-depth SEO strategies, consider looking at Search Engine Optimization For Dummies, by Peter Kent.

Understanding How Search Engines Find You

Have you ever wondered why some companies manage to find their way to the top of a page of search engine results – and occasionally pop up several times on the same page – while others get buried deep within pages and pages of website listings? In an ideal world, search engines would rank e-commerce sites by their design, functionality and whether the businesses behind them give the best possible deals. In fact, technology has enabled search engines to place *some* importance on these factors, but with so many millions of websites crowding the Internet, the job of processing searches and indexing website URLs and contents has to be automated. Because it's computerised, you can perform some magic with the way your web pages are written that can help you improve your placement in a set of search results.

Your site doesn't necessarily need to appear right at the top of the first search results page. The important thing is to ensure that your site appears before that of your competition. You need to think like a searcher, which is probably easy because you no doubt do plenty of web-based searches yourself. How do you find the websites you want? Two things are of paramount importance: keywords and links.

Keywords are key

A *keyword* is a word describing a subject that you enter in a search box in order to find information on a website or on the wider Internet. Suppose that you're trying to find where to buy a herbal sleep aid called Nightol. You'd naturally enter the term *Nightol* in the search box on your search service of choice, click a button called Search, Search Now, Go or something similar, and wait a few seconds for search results to be gathered.

When you send a keyword (or keywords) to a search service, you set a number of possible actions in motion. One thing that happens for sure is that the search engine processes the keyword. Rather than sift through the entire live web, the search engine churns the keyword through its huge index containing contents culled from billions of web pages. The whole process usually takes less than a second.

Web pages are so ubiquitous and changeable that most of the indexing work is actually done by computer programs called *bots* or *spiders* automatically scouring the web for content. These programs don't necessarily record every word on every web page. Some take words from the headings; others index the first 50 or 100 words on a website. In some cases, search engines look at site descriptions from services such as the DMOZ Open Directory Project, a human-edited directory of web pages that only lists what it thinks are quality websites.

Search engines are increasingly indexing alternative content to bog-standard, static web pages. Videos, news articles, Flash animations, books, images, maps, audio and blogs are just some of the things you can search through these days. (Google even includes real-time tweets from Twitter users and current news articles if you're searching for something timely, such as a breaking news story or celebrity gossip.)

Accordingly, when Kim did a search for *Kit Kat* on Google.co.uk, the sites that were listed at the top of the first page of search results had several attributes:

- ✔ Some sites had the brand name *Kit Kat* in the URL, such as `www.kitkat.com` or `en.wikipedia.org/wiki/Kit_Kat`.

- ✔ Other sites mentioned the word *Kit Kat* several times at the top of the home page or in the title.

- ✔ A number of Kit Kat images appeared at the top of the search. These in turn came from websites that used the phrase Kit Kat when describing their image.

Businesses that advertise using Google AdWords use a fantastic, free tool that tracks keyword queries made to the popular search engine. This helps businesses see what people are searching for so they can target sponsored ads to audiences who are looking for those specific keywords (see the box 'Paying for search listings can pay off', later in this chapter). But a little-known fact is that the keyword tool is just as useful for your business, because you can tailor your online content depending on what people are searching for to maximise the number of visits to your site or just make your site more prominent in a list of search results. You may do well to know what's trendy and write your text accordingly.

The Google AdWords keyword tool is accessible either from the Google AdWords console at `www.google.co.uk/adwords` or from `https://adwords.google.com/select/KeywordToolExternal`. Other popular services worth looking at include Wordtracker (`www.wordtracker.com`), which includes a seven-day free trial, and the free Trellian Keyword Discovery tool at `www.keyworddiscovery.com`.

A number of parameters

Google says it asks more than 200 questions to gauge a website's importance, including how many times the keywords are mentioned on the website. Google also looks at the country you're searching from and the date and time of your search query. As Google learns more about how people search, its secret computer algorithms constantly improve on delivering relevant search results (think of it as a mysterious blend of herbs and spices – you don't know what's in it, but it works). Take the example Google gave Kim a few years back, when she interviewed the search giant for an article. When Americans look up the word *Turkey* outside of Thanksgiving season, they're probably looking up the country as a holiday destination. But come November, search results will most likely relate to the bird. So, the results Google dishes up vary depending on the time of year.

Adding your site's most important keyword to the URL is one solution to better search placement. But you can't always do this. When it comes to keywords, your job is to load your website with as many words as you can find that are relevant to what you sell. You can do so by:

- Making use of the descriptive <META> tag in the HTML for your home page so that the spiders that index web pages know what your page is about (before you get confused, we include a section on this called 'Adding descriptions to your HTML', later in this chapter). Search engines could use this description as a summary or snippet in your website's search engine result listing, so getting it right is important. Using a different meta description for each page is even better.

- Adding keywords to the initial body text on your pages, as we describe in the 'Adding keywords to key pages' section, later in this chapter.

- Using your keywords in your website's headings and subtitles, so search engines realise they're important. For more on how to do this, refer to the 'Adding keywords to key pages' section, later in this chapter.

A keyword doesn't have to be a single word. You can also use a phrase containing two or more words. Think beyond single words to consider phrases people may enter when they're trying to find products or services you're offering. Be sure to check out the Google AdWords keyword tool or other similar service (see the previous section for details).

Links help searchers connect to you

Keywords aren't the only things that point search services to websites. Services like Google keep track of the number of links that point to a site. The greater the number of links, the higher that site's ranking in a set of Google search listings. It's especially good if the URLs that form the links make use of your keywords.

Suppose that your ideal keywords are 'Dan's Shoe Shop'. The ideal URLs would be www.dansshoesshop.co.uk, www.dansshoeshop.com and so on. You can create the following HTML link to your e-commerce website on a personal web page, or an eBay About Me page (see Chapter 10):

```
<a href="http://www.dansshoeshop.com"> Visit Dan's Shoe
        Shop </a>
```

Such a link would be doubly useful: a search service such as Google.co.uk would find your desired keywords ('Dan's Shoe Shop') in the visible, clickable link on your webpage, as well as in the HTML for the link.

Never use phrases such as 'Click here' to link to websites – they don't mean anything to search engines. If Dan spends two paragraphs describing his shoe shop, then a link saying 'Visit Dan's Shoe Shop' is more meaningful than 'Click here for more information'. It also tells Google that the link is to Dan's Shoe Shop.

We know that Google looks at the words people use to link to other articles when gauging their relevance, and this provides potential for manipulation of the system. Back in 2003 a horde of bloggers linked the phrase 'miserable failure' on their websites to then-president George W. Bush's biography on the White House website. Whenever anyone Googled 'miserable failure', the first link went to that page. This was all because of Google's automated system that lent more weight to the phrases used in link text. Eventually, Google cottoned on to this and similar pranks. It then changed its algorithm to minimise these kinds of 'cheats'. (We also assume the company didn't want people to think it was endorsing this kind of behaviour!)

Taking the initiative: Paying for ads

You can't get much better placement than right at the top of the first page of a set of search results, either at the top of the page or in a column on the right-hand side. It's even better if your site's name and URL are highlighted in a colour.

Unfortunately, the only way to get such preferred treatment is to pay for it. And that's just what a growing number of online businesses are doing – paying search engines to list their sites in a prominent location. Be careful you don't fritter your money away by continuing with an inefficient advertising technique, though. Target niche markets, set a budget and stick with it. If paying for ads doesn't work out, it might be time to adopt a different strategy or continue to focus on improving your natural placement in search results. See the 'Paying for search listings can pay off' sidebar, later in this chapter, for more information.

The wisdom of crowds

Back in the web's early days Yahoo!, one of the oldest search engines around, started out by providing a human-edited directory of links to what its editors considered the most reputable or noteworthy websites. (When Kim was at university in 1995, this was the main way she discovered her two favourite diversions from study: a now-defunct web-based chat room called Doug's, and the Internet Movie Database, which still exists today.)

Having a sense-check by real live editors was, until quite recently, highly beneficial for websites because it lent their destinations some weight. Yahoo! even had a coveted cool pick of the day that drove traffic to featured sites.

Eventually, search engines became much more adept at delivering relevant results. Yahoo! quietly retired its directory (although you can still access it at http://dir.yahoo.com) and its cool recommendations a couple of years back.

So, have search engine spiders completely replaced real-life recommendations? Far from it. The general public are now the ones taking the lead and publicising noteworthy websites. Take a look at your friends sharing links on Facebook every day or recommending links on Twitter. And giving a YouTube video of the next teen singing sensation the thumbs up or the thumbs down literally takes just a click of a button.

Services like Digg, Delicious and Reddit also showcase what's hot – and the users of these sites decide what's cool. Thanks to Digg (www.digg.com), computer programmer and author Andy Geldman received over 10,000 visitors to Slurls (www.slurls.com), the website of his humorous book that lists unfortunate website names with double meanings.

He explains: 'Digg works by promoting stories and people vote on them if they like them. As you get more votes, your story moves up in popularity and if you're lucky you get on the front page and can get literally tens of thousands of visitors. So you have to have a good story that captures people's interest. I got around 10,000 visitors from Digg, plus the knock-on effect to other sites.' Sure, not every single one of those visitors were driven to spontaneously buy a copy of his book, but a few did – best of all, it created a huge, positive buzz and got his name out there. Who can complain about that?

Knowing who supplies the search results

Another important thing to remember about search engines is that they often gather results from *other* search services. You may be surprised to find out that if you do a search of the web on Orange, your search results are primarily gathered from Google. That's because Orange has a contract from Google to supply such results. The same applies to thousands of major websites that have taken advantage of Google's powerful search capabilities. And Microsoft owns a stake in Facebook, so whenever you use Facebook to conduct a keyword search you find results from Bing, Microsoft's search engine.

Just what are the most popular search services in the UK? A rundown appears in Table 13-1. We present the services in rank order, beginning in the first row with Google, which is No. 1. Rankings were reported by Hitwise in

January 2011. As you can see, Google is massively dominant, with the Google US site even outstripping Yahoo! UK and Ireland's popularity.

Table 13-1	Internet Search Services	
Search Service	*URL*	*Proportion of visits*
Google UK	`www.google.co.uk`	75.58%
Google (US)	`www.google.com`	7.37%
Bing	`www.bing.com`	5.18%
Yahoo UK and Ireland	`uk.search.yahoo.com`	3.16%
Ask Jeeves UK	`www.uk.ask.com`	2.05%

These search services are by no means the only ones around, but they're the ones you should focus on. Depending on the nature of your business, other popular search engines are around in emerging markets such as China, where Google trails behind the search engine Baidu (`www.baidu.com`).

Following Google's Guidelines

When it comes to search engines, Google is at the top of the heap. Back in the day, it was Yahoo! that was setting the pace, but Google's lightening quick searches and its comprehensive documenting of the web has made it favourite.

Google is a runaway success thanks to its effectiveness. Competitors like Microsoft's Bing are yapping at its heels, but in our opinion you're simply more likely to find something on Google, and more quickly, than you are anywhere else. Any search engine placement strategy has to address Google first and foremost. But that doesn't mean you should ignore Google's competitors. In fact, Yahoo! has put out a brilliant style guide book covering all aspects on how to write for the web – and you can read highlights, including the company's common sense SEO tips, at `http://styleguide.yahoo.com`.

Meanwhile, Google also has some clever tips and guidelines that'll help your website gain a better place in its search results. And not only that: many of the practical tips relate to improving the structure and layout of your website as a whole.

Google's technical tips are worth investigating by you (or your appointed expert). Failing to follow the right sort of guidelines could see your website being penalised for something you might not realise is happening (such as an unpatched security hole, or spammers leaving unsolicited advertising links on your blog posts).

Where to find these tips? We encourage you to download Google's SEO starter guide, which includes all you need to get started. It's an Adobe PDF file so you can either read it on screen or print it out as a nifty booklet (note that it runs to around 30 pages, so you might want to print double-sided). At the time of writing, you can access the guide at `www.google.com/webmasters/docs/search-engine-optimization-starter-guide.pdf`.

Always make sure that you've exhausted all the free channels of search optimisation before you shell out any cash for SEO. And tread carefully when choosing an SEO company to work with. Plenty of SEO companies and consultants are about, and we know that the vast majority are perfectly legitimate (Kim's spoken – and worked with – plenty of folk who adopt a realistic and helpful approach to the technique). But beware of companies that adopt automatic methods to try to improve your ranking. Dodgy software exists that does things like link to your website from dozens of fake websites or news articles in a bid to artificially inflate its importance and improve your ranking.

People adopt all sorts of sneaky techniques to cheat the search engines. For example, some repeat keywords dozens of times on a page but change the font colour to the same shade as the background so it can't be seen. Google tries its best to detect duplicate or bogus websites that are trying to beat the system – if it doesn't catch you at first, it's likely it eventually will, and then Google will drop your website from its index altogether. The best way to increase your ranking is to build up a bona fide reputation and forge genuine partnerships with websites that endorse you. You've been warned!

Googling yourself

If you want to evaluate the quality of your search results placement on Google, you have to start by taking stock of where you currently stand. That's easily done: just go to Google's UK home page (`www.google.co.uk`) and 'Google' yourself. (In other words, do a search for your own name or your business's name – a pastime that's called *egosurfing*.) See where your website turns up in the results and also make a note of which other sites mention yours. Next, click Advanced Search or go directly to `www.google.co.uk/advanced_search`. Click 'Date, usage rights, numeric range and more' to bring up a host of different search parameters. Under 'Page-specific tools', enter your URL in the box 'Find pages that link to the page' and click Search. The results that appear in a couple of seconds consist of websites that link to yours. The list suggests to you the kinds of sites you should approach to solicit links.

Google Webmaster tools

Another essential place to visit is Google Webmaster Central, at `www.google.com/webmasters`. After registering your site (see the box 'Be an instant webmaster' in Chapter 8 for how to do this) and waiting a few days until it collects enough data, you can find out exactly how Google sees your site and thus improve its efficiency. Things Google Webmaster tell you include:

- ✔ **Search queries:** The search terms people use to find your site. For more on analysing this information, see the section later in this chapter, 'Monitoring Traffic: The Science of Web Analytics'.

- ✔ **Keywords:** These are the descriptive words Google thinks are relevant to your site. Should these be wide of the mark, then you should rethink your content strategy.

- ✔ **Diagnostics:** Do any security holes exist in your site that could result in malicious activity? Are there any links to pages that no longer exist, which could confuse the Google robot and deter your visitors? What about any improvements to your HTML, such as avoiding duplicate meta descriptions? Find the answers here.

- ✔ **Fetch as Googlebot:** How does the Google robot see a particular page of your site? Enter its URL and Google will 'fetch' your page and bring you the result within a few minutes.

Even more advanced tools are at your fingertips here. In Figure 13-1, you can see the search terms people have used to find Kim's site. Kim's sorted them so that the keywords at the top are those that have attracted the greatest proportion of clicks, known as the *click-through rate*, or CTR. In this case, the keywords *pinhole photo* have attracted a high CTR of 26 per cent. Kim discovered that this is because, at the time of writing, her image appears in the first search results for *pinhole photo* on Google. *London photos* has a CTR of 11 per cent. (See the later section 'Adding keywords to key pages' for how to add keywords to your HTML.)

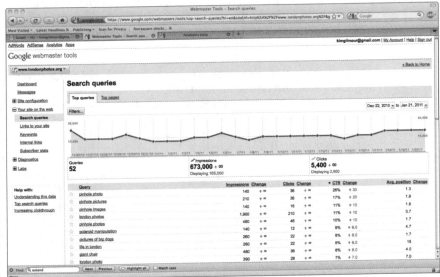

Figure 13-1: By finding out when your website appears in search results and whether people click through to it, you can experiment with making your content more enticing.

©2011 Google

Leaving a Trail of Crumbs

In order to improve your site's search placement, you need to make it easy for searchers to find you. You leave a trail of digital crumbs. You add keywords throughout your web pages, and you make sure that your site is included in the databases of the most popular services.

Keep in mind that most web surfers don't enter single words in search boxes. They tend to enter phrases. Combinations of keywords are extra effective. If you sell tools, don't just enter *tools* as a keyword. Enter keywords such as *tool box*, *power tool*, *tool caddy*, *pneumatic tool*, *electric tool* and so on.

Search Engine Watch (`www.searchenginewatch.com`) is the ultimate place to go for tips on how search engines and indexes work, and how to get listed on them.

Adding descriptions to your HTML

Describing your website in a couple of snappy sentences sounds easy. But when you consider that this tagline could be displayed underneath your website's search result, that's when it sounds a little daunting. Essentially, you're penning a mini-sales pitch with the aim of attracting customers to your site – you don't want your competitors thinking of something more enticing!

So, grab an old-fashioned pencil and paper and write down all the words you can think of that are related to your site, your products, your services or you – whatever you want to promote, in other words. You may also enlist the help of a thesaurus or the one online at Dictionary.com (`www.dictionary.com`). Look up one term associated with your goods or services, and you're likely to find a number of similar terms.

After you have a set of keywords, you need to weave them into some concise summary text and add it to the HTML for your web pages. Website *descriptions* are contained within HTML commands that begin with `<META>`. If you type the commands by hand using a text editor, you need to locate the meta descriptions command in between the `<HEAD>` and `</HEAD>` tags at the head of the document. It looks like this:

```
<META NAME="description" content="Insert your tagline
        here">
```

The `<META>` tag is most important when relating to this `description` command. Make sure you create one that includes as many keywords and synonyms as you can in order to get visitors clicking!

Retail giant Amazon.co.uk has a meta description that reads:

```
<META NAME="description" content="Low prices on digital
        cameras, MP3, sports equipment, books, music,
        DVDs, video games, home, garden and much more.
        Free UK delivery on Amazon orders.">
```

Adding meta descriptions is easy with most web page editors. You can type your information in specially designated boxes or even fill in a box with your tagline, although it's a good idea to have *several* meta descriptions throughout your website depending on the page content. Google likes this sort of thing.

If you use Wordpress to publish your website, a special plugin lets you do this whenever you post new content. For information on this and on adding meta descriptions to Wordpress, go to http://codex.wordpress.org/Meta_Tags_in_WordPress.

When you search for your competitors' websites, take a look to see whether search engines have taken their meta description and used it as a summary snippet in their search result. In some cases, depending on the keywords you've searched for and whether some summary text exists, Google displays a relevant snippet of information taken directly from the content on their website.

You can spy on your competitors' websites to see whether they've added any meta descriptions or keywords to their web pages by following these steps:

1. **Go to your competitor's home page and choose View⇨Source/ Page source, depending on the browser you're using.**

   A new window opens with the page source supplied.

2. **Scroll through the code, looking for the <META> tags if they're present. (Press Ctrl+F, enter META and click the Find button if you can't find them on your own.)**

   If the page's author used <META> tags to enter a description, you see it on screen.

3. **Make a note of the keywords supplied and see whether you can apply any to your own website.**

With a <META> Keyword command you can literally list all the relevant key-words you can think of in your HTML – this list is kept from view to the casual surfer, but search engines can scan it. Meta keywords used to carry more weight before search engines were smart enough to pick up the important words located on a website, but the system is easily abused. Google doesn't even take it into account any more. These days, search engines just analyse the actual content of your website for keywords.

Registering your site with Google.co.uk

Google's robot automatically indexes web pages all over the Internet. The robot actually has a name: Googlebot. (It even has a smaller brother, a robot that trawls sites designed for mobile devices called Googlebot-mobile.) However, you don't have to wait for Googlebot to find your site: you can fill out a simple form that adds your URL to the sites that are indexed by this program. Go to www.google.co.uk/addurl.html, enter your URL and a few comments about your site, type the security word you see in the box and click the Add URL button. That's all there is to it. Expect to wait a few weeks for your site to appear among Google's search results.

Get listed in local indexes

While we're often wary of automated services that get you 'listed' on hundreds of often spammy directories, it's definitely worth submitting your business to Google Maps and to Yell.com.

When you submit your business to Google Maps, then anyone looking for your business sees your business name appear on the map as a pinpointed location, along with your phone number and a website, if you have one. If Google has photographed your area, you may even see a picture of your front door! To get started, go to http://maps.google.co.uk and click 'Put your business on Google Maps'. Then follow the instructions. If you need even *more* convincing about the benefits of putting a business on Google Maps, see the video at www.youtube.com/googleplaces.

Meanwhile, it's well worth getting a free, standard listing on Yell.com, the UK's local business search engine. Yell.com results also appear on Google Maps and others; and the site is regularly used as a specialist business search engine in its own right. You can pay to get a higher priority listing in Yell.com searches, but we recommend seeing how well the free one goes first – it includes your business name and contact details, as well as a map location. To sign your business up and find out more about the paid-for products, go to www.yelldirect.com.

Businesses on the web can get obsessed with how high their sites appear on the list of search results pages. Of the millions of sites listed in a search service's database, the chances are good that at least one has the same name as yours (or something close to it) or that a page contains a combination of the same words that make up your organisation's name. Don't be overly concerned with hitting the top of the search-hit charts. Yes, you need to be making sure you're attracting customers from search queries, but concentrate on creating a top-notch website, making sales and generating genuine buzz. That way, search engines realise just how great you are without you worrying about whether you've placed your keywords in the right places.

Google can read your mind!

In the last couple of years, Google has intro-duced a number of mind-blowing tools that are based purely on what it's learned from people who use its service every day – people just like you and us. The first, Google Autocomplete, you're probably familiar with. As you start typing keywords into the search box, a number of options automatically appear from a drop-down menu. It's like predictive text, but far more accurate! The second, called Google Instant, literally delivers search results to you on screen as you type! You need to be logged in using your Google Account login details to see this (if you've got a Gmail or YouTube account then you can use these credentials as your Google Account). Worth checking out.

Adding keywords to key pages

Earlier in this chapter (see 'Adding keywords to your HTML'), we show you how to add meaningful descriptions to the HTML for your web pages. You can add other keywords to parts of your web page that are visible – parts of the page that those programs called *robots* or *spiders* scan and index:

- ✔ **The title:** Be sure to create a title for your page. The title appears in the title bar at the very top of the browser window between the tags <TITLE> and </TITLE>. Many search engines index the contents of the title because it appears not only at the top of the browser window, but at the top of the HTML too.

- ✔ **Headings:** Your web page's headings should be specific about what you sell and what you do. Place them between your HTML heading tags where <H1> signifies the most important heading, <H2> a secondary heading and so on down to <H6>. The more important the heading, the larger it appears on the page. Your <H1> heading tag might read:

  ```
  <H1>Handmade artisan chocolates: true gourmet delights
       delivered!</H1>
  ```

- ✔ **The first line of text:** Sometimes, search services index every word on every page, but others limit the amount of text they index. So the first lines may be indexed, but others aren't. Get your message across quickly; pack your first sentences with nouns that list what you have for sale.

- ✔ **On all your URLs:** Make every directory in your website count as a keyword. Going to www.dansshoeshop.com/mens/boots is more meaningful to a visitor and a search engine than www.dansshoeshop.com/3456/page2.html. The same goes for blogs – you can jazz up your *permalinks*, the permanent link for a blog post, so that it reflects the date and content, such as http://mashable.com/2011/01/24/the-history-of-social-media-infographic.

Paying for search listings can pay off

Listing with search sites is growing more complex all the time. Whenever you do a search you see *sponsored results* appear alongside or above and below the regular (or what's known in the trade as *organic*) search engine results pages. These aren't appearing just like magic: the listings are always relevant to the search terms entered, such as *used cars*.

These sponsored results are called *pay per click* (PPC) or *paid search* ads, and advertisers only pay their host when a visitor clicks on the sponsored search result.

But how much money do advertisers pay? Well, it depends on the host's PPC model. Search engines usually operate an auction-style bidding system, where advertisers compete with rivals for certain search terms (keywords). Advertisers who bid higher maximum amounts for keywords tend to get a more prominent listing, and their ad appears more often. The quality of the advertiser's link and the amount of times it gets clicked on also contribute to its prominence in the sponsored results.

Search engines also use technology to locate a user's approximate location, so local businesses can target advertising to people in their town.

PPC is an art form, and this book isn't the place to delve into immense detail about how to go

about conducting an advertising campaign and choosing the right keywords – it's hard enough figuring this out for your own site. But the good news is, it's relatively inexpensive to start dipping your toes in the water because you can specify a maximum daily amount to ensure that you won't go over budget if too many people click on your ad.

You may need to experiment with PPC to see whether it'll work for you. As Christianne James, founder of nursery website 4Little1s (www.4little1s.com) that we profile in Chapter 1, says: 'We started by using Google AdWords and Microsoft Adcenter to get our website on page one of the search engines. This was very expensive and we learned a very valuable lesson in ensuring that if you are paying for each "click", you have to ensure you target the page your customer arrives at. No point in advertising nursery furniture with the advert that takes your customer to the home page of your website. It needs to take the customer directly to the section on nursery furniture.'

The key (excuse the pun) is to get creative and think about the quality of the people clicking on your link, rather than the number of people who'll click on your ad.

The best way to ensure that your site gets indexed is to pack it with useful content. We're talking about textual content and, for images, *ALT text* that describes what they're about (see further on in this chapter for more). Make sure that your pages contain a significant amount of text as well as these other types of content.

Websites that specialise in search-engine optimisation talk about something called *keyword density:* the number of keywords on your page, multiplied by the number of times each one is used. Keyword density is a way to gain a good search engine ranking. In other words, if you sell shoes and you use ten different shoe-related terms once, you won't get as good a ranking compared to the use of six of seven words that appear twice, or a handful of well-chosen keywords used several times each.

It's a fine balance, though. Go overboard on the keyword density and the search engine might just think you're trying to cheat the system. As a result, your website's position in search engine rankings could actually be *penalised*. Do a sense-check on how much is too much. Read your text out loud. If it sounds pretty natural, you're probably safe.

Take the following passage taken from the home page of Startups.co.uk, which Dan used to be the editor of. It serves people who are considering starting a business, or those who've just taken the plunge. Notice how many times *business*, *start* and *entrepreneur* are used. (The actual text is a lot longer, and the words are repeated several more times.)

> *Whether you are a budding entrepreneur ready to start a business for the first time or you are an established entrepreneur looking to do it a second time, we have all the news and information you need to get your business starting on the right foot.*

Don't make your pages hard to index

Sometimes, the key to making things work is simply being certain that you aren't putting roadblocks in the way of success. The way you format web pages can prevent search services from recording your text and the keywords you want your customers to enter. Avoid these obvious hindrances:

- ✔ **Your text begins too far down the page.** If you load the top of your page with images that can't be indexed, your text is indexed that much slower, and your rankings suffer.

- ✔ **Your pages are loaded with Java applets, animations and other objects that can't be indexed.** Content that slows down the automatic indexing programs reduces your rankings too.

- ✔ **Your pages don't actually include the ideal keyword phrase you want your searchers to use.** If you have a business converting LP records to CDs, you want the phrases 'LP to CD' or 'convert LPs to CDs' somewhere on your home page and on other pages as well.

You can potentially assign every image on your web page a textual label (also known as *ALT* (alternative) *text* because the ALT element in HTML enables it to be used). The immediate purpose of the label is to tell visitors what the image depicts in case it can't be displayed in the browser window. They can also be read out by screen readers for people with visual impairments. Always describe your images accurately, because they're indexed and displayed for potential visitors. They also help search engines figure out what your page is about.

Monitoring Traffic: The Science of Web Analytics

How do you improve the number of times your site is found by search engines? One way is to analyse the traffic that comes to your site, a practice often called *web analytics*. Even if you don't like playing with numbers or looking at facts and figures, it's often a great joy seeing who's coming to your website, what they've been searching for and where they go when they're on there.

Plenty of excellent tools exist that can magically sort all of this data out for you and present it in a form that anyone who isn't Stephen Hawking can understand. Here are two common options:

- **Google Analytics:** The most popular, free tool is Google Analytics (yes, the search engine giant does it again). It uses a method called *page tagging*, which involves you placing a snippet of code on all your web pages. This shouldn't be laborious if you have a dynamic website that uses templates in its design, because including the snippet of code on your templates saves you the trouble of having to edit every one of your current and subsequent pages. Google hosts all the information about who's visiting your site, and you can access the data from any web browser, wherever you are in the world.

- **Log file analysis:** Log file analysis produces the same result as Google Analytics. It's more technical, but an expert should be able to help you. Every website records (or logs) information such as which resources on your website people visit most, what pages people look at, where visitors roughly come from, failed page requests and so on. You can pull all this raw data into more meaningful information.

  Log files and tagged pages typically record information such as the IP address of the computer that accesses a web page. They don't tell you the name and address of the person using the machine at the time. They give you an idea of where the computer is located geographically, based on the suffix at the end of a domain name (such as `.de` for Germany or `.fr` for France). They also know the website the visitors came from, such as a Google search results page, or via a link from another site.

Web analytics software is very sophisticated. Some of the things you can discover and do include:

- **Human versus non-human visitors:** You can see which visitors are human and which are search engine spiders. Both are useful to know, particularly if you're concerned about whether or not search engines are indexing your site.

✔ **Unique visitors:** When people visit your site, do something and come back to it again a few minutes later, they might be counted as two separate visits. But by using a small tracking file called a *cookie*, the analytics software can determine unique visitors within a certain timeframe.

✔ **Bounce rate:** The percentage of people who visit your site and then leave right away, probably because it either doesn't contain the information they're looking for or they can't find it. In online business parlance, you want to make your site *sticky* – that means keep people sticking around!

✔ **Discover success rates:** On Google Analytics, you can set some parameters you'd like to achieve, such as someone registering on your website, making a purchase or ending up at a certain URL. You can then identify your website's *conversion rate* – a percentage defined by the number of visits that result in your goal divided by the number of visitors to your website.

✔ **Referrer reporting:** This information gives you the site your visitor came from. That way, you'll know what sites are directing visitors to yours.

✔ **Apply segments:** You can create segments to analyse certain traffic, such as visits from certain regions that end up in purchases, or visits to certain areas of your site.

✔ **E-commerce analysis:** See where your revenue is coming from, and how your customers got there. Was it thanks to an advertising campaign or perhaps a Google search? Did the visitor type your website name in directly?

✔ **Benchmarking:** Measure how well your website is stacking up against other similar-sized sites. Kim's blog at www.londonphotos.org hasn't been updated for a while, so sadly 70 per cent of visitors leave as soon as they realise that. According to Google, Kim should be aiming for a bounce rate of 49 per cent. Keeping the blog fresh should narrow the gap somewhat. Similarly, her site attracted 1,900 unique visitors in a month, when she should be aiming for 3,755. This, recalls Kim, was what levels were like back when she was regularly updating the site in the mid-2000s.

These are just a few of the dozens of parameters available for you to analyse. Google also has no shortage of resources to help you sift through all this data. In Figure 13-2 you can see the Google Analytics dashboard, which gives a nice overview of how your site is doing.

Web analytics can help improve your website traffic, but you can also use it to find out more about your visitors for market research purposes. Where they come from, what pages they look at and whether they buy something are all useful parameters.

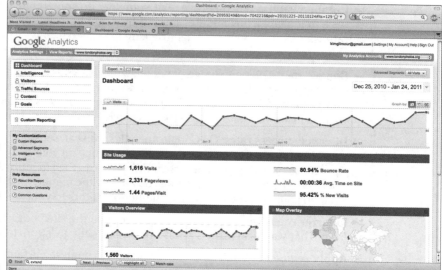

Figure 13-2:
Google
Analytics
gives you
a virtual
report card
for your site.

Part IV
The Necessary Evils: Law and Accounting

In this part . . .

Before you can start raking in the big (or at least moderate) bucks on the Web, you've got to get your ducks in a row. Along with the flashy parts of an online business – the ads, the Web pages, the catalog listings – you have to add up numbers and obtain the necessary licenses.

This part addresses the aspects of doing business online that have to be covered in order to pay taxes, take deductions, and observe the law. You may think of them as necessary evils that help you avoid trouble, but they're also ways to help you boost your bottom line and help you stand out from your competitors, too. In this part, you read about taxes, licensing, accounting, copyright, and other scintillating legal and financial must-haves for your online business.

Chapter 14

Making It All Legal

In This Chapter

▶ Understanding the laws you must follow

▶ Using trade marks to protect your company's identity

▶ Avoiding copyright infringement

▶ Deciding whether to incorporate

▶ Keeping your website on the right side of the law

A s the field of e-commerce becomes more competitive, online patents and trade marks, along with other means of legal protection, multiply correspondingly. The courts are increasingly being called upon to resolve smaller e-squabbles and, literally, to lay down the e-law.

For example, when Google purchased the video-sharing website YouTube for $1.65 billion, it was forced to pull large numbers of video files from its archive. Why? Because users were uploading all sorts of copyrighted material that they had no licence to broadcast. Today, YouTube uses technology to identify copyrighted files that have been have been uploaded without the owner's consent and responds swiftly to legal takedown requests. Nominet, the registry of .uk domain names, receives about 50 to 60 domain name disputes every month through its Dispute Resolution Service. Meanwhile in 2010, the WIPO Arbitration and Mediation Center was confronted with 2,696 domain name disputes – an average of 7 per day. Many of these were filed by large corporations seeking to gain control over domain names that were allegedly being held by small business cybersquatters. And in summer 2004, Microsoft settled a lawsuit it had filed in US district court by paying $20 million to stop a company called Lindows.com from infringing on its trade-marked name Windows.

In the world of online business, copyright issues and trade mark disputes aren't the only things you need to consider. The E-commerce Regulations, Distance Selling Regulations, Privacy and Electronic Communications Regulations and the Data Protection Act all have a big impact on an online business. Protecting your customer information, following e-commerce law and sticking to distance selling regulations are all crucial things to familiarise yourself with. You also need to exercise caution when marketing to customers using emails or texts.

As a new business owner, you need to remember that ignorance isn't an excuse in law. This area may well make you nervous because you lack experience in business law and you don't have lots of money with which to hire lawyers and accountants. You don't want to be discovering the ins and out of copyright or the law behind distance selling for the first time when you're in the midst of a dispute.

In this chapter, we give you a snapshot of legal issues that you can't afford to ignore. This chapter is no substitute for proper legal advice, but hopefully, this information can help you head off trouble before it occurs.

In this chapter, we often mention Business Link (www.businesslink.gov. uk) as a resource for legal guidelines, sample privacy policy templates and good practice legal tips. At the time of writing, the site was set to undergo a massive redesign, so you may need to hunt around if some things aren't in the exact place we tell you.

Abiding by Key Regulations

There are a number of crucial rules you need to follow when you operate an online business, particularly when it comes to distance selling and abiding by privacy regulations. The main regulations you need to familiarise yourself and the relevant website requirements are listed below.

E-commerce Regulations

The E-commerce (EC Directive) Regulations 2002 help ensure that online businesses provide a minimum quality of service to customers, big and small. Contrary to what the name implies, the law doesn't just cover e-commerce related issues.

In fact, every site that provides a commercial service needs to comply with the E-commerce Regulations, even if you're just using the website to advertise your services. According to the Regulations, this includes companies that:

- ✔ Sell goods or services online (including text messages and email)
- ✔ Advertise online (including text messages and email)
- ✔ Store or convey electronic content for customers or provide access to a communications network

And you can't avoid complying with the Regulations if you're based in the UK but use an overseas host to store your content. You need to comply with UK law.

In this section, we provide a snapshot summary of the legislation. To view it in full, go to www.legislation.gov.uk/uksi/2002/2013.

Providing comprehensive contact details

No one wants to visit an online shop only to discover that the seller hasn't provided a name, phone number or physical address – just a link to a random, free webmail account. Who knows if the seller even checks this account? Where might your money end up? Or will your goods arrive at all?

Making sure you supply full contact details, including those of your company (if you're a registered business), is a must so that your customers can have faith in your business and your products. At the very least, these are the accepted details you need to include (this also covers requirements under the Companies Act 2006):

✔ Your company name (even if it's not your trading name)

✔ An email address

✔ A physical contact address (in other words, no PO boxes!); your registered office address is acceptable

✔ Your company number, if applicable

✔ Place of registration

✔ Your VAT number, if you have one

✔ Details of any professional body you're a member of, such as a licence number

✔ Details of any supervisory authority, if your services are subject to an authorisation scheme (such as the Financial Services Authority)

Visitors to your website need to be able to find these contact details easily, but you don't need to repeat all the information on every page. A common method is to put everything on a separate 'Contact Us' page.

Online contracting and pricing information

Always specify whether or not prices include VAT, and include a clear indication of delivery costs and other applicable taxes.

Anyone who buys a product from you is entering into a contract, so you need to make it easy for the customer to access and store or print these contract details. The regulations state that you need to provide the following in a 'clear, comprehensible and unambiguous manner':

✔ The technical steps needed to conclude the contract (Amazon emails you after you've placed an order, and says your contract will complete after goods are dispatched to you)

✔ Details as to whether or not the business will file the concluded contract, and how the customer can access the contract

✔ Technical means for people to go back and correct input errors prior to placing an order (such as deleting something from their shopping basket)

✔ A link to any relevant codes of conduct to which you subscribe (unless the contract is concluded by email)

✔ Terms and conditions that are in a format that lets people store and reproduce them, such as sending an email confirmation or providing an online page that people can print

✔ An acknowledgement email as soon as an order is placed without delay

The Privacy and Electronic Communications (EC Directive) (Amendment) Regulations 2011

The Privacy and Electronic Communications (EC Directive) (Amendment) Regulations 2011 are overseen by the Information Commissioner's Office (www.ico.gov.uk), an independent public body whose sponsoring department is the Ministry of Justice.

Marketing

Unsolicited junk mail, or spam, comes under these rules. But how about legitimate marketing email that might interest your customers? The guidelines are clearly defined, with the latest information all accessible from the Information Commissioner's site. Go to the section for organisations to find out what you need to do as a business to comply with the regulations (and whether they apply to your business). Some decent FAQs and easy navigation should help you along.

In the UK, if an individual buys something from you online or expresses interest in your product or service (by registering on your website, for example), you're allowed to email the person promotional messages if she hasn't objected to this in the course of the transaction. In marketing speak, this is called a *soft opt-in*. The person hasn't been jumping for joy going, 'Yes! I'll be happy to receive emails about your wonderful products!', but she hasn't ticked the box that says she *doesn't* want to receive those messages either – so consent is assumed.

'The crucial consideration is that individuals must fully appreciate that they are consenting and must fully appreciate what they are consenting to,' the Information Commissioner's Office website states. The way you assume someone's consented or not to receiving marketing messages varies. The person might need to tick a box to opt out of your emails. For instance, you can assume that someone's consented to receiving further information from you when you've placed a message on your site that says something like:

By registering with our website, you indicate your consent to receive email marketing from us unless you have indicated an objection to receiving such messages by ticking this box.

In any case, each email you send needs to include an opportunity for people to opt out of such messages in the future. This could be by clicking an *unsubscribe* link managed by the email marketing software, or replying to the email with the word *unsubscribe*.

Let's face it, a lot of people fail to read everything properly and end up giving consent by accident, but so long as you clearly abide by the guidelines and give people an opportunity to avoid receiving such messages next time, you won't be breaking any rules.

The soft opt-in rule is a good way to start compiling a decent mailing list, particularly if someone's just made her first purchase from your site. But always letting people opt in to receiving marketing messages from you is, in our opinion, the preferred method. Give them some great incentives to do so, and you'll soon gain quality subscribers.

Using cookies and other web tracking tools

In May 2011, the privacy law in Europe was amended to include changes on using *cookies* and other web tracking tools on your website. Cookies are small text files that websites place on your computer. Among other things, they store information about the device you're using, and remember who you are and your display preferences when you return to a site, so you don't have to re-enter information. Cookies are also used to deliver advertising and advertising campaigns across a range of websites that the ad appears on.

Without cookies, many websites simply would not work properly. But new legislation now requires websites to gain users' consent before they can use cookies. Previously, consumers had the choice to opt-out of websites storing information on their computers, but the websites were allowed to place the cookies first.

If you're building a website from scratch, you need to consider what kind of cookies you're going to be using and how intrusive they might be. In addition, even if you use *third-party* cookies, such as ones placed by advertisers, it will also still be necessary to obtain users' consent.

There have been many critics of the legislation who consider it impractical to have to ask for consent when using cookies, but the ICO says you cannot ignore these rules.

When you go to the ICO website, you'll see the ICO's own notice at the top of the screen about cookies which you can adapt for your own site. It reads, "The ICO would like to use cookies to store information on your computer, to improve our website. One of the cookies we use is essential for parts of the site to operate and has already been set. You may delete and block all cookies from this site, but parts of the site will not work. To find out more about the cookies we use and how to delete them, see our privacy notice." There's a box you need to tick to say you accept the use of cookies on the site.

For more plain-English information on cookies, see www.allaboutcookies.org. For guidance from the ICO about cookies and your website and a downloadable PDF, see www.ico.gov.uk/for_organisations/privacy_and_electronic_communications/cookie_rules_prepare.aspx.

Data Protection Act 1998

The Information Commission's Office oversees the Data Protection Act. This Act, which came into force in 2000, overlaps slightly with the Privacy and Electronic Communications Act (see the previous section) because they both cover personal information. The Data Protection Act aims to ensure that any company that collects personal information stores it with the utmost care.

In April 2010 the ICO was granted the power to issue fines of up to £500,000 to companies that breached the Data Protection Act. Before that, its powers were largely limited to issuing enforcement notices. The first fines went out in November 2010. Employment services company A4e was fined £60,000 after a laptop – containing unencrypted information on 24,000 people – was stolen from an employee who was using it to work from home. The information included sensitive information including whether individuals had a criminal record.

Go to www.ico.gov.uk/for_organisations/data_protection/the_guide/key_definitions.aspx to find comprehensive information on data protection, particularly as it relates to your sector.

The website also has a checklist for small businesses on good practice when it comes to customer security. You probably realise that storing sensitive information in raw form on transportable memory sticks isn't the greatest idea. But does your business have a security policy for permanently deleting customer data? Just deleting it from the Recycle Bin on a computer isn't enough, because someone can often recover the data. On the website, go to Tools and resources⇨Document library⇨Data protection, and download the PDF file entitled *Data Protection Good Practice Note: Security of personal information.*

Apart from storing data safely, your company needs to provide a clear privacy policy indicating how and why you use your customer information. You also need to indicate whether information needs to be disclosed to third parties and why (for example, you might use a separate company to process credit card payments). You can download a sample privacy policy that you can adapt from the Business Link website (www.businesslink.gov.uk) under IT and e-commerce⇨Legal issues⇨Sample Internet policies and notices⇨Sample privacy policy.

We've heard of plenty of stories where customers' credit card details have been unwillingly exposed, or websites hacked into and details stolen. Storing customer information in an encrypted form and abiding by industry standards are essential. You won't necessarily protect your business from being an unlikely victim of hacking – but if you can demonstrate that you handled customer data with the utmost care, then the incident should only be a criminal matter for the police, not the Information Commissioner's Office.

If a third party provider handles any customer information, your business is still responsible for the handling of that information. So choose your partners wisely – trusted, respected industry names; or companies that trusted people can recommend.

Consumer Protection (Distance Selling) Regulations 2000

Selling over the Internet means you don't get face-to-face contact with the buyer. In the real world, you can try clothes on in a fitting room – but the Internet cabling isn't quite big enough to squeeze over a new pair of jeans to your living room! So you face more room for disappointment; higher chances of an unwanted item.

This isn't a new problem – people have been selling via mail order, catalogues, phone and fax way before the web. But the Internet has seen distance selling explode, which is why legislation is in place to allow people to return items within seven days of receipt if they aren't satisfied. The Consumer Protection Regulations cover most items sold online apart from land and property; accommodation, travel, catering or leisure; financial services (which are covered by the Financial Services (Distance Marketing) Regulations 2004) and timeshares.

Apart from the contact and delivery details we mention in the earlier section 'E-commerce Regulations', you must also provide information on how customers can make payments.

Cooling-off period

The seven-day *cooling-off period* means buyers can return goods within seven days if they aren't satisfied. Some exceptions to this exist that are beyond the scope of this book but include things such as shrink-wrapped software or DVDs and CDs with seals that have been removed. The Office of Fair Trading's website (www.oft.gov.uk) has full details.

You need to provide sufficient information on a consumers' right to cancel in what's called a *durable medium* – no official definition of this exists, but it's generally thought to be a medium that you can't edit, such as an email that could later be printed. (A website can be edited any time so it's not considered durable.) You need to include details on:

- ✔ Whether goods should be returned by the customer, and who pays for this – if you don't mention this upfront, you have to foot the bill (you also pay if the returned goods are faulty)
- ✔ A physical address where customers can complain, and any guarantee details

Slightly different rules apply for services, particularly those that start within the seven working day cooling-off period. The customer's right to cancel can end as soon as the service starts, so long as you specify this in writing at the time of purchase.

The Distance Selling Regulations apply to any *business* selling *fixed-price* goods over the Internet. So that includes eBay too, but only for registered businesses listing items under Buy It Now; not auctions.

Read the Office of Fair Trading's *Home Shopping: Distance Regulations Guide*. You can download it from the website in PDF form via `www.oft.gov.uk/about-the-oft/legal-powers/legal/distance-selling-regulations`.

You may have heard stories of pricing errors on websites – back in 2003, the electronics store Dixons advertised a top-end digital camera at £1 each, and thousands of people flocked to the site to place an order. People protested when Dixons wouldn't honour their orders, but Dixons stood its ground and won out. Make sure that your terms and conditions clarify when a customer's order becomes a binding contract. For instance, Amazon only confirms a contract when the goods have been dispatched. It makes sense. Think about going into a real-life store and seeing a camera for £1. The assistant will probably scan the item and, before she takes your money, declare that a pricing error has occurred and apologise for being unable to sell the item at that price (unless she was feeling *really* nice). Until the transaction changes hands, neither party is obliged to buy or sell the item.

We also recommend that you included a statement on your website that says something like, 'Prices are subject to confirmation.'

Refunds

You should refund customers as soon as they cancel orders. You aren't allowed to wait and wait until they've returned your goods (but strictly speaking, you do have 30 days at the most to refund their money).

We mention in the previous section that you don't have to pay the cost of returning an unwanted item if you specify in the contract that the customer must pay. However, you *do* need to refund the original delivery cost of the item.

Customers have legal rights too – to understand these, check out the Sale of Goods Act hub for businesses at www.oft.gov.uk/business-advice/ treating-customers-fairly/sogahome. This website includes tutorials for businesses on consumer rights, as well as a raft of downloadable materials, how the law applies in real-life situations, a multiple-choice quiz, glossary and much more. It (almost) makes learning about legal issues fun!

Thinking about Trade Marks

Under UK law, a *trade mark* is a visual element that accompanies a particular tangible product or line of goods and serves to identify and distinguish it from products sold by other sources. In other words, a trade mark isn't necessarily just for your business's trade name. In fact, you can trade mark letters, words, names, phrases, slogans, numbers, colours, symbols, designs or shapes. For example, take a look at the cover of the book you're reading right now. Look closely and see how many trade mark (™) or registered trade mark (®) symbols feature. The same trade-marked items appear on the Dummies website, as you can see in Figure 14-1.

Figure 14-1: You don't have to use special symbols to designate logos or phrases on your website, but you may want to.

You need to distinguish between the two ™ and ® symbols, says publishing lawyer Bernie Nyman of BM Nyman and Co. 'The former can be used to denote a claim to trade mark ownership where the mark is not registered. The latter can only be used in conjunction with a registered trade mark. If you use it with an unregistered trade mark, that is a criminal offence under UK law.'

Although you're unlikely to ever get involved in a trade mark battle yourself, and you may never trade mark a name, you need to be careful which trade name you pick and how you use it. Choose a name that's easy to remember so that people can associate it with your company and return to you often when they're looking for the products or services that you provide. Also, as part of taking your new business seriously and planning for success, you may want to protect your right to use your name by registering the trade mark, which is a relatively easy and inexpensive process.

When registering a trade mark you get legal protection only in the areas in which you register it. To register a trade mark in this country, you file an application with the UK Intellectual Property Office. Online applications are £170 plus £30 for one class of trade mark. Extra classes of trade mark cost £50. What's a *class*? Take the example of Julian Assange, founder of whistleblower website WikiLeaks. In February 2001, he applied to trade mark his name under class 41, which covers 'Public speaking services; news reporter services; journalism; publication of texts other than publicity texts; education services; entertainment services'. At the time of writing, he was still waiting for approval on the trade mark.

A Right Start application procedure involves paying half of the application fee up front and obtaining a report from the UK Intellectual Property Office as to whether your application meets the filing requirements. You pay the balance of the filing fees if you choose to proceed after receiving the report. For more on fees go to www.ipo.gov.uk/pro-types/pro-tm/t-law/t-notice/t-notice-feeservice.htm.

All the forms and guidance you need are at the UK Intellectual Property Office website at www.ipo.gov.uk, shown in Figure 14-2. The step-by-step process is easy and you can benefit from incentives for filing online, including an online discount.

Having to register a trade mark in every country can be costly and probably unnecessary for a startup, but you can get around this. The European Union's Community Trade Mark (CTM) can provide a trade mark valid across the EU. The Madrid Protocol expands to include the US, and is operated by the World Intellectual Property Organisation (WIPO). For more information, check out publishing lawyer Bernie Nyman's website at www.bmnyman.co.uk/trade-marks.

A trade by any other name

A *trade name* is the name by which a business is known in the marketplace. A trade name can also be *trade marked,* which means that a business has taken the extra step of registering its trade name so that others can't use it. At the same time, it's important to realise that a trade name can be a trade mark even though it hasn't been registered as such. Big corporations protect their trade names and trade marks jealously, and sometimes court battles erupt over who can legally use a name.

Figure 14-2:
You can
quickly
apply for
your own
registered
trade mark
online by
using
this site.

For most small businesses, the problem with trade marks isn't so much protecting your own as it is stepping on someone else's. Research the name you
want to use to make sure that you don't run into trouble. A good place to start
is by checking out Companies House's website (www.companieshouse.gov.
uk), which has the definite list of businesses operating (and recently folded)
in the UK. It doesn't list sole traders or ordinary partnerships, but it tells you
what company names are currently taken, and which you can use. You can
also register your own business name through the site, at a cost of £20.

Determining whether a trade mark is up for grabs

To avoid getting sued for trade mark infringement and having to change your
trade name or even pay damages if you lose, you should conduct a trade
mark search before you settle on a trade name. The goal of a trade mark
search is to discover any potential conflicts between your trade name and
someone else's. Ideally, you conduct the search before you actually use your
trade name or register for an official trade mark.

Far and away the best method of searching for trade mark information is to do
a search at the Intellectual Property Office (www.ipo.gov.uk). You'll find all
UK registered trade marks, as well as community trade marks covering the EU.

Other websites to try, if you're interested in looking at trade marks inter-
nationally, are the World Intellectual Property Office trade mark search

at `www.wipo.int/trademarks/en` and the United States Patent and Trademark Office at `www.uspot.gov`.

The consequences of failing to conduct a reasonably thorough trade mark search can be severe. In part, the consequences depend on how widely you distribute the protected item – and on the Internet, you can distribute it worldwide. If you attempt to use a trade mark that someone else has registered, you could be taken to court and be prevented from using the trade mark again. You may even be liable for damages and solicitors' fees. So being careful is best.

Be prepared for a lengthy approval process after you file your application. Trade mark registration can take months, and it's not uncommon to have an application returned. Sometimes, an applicant receives a correspondence that either rejects part of the application or raises a question about it. If you receive such a letter, don't panic. You need to go to a lawyer who specialises in or is familiar with trade mark law and who can help you respond to the correspondence. In the meantime, you can still operate your business with your trade name.

Ensuring that your domain name stays yours

The practice of choosing a domain name for an online business is related to the concept of trade names and trade marks. By now, with cybersquatters and other businesspeople snapping up domain names since 1994 or so, it's unlikely that your ideal name is available in the popular `.com` or `.co.uk` domain. It's also likely that another business has a domain name very similar to yours or to the name of your business. Two common problems exist:

- ✔ Someone else has already taken the domain name related to the name of your existing business.

- ✔ The domain name you choose is close to one that already exists or to another company with a similar name (check out the Microsoft Windows/Lindows.com dispute that we detail in the introduction to this chapter).

If the domain name that you think is perfect for your online business is already taken, you have options. You can contact the owner of the domain name and offer to buy it. Alternatively, you can choose a domain name with another suffix. If a `.com` name isn't available, try the old standby alternatives, `.org.uk` (which, in theory at least, is for nonprofit organisations) and `.net` (which is for network providers).

You can also choose one of the newer Top-Level Domains (TLDs), domain name suffixes, which include the following:

- ✔ `.biz` for businesses

- ✔ `.info` for information or general use

- ✔ `.name` for personal names

- ✔ `.eu` for websites aimed at European Union countries

A massive change is set for domain names, allowing pretty much *any* ending to a website domain. You can find out more about the biggest shake-up to Internet naming yet in Chapter 8, and at `www.icann.org`, the website of the world's Internet naming authority, ICANN.

You can always get around the fact that your perfect domain name isn't available by changing the name slightly. Rather than `treesurgeon.com`, you can choose `tree-surgeon.com` or `treesurgery.com`. But be careful, lest you violate someone else's trade mark and get into a dispute with the holder of the other domain name.

Practising Safe Copyright

Copyright refers to the creator's ownership of creative works, such as writing, art, software, video or cinema (but not names, titles or short phrases). As lawyer Bernie Nyman explains on his website at `www.bmnyman.co.uk/copyright`, 'It is a property right, and this means that it is capable of being owned, it is capable of being sold and it is capable of being licensed. In short, it is a very valuable commodity.'

Copyright also provides the owner with redress in case someone copies the works without the owner's permission. Copyright is a legal device that enables the creator of a work to control how people use the work.

Although copyright protects the way ideas, systems and processes are embodied in the book, record, photo or whatever, it doesn't protect the idea, system or process itself. In other words, if William Shakespeare were writing *Romeo and Juliet* today, his exact words would be copyrighted, but the general ideas he expressed would not be.

Even if nobody ever called you a nerd, as a businessperson who produces goods and services of economic value, you may be the owner of intellectual property. *Intellectual property* refers to works of authorship as well as certain inventions. Because intellectual property may be owned, bought and sold just like other types of property, it's important that you know something about the copyright laws governing intellectual property. Having this information maximises the value of your products and keeps you from throwing away potentially valuable assets or finding yourself at the wrong end of an expensive lawsuit.

Copyright you can count on

Strictly speaking, not everything you see on the Internet is copyrighted – some really old works may be out of copyright and deemed 'in the public domain'. But this phrase is misleading, because not everything you see online is in the public domain in the sense that someone else can copy and republish it.

Copyright exists from the moment a work is fixed in a tangible medium, including a web page. For example, plenty of art is available for the taking on the web, but look before you grab. Unless an image on the web is specified as being copyright free, you'll be violating copyright law if you take it. HTML tags themselves aren't copyrighted, but the content of the HTML-formatted page is. General techniques for designing web pages aren't copyrighted, but certain elements (such as logos) are.

Fair dealing . . . and how not to abuse it

Copyright law doesn't cover everything. According to Business Link (www.business link.gov.uk), the government group that gives advice to businesses, you can make *limited use* of copyrighted material without the author's permission in the following circumstances:

✔ For use as teaching material

✔ For criticising and reviewing

✔ For news reporting

✔ When it applies to court proceedings

Fair dealing, as some people refer to it in the UK, has some big grey areas that can be traps for people who provide information on the Internet.

Don't fall into one of these traps. Shooting off a quick email asking someone for permission to reproduce her work isn't difficult. Chances are that person will be flattered and will let you make a copy as long as you give her credit on your site. Fair dealing is entirely dependent on the unique circumstances of each individual case, and this is an area where, if you have any questions, you should consult a solicitor.

To be on the safe side, always include a "sufficient acknowledgement" as recommended by the May 2011 Hargreaves Review on Intellectual Property, which can be found at www.ipo.gov.uk.

Keep in mind that using a work for criticism, comment, news reporting, teaching, scholarship or research is okay. That comes under the *fair dealing* limitation. (See the nearby sidebar 'Fair dealing . . . and how not to abuse it' for more information.) However, we still contend that getting permission or citing your source is best in these cases, just to be safe.

We talk about the Creative Commons Licence and how it lets people reuse and reproduce material in Chapter 5.

Making copyright work for you

A copyright – which protects original works of authorship – costs nothing, applies automatically and (across the EU) lasts for the life of the author plus 70 years from the end of the year in which the author dies. When you affix a copyright notice to your newsletter or website, you make your readers think twice about unauthorised copying and put them on notice that you take copyright seriously.

Creating a good copyright notice

Even though any work you do is automatically protected by copyright, having some sort of notice expresses your copyright authority in a more official way. Copyright notices identify the author of a given work (such as writing or software) and then spell out the terms by which that author grants others the right (or the licence) to copy that work to their computer and read it (or use it). The usual copyright notice is pretty simple and takes this form:

```
Copyright 2012 [Your Name] All rights reserved
```

You don't have to use the © symbol, but it does have far more impact and makes your notice look more official. In order to create a copyright symbol that appears on a web page, you have to enter a special series of characters in the HTML source code for your page. For example, web browsers translate the characters © as the copyright symbol, which is displayed as © in the web browser window. Most web page creation tools provide menu options for inserting special symbols such as this one.

Protecting with digital watermarks

In traditional offset printing, a *watermark* is a faint image embedded in stationery or other paper. The watermark usually bears the name of the paper manufacturer, but it can also identify the organisation for which the stationery was made.

Watermarking has its equivalent in the online world. Graphic artists sometimes use a technique called *digital watermarking* to protect images they create. This process involves adding copyright or other information about the image's owner to the digital image file. The information added may or may not be visible. (Some images have copyright information added, not visible in the body of the web page but in the image file itself.) Other images, such as the one shown in Figure 14-3, have a watermark pasted right into the visible area, which makes it difficult for others to copy and reuse them.

Figure 14-3:
If your products are particularly precious, such as unique works of art, assert your copyright over them on your web site.

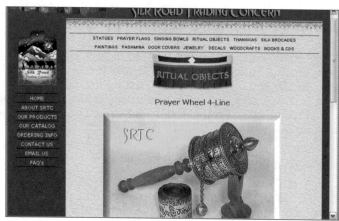

Digimarc (www.digimarc.com), which functions as a plugin application with the popular graphics tools Adobe Photoshop (www.adobe.com) and Corel Paint Shop Pro (www.corel.com), is one of the most widely used watermarking tools.

Doing the paperwork on your copyright

No official copyright registrar exists in the UK, because copyright is automatic, but a number of unofficial companies will log your claim to a copyright for you. That step helps if you ever have the misfortune of falling into a dispute with another party, but you should think very carefully before handing over your hard-earned cash. You can guard copyrighted material for a much lower cost in several other ways.

The most common method is to send material to yourself via recorded delivery, and not open the package when you receive it. That gives a clear date before which the material must have been created. When it comes to digital information, designs, logos and so on, you can protect your copyright by printing screen grabs of your work and following the process from there.

Understanding Legal Basics

The UK prides itself on the ease with which you can start a business. If you know what you're doing, you can start up in just a couple of days compared to weeks and months elsewhere in the world. That's not to say you can just set up shop and start trading, however. To start with, restrictions regulate the selling of certain types of products, such as food and agricultural products, and your own software, as well as running businesses where you're responsible for the well-being of others (say, if you run a paintball business, where you teach your customers how to use the guns, you oversee games or where you may need to use basic first aid).

You must also register your business with Her Majesty's Revenue and Customs (HMRC), an organisation that takes a close interest in any money you make from the business. If your annual turnover reaches £73,000 you need to register for Value Added Tax (VAT). But even at the very beginning, you have to register yourself as self-employed for tax purposes – even if your business is part time or you have a nine-to-five job too. You have to start filling in your own self-assessment tax forms annually and must declare your earnings each year.

So, you need accounting software to keep track of your finances and a business bank account that's separate from your current account. These elements, along with any special qualifications you may require to start your business, are essential. They're as important as your product, promotional material and informing the tax authorities; all are required before you start a business.

Business Link's website (`www.businesslink.gov.uk`) includes a fantastic range of content and we recommend you go there because we can't fit it all here. Our advice is to read all the information relevant to you as thoroughly as possible and check out links to organisations that cover your sector well before you start your own business venture. Remember: forewarned is forearmed!

Understanding Your Business in the Eyes of the Law

No two businesses are alike, but you have the option of picking not only your product, marketing material and web design, but also the legal form that your business takes. You have a number of options from which to choose, and the choice can affect the amount of taxes you pay and your liability in case of loss. The following sections describe your alternatives.

Sole trader

If you're a *sole trader*, you're the only boss. You make all the decisions, and you get all the benefits. On the other hand, you take all the risk too. This setup is the simplest and least expensive type of business because you can run it yourself. You don't need an accountant or lawyer to help you form the business, and you don't have to answer to partners or shareholders either. To become a trader, you just have to declare yourself as such with Her Majesty's Revenue and Customs (www.hmrc.gov.uk).

Partnership

In a *partnership*, you share the risk and profit with at least one other person. Ideally, your partners bring skills to the endeavour that complement your own contributions. One obvious advantage to a partnership is that you can discuss decisions and problems with your partners. All partners are held jointly liable for losses. The rate of taxes that each partner pays is based on the partner's individual tax position.

If you decide to strike up a partnership with someone, drawing up a *partnership agreement* is a good idea. Although you aren't legally required to do so, such an agreement clearly spells out the duration of the partnership and the responsibilities of each person involved. Make sure you deal with division of profits and liabilities and also what happens if a partner leaves or joins the partnership and what happens when the partnership is wound up.

If no agreement exists, then you're bound by the ancient Partnership Act 1890, which dates back to when people were using telegraphs to communicate with each other, rather than Blackberrys!

Another type of partnership exists, called a limited liability partnership (LLP). Unlike members of ordinary partnerships, the LLP itself, rather than the individual partners, is responsible for any debts that it incurs.

Limited companies

A number of different company types are around. These include a private limited company, public limited company and unlimited company. As a startup, you'll most likely be registering as a private limited company.

If sole traders and partnerships (see the previous sections) are so simple to start up and operate, why would you consider becoming a private limited company? After all, you may undergo a type of *double taxation*: if your company earns profits, those profits are taxed at the corporate rate, and any shareholders have to pay income tax too.

Well, the process is amazingly quick (unless you're transitioning from a sole trader or partnership). It just takes a couple of hours after you go to a company formation agent. The Companies House website (www.companies house.gov.uk) includes all the information. Other top reasons include:

✔ If you have employees, you can deduct any health and disability insurance premiums that you pay.

✔ You can raise money by offering stock for sale.

✔ Transferring ownership from one shareholder to another is easier.

✔ The company's principals are shielded from liability in case of lawsuits. The main difference between a limited liability company and a partnership is that the liabilities of the business aren't passed on to the owners. You're only liable for any debt you incur (say, if the founders jointly take out a loan), but you don't have liability for the company's taxes.

A limited liability company gets taxed on its profits (corporation tax), and its shareholders get taxed on the dividends received by the company. Check out www.hmrc.gov.uk for more on the taxing matter of taxes, as well as the following chapter for more on accounting tools.

Keeping Out of Legal Trouble

A big part of keeping your online business legal is steering clear of so-called business opportunities that can turn into big problems. In the following list, we highlight some areas to watch out for.

✔ **Get it in writing!** Perhaps the most important way to avoid legal trouble is to get all your agreements in writing. (Notice how lawyers always do that?) Even if the parties involved type and sign a simple one-page sheet describing what's to be done and what's to be paid, that's far better than a verbal agreement. It's also better than an email message – an email doesn't enable signatures, and a single message doesn't clearly point out that both parties have actually agreed to something. A qualified lawyer can help you prepare contracts that you can send to both suppliers and customers who engage your services.

The other important things to get in writing are the points covering data protection and privacy policies that we mention in the earlier section 'Abiding by Key Regulations'. Remember that when you publish a policy

statement on your website, you need to actually follow what it pre-
scribes; you can be sued if you violate it.

- **Ever thought of health and safety?** It may come as a surprise, but as soon
  as you set up and register your online business, you must create a safe
  and risk free environment for your employees (even if the only employee
  is you!). It sounds silly, but the Health and Safety Executive is taking no
  chances – it's ultimately responsible for the welfare of British workers
  and is charged with keeping levels of accidents and illness down. Follow
  this link to the Health and Safety Executive website (www.hse.gov.uk/
  businesses.htm) for the lowdown on your responsibilities.

- **Remember the red tape or form-filing.** People in the UK make a big deal
  about red tape (for example, the various regulations defining what you
  can and can't do). The reams of forms that you have to fill in to show
  you've complied can be a real pain. Take Dan's pals who run a husband-
  and-wife window-cleaning company, number of employees: two. They
  recently had to fill in a form describing the demographic makeup of their
  business. In other words they had to declare that their business was
  50 per cent men (the husband) and 50 per cent female (the wife), that
  the business was exclusively made up of British people and that all the
  staff were in their 40s.

  Of course, in a business of two people, you'd be forgiven for employing
  only 40-something Brits, but small business are not exempt from dis-
  crimination. You can scoff at these documents, but (unfortunately) you
  still have to fill them in and return them to the authorities. You'll also
  need to comply with employment law legislation if you employ people.

- **Make your site accessible.** Under the Equality Act (which replaced
  almost all previous anti-discrimination legislation in October 2010), you
  have to take reasonable steps make your website accessible to people.
  The RNIB charity has an excellent summary and guidelines on what you
  need to know, in the absence of any case law, at www.rnib.org.uk/
  professionals/webaccessibility/lawsandstandards/Pages/
  uk_law.aspx. As a general rule, all text should be able to be read by a
  screen reader. Also check out the World Wide Web Consortium's latest
  guidelines via www.w3c.org.

- **Adult content is risky business.** Be careful if you provide so-called adult
  content. There's no doubt about it: cyberspace is full of X-rated sites,
  many of which do make money. (Porn is one of the Net's most successful industries!) But this area is risky.

  If you do sell adult items online, always put up a front page warning
  users that entering the site will expose them to adult content, and in
  general do all you can to protect youngsters – you've been warned.

✔ **What you don't know about acceptable use policies can hurt you.** Be aware of acceptable use policies set up by agencies that control what goes out online. Usually, the company that hosts your website has a set of acceptable use guidelines spelling out what kind of material you can and can't publish.

Another important kind of acceptable use policy that you need to know about is the acceptable use policy issued by your Internet Service Provider (ISP). The most common restriction is one against *spamming* (sending unsolicited bulk mailings). Not following your web host's or your ISP's guidelines can get you kicked off the Internet, so make sure that you're aware of any restrictions by reading the guidelines posted on your ISP's or web host's site.

Chapter 15

Accounting Tools for Online Businesses

Some people have a gift for keeping track of expenses, recording financial information and performing other fiscal functions. Unfortunately, we, and many of you, don't have these rare skills. Yet we know (and you should know) the value of accounting procedures, especially those that relate to an online business.

Without having at least some minimal records of your day-to-day operations, you won't have any way – other than the proverbial gut feeling – of knowing whether your business is truly successful. Besides that, banks and the tax authorities don't put much stock in gut feelings. When the time comes to ask for a loan or to pay taxes, you'll regret not having watertight records close at hand.

In this chapter, we introduce you to simple, straightforward ways to handle your online business's financial information – and all businesspeople know that accurate record keeping is essential when revenues dwindle and expenses must be reduced. In this chapter, you discover the most important accounting practices and find out about simple software that can help you tackle the essential fiscal tasks that you need to undertake to keep your new business viable. (For more information on these topics, also see *Bookkeeping For Dummies*, By Jane Kelly.)

ABCs: Accounting Basics for Commerce

We can summarise the most important accounting practices for your online business as follows:

- ✓ **Deciding what type of business you're going to be:** Are you going to be a sole trader, partnership, or a limited company? (See more about determining a legal form for your business in Chapter 14.)

- ✓ **Establishing good record-keeping practices:** Record expenses and income in ways that will help you at tax time.

- ✓ **Obtaining financing when you need it:** Although getting started in business online doesn't cost a lot, you may want to expand someday, or borrow money to buy stock, and good accounting can help.

Number crunching and keeping records of what you spend is dull but necessary. There's nothing fun about unexpected cash shortages or other problems that can result from bad record keeping.

Good accounting is the key to order and good management for your business. How else can you know how you're doing? Yet many new businesspeople are intimidated by the numbers game. Use the tool at hand – your computer – to help you overcome your fear. Start keeping those books!

Choosing an accounting method

Accepting that you have to keep track of your business's accounting is only half the battle; next, you need to decide how to do it. The point at which you make note of each transaction in your books and the period of time over which you record the data make a difference not only to your accountant but also to agencies such as HM Revenue & Customs (HMRC). Even if you hire someone to keep the books for you, you need to know what options are open to you.

 Consult the HMRC website (www.hmrc.gov.uk) and check out the section on Businesses & Corporations, which has a whole host of information telling you how and when accounting procedures come into play. You may also want to check out the Chartered Institute of Taxation (www.tax.org.uk) or an accountancy firm like TaxAssist Accountants (www.taxassist.co.uk).

Cash-basis versus accrual-basis accounting

Don't be intimidated by the terms in this section: they're simply two methods of totalling up income and expenses. Exactly where and how you do the recording is up to you. You can take a piece of paper, divide it into two columns labelled *Income* and *Expenses* and do it that way. (We describe some more high-tech tools later in this chapter.) These methods are just two standard ways of deciding when to report them:

- ✔ **Cash-basis accounting:** You report income when you actually receive it and write off expenses when you pay them. This is the easy way to report income and expenses, and probably the way most new small businesses do it.

- ✔ **Accrual-basis accounting:** This method is more complicated than the cash-basis method, but if your online business maintains an inventory, you must use the accrual method. You report income when you actually receive the payment; you write down expenses *when services are rendered* (even though you may not have made the cash payment yet). For example, if a payment is due on 1 December, but you send the cheque out on 8 December, you record the bill as being paid on 1 December, when the payment was originally due.

Accrual-basis accounting creates a more accurate picture of a business's financial situation. If a business is experiencing cash flow problems and is extending payments on some of its bills, cash-basis accounting provides an unduly rosy financial picture, whereas the accrual-basis method is more accurate.

Choosing an accounting period

The other choice you need to make when it comes to deciding how to keep your books is the accounting period you're going to use. What date you choose is up to you:

- ✔ **Calendar year:** The calendar year ends on 31 December. This is the period with which you're probably most familiar and the one many small or home-based businesses choose because it's the easiest to work with.

- ✔ **Fiscal year:** In this case, the business picks a date other than 31 December to function as the end of the fiscal year. In the UK, the corporation tax year runs from 1 April to 31 March, and many businesses choose to coincide their accounting period with the official corporation tax year to make it easier to do the tax calculations. Many large organisations pick a date that coincides with the end of their business cycle. Some pick 31 March as the end, others 30 June and still others 30 September.

You need to pay your corporation tax before you file your tax return; nine months after your company's accounting period ends. You must file your tax return 12 months after your company's account period.

If you're a registered corporation, as of 1 April 2011 you must file your tax return electronically for any accounting period. Similarly, you must file your company tax return online for any account period ending after 31 March 2010.

Your accountant is probably doing it all for you but to read more about corporations and corporation tax – and to find a link on registering for online services – go to www.hmrc.gov.uk/ct.

Alerting Companies House

Don't forget, too, that you must file your accounts with Companies House (the register of UK companies) and be aware of your filing deadlines. You don't want to miss any of these and have the registrar think that you've gone out of business. After you're struck off the register, your assets become Crown property!

The Companies House website has up-to-the-minute booklets and guidance notes, and you can lodge company information, such as annual returns, through the site and check out your filing deadlines. Go to www.companieshouse.gov.uk.

Those with more straightforward financial affairs can file company account information to both HMRC and Companies House at the same time. Take a look here: www.hmrc.gov.uk/ct/ct-online/file-return/joint-filing.htm.

Knowing what records to keep

When you run your own business, it pays to be meticulous about recording everything that pertains to your commercial activities. The more you understand what you have to record, the more accurate your records are – and the more deductions you can take too. Go to the office supply retailer and get a financial record book (or *journal*), which is set up with columns for income and expenses.

Tracking income

Receiving cheques, bank transfers and credit-card payments for your goods or services is the fun part of doing business, and so income is probably the kind of data that you'll be happiest about recording.

You need to keep track of your company's income (or, as it's sometimes called, your *gross receipts*) carefully. Not all the income your business receives is taxable. What you receive as a result of sales (your *revenue*) is taxable, but loans that you receive aren't. Be sure to separate the two and pay tax only on the sales income. But keep good records: if you can't accurately report the source of income that you didn't pay taxes on, HRMC labels it *unreported income* and you have to pay taxes, and possibly fines, on it.

Just how should you record your revenue? For each item, write down a brief, informal statement. This statement is a personal record that you may make on a slip of paper or even on the back of a cancelled cheque. Be sure to include the following information:

- ✔ Amount received
- ✔ Type of payment (credit card, electronic cash or cheque)
- ✔ Date of the transaction
- ✔ Name of client or customer
- ✔ Goods or services you provided in exchange for the payment

Collect all your cheque stubs and revenue statements in a folder labelled *Income* so that you can find them easily at tax time.

Capital allowances and assets

Assets are resources that your business owns, such as your office and computer equipment. You can claim tax relief on some of your assets provided they meet certain criteria; these are known as *capital allowances*. What you can claim and how much you can claim does change from year to year, so we advise you to check out the HMRC's guide to capital allowances at www.hmrc.gov.uk/ct/forms-rates/claims/capital-allowance.htm. In any case, you should keep records of your assets that include the following information:

- ✔ Name, model number and description
- ✔ Purchase date
- ✔ Purchase price, including fees
- ✔ Date the item went into service
- ✔ Amount of time the item is put to personal (as opposed to business) use

File these records in a safe location along with your other tax-related information.

Recording payments

Even a lone entrepreneur doesn't work in a vacuum. An online business owner needs to pay a web host, an Internet service provider (ISP) and possibly web page designers and other consultants. If you take on partners or employees, things get more complicated. But in general you need to record all payments in detail as well.

Your accountant is likely to bring up the question of how you pay the people who work for you. Depending on the circumstances, they may betreated as full- or part-time employees, which means that you'll be responsible for working out and collecting income tax and National Insurance contributions (NICs) from them under the Pay As You Go (PAYG) regime. Or, they may be treated as independent contractors, working through their own business. In this case, you'll be able to pay them a gross amount (without deductions for tax or NICs), and they will be responsible for settling their own liabilities with HMRC. HMRC uses a stringent series of guidelines to determine who's a contractor and who's a full-time employee. Check out the following link, which describes the legal difference between contractors and employees: www.hmrc.gov.uk/employment-status/index.htm.

Hiring independent contractors rather than salaried workers is far simpler for you: you don't have to pay benefits to independent contractors, for one thing, plus you don't have to schedule their holidays, pension payments or life insurance policies. Just be sure to get invoices from any independent contractor who works for you. If you have full-time employees whom you pay an hourly wage or annual salary, things get more complicated, and you'd best consult an accountant to help you set up the salary payments.

Listing expenses

Get a big folder and use it to hold any receipts, contracts, cancelled cheques, credit-card statements or invoices that represent expenses. It's also a great idea to maintain a record of expenses that includes the following information:

- ✔ Date the expense occurred
- ✔ Name of the person or company that received payment from you
- ✔ Type of expense incurred (equipment, utilities, supplies and so on)

Recalling exactly what some receipts are for is often difficult a year or even just a month after the fact. Be sure to jot down a quick note on all cancelled cheques and copies of receipts to remind you of what the expense involved.

Understanding the Ps and Qs of P&Ls

You're likely to hear the term *profit-and-loss statement* (also called a P&L) thrown around when discussing your online business with financial people. A profit and loss statement is a report that measures the operation of a business over a given period of time, such as a week, a month or a year. The person who prepares the profit and loss statement (either you or your accountant) adds up your business revenues and subtracts the operating expenses. What's left are either the profits or the losses.

Most of the accounting programs we list in the following section include some way of presenting profit and loss statements and enable you to customise the statements to fit your needs.

Accounting Software for Your Business

The well-known commercial accounting packages, such as QuickBooks and Sage, let you prepare statements and reports and even tie into a tax preparation system. Stick with these programs if you like setting up systems such as databases on your computer. Otherwise, go for a simpler method and hire an accountant to help you.

Whatever program you choose, make sure that you're able to keep accurate books and set up privacy and backup schemes that prevent your kids from zapping your business records.

If your business is a relatively simple one – say, if you're a sole trader – you can record expenses and income on a spreadsheet or by hand and add them up at tax time. (That's what Kim does.) Then input them into a HMRC tax return. Alternatively, you can record your entries and turn them over to a tax advisor who can prepare a profit and loss statement and tell you the balance due on your tax payment.

If you're looking to save a few quid and want an extra-simple accounting program that you can set up right now, look no further than Microsoft's own Excel spreadsheet software, which comes with your standard Microsoft Office package. It can help you tot up your earnings and deduct tax, but you need some practice to get it right.

TurboCASH (www.turbocashuk.com) is a step up from a spreadsheet, but so simple that even financially impaired people like us can pick it up quickly. TurboCASH is *open source* (meaning anyone can use it under the terms of the General Public Licence) and is designed to enable people with no prior accounting experience to keep track of income and expenses. Go to the website to see how TurboCASH stands up against more established players like QuickBooks and Sage.

Another popular, basic and cheap accounting tool is OWL Simple Business Accounting (SBA), compatible from Windows 95 all the way to Windows 7. The following steps illustrate how easy it is to start keeping books with SBA. These instructions assume that you've downloaded and installed the software from the OWL Software website (www.owlsoftware.com/sba.htm). You can download a 30-day evaluation version before you buy, which we're using here. Upgrading to a full version of the software costs about £36.

1. Choose Start⇨Programs⇨OWL Business Apps⇨SB Accounting 4.

The main OWL Simple Business Accounting window appears, as shown in Figure 15-1.

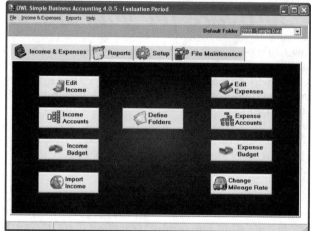

Figure 15-1:
SBA uses folders to contain income and expense data that you report.

The program comes with a set of sample data already entered to help you get accustomed to its features. Choose Help and then User's Guide to open the SBA User's Guide help file, which is in PDF format. Click the topic Getting Started if you want an overview of how the program operates.

2. Click the Setup tab to bring it to the front and than make any custom changes you may want:

- If you want to operate in a fiscal year different from the pre-entered 1 January, enter the number for the new month that you want to set as the beginning of your fiscal year.

- If you want your on-screen and printed reports to be in a different font than the pre-selected one (MS Sans Serif), click the Report Font button, choose the font you want, and then click OK to close the Font dialog box. Times New Roman is usually a good choice because it's relatively compact.

3. Click the File Maintenance tab to bring it to the front and then click the Erase Data button. When asked whether you want to erase expense data or other information, you may click OK.

This step erases the sample data that was pre-entered to show you how the program works.

4. **Select the Income and Expenses tab to bring it to the front and then click the Define Folders button to create folders for your business data.**

   The PickFol dialog box appears, as shown in Figure 15-2. This dialog box lists any folders that you've created.

Figure 15-2:
Use this dialog box to add, delete or edit folders that hold your business data.

5. **Click New.**

   The Folder Definition dialog box appears.

6. **Enter a new name in the Description box and click Save.**

   A Confirm dialog box appears, asking whether you want to add another folder.

7. **If you do, click Yes and repeat Step 6; when you're done, click No.**

   The Folder Definition dialog box closes, and you return to the PickFol dialog box, where your renamed folder or folders appear.

   You may want to create separate folders for your personal or business finances, for example. After your folders are set up, you can record data as the following steps describe.

8. **Click Exit.**

   The PickFol dialog box closes and you return to the main OWL Simple Business Accounting window.

9. **Select the Income and Expenses tab to bring it to the front and then click either the Income Accounts or Expense Accounts button to create an Income or Expense Account.**

   The Select Account dialog box appears.

10. **Click New.**

    The Account Definition dialog box appears.

11. **Enter a name for the account in the Description dialog box and then click Save.**

    A dialog box appears, asking whether you want to create another account.

12. **If you do, click Yes and repeat Step 11; when you're done, click No.**

    The Select Account dialog box appears, listing the items you just created.

13. **Click Exit.**

    You return to the main OWL Simple Business Accounting window.

14. **When you've created Income and Expense Accounts, click either the Edit Income button or the Edit Expense button, depending on the type of data you want to enter.**

    Depending on the button you clicked, the Select Income or Select Expense dialog box appears.

15. **Click New to enter a new item.**

    A dialog box named either Income or Expense appears, depending on the button you selected in Step 14.

16. **Enter the amount and description in the appropriate fields and click Save.**

    The Confirm dialog box appears, asking you to confirm that you either want to add or delete a record.

17. **If you do, click Yes and repeat step 16; when you're done, click No.**

    You return to the Income or Expense dialog box, where you can review more entries.

18. **Click Exit.**

    You return to the Income and Expenses options.

19. **When you're all finished, choose File➪Exit to exit the program until your next accounting session.**

After entering some data, you can select the Reports tab, run each of the reports provided by SBA (including income, profit, general ledger, mileage log, expense reports and budget reports) and examine the output. When running the reports, be sure to select a reporting period within the current calendar year.

The Taxman Cometh: Concerns for Small Business

After you make it through the startup phase of your business, it's time to be concerned with taxes. Here, too, a little preparation up front can save you lots of headaches down the road. But as a hard-working entrepreneur, time is your biggest obstacle.

Successive surveys reveal that a large number of entrepreneurs leave filing their tax return until the last minute. A few submit their tax returns late and incur fines from HM Revenue and Customs. Planning is really important for taxes. In fact, HMRC rules state that businesses must keep records appropriate to their trade or business for six years after the transactions are made. HMRC has the right to view these records if it wants to audit your business's (or your personal) tax return. If your records aren't to HMRC's satisfaction, the penalties can be serious.

Should you charge VAT?

Here's one of the most frequently asked questions we receive from readers: should I charge sales tax for what I sell online? The short answer is that, as always, it depends. VAT is a tax that applies to the transfer of goods and services. You have to register for VAT when your turnover reaches £70,000 per year, but you can register before your business gets to this stage.

The annual VAT threshold is determined by *total sales* and is not the same as *total profits* (which is generally sales minus expenses). You can make a loss and still need to register for VAT.

The threshold operates on a month-by-month basis, so you need to check at the end of each month to make sure you haven't gone over the limit (currently £70,000) in the previous 12 months. You also need to think about whether you're going to go over that limit in the following 12 months. If you think your total sales may exceed the VAT threshold, you need to register.

You must register with HMRC within 30 days of being aware that you're going to exceed the threshold. If you fail to register you're charged a penalty, which can eventually be up to 15 per cent of the VAT owed and is in addition to the actual VAT due. So make sure that you register on time and avoid incurring costly penalties. After you've registered, you must charge varying levels of VAT, depending on what you sell. You must also keep records of what you charge for what products or services. This is called your *output tax*. There's a comprehensive guide to VAT on the HMRC website. Follow these steps to find it:

1. **Log on to www.hmrc.gov.uk.**

   Look toward the top right-hand corner of the home page and locate the VAT link under Businesses & Corporations. Clicking the link takes you to the VAT home page.

2. **Locate Getting Started with VAT.**

   Under this section click Introduction to VAT.

3. **Jump to Who Charges VAT and What VAT is Charged On.**

   You'll see a link to what products and services are VAT taxable. Further down, you can read about the various rates of VAT (including the zero rate), what you can charge (and be charged) VAT on, what isn't covered by VAT and where to go for more information.

Familiarising yourself with this and other guides on the website is a good idea because they help shed light on seemingly complex issues. Bookmark this section and refer back to it when you need to.

Remembering other business taxes

You have to consider, if not always pay, a whole range of taxes. As your business grows, the number and complexity of taxes you must deal with grows too. That's why businesses often start up using accountancy software, then hire a part-time bookkeeper, then a full-time accountant and then eventually an accounts department and outsourced consultants.

To start with, however, you just need to think about taxable income. Anything you make money from is taxable in theory, but the authorities don't get interested until you're making a few thousand pounds a year (which, of course, you must make to survive). That's where income or corporation tax comes in, depending on the business model you choose to adopt. (See Chapter 14 for more on the types of businesses you can start.)

Another area that adds to tax considerations is the business costs you incur, many of which are tax deductible. Then you have business rates, or council tax, the level of which depends on the size and location of your premises, as well as staff pay – it's down to you to organise their income tax and national insurance contributions.

Happily, this confusing-sounding series of taxes is nicely summarised on Business Link's website (www.businesslink.gov.uk), where you can find accessible information on what you have to pay and what you don't.

Self-assessment: Doing your tax return online

Many of you reading this chapter may think: 'Well, I haven't yet registered my business as a company; I'm happy being a sole trader and operating on a self-employed basis for now.'

The good news is that doing your own accounts and filing them online isn't that scary. If you're self-employed, the advantage of doing your tax return online is that it's secure and HMRC's system does the correct calculations for during the process of completing the form. HMRC also receives your submission straight away, and you can set up a direct debit so you won't miss any payment deadlines.

Kim uses Self Assessment Online to file her tax return. She likes how she can save her details and come back to them later, print her records, look at past statements and change her address details online from one convenient location.

To register for Self Assessment Online, go to www.hmrc.gov.uk/sa/file-online.htm and click the following link path: Self Assessment Online Login Page⇨Register⇨Individual⇨Tick Self Assessment then click Next⇨Next. In order to enrol from this point you need your Unique Taxpayer Reference (UTR) as well as either your national insurance number or postcode to hand. You find your UTR on all relevant correspondence from HMRC.

The registration process only takes a few minutes but you won't be able to use the service straight away. You'll receive an activation personal identification number (PIN) by post in about a week's time, which you'll need to enter when first logging in. This is sent to your registered address for security reasons. From then on, all you'll need is your user ID and password (never record your password on paper).

Part V
The Part of Tens

'Hey, honey, I've just bought a little old place
in England called Cornwall from a guy
called Charlie Windsor.'

In this part . . .

If you're like us, you have one drawer in the kitchen filled with utensils and other assorted objects that don't belong anywhere else. Strangely enough, that's the place we can almost always find something to perform the task at hand.

Part V of this book is called The Part of Tens because it's a collection of miscellaneous secrets arranged in sets of ten. Filled with tips, cautions, suggestions, and examples of new ways to make money online, this part presents many kinds of information that can help you plan and create your own business presence on the Internet.

Chapter 16

Ten Must-Have Features for Your Website

In This Chapter

▶ Boosting the security of your website

▶ Offering products and services that people want

▶ Getting personal with your customer

▶ Promoting yourself

*Y*ou can put any number of snazzy features on your website. If you ever meet with a web design firm, you're sure to hear about all the cool scripts, widgets, buttons, badges, animations and other interactive add-ons that can go on your pages. Some pizzazz isn't a bad thing, especially if you're just starting out and need to set yourself apart from the competition. Interactive features and a well-designed website give you an air of competence and experience, even if your online business is brand new.

But the website features that count toward your bottom line are the ones that attract and retain customers and entice them back to you regularly. Along with the bells and whistles, your business home on the web needs to have some basic must-haves that shoppers expect. Make sure that your site meets the minimum daily requirements: it needs to be easy to find, loaded with content, include contact and background information about you and include features that make shopping (if that's what you do) easy and secure.

Thanks to the proliferation of social media like Twitter, Facebook and YouTube – and selected tools that easily let you list your business on these websites – giving your website the extra exposure it needs has never been easier.

This chapter describes ten specific features that help you achieve these objectives.

Secure Easy-to-Remember URLs

Names are critical to the success of any business. A name becomes identified with a business, and people associate the name with its products and its level of customer service. When a small company developed a software product called Lindows, giant Microsoft sued initially, but eventually paid $20 million to stop the infringement on its well-known trademarked product Windows.

Write down five or six names that are short and easy to remember and that would represent your business if included in an URL. Do a domain name search and try to find the one you want. (A good place to search is Network Solutions, www.networksolutions.com/whois/index.jsp). Try to keep your site's potential name short and free of elements like numbers and hyphens where possible. A single four- to ten-character name in between the www. and the .com or .co.uk sections of the URL is easy to remember. With the hundreds of millions of registered domain names out there, we know this is easier said than done!

Domain names are cheap to register and renew, especially if you're able to lock them up for several years at a time. Names in the .com and .co.uk domains are still the most desirable type of URL suffixes because they're the ones that most consumers expect to see when they're trying to find your website's URL. Even if you're able to get a .com name, purchase domain names in other popular domains such as .net and .org.uk. That way, you protect your URL from being 'poached' by competitors who are trying to copy you. If your URL is easily misspelled, consider purchasing a domain name that represents a common misspelling. That way, if shoppers make a typing error, they're still directed to your site.

If you've already trademarked a name and find that someone else has taken it for their own website, you have the right to dispute this. The body that oversees domain names ending in .uk, Nominet, offers a dispute resolution service as an alternative to the courts. It claims that about one in 2,000 .uk domain name registrations causes someone to make a complaint. For more on the process, see www.nic.uk/disputes.

Provide a Convenient Payment Method

Shoppers go online for many reasons, but those reasons don't include a desire for things to be complex and time consuming. No matter how technically complex it may be to get your computer on the Internet, shoppers still want things to be quick and seamless. At the top of the list of seamless processes is the ability to pay for merchandise purchased online.

You don't necessarily need a merchant account from a bank to process your own credit-card payments, as we describe in Chapter 11. You don't need to get point-of-sale hardware either. The other day, Kim went online to buy some specialist cleaning products for her new kitchen bench. At the online checkout, the company website redirected her to PayPal to complete the purchase . All she needed to do was log into PayPal (www.paypal.com) and she received the products in a couple of days. eBay bought the payment provider after the service became so popular among members of its website, and it's now mandatory for UK sellers to provide PayPal as a payment option for practically all items. Chances are that many of your prospective customers already have accounts with PayPal if they use eBay. Set yourself up as a seller with PayPal or Google Checkout and accept postal orders and personal cheques. If you can take the additional step of getting a shopping trolley and a credit-card payment system, particularly as your turnover increases, so much the better.

Promote Security, Privacy and Trust

Even shoppers who've been making purchases online for years at a time still feel uncertainty when they type their credit-card number and click a button labelled Pay Now, Purchase or Submit on a commercial website.

What promotes trust? Information and communication. Shoppers online love getting information that goes beyond what they can find in a printed catalogue. Be sure to include all the following details that can make shoppers feel good about pressing your Buy Now button:

- ✔ Not only is it good practice to include your contact details, it's the law. Under the E-Commerce Directive, businesses should clearly include their name, email address, a physical address, VAT number if applicable, place of company registration (if this applies to you) and any official information pertaining to the business, such as registered licence numbers if you're a tradesperson. For more, see Chapter 14.

- ✔ A privacy statement that explains how you're going to handle customers' personal information is essential if you handle customer data, because you need to assure shoppers that you're adhering to the Data Protection Act 1998.

- ✔ Detailed product descriptions show you're knowledgeable about a product.

- ✔ Include a plain English terms and conditions section on your website explaining how orders are processed and clearly outlining your returns policy. For an example of an e-commerce policy that you can adapt to your business, go to the Business Link website (`www.businesslink.gov.uk`) and under Starting Up ➪ IT & e-commerce for start ups you can find a sample policy.

✔ Strive to make your site work from the outset: no missing links or images, errors with code and accessibility problems.

✔ Grab testimonials from customers and endorsements from high-profile organisations or those that promote good business practices such as Investors in People. List any business awards you may have under your belt.

Another thing that promotes trust is information about who you are and why you love what you do, as we describe in the 'Blow Your Own Trumpet' section, later in this chapter.

Choose Goods and Services That Buyers Want

All merchants would love to be able to read the minds of their prospective customers. On the Internet, you have as much chance of reading someone's mind as you have of meeting that person face to face. Nevertheless, the Internet does give potential buyers several ways to tell you what they want:

✔ Come right out and ask them. On your website, invite requests for merchandise of one sort or another.

✔ After a purchase, ask customers for suggestions about other items they'd like to buy from you.

✔ Include a means for customers to review your product. Or gauge opinion about its popularity by including a Tweet button that lets people share the item on Twitter without having to leave your page (`http://twitter.com/about/resources/tweetbutton`). You can also adorn your website with a badge that lets you display content from your business's Facebook page (`www.facebook.com/badges`).

✔ Visit message boards, Facebook pages and websites related to the item you want to sell. Take a look at what people are saying about the product on Twitter. Check Google Trends to see how popular the keywords describing your item have fared over a certain period (see `www.google.com/trends`).

✔ Make a weekly (remember that Saturdays and Sundays are the best days for auctions to end) search of eBay.co.uk's completed auctions to see what's sold, and which types of items have fetched the highest prices.

Have a Regular Influx of New Products

With a printed catalogue, changes to sales items can be major. The biggest problem is the need to physically reprint the catalogue when inventory changes (and the cost involved with this). One of the biggest advantages associated with having an online sales catalogue is the ability to alter your product line in a matter of minutes, without sending artwork to a printer. You can easily post new sale items online each day, as soon as you get new sales figures. One reason to keep changing your products on a regular basis is that your larger competitors are doing so. Lands' End, which has a well-designed and popular online sales catalogue (`www.landsend.co.uk`), puts out new products on a regular basis and announces them in an email newsletter to which loyal customers can subscribe. And Argos is famous for its hefty printed catalogue, yet the company still issues one on a seasonal basis. Argos also highlights special deals on its website, and you can search for all products online using keywords or the catalogue number.

Changing product lines is great for seasonal items like clothes and gift ideas, but don't forget to keep stock of those staple items your customers keep coming back to. Marks & Spencer wouldn't be Marks & Spencer if it got rid of its trusty underwear section!

Be Current with Upkeep and Improvements

Do you have a favourite blog, comic strip or newspaper columnist that you like to visit each day? We certainly do. If these content providers don't come up with a new material on a regular basis, you get discouraged. Your loyal customers will hopefully feel the same way about your website, eBay shop or other sales venue.

We know what you're thinking: you've got so many things to do that you can't possibly be revisiting your website every day and changing headings or putting new sales online. You have to get the kids off to school, pack up merchandise, run to the post office, clean the house – the list goes on and on. You can't be two places at once. But here's what you can do:

✔ When pressed for time, update your website on the move. For example, access Twitter using your phone and update your Twitter feed while you're in the post office queue. Give customers some information about what you're up to. Perhaps you'd like to recommend some gift ideas for Christmas.

✔ Help your customers generate their own content. By providing the ability for people to comment on your blog or Facebook posts, you facilitate a forum for discussion with minimal effort. Some of the posts on Anything Left Handed's blog (`www.anythinglefthanded.co.uk/blog-home.html`) get hundreds of replies. Whatever programme you use to write your blog lets you enable comments on your website.

✔ Get friends or a student to help. Hire someone to run your site and suggest new content for you. In a five-minute phone conversation, you can tell your assistant what to do that day, and you can move on to the rest of your many responsibilities.

Personally Interact with Your Customers

The fact that personal touch counts for so much in Internet communication is a paradox. With rare exceptions, you never meet face to face with the people with whom you exchange messages. Maybe it's the lack of body language and visual clues that make shoppers and other web surfers so hungry for attention. But the fact is that impersonal, mass email marketing messages (in other words, *spam*) are reviled while quick responses with courteous thank-yous are eagerly welcomed.

Customers welcome personal emails, just as they appreciate a human being responding to a query in a shop. Automatic checkouts in supermarkets may be handy when they work, but they aren't yet advanced enough to tell you whether a smaller tub of margarine is available, or whether you can benefit from a special deal if you buy more than two cans of baked beans. Nor will they help an elderly lady get her shopping to her car.

Perhaps we may be a little cynical these days towards sincerity when salespeople are trying to be nice to us, but it's always best to be extra courteous to your customers and never put the pressure on them to make a purchase.

Facebook, Twitter and YouTube have revolutionised the personal touch, particularly when it comes to celebrities and businesses interacting with their fans. When one of Kim's friends received a personal response on Twitter from TV personality Jonathan Ross, he was chuffed.

If you're a busy person, yet you've found time to respond personally to your customers without using a robotic form letter, they'll be grateful for the effort. Word of mouth really is one of the best ways to get your product noticed (see the following section).

Don't be afraid to pour on the extra courtesy and provide complete answers to every question: just tell yourself each answer is worth an extra pound or two in sales. It probably is.

Post Advertisements in the Right Places

When most people think about advertising on the Internet, they automatically think about banner advertisements placed on someone else's web page. A banner advertisement is only one kind of online ad, and possibly the least effective. Even though these ads can now track web surfers' movements during a session and try to show them relevant content depending on the pages they like to visit, it's still a relatively passive medium. The Internet can make marketing so much more personal. Make use of all the advertising options going online brings you, including the following:

- **Use word of mouth.** When US actress Demi Moore mentions a product she likes on her Twitter page (such as the online music service Spotify) her millions of followers take notice. When someone's post on Twitter is replicated by one of their followers (known as a *retweet*), word spreads like wildfire. Bloggers use this method all the time too: one person mentions something in another blog, that blogger mentions someone else, and so on. On Facebook you can broadcast a status update or link to all your followers and they can share it with their friends.

- **Exchange links.** 'You link to my website, and I'll link to yours', in other words. This option is especially effective if you're linking to a business whose products and services complement your own. Only exchange links with relevant websites; otherwise people will leave your site in droves if they're being presented with content that's far from useful. Additionally, search engines will rank your site higher in the page results (see the next bullet point) only if other *important* websites have given yours the thumbs up, so choose quality over quantity here.

- **Get listed in search engines.** Make sure that your site is listed in the databases maintained by Google and the other search engines (see Chapter 13 for more techniques and information).

- **Try paid-for advertising.** Google, Microsoft and Yahoo! let you advertise your sites on their search engines and throughout their content networks by using text-based, pay-per-click (PPC) advertising. You only pay when someone clicks on your ad. Facebook is another medium you can try for marketing your website. For more on how PPC works, see Chapter 13. You may see limited success depending on the type of website you have, but you can target the people you want to market to, set your own budget and see whether it works for you.

 Make sure that your home page contains keywords in text and headings that search engines can use to index it and add it to their database. The more keywords you add, the better your chances of having your site turn up in search results.

Blow Your Own Trumpet

Sam Walton founded Wal-Mart (which owns Asda), and the Walton family still runs it, but 99 per cent of the shoppers who flock to the megastores every day don't know or care about that fact. Wal-Mart is a well-established brand with a physical presence. Your fledgling online business has neither of those advantages. You need to use your website to provide essential background about yourself, why you started your business and what your goals are.

Your immediate aim is to answer the question that naturally arises when a consumer visits your online business: 'Who are these people?' or 'Who is this guy?' The indirect goal is to answer a question that the shopper doesn't necessarily ask consciously, but that is present nonetheless: 'Why should I trust this place?' Be sure to tout your experience, your background, your family or your hobbies – anything to reassure online shoppers that you're a reputable person who's looking out for their interests.

Create a Well-organised Website

A well-organised website is absolutely essential. Yes, you can establish a regular income on eBay without having any website at all. But in such a competitive sales environment, setting up a website so potential buyers can click through and learn more is worth the effort. Map out your website well before you start building it, and ensure that you have simplicity and usability at the forefront of your mind. How do you make your site well organised and functional? Make sure your site incorporates these essential features:

- ✔ **Clear signposting:** Time-poor customers expect to see a row of navigation buttons along the top or one of the sides of your home page. Don't make them hunt; put them there.

- ✔ **Links that actually work:** Nothing is more frustrating than clicking a link that's supposed to lead to a photo and/or a bit of information that you really want and coming up with the generic `Page not found` error message.

- ✔ **Links that indicate where you are on the site:** Such links are helpful because, like a trail of breadcrumbs, they show how the customer got to a particular page. Here's an example: Clothing > Men's > Sportswear > Shoes > Running. When your site grows to contain dozens of pages and several main categories, links that look like this one can help people move up to a main category and find more subcategories. They can also backtrack and find their way home, because unlike Hansel and Gretel in the famous fairytale, there aren't any birds eating all the breadcrumbs!

✔ **A site map:** Well-organised websites shouldn't really need one, but they can come in handy if your site is very complex. A site map is a page that leads visitors to all areas of your site and can prevent them from going elsewhere if they get lost. See Google's site map at `www.google.com/sitemap.html`.

✔ **Every page counts:** Yes, the main part of your website – the home page – is where people 'land' whenever they type in your web address. But not everyone arrives at your home page if they've searched for something on Google and are directed to an obscure subsection of your site. When designing your website, make sure that you retain consistent signposting throughout every page. This means navigation buttons and a clear link to the home page on *every page*. Don't assume that people know what your website is all about if they land at a different part of your site. There's no need to fear: it's not hard work to achieve this when first establishing your site. You or your web designer should be using a language called Cascading Style Sheets (CSS) to maintain consistent formatting on your site (for more on this, see the overview in Chapter 1, and Chapter 5).

Be the first to visit your website and test it to make sure that the forms, email addresses and other features function correctly. If someone sends you an email message only to have it bounce back, you'll probably lose that customer, who may well conclude that you aren't monitoring your website or your business. At the very least, open your site in the latest versions of Microsoft Internet Explorer and Firefox browsers to make sure that your text and images load correctly. Kim's web design mates on Facebook often post links to their work in progress and ask for constructive feedback from friends. Also check out Google's excellent webmaster tools to see how visible your site is on Google, and what can be done to improve your site's visibility. See `www.google.com/webmasters` for more.

Chapter 17

Ten Hot Steps to Entrepreneurial Success

In This Chapter

▶ Sharing your expertise on a directory or forum

▶ Turning what you love doing into a business

▶ Understanding how customers can contribute to your business

*N*ot so long ago, starting an online business primarily meant creating a website and organising it in a businesslike manner. You'd create a catalogue, add a shopping trolley and payment system, and hope customers would find you.

These days, you don't have to create a fully-fledged website to sell online. The hottest way to make money is to sign up with an online service that helps individuals get their content online and market themselves or their products and services before the public. These services exist in the 'cloud' – hosted somewhere in the virtual Internet sky, accessible wherever you are. You may have to pay a small monthly hosting fee or a sales commission. But the benefits are huge: you don't have to do all the work of creating a catalogue and payment system because your host does the work for you. You may need to sign up with a company that streamlines the process of setting up a blog or creating a shop on eBay.

This chapter presents ten innovative approaches to making money online. By following one or more of these relatively simple options (or by thinking creatively about how these ideas could help you get your business on its way), you can start generating income quickly and painlessly. You may not make a fortune, but focusing attention on yourself and your business can brighten your life even as it puts extra cash in your pocket.

It doesn't take much effort just to make your presence felt on the web, even if you already have an existing offline business. A large percentage of the population is sitting at the computer already hooked up to the Internet. When they suddenly realise that they need their suit pressed for a meeting the next day or that their kids need school supplies, they're more likely to call up information on service providers by using a search engine than they are to flip through the phone book and make a call to find out locations and hours.

Start a Blog

In many cases, adding the personal touch separates the successful businesses shops from soulless warehouses. Nowadays, however, you're likely to be greeted with a cheery hello even when you wander into a pound shop. The precedent has definitely been set for mixing the family into business.

Blogs might seem a bit old school now next to all the hot, up-and-coming Web 2.0 concepts out there, but they're still as influential as ever and it's easy to share blog links via social networks like Facebook or Google+. Blogs differ from starting a Twitter feed because you can make your posts as long as you like, and they encourage comments from readers (your customers). By giving customers a window into your mind, you can build trust, which in turn can build business. You may not want to define yourself with your strong religious preferences or passionate view on the results of the latest election, but it can be a definite asset to post a few photos of your children or what it looks like in your 'real world' office when you're enjoying a cup of coffee. On a slightly more businesslike side, consider a link to the text of a paper you presented at the latest professional conference you attended, or a discussion of an interesting news article or statistic relating to your field of expertise. Of even more relevance may be a series of photos showing the happy day that the new press was delivered to your printing plant, accompanied by examples of new brochures that feature the results of its bells and whistles. Whatever the subject, the goal is to keep the tone of the text upbeat and breezy, friend to friend.

Turn Your Hobby into a Business

Your authors are perfect examples of people who were able to start a new career thanks to the Internet. We started when the World Wide Web was new, and lots of people who were previously not all that comfortable with the computer were trying to go online. Nowadays, there's not such a need for beginners' books, especially now that modern babies seem to be born with computer mice in their hands (when Kim's daughter Audrey was barely a year old, she managed to work out how to unlock her mum's iPhone by pressing the button and using her finger to unlock the slider on the touch screen!). So we're not recommending that you follow in our exact footsteps. But the point is that you should take anything you love and are good at and turn it into a website.

On the web, you're limited only by your imagination as to what you can sell. Take what you know and love and run with it.

The gothic rock star Marilyn Manson sells his artwork on his website (www.marilynmansonartworkonline.com). One of Greg's favourite online people, a Wisconsin woman who calls herself The Butter Cow Lady and who has gained local fame through her butter sculptures, sells her life story on her site (www.thebuttercowlady.com). If you enjoy photography, you can upload your photos to Flickr and sign up as a Getty Images partner; or put them on a stock photo library like Alamy (www.alamy.com). Kim has sold a few photos through both Flickr and Alamy without trying too hard, so think of what a professional photographer could achieve!

Get Other People to Contribute

Many websites work by soliciting contributions from interested visitors. If you build a website, others will come. The most obvious example is eBay: the site's success is due almost entirely to content submitted by sellers around the world. Another great example is Trip Advisor (www.tripadvisor.com), which lets people rate and review hotels, B&Bs, restaurants and attractions all around the world. You can see the highest-rated hotels for each city you plan to visit, and sort them by price and proximity to the city centre. The site makes its money by getting an affiliate commission from the booking agents that the site links to, as well as from other advertisements.

You can emulate eBay and Trip Advisor's success on a smaller scale. Say that you'd like to sell greeting cards. You might post the images from folks who take photographs of scenery, make block prints of jungle animals or collect drawings and paintings. Or quilting may be your passion. Why not set up a website that offers the work of those who create different patterns, use different fabrics, collect antique quilts or do repairs? Another brilliant website, Not On The High Street (www.notonthehighstreet.com) acts as a conduit for small businesses who create handmade craft designs or one-off pieces.

What about a forum dedicated to collecting something, like art books or pin badges? The web is the perfect place to bring like-minded individuals together, and contributions from others can keep your site current and successful while giving you time to focus on design and marketing issues.

Sites like Lulu.com (www.lulu.com) allow unpublished authors to have their work bound in an attractive fashion and put up for sale. Kim published a fiction book she wrote in this manner and was highly impressed by the quality. Books are printed on demand, so you only pay for the copies you need – or nothing at all, if customers order direct from Lulu. You can create a sales page for your book, set a price and earn money on the profits. For an extra fee, you can even purchase ISBN numbers for your book and have them officially published and sold through outlets like Amazon.co.uk. You get a smaller cut for each sale of your book than you would if you sold directly through Lulu, but greater exposure.

Slashdot (slashdot.org), a popular news-and-views site for computer nerds, depends on those very same nerds for many of its stories and reviews and gains credibility for welcoming opinions from far and wide.

Inspire Others with Your Thoughts

Sometimes, you end up making a huge change in your life without really trying. You put something online that's sincere and heartfelt, and that you think may help some other people. You find out that tons of people out there feel the same way.

Salam Pax, an Iraqi citizen writing under a pseudonym, also known as the 'Baghdad Blogger', didn't use his writing to make money online initially, yet his words were read the world over. He wrote a personal account of the goings on in Iraq during the war with Britain and America in 2003. The blog was popular because it cut through media and political spin and told readers exactly what was happening on the ground, as well as how the war was affecting ordinary families.

Despite not setting out to enrich himself, Pax later converted his blog into a column on the Guardian Unlimited website and later published a successful book with his collective thoughts. It just goes to show what you can achieve if you capture people's imaginations.

Offer Your Services on a Directory

If you say the phrase 'making money online', what comes to most people's minds is selling small, easily transportable objects. But merchandise is only one type of product you can make available in the marketplace; you can also market your services and your knowledge. Place an ad on your local version of Craigslist (www.craigslist.org) or Gumtree (www.gumtree.com). Then register with a directory like the one on RealBusiness.co.uk (www.realbusiness.co.uk) or Yell (www.yell.com). Why not also consider specialist ones depending on your area of expertise such as the UK baby and toddler directory (www.babydirectory.com), a solicitor database (www.lawsociety.org.uk), a music teacher resource (www.musicteachers.co.uk), a vegetarian restaurant listings site (www.happycow.net) and so on.

Ask for Contributions

You can earn money through the web in more than one way, and you don't necessarily have to 'charge' for services rendered. Relying on the kindness of strangers, as sites like Wikipedia do, is one way of earning an income without demanding cash upfront.

This model is less reliable than the standard 'money for products' approach, and you have to be pretty special to get people to part with their money voluntarily, but in some cases it can earn you some extra cash.

eBay and Amazon would struggle if they asked for contributions, because they already have healthy takings. The sites that are most likely to get people reaching for their wallets are expert blogs, sources of accurate information (like Wikipedia) or those that display artistic works (like pictures, novels or poetry).

Non-profit organisations flourish when it comes to obtaining funds online and we can learn much from them. The microfinance site Kiva (www.kiva.org) lets you loan, rather than donate, money to third-world entrepreneurs in countries like Cambodia through global field partners. The scheme helps them become self-sufficient rather than rely on charity. You get your money back once the entrepreneur pays off the loan to the field partner, which happens in the vast majority of cases. Whenever you loan out some money, Kiva asks whether you'd like to add an optional extra donation to help with the site's running costs – which many people are happy to pay. Once a loan has been paid back you can use it to fund another loan.

Give Out Not-So-Free Advice

The Internet has always been a great place to get questions answered. Over the years, sites like Yahoo! Answers and eHow.com have been the primary resources for answers and support. You can also start a website on which you offer your consulting services. You can gather tips, tricks and instructions pertaining to your field of interest. Over the last eight years the technology blog Read Write Web (www.readwriteweb.com) has evolved from a simple, one-man operation about the latest tech trends to one boasting an 'international team of journalists'.

Become a Video Star

Back in 2010, Paul Vasquez got very, *very* excited when he saw a 'double rainbow' in the skies of Yosemite National Park – and posted the vid on YouTube. His ecstatic, tearful exclamations of 'Double rainbow all the way across the sky!', 'What does this mean?' and 'Oh my God, it's so bright!' led to many parodies and much viral coverage – to date, it has had more than 28 million views on YouTube (look it up if you don't believe us; no doubt the figure will be millions higher). Soon enough he caught Microsoft's eye, who recruited him to star in an advertising campaign for its photo gallery application. (In the ad, Paul can't fit the double rainbow photo into one frame, so uses the panoramic stitching tool to piece several photos together.)

With most modern phones, laptops and digital cameras pre-equipped with the ability to record moving images, it makes sense to record your viewpoints or observations on video. You could even go around interviewing people in your trade and putting the edited highlights online!

If your original YouTube video is popular and original enough, you can apply to be in YouTube's partner programme, which lets you share in ad revenue with the Google-owned video giant.

When you only want to do light editing of your video, such as cutting out a few dull scenes or adding some basic titles, then you can use the free video editing software that comes equipped with today's Windows and Mac systems – Windows Live Movie Maker and iMovie. They also provide direct links to YouTube, so you needn't worry about converting the video type or compressing its size.

Be a Mine of Information

What's that you say? You can't draw, you don't have any products to sell and you aren't a professional contractor? Never fear. On the web, information sells. Chances are you have a mine of information about one topic in particular. You know a lot about your family history, you know everything there is to know about collecting coins, you're a genius with identifying rocks or you're an avid birdwatcher. Create a website on which you put every bit of information you have online. Make your site the one and only greatest resource ever devoted to this topic.

Follow the example of the Urban Legend Reference Pages (`www.snopes.com`), a website started back in 1995 by a husband-and-wife team living in California. The site collects urban legends of all sorts and reports on whether or not they're actually true; it makes enough money from ads to keep it going. But the main thing is that it's a labour of love for its creators. Whenever we receive a chain email with a bizarre warning that more people get sick from contaminated cut onions than spoiled mayo, a doctored photo of a document showing Barack Obama was 'born in Kenya', a plea from the parents of a missing child we've never heard of who needs our money or a warning about a plague we've heard nothing about, we turn to Snopes just to make sure it's a fake.

Need Income? Just Ask!

It sounds odd, but if you present yourself in the right way on the web, and you simply ask for money, you just might get it. One of the earliest and still most famous cases is that of Karyn Bosnak. When she found herself buried in £10,000 of credit-card debt, she created a website called SaveKaryn.com (now archived at `www.savekaryn-originalsite.com`). She asked for donations to help her out of debt. In just 20 weeks, her site received nearly two million visits, and she wasn't in debt any more – especially because her book *Save Karyn* (Corgi Adult) was published in several languages too.

When blogger Andrew Sullivan was in need of funds to keep his blog online, faithful readers donated more than £35,000. Sullivan was well established by that time; people knew he'd use the money to keep providing them with the opinions and insights they were used to. Present yourself in an open, positive manner, and readers will respond to you too.

You can accept donations via the payment service PayPal by displaying a Donate button on your website. You don't need scripting experience – PayPal gives you the HTML code you can put on your website and you can even choose from a selection of donation buttons. To find out how, just look under 'Merchant tools' after you're logged into PayPal. In order to access funds, you need a Premier or Business account. For more on PayPal, see Chapters 10 and Chapter 11.

Chapter 18

Ten Must-See Websites for Online Entrepreneurs

. . . .

In This Chapter

▶ Keep up with the latest technology trends

▶ Access resources to help you with the day-to-day running of your site

▶ Connect with fellow entrepreneurs

. . . .

Keeping up to speed with the ever-changing world of online business can be challenging, but here are ten brilliant sites you can bookmark to keep things running smoothly. Understanding business legalities, reaching the top of Google rankings, getting down with the kids and finding support where you need it are just some of the wonderful things you can do within these sites.

You're starting an online business, so it's important that you understand the Internet and all it has to offer. You should know by now that it's a great learning resource and it can teach you an awful lot about how to run your own web business.

Realbusiness.co.uk

In need of some inspiration? Realbusiness.co.uk (www.realbusiness.co.uk) is the website of *Real Business* magazine, and it's a good place place to start your journey. The website is full of great features, profiles and interviews with entrepreneurs from all walks of life. There's all the latest business news, a busy forum where you can ask questions or express your views, regular columnists, how-to guides, legal advice – everything you need to understand who entrepreneurs are, what they strive for and what you can achieve too.

Find them on Twitter at http://twitter.com/real_business.

Google.co.uk

Well, before you start your online business, you need to do plenty of research. Take your knock-out business idea and consider whether others are doing something similar – is there room for your idea in the market? You must work out who'll build your website: will it be you, a friend or a professional company? You also have to think about who'll host your website, how you'll promote it and how you'll make it visible amongst all the other web-based businesses out there.

Google.co.uk (`www.google.co.uk`) is your ally in this research. The great thing about finding reputable businesses to help you is that they're likely to have a higher Google rating (they appear on the first page of a search on the website). A company providing search engine optimisation and online marketing, for example, should be easy to find in a web search. If you don't find such a company easily, then they're not very good at their job, and you should leave them well alone.

Google's assistance when it comes to your business doesn't end there. We could go on and on about its other useful tools (and we do throughout the book, particularly in Chapter 13): online documents and spreadsheets, email, photo sharing, maps, directions, translators, news alerts, a lightning-fast web browser, blogs, AdWords, website statistics and analytics . . . the list never ends at this innovative organisation.

W3.org

Your car may look good on the outside, but if its engine isn't up to standard, you could run into a lot of trouble when you aren't expecting it. Same goes for your website. Making sure your site – the hub of your business – meets certain agreed standards when it comes to its creation and design isn't just advisable, but crucial if you want to retain visitors, keep your site looking as it should and make sure it can evolve whenever the web does. The World Wide Web Consortium (W3C) exists to create and maintain these standards. Headed up by inventor of the web, Tim Berners-Lee, its mission and principles are simply 'Web for All'.

Although some of the technical articles on the W3C site (`www.w3.org`) may seem daunting, it has plenty of plain English guides to HMTL and CSS (for more on these, see Chapter 5) and a comprehensive guide to accessibility.

So, although you won't need to know all the underlying jargon touted in the depths of this extensive site, it's well worth keeping up to date with the latest web standards and knowing how important they are to ensure the web runs smoothly.

Businesslink.gov.uk

Your one-stop shop for information on the mechanics of starting a business is Business Link's website (www.businesslink.gov.uk). The government-funded website offers hundreds of official guides that are updated constantly. The site doesn't just cover rules and regulations (although these are vitally important), but also offers advice on how to start your business, how to maintain it and how to grow it. All in all, a highly practical resource.

As of April 2012, Business Link's 'real life' presence in regional centres across the UK will sadly be axed as part of the government's spending cuts; but this website, we're told, will be even more improved as a result – so keep it bookmarked!

 Another website we recommend is the Information Commissioner's (www.ico.gov.uk). Here you find your legal obligations as a business (and not just an online business) under the Data Protection Act clearly outlined. The website has some great checklists to download and keep to hand, such as a checklist on how to comply with the Act, and much more.

HMRC.gov.uk

Like Business Link, HM Revenue & Customs is a government organisation, meaning that the content on its website (www.hmrc.gov.uk) is trustworthy and chimes with UK rules and regulations. The site doesn't have the same number of guides as Business Link, nor does it offer as much advice. But it's the ideal source of information on your business, tax and record-keeping commitments. The website has quick links to printable forms, glossaries, calculators and other valuable resources. It's also the place to go if you're filing your tax return online.

Chances are you're not a tax expert; you just have a good business idea that you think could earn you some money and perhaps develop into something big. But you do need a grasp of what you must pay back to the government; the amounts vary depending on the nature of your business and the amount of money you make. This website tells you everything you need to know to get started – and more.

Ebay.co.uk

In today's ultra-competitive world, the customer really is king. Sites like Play.com (www.play.com), CD Wow (www.cdwow.com) and Firebox (www.firebox.com) force down the price of items that cost a lot more in high street stores. Their profit margins are pretty tight, but they shift so much stock that they can earn a tidy living for their directors.

Furthermore, price comparison websites like Kelkoo (`www.kelkoo.com`) and PriceRunner (`www.pricerunner.co.uk`) let consumers know exactly where they can find the cheapest goods. You have to be sure that you can either offer products cheaper (very unlikely nowadays) or that you offer a bespoke service and good customer care.

Apart from the sites we list in the preceding paragraphs, the best way to assess whether your business will sink or swim is to check out the competition on eBay.co.uk (`www.ebay.co.uk`). Study your competitors like a hawk. What makes them professional? How much do their products usually sell for and how can you improve on the customer's experience? If you can't do something cheaper or better, then maybe it's not worth doing at all!

Startups.co.uk

Startups.co.uk (`www.startups.co.uk`) is another great information resource for people thinking about starting a business (of course, Dan would say that, because he's partly responsible for creating it). Arguably the best thing about the site isn't its daily small business newsfeed, or its large mine of how-to guides. The best thing is its real life start-up stories and its busy online forum where you can ask questions and make suggestions to its many users, some of whom are lawyers, accountants and other advisers who give their advice away for free. We particularly like the 'Rate My Website' section, where others can give their (honest) opinion on your website.

Technology Blogs

It's vitally important to keep up with the times when you start your online business. There's nothing worse than trawling through a site that feels like it was developed in 1996. Innovative super sites like Youtube (`www.youtube.com`), Google (`www.google.co.uk`) and Facebook (`www.facebook.com`) are distant cousins of your own site and you must pay attention to the jazzy new tools they keep producing.

Keep track of redesigns, new services and product ideas, and try to apply them to your own website. But instead of trawling around the Internet all day waiting for sites to do something new, keep track through a news service like the Guardian's Technology website (`http://technology.guardian.co.uk`),

BBC Technology (www.bbc.co.uk/news/technology) or one of the many blogs on the subject such as Techcrunch (www.techcrunch.com) and Mashable (see the section on this blog in this chapter).

Mashable.com

Not knowing what the cool kids are up to online might cost you a few customers, right? Step in Mashable (www.mashable.com), a blog established in 2005 by then 19-year-old Pete Cashmore in north Scotland. Within no time, it's become *the* definitive source for up-to-the-minute news on social media, technology and major developments in the cutting-edge world of Web 2.0. At Mashable you can find out what's hot and how you can promote your business using the best new tools and services around.

Mashable is now US-based, funded by advertising from the world's biggest technology brands and syndication of its content. Be one of its millions of Twitter subscribers at http://twitter.com/mashable or subscribe to one of its many regular email newsletter.

Other similar sites include Ars Technica (www.arstechnica.com), The Next Web (www.thenextweb.com) and GigaOM (www.gigaom.com), although these are quite US-oriented.

UKbusinessforums.co.uk

Having support from other entrepreneurs is a great help – so why not engage in some friendly banter with like-minded individuals at UKbusinessforums. co.uk (www.ukbusinessforums.co.uk)? Dozens of people are on the forums at any time, discussing anything from accounting to e-commerce software, website promotion and legal issues.

Targeted specifically towards small businesses and entrepreneurs, UK Business Forums boasts more than 80,000 members. You need to register in order to post a query (basic membership is free and lets you post and reply to topics), and if you like the community you can upgrade to become a paid-up member. Full membership is £36 a year, and lets you access the marketplace, list in the business directory, add a link to your site in your forum signature, access the private forums in order to request a review of your website and much more.

Index